Your College Experience

Strategies for Success

Seventh Edition

John N. Gardner

Senior Fellow
National Resource Center for The First-Year Experience and Students in Transition
University of South Carolina, Columbia

Executive Director, Policy Center on the First Year of College
Brevard, North Carolina

A. Jerome Jewler

Distinguished Professor Emeritus
College of Mass Communications and Information Studies
University of South Carolina, Columbia

Betsy O. Barefoot

Co-Director and Senior Scholar
Policy Center on the First Year of College
Brevard, North Carolina

THOMSON
WADSWORTH

Australia • Brazil • Canada • Mexico • Singapore • Spain • United Kingdom • United States

THOMSON

★
™

WADSWORTH

Your College Experience: Strategies for Success, **Seventh Edition**
Gardner/Jewler/Barefoot

Executive Editor: *Carolyn Merrill*
Development Editor: *Cathy Murphy*
Assistant Editor: *Eden Kram*
Technology Project Manager: *Joe Gallagher*
Marketing Communications Manager: *Brian Chaffee*
Senior Project Manager, Editorial Production: *Samantha Ross*
Senior Art Director: *Bruce Bond*
Senior Print Buyer: *Mary Beth Hennebury*

Senior Permissions Editor: *Isabel Alves*
Production Service/Compositor: *Pre-Press Company*
Text Designer: *Will Tenney, Perspectives*
Photo Manager: *Sheri Blaney*
Photo Researcher: *Christina Micek*
Cover Designer: *Linda Beaupré*
Printer: *Transcontinental Beauceville*

Cover Art: *top left*: Stockbyte/Getty, *right*: Matthias Tunger/DigitalVision/Getty; *2nd row: left, middle*: DigitalVision/Getty, *right*: Stockbyte Platinum/Getty; *3rd row: left*: Stockbyte/Getty, *right*: DigitalVision/Getty; *bottom, all*: BananaStock Ltd./RF.

Printed in Canada
1 2 3 4 5 6 7 09 08 07 06 05

Library of Congress Control Number: 2005904923

Student Edition: ISBN 1-4130-1856-4

Loose-leaf Edition: ISBN 1-4130-2071-2

Thomson Higher Education
25 Thomson Place
Boston, MA 02210-1202
USA

For more information about our products, contact us at:
Thomson Learning Academic Resource Center
1-800-423-0563

For permission to use material from this text or product, submit a request online at **http://www.thomsonrights.com** Any additional questions about permissions can be submitted by e-mail to **thomsonrights@thomson.com**

Credits appear on page 351, which constitutes a continuation of the copyright page.

About the Authors

John N. Gardner brings unparalleled experience to this writing partnership for American higher education's authoritative text for first-year seminar courses. John is the recipient of his institution's highest award for teaching excellence. He has twenty-five years of experience directing and teaching in the most respected and widely emulated first-year seminar in the country, the University 101 course at the University of South Carolina. John is universally recognized as one of the country's leading university educators for his role in initiating and orchestrating an international reform movement to improve the beginning college experience, a concept he coined as "the first-year experience." He is the founding executive director of two influential higher education centers that support campuses in their efforts to improve the learning and retention of beginning college students: the National Resource Center for The First-Year Experience and Students in Transition at the University of South Carolina (www.sc.edu/fye), and the Policy Center on the First Year of College in Brevard, NC (www.fyfoundations.org). The experiential basis for all of his work is his own miserable first year of college on academic probation, an experience he hopes to prevent for this book's readers.

A. Jerome Jewler is a best-selling author, educator, and friend to students. As a distinguished professor emeritus of the College of Mass Communications and Information Studies as well as co-director of the University 101 first-year seminar, including its faculty development component, at the University of

South Carolina, Columbia, he has guided advertising students through the creative and writing processes and has helped hundreds of new students determine their goals. As University 101 co-director, he planned and conducted training workshops for first-year seminar instructors, has won a Mortar Board award for teaching excellence, and was recognized as USC Advisor of the Year and nationally as the Distinguished Advertising Educator in 2000. While not working on this book—which isn't very often!—he teaches younger children as a docent for the South Carolina State Museum.

Betsy O. Barefoot is a writer, researcher, and teacher whose special area of scholarship is the first-year seminar. During her tenure at the University of South Carolina from 1988 to 1999, she served as co-director for research and publications at the National Resource Center for The First-Year Experience and Students in Transition. She taught University 101, in addition to special-topics graduate courses on the "first-year experience" and the principles of college teaching. She conducts first-year seminar faculty training workshops around the U.S. and in other countries and is frequently called on to evaluate first-year seminar outcomes. Betsy currently serves as co-director and senior scholar in the Policy Center on the First Year of College in Brevard, NC. In this role she led a major national research project to identify "institutions of excellence" in the first college year. She currently works with both two- and four-year campuses in evaluating all components of the first year.

Brief Contents

Contents

Preface to Students

This book is different from all your other textbooks. In fact, it may be the most important book you'll read as you begin your college experience because it's about you and improving your chances for success in college and beyond.

We know that college can be very difficult and that you will face many challenges ahead. But we also know that if you read this book carefully and act upon its many suggestions, you will immediately improve your chances of doing well in college and in life.

The very fact that you even have this book means that your campus offers a course designed to help first-year college students. One thing we have learned is that if you successfully complete this course, your chances of continuing in college and completing your degree are greater than those for students who do not take advantage of this opportunity. So we hope you will take this course seriously and let the course and this book help you navigate smoothly through your beginning college experience.

Why listen to us? For one thing, all three of us have dedicated our higher education careers to helping improve what educators have come to call "the first-year experience." Many professionals in our field would probably describe us as three of the country's leading experts on promoting student success in college and as champions for new college students. All three of us met and became friends and coworkers at the University of South Carolina. All three of us taught USC's well-known University 101 first-year seminar, where we practiced many of the strategies we now recommend in this book.

While we know a great deal about student success, there is no way the three of us could know everything. So we have sought and found a number of expert contributors. You will see them acknowledged at the beginning of many chapters. We believe there is no other book on the topic of college success that can give you a wider range of knowledge and experience.

Enhanced Strategies for Success

We open this book by introducing a comprehensive set of strategies for success and elaborate on them throughout the book. These strategies are grouped around five topics to underscore the book's major concepts.

Plan Ahead! Among the most important things you must learn in college is how to be prepared. This means knowing how to manage your time, showing up for class on time, having work done on time, and sticking to a weekly schedule, among other things. You can see we're going to be serious about time!

Take Charge of Learning! We all learn differently; in this section you'll find how you learn best. You will be introduced to many types of learning theories and have the chance to try a number of different learning styles and techniques. Other chapters in this section will introduce you to critical thinking and engagement with learning—two very important skills you should understand and practice.

Sharpen Your Skills! More specifically, we're talking about taking notes, reading textbooks, developing memory skills, taking exams, improving your writing and speaking, and learning how to research a topic. Sounds like a tall order, but you will be better able to manage these skills after reading these six chapters that will walk you step-by-step through critical processes that can mean the difference between success and failure.

Get Connected! Going to college will help you plan for the future, select friends wisely, and appreciate people of different cultures. In this section, you'll learn how to begin the career planning process, choose friends who will have a positive impact on your life, and interact with others whose backgrounds and cultures are different from yours.

Know Yourself! To conclude, we cover two topics that will help you understand yourself better. One—values—is philosophical, but develops into a discussion of such practical things as service learning and money management. The second—wellness—is straightforward "talk" about caring for your body and your mind. If those aren't in good working order, how can you manage to do well in your courses?

With the purchase of a new textbook, you receive a valuable passcode that allows you access to the website for **iLrn® College Success**.

iLrn College Success is an exciting new online learning and teaching tool designed to increase student success in the classroom. **iLrn** will grant students and instructors quick and easy admission to numerous resources: Assess! (self-assessments); Write! (electronic journals that encourage students to reflect on their progress); Consider! (essay questions and exercises); Practice! (Test Your Knowledge interactive quizzes); and Test Yourself! (practice test questions).

The **College Success Factors Index (CSFI)** is accessible via the **iLrn College Success** website. This exclusive student assessment tool measures eight indices that can affect student adjustment to college life. This program is an excellent pre- and post-test for incoming students and helps individual instructors tailor their course topics to appropriately address student needs.

So, armed with this textbook and **iLrn College Success**, you are ready to begin.

Welcome to college! We sincerely believe that this textbook can help you move closer to achieving your life goals.

John N. Gardner
A. Jerome Jewler
Betsy O. Barefoot

Preface to Instructors

The most widely emulated course aimed at helping first-year students succeed—University 101—was born in 1972 on the Columbia campus of the University of South Carolina. John Gardner, one of the authors of this text, was appointed to direct the course; the coauthors of this edition have joined the program across the years. The course has grown into an international movement known as The First-Year Experience®. Now versions of University 101 are taught at hundreds of campuses around the world. This book is based on our collective experience in teaching thousands of first-year students, and we are confident that if students read and heed the information herein, they will be more successful in college.

Seeing what an immediate difference this course had made for our own students at a major public research university, we set out to bring this same critical information to a wider audience of students in two-year and four-year, not-for-profit, and proprietary higher education settings. We also saw our work as contributing to this country's overall efforts to enhance student retention and graduation rates.

The content of this book, its topics and strategies, are based on a growing body of literature about the kinds of experiences that are more likely to enhance student success and retention in college. Our intent always has been to write in a way that conveys both respect and admiration for students by treating them as the adults we know they are, while recognizing their continued need for challenge and support.

Whether you are considering this textbook for use in your first-year seminar or already have made a decision to adopt it, we thank you for your interest and trust that you will find *Your College Experience: Strategies for Success* a valuable teaching aid. While our text was written primarily for students in first-year seminar courses, we hope it will also guide you and your campus in understanding the range of issues that, for better or for worse, can affect student success. Whether you are a first-time adopter of *Your College Experience* or someone who has used previous editions, we want you to know the essential features of this text and the major differences between this edition and the previous ones:

Organization

We open this book by presenting a comprehensive set of strategies for student success. In this new edition, these strategies are grouped into five sections to underscore the book's major concepts.

Plan Ahead! Among the most important lessons in college is how to be prepared. This means knowing how to manage time, showing up for class on time, having work done on time, and sticking to a weekly schedule, among other things. You can see we're going to be serious about time!

Take Charge of Learning! We all learn differently; in this section your students will find how they learn best. In a new and expanded chapter, "How We Learn," they will be introduced to many types of learning theories and have the chance to try a number of different learning style instruments. Other chapters in this section introduce the concepts of critical thinking and engagement with learning.

Sharpen Your Skills! More specifically, we're talking about taking notes, reading textbooks, developing memory skills, taking exams, improving writing and speaking, and learning how to research a topic. This may initially sound like a tall order to your students, but in six chapters we walk them step-by-step through the critical processes that can mean the difference between success and failure.

Get Connected! Going to college should help students plan for the future, appreciate people of different cultures, and choose friends wisely. In this section, your students will learn how to begin the career planning process, how to choose friends who will have positive impacts on their lives, and the value of living as part of a diverse community.

Know Yourself! To conclude, we offer two topics that will help students understand themselves better: One—values—is philosophical, but develops into a discussion of such practical things as service learning and money management. The second—wellness—is simply straight talk about caring for mind and body.

Chapter Features

Each chapter includes these distinctive features:

- **In this chapter you will learn**: This summary of key concepts guides the student through the chapter content to follow.

- **Self-assessments**: This brief exercise asks students to evaluate their initial level of understanding of the chapter topic. In the seventh edition, the self-assessments that open each chapter consistently use positive statements.

- **Turning Point**: In this edition, we feature authentic student voices and photos, commenting in a few short sentences on a major "turning point" in their first year of college.

- **Where to Go for Help**: This feature directs students to helpful resources on campus and online.

- **Achieve It! Setting Goals for Success**: This new goal-setting instrument appears at the end of the main body text of each chapter. This feature asks students to think of a goal related to the chapter content, to devise a plan for achieving the goal, and to write the plan down.

- **Try It! Exercises**: Each chapter includes short-answer exercises and a group exercise called "Working Together."

- **Write about It! Your Personal Journal**: This end-of-chapter feature invites students to comment on their personal and academic progress (and anything else they want to write about).

What's New in the Seventh Edition

Chapter 1: Strategies for Success
- This chapter includes new content about making sensible choices for college success.
- Students are now advised to use a computer calendar or PDA as a backup planning device.

- The chapter provides additional advice on avoiding plagiarism.
- Students are now encouraged to change advisors if the relationship is not a good one.
- A broader comparison of high school vs. college mentions diversity and the difficulty of managing time in college.

Chapter 2: Time Management

- The Self-Assessment exercise is all new.
- There is a new section on setting priorities.
- A new section focuses on overcoming procrastination and includes material on the psychological reasons behind the problem.
- A new exercise focuses on "Comparing Class Schedules."

Chapter 3: How We Learn

This chapter has been almost completely rewritten to include:

- New coverage of these learning styles models: field dependence/independence; Kolb inventory; multiple intelligences; and VARK. With the Myers-Briggs Type Indicator™, the chapter now includes five learning styles models.
- Coverage of learning disabilities: types of disabilities, warning signs that a student may have LD, and where to go for help with LD.

Chapter 4: Engagement with Learning

This chapter underwent a major revision, moving the focus from *active learning* to *engagement with learning*. Updates include:

- A new section on the benefits of engagement.
- Material on using study groups in math and science courses, moved from the previous edition's Chapter 11.
- A new section titled "A Good Teacher Wants You to Succeed."
- A new exercise, "Ways to Be Engaged."

Chapter 5: Critical Thinking

The chapter places greater emphasis on the importance of critical thinking for job candidates and in the workplace, including:

- A new section on appreciating the value of a liberal education.
- Enhanced coverage of logical fallacies.
- Coverage of how to generate creative ideas.
- A new exercise on learning about liberal education.

Chapter 6: Listening, Note-Taking, and Participating

- The Self-Assessment includes a question about downloading material from teachers' websites before class.
- "The Before Class: Prepare to Remember" section advises students to use active learning to gain a better understanding of what the instructor thinks is important.
- New figures demonstrate outline, paragraph, and list forms of note-taking, all using the same lecture. These supplement an example showing the Cornell method.

- Material has been incorporated from the previous edition's Chapter 11, providing coverage on taking notes in math and science courses.
- The "After Class" section advises students to refer back to the textbook for diagrams and other figures that will supplement lecture material.
- Two new exercises have been added, "Using Your Five Senses to Learn" and "What System of Note-Taking Works for You?"

Chapter 7: Reading Strategies
- The chapter includes new material on reading textbooks, including specific sections on social science and humanities texts.
- Material on reading math and science texts has been incorporated from the previous edition's "Thinking Mathematically and Scientifically" chapter.
- There is a new section on reading primary source material.
- Specific material on reading for ESL students has been added.
- A new exercise focuses on the differences between high school reading and college reading.

Chapter 8: Improving Your Memory
This topic is new to the seventh edition. The chapter includes:

- New material on how memory works and myths about memory.
- Strategies for improving memory, aids to memory, mnemonics, and whether technology is a help or a hindrance to memory.

Chapter 9: Taking Exams and Tests
- This chapter features a new section on the advantages of using flash cards to study.
- There is a new, extensive section on test anxiety.
- The chapter provides extensive coverage of the following types of tests: fill-in-the-blank, machine-scored, computerized, open-book, and take-home.
- Coverage of problem-solving tests and laboratory tests has been moved here from the previous edition's Chapter 11, "Thinking Mathematically and Scientifically."

Chapter 10: Effective Writing and Speaking
- More intensive focus is given to the writing process.
- Material drawn from the work of Peter Elbow and Niko Silvester has been added.
- The chapter includes a new section on e-mail, and the difference between it and formal writing.
- Also new is an end-of-chapter exercise, "Write, Pair, Write, Share."

Chapter 11: Research and College Libraries
This chapter includes two new exercises on ethical behavior and research.

Chapter 12: Majors and Careers: Making the Right Choices
Features include:

- New material on careers in the new economy—with a focus on the need for innovation.
- A new section on the two-year college student's career timetable.
- More emphasis on how values affect a student's choice of major and career.

- A new section on types of skills, including content skills, transferable skills, and soft skills.
- Several new exercises: "Work Shadowing," "Using Your Career Library," "Investigating an Occupation," and "My Current Thinking about Career Choice."

Chapter 13: Relationships
- The chapter includes a new section on college and friendships.
- There is an enhanced marriage and parenting section.
- "You and Your Parents" now includes new material on "helicopter parents" and blended families.
- New material has been added on living safely on campus.
- A new exercise, "Looking for Love," asks students to evaluate what people see as their "ideal" by examining personal ads.

Chapter 14: Diversity: Appreciating Differences among Us
The chapter examines the concept of diversity, how our beliefs are formed, ethnicity and culture, multiculturalism and diversity in higher education, the history of diversity on campus, and groups on campus that can broaden one's views of diversity. There are new sections on discrimination, insensitivity, and prejudice on campus and how to fight hate. All of the exercises are new.

Chapter 15: Exploring Your Values
- Statistics comparing American quality of life since 1970 have been updated.
- Additional material is provided on service learning's value.
- New information is given on how values relate to money management.

Chapter 16: Staying Healthy
This chapter has been extensively rewritten with the help of a new contributor, Michelle Murphy Burcin of the University of South Carolina.

- The chapter now includes coverage of emergency contraception.
- A new birth control table is more concise and easier to understand.
- Coverage is provided on how to help a drunk friend.
- New statistics on tobacco use in college are given.
- Warnings on the dangers of ritalin abuse have been added.
- Heroin and methamphetamine abuse are now covered.
- New exercises include "Doing a Weekly Check" and "Working Together: Recommendations for Stress Management."

Supplements: Teaching Aids for Instructors

Annotated Instructor's Edition, Your College Experience: Strategies for Success, Seventh Edition (1-4130-2072-0)
This full textbook includes annotations and suggestions for teaching, annotated by Jason Finkelstein of Bronx Community College.

Your College Experience: Strategies for Success, Seventh Edition, Loose-leaf Version (1-4130-2071-2)
Customize *Your College Experience* with your own campus-specific materials using this three-hole punch version of the text. This version is unbound and comes with a front and back cover, with each page three-hole punched for easy customization.

Instructor's Manual and Test Bank, Your College Experience: Strategies for Success, Seventh Edition (1-4130-2067-4)

Prepared by Suzanne Hamid of Lee University, the Instructor's Manual and Test Bank includes chapter objectives, teaching suggestions, additional exercises, test questions, a list of common concerns of first-year students, an introduction to the first-year experience course, a sample lesson plan for each chapter, and various case studies relevant to the topics covered. New to this edition is material on how to run a peer mentoring program.

ExamView® Computerized Test Bank, Your College Experience: Strategies for Success, Seventh Edition (1-4130-2069-0)

Create, deliver, and customize tests (both print and online) in minutes with this easy-to-use assessment and tutorial system. ExamView offers both a Quick Test Wizard and an Online Test Wizard that guide you step-by-step through the process of creating tests, while the unique "WYSIWYG" capability allows you to see the test you are creating on the screen exactly as it will print or display online. You can build tests of up to 250 questions using up to twelve question types. Using ExamView's complete word processing capabilities, you can enter an unlimited number of new questions or edit existing questions.

Multimedia Manager 2007 (1-4130-2791-1)

Whether you want to create a lecture from scratch or use a customizable template, our **Multimedia Manager for College Success** makes preparation a snap. With content that is easy to customize, this one-step presentation tool makes course preparation faster and simpler—and lectures more engaging. FREE to qualified adopters and organized by fourteen common college success topics, the Multimedia Manager helps you assemble, edit, and present tailored multimedia lectures for your course. We have updated the Multimedia Manager with new PowerPoint presentations, new video clips, new images, and new web links that can supplement your College Success course.

JoinIn™ (1-4130-2070-4)

We are pleased to offer book-specific JoinIn™ content for Response Systems tailored to specific Wadsworth College Success texts. Transform any lecture into an interactive experience for students with **JoinIn™** on **TurningPoint®** software—our multimedia content created specifically for use with personal response systems. Combined with your choice of several leading keypad systems, JoinIn turns an ordinary PowerPoint application into powerful audience response software. With just a click on a handheld device, your students can immediately respond to multiple-choice questions, polls, and interactive exercises. Available to qualified college and university adopters.

Turnitin®

See your Wadsworth sales representative if you are interested in learning more about **Turnitin®**. This proven online plagiarism prevention software promotes fairness in the classroom by helping students learn to correctly cite sources and allowing instructors to check for originality before reading and grading papers. Turnitin quickly checks student papers against billions of pages of Internet content, millions of published works, and millions of student papers. Access to Turnitin can be provided with your textbook under special order.

Videos

See your local Thomson (Wadsworth) sales representative for more information.

10 Things Every Student Needs to Know to Study (1-4130-1533-6)

This 60-minute video covers such practical skills as note-taking, test-taking, and listening, among others.

10 Things Every Student Needs to Succeed in College (1-4130-2907-8)

This 60-minute video compilation illustrates ten valuable and highly effective practices every student needs in order to engage in a successful college experience. Topics include successful time management, recognizing and understanding learning styles, and written/spoken communication.

Student Resources

iLrn® College Success

iLrn College Success is an exciting new learning and teaching tool designed to increase student success in the classroom. Accessed through a PIN-coded website available with the purchase of a new textbook, **iLrn** will grant students and instructors quick and easy admission to numerous resources: Assess! (self-assessments); Write! (electronic journals that encourage students to reflect on their progress); Consider! (essay questions and exercises); Practice! (interactive quizzes); and Test Yourself! (practice test questions).

The College Success Factors Index (CSFI), accessible via the iLrn College Success website

This exclusive student assessment tool measures eight indices that can affect student adjustment to college life. This program is an excellent pre- and post-test for incoming students and helps individual instructors tailor their course topics to appropriately address student needs. For more information about the CSFI, please visit **www.success.wadsworth.com** and click on the link to the College Success Factors Index website. The Instructor's Manual and Test Bank that accompanies this text offers detailed information about CSFI.

See www.success.wadsworth.com for more information about **iLrn College Success** today!

Acknowledgments

Chapters 2, 6, 7, 9: Jeanne L. Higbee, *University of Minnesota, Twin Cities*

Chapter 3: Tom Carskadon, *Mississippi State University*

Chapter 10: Constance Staley, *University of Colorado, Colorado Springs*; and Robert Stephen Staley II, *Colorado Technical University*

Chapter 11: Charles Curran and Rose Marshall, *University of South Carolina, Columbia*

Chapter 12: Philip Gardner, *Michigan State University*; Linda Salane, *Columbia College, South Carolina*; Stuart Hunter, *University of South Carolina, Columbia*

Chapter 13: Tom Carskadon

Chapter 14: Juan Flores, *Folsom Lake College*

Chapter 15: John M. Whiteley and James B. Craig, *University of California, Irvine*; Edward Zlotkowski, *Bentley College*; and Andrew Luptak, Steve Crook, and Karl Knorr, *Concordia University, Wisconsin*

Chapter 16: Michelle Murphy Burcin, *Providence Hospitals* and the *University of South Carolina, Columbia*; Sara J. Corwin, JoAnne Herman, Bradley H. Smith, Rick L. Gant, and Georgeann Stamper, *University of South Carolina, Columbia*

Special thanks also to reviewers of this edition whose wisdom and suggestions guided the creation of this text:

Richard Conway, *Nassau Community College*
Joyce Deaton, *Jackson State Community College*
Gigi Derballa, *Asheville Buncombe Technical Community College*
Lisa Donato, *Essex Community College*
Diane Frazier, *Colby Community College*
Charles Frederick, *Indiana University*
Melanie Harring, *University of Wisconsin, Oshkosh*
Judy Jackman, *Amarillo College*
Rebecca Jordan, *University of Kentucky*
Harriet McQueen, *Austin Peay State University*
Jaseon Outlaw, *Arizona State University*
Bea Rogers, *Monmouth University*
Christel Taylor, *University of Wisconsin–Waukesha*
Susan M. Vladika, *Marywood University*
Linda S. York, *Wallace Community College*

Reviewers of the previous edition:

Anne Hawthorne, *Cuyahoga Community College*
Bill Horstman, *Mesa State College*
Elizabeth S. Kennedy, *Florida Atlantic University*
Karen M. Kus, *East Carolina University*
Judith M. Lang, *Whitworth College*
Polly McMahon, *Spokane Falls Community College*
Anna Roope, *Virginia Tech*
Diane L. Savoca, *St. Louis Community College*
Vicki Stieha, *Northern Kentucky University*
Mary Walz-Chojnacki, *University of Wisconsin–Milwaukee*
Phyllis N. Weatherly, *Floyd College*

Finally, all this could not have happened without the Thomson Wadsworth team that supported our text, guided us through the writing and production, and worked at least as hard as we did to make *Your College Experience* the premier text in its field. Our special thanks to:

Carolyn Merrill, Executive Manager for College Success, for her exceptional editorial vision of what this text could be, her vast knowledge of the market—especially what first-year seminar instructors want and what the students need—and her consummate professional skills in leading a complex project with a large author/production staff and keeping us all focused on the task at hand.

Cathy Murphy, Development Editor, for her significant investment in this project, her high standards, and her creative and thoughtful contributions.

We also thank Susan Badger, CEO of Thomson Higher Education; Sean Wakely, President of Thomson Higher Education; Eden Kram, Assistant Editor; Joe Gallagher, Technology Project Manager; Samantha Ross, Senior Production Project Manager; Abigail Greshik, Project Manager, Pre-Press Company, Inc.

Most of all, we thank you, the users of our book, for you are the true inspirations for this work.

PART
1
Plan Ahead!

Strategies for Success
· ·

in this chapter YOU WILL LEARN

- How to make sensible choices for college success
- Why some students don't graduate
- The impact of college on your future earnings
- Typical questions first-year students ask
- The many differences between high school and college
- What concerns returning students
- The advantages of a college education
- How to set your own goals for success

Does this look like your campus? What is similar and what is different?

SELF-ASSESSMENT
STRATEGIES FOR SUCCESS

Check the items that apply to you:

1. ____ **I plan to arrive for class on time or earlier.**

2. ____ **I understand that people learn in different ways. That's why it may be difficult for me to understand some teachers.**

3. ____ **I know how to set up a time management plan and stick to it.**

4. ____ **I write as often as possible to improve my writing.**

5. ____ **I'm comfortable participating in class discussion.**

6. ____ **I welcome constructive criticism about my work.**

7. ____ **I know how to take effective notes and how to memorize important points for an exam.**

8. ____ **I plan to connect with a group so that I can study better.**

9. ____ **I plan to meet with my academic advisor or counselor often.**

10. ____ **I maintain a budget, stay on top of my financial aid, and avoid debt so that I don't run out of money in college.**

If you checked seven or fewer of the items, find someone who can help you understand why all ten items are critical. At the end of this chapter, you will be asked to set personal goals for one or more of your unchecked items. If you checked all items, you will be asked to set other goals.

No matter your age, no matter your background, the fact that you were admitted to college means you realize how dramatically your college experience can change your life for the better.

Yet the sad fact is that many entering students drop out or flunk out. And the highest college dropout rate occurs during the first year.

If new students are determined to succeed, why do some of them make questionable choices? Take the student who left campus before the first day of classes because she was intimidated by the social activities the school had arranged for new students. Or the guy who wanted to meet other students so much that he went out every night and never cracked a book. Or the one who maxed out his credit card the first week of the term. Or those who lacked clear goals for college or couldn't manage their time or never learned how to study for an exam or use the library, the Internet, and other research sources. Or the student of color who felt out of place on a predominantly white campus. Or the returning student who found it was nearly impossible to balance the responsibilities of work, family, and studies.

This book, as you will see, is a game plan for engagement in those experiences that will help you succeed in college. It is a package of strategies that, if followed, can help you achieve more than you ever dreamed possible. We've grouped those strategies under five topics:

Plan Ahead!

Take Charge of Learning!

Sharpen Your Skills!

Get Connected!

Know Yourself!

Following are a number of specific suggestions for each of the five topics. Many of them may strike you as common sense—and many of them are. Nonetheless, you will benefit from carefully reading them and thinking about what they mean to you. You will also find that, since they serve as the five parts of this text, they serve as a preview to the remainder of the book.

Strategies for Success

Plan Ahead!

1. **Show up and be on time for class.** When you miss even one day, you're missing something. You're also sending your instructor a message that you don't care. If you know you are going to miss class or arrive late, contact your instructor as soon as possible and certainly before the next class meeting. The most dangerous classes to miss are those at the start of the term.
2. **Have work done on time.** You may face a grade penalty, and you will most certainly irritate some of your teachers if you are perpetually late with assignments. Some instructors may have a policy of not accepting late work or penalizing you for it. Ask to be certain. If your work is late because of illness or an emergency, let your instructor know. It may help.
3. **Set up a weekly schedule.** And stick to it. Learning how to manage your time can make the difference between success and frustration. Get a portable appointment calendar from your campus bookstore this week and always keep it handy. Consider using a computer calendar program or PDA as a backup to your written one.
4. **If you are a full-time student, limit your work week to fifteen hours.** Most students begin a downhill slide after that. Need more money? Consult a financial aid officer. We suggest that, whenever possible, you look for

a job on campus. Students who do and who work less than fifteen hours have a higher graduation rate than those who work off campus and/or more than 15 hours.

5. **If stressed, enroll part-time.** Stress is the enemy of learning. You're likely do better in all classes if you adjust the number of courses you're taking to reduce your stress.

Take Charge of Learning!

6. **Discover how you learn best.** Explore learning style theory, which suggests that we employ differing approaches to make sense of the world around us and the information we receive, and to understand the decisions we make and the way we choose to live. Perhaps you'll understand why you hate being alone and love to plan things in detail, while your best friend or even your instructor is just the other way around.

7. **Improve your study habits.** Starting with a time management plan, make every minute of every day count. Master the most effective methods for reading textbooks, listening, taking notes in class, studying for exams, and using information sources on campus. If your campus has an academic skills center, visit it whenever you need help with your studies.

8. **Develop critical thinking skills.** Challenge statements. Ask why. Seek dependable information to prove your point. Look for unusual solutions to ordinary problems. Never accept something as fact simply because you found it on the Internet or someone tells you it's true. And don't be swayed by your emotions; keep your logical thinking powers at work.

9. **Improve your writing and speaking.** Instructors—and employers—want people who can think *and* write *and* speak. Learn to rehearse your thoughts, put them on paper, and revise until your words clearly say exactly what you want them to say. Remember, the more you write, the better you'll write and the more you'll want to write. The same goes for speaking.

Sharpen Your Skills!

10. **Participate in class.** Research indicates that students usually remember more about class discussion when they involve themselves in it. As a result, they usually enjoy the class more and earn higher grades. Seek teachers who favor this engagement in learning; you'll find learning is more fun this way.

11. **Learn how to remember more from every class.** Effective listening not only results in better notes but also helps you improve memory techniques—an important skill as exams approach.

12. **Learn from criticism.** Criticism can be healthy and helpful. It's how we all learn. If you get a low grade, ask to meet with your instructor to discuss what you should do to improve your work.

13. **Take workshops on how to study,** especially if you've been out of school for a while. Even after reviewing the study skills in this book, you may decide to take a comprehensive study skills course. You also may need to review basic math or writing skills. Fortunately, relearning something is much easier than learning new material.

14. **Learn how to use the library and computer resources to conduct research.** That means not only knowing how to do a conventional library search, but also getting comfortable with databases and the Internet—and

with librarians, who are there to help you. For some of your research, all you may need is a computer terminal anywhere on campus or at home. Know how to cite your sources. Never take another's words and call them your own. That's **plagiarism**, a cause for severe disciplinary action, including dismissal from school.

Get Connected!

15. **Study with a group.** Research shows that students who collaborate in study groups often earn the highest grades and survive college with fewer academic problems. If you have family responsibilities, consider inviting several other students to your home for a study group session.

16. **Get to know at least one person on campus who cares about you.** It might be the teacher of this course, some other instructor, your academic advisor, someone at the counseling or career center, an advisor to a student organization, or an older student. You may have to take the initiative to establish this relationship, but it will be worth it.

17. **Become engaged in campus activities.** Visit the student activities office. Work for the campus newspaper or radio station. Join a club or support group. Play intramural sports. Most campus organizations crave newcomers—you're their lifeblood.

18. **Become engaged in campus life and work.** You can do this through a practicum, an internship, or a field experience. Or you can perform community service as a volunteer. Or work with a faculty member on his or her research. Or think ahead about enrolling in a Study Abroad program in the future. Going the extra mile is what *engagement* or connection is all about. And students who are more engaged report they had a more beneficial college experience.

19. **Learn about campus helping resources.** Find out where they are. Academic and personal support services are usually free and confidential. Successful students use them. Check each chapter in this book for suggestions on "Where to Go for Help."

20. **Meet with your instructors.** This isn't high school. You should make it a point to meet with an instructor if you have something to discuss. Students who do tend to stay in college longer. Your instructors are required to have office hours; they expect you to visit.

21. **Find a great academic advisor or counselor.** Be sure he or she is someone you can turn to for both academic and personal guidance and support. If your personalities clash, ask the department office to find another advisor for you.

22. **Visit your campus career center.** A career counselor can help you learn more about your academic major or find another major that suits you better. If you can't decide on a major immediately, remember that many first-year students are in the same boat. Talk about your options.

23. **Take advantage of minority support services.** If you are a minority student, find out if your campus has centers for minority students. Pay a visit and introduce yourself. Take advantage of mentoring programs a center might offer.

24. **Use services designed for returning students.** Find out if there is an office for returning students, or if someone in student affairs specializes in this field. Use the counseling center on campus if you need to work through some problems.

25. **Enlist support of your spouse, partner, or family.** A returning student may need to adjust household routines and duties. Let others know when you need extra time to study. A supportive partner is a great ally, but a nonsupportive partner can threaten your success in college. If your partner feels threatened and tries to undermine what you are doing, sit down and talk it over, or seek counseling.

Know Yourself!

26. **Take your health seriously.** How much sleep you get, what you eat, whether you exercise, and what decisions you make about drugs, alcohol, and sex all will affect your well-being and how well you will do in classes. Find healthy ways to deal with stress. Your counseling center can help.

27. **Have realistic expectations.** At first you may be disappointed in the grades you make, but remember that college is a new experience and things can, and probably will, improve. Remember you are not alone. Millions of other students have faced the same uncertainties you may be facing. Hang on to that positive attitude. It makes a difference.

28. **Learn how to be assertive, yet tactful.** If you don't, others may walk all over you. If it's difficult for you to stand up for yourself, take assertiveness training. Your counseling center probably offers workshops that can teach you to stand up for your rights in a way that respects the rights of others.

29. **Be proud of your heritage.** No matter your heritage, you may hear ugly remarks and witness or be the target of bigotry caused by ignorance or fear. Stand tall. Be proud. Refuse to tolerate disrespect. And remember that most of the college population embraces tolerance.

First-Year Commitment: Hangin' In

Why do so many students drop out of college in the first year? Columbia University professor Andrew Delbanco explains:

> *Every year I read that our incoming students have better grades and better SAT scores than in the past. But in the classroom, I do not find a commensurate increase in the number of students who are intellectually curious. . . . Many students are chronically stressed, grade-obsessed and, for fear of jeopardizing their ambitions, reluctant to explore subjects in which they doubt their proficiency.*[1]

Think about that. When you "doubt your proficiency" in a certain subject, are you creating a negative "self-fulfilling prophecy," an attitude that could help your worst nightmare come true?

What other circumstances make the first-year dropout rate so high?

For those fresh out of high school, a major problem involves newfound freedom. Your college teachers are not going to tell you what, how, or when to study. If you live on campus, your parents can't wake you in the morning, see that you eat properly and get enough sleep, monitor whether or how well you do your homework, or remind you to allow enough time to get to school. In almost every aspect of your life, getting it done now depends on you.

For returning students, the opposite is true: they experience a daunting lack of freedom. Working, caring for a family, and meeting other adult commitments and responsibilities compete for the time and attention it takes to do your best or even simply to persist in college.

Whichever problem you are facing, what will motivate you to hang in? And what about the enormous investment of time and money that getting a college degree requires? Are you convinced that the investment will pay off? Or are you having thoughts such as these:

- This is the first time someone has not been there to tell me I had to do something. Will I be able to handle all this freedom? Or will I just waste time?

- I've never been away from home before, and I don't know anybody. How am I going to make friends? How can I get involved in some activities? Who do I go to for help when I need it?

- I have responsibilities at home. Can I get through college and still manage to take care of my family? What will my family think about all the time I'll have to spend in classes and studying?

- As a minority, will I be in for some unpleasant surprises?

- Maybe college will be too difficult for me. I hear college teachers are much more demanding than high school teachers.

  See Exercise 1.1: Solving a Problem

- I hope I won't disappoint the people I care about and who expect so much of me.

- In high school, I got by without working too hard. Now I'll really have to study. Will I be tempted to cut corners, maybe even cheat?

- Will I like my roommate? What if he or she is from a different culture?

- What if I don't pick the right major? What if I don't know which major is right for me?

[1] Andrew Delbanco, "Academia's Overheated Competition," *New York Times*, March 16 , 2001.

- Can I afford this? Can my parents afford this? I wouldn't want them to spend this much and then have me fail.

- Maybe I'm the only one who's feeling like this. Maybe everyone else is just smarter than I am.

- Looking around class makes me feel so old! Will I be able to keep up at my age?

- Will some teachers be biased toward students of my culture?

High School versus College

Besides what we've already said, the differences between high school and college can also make starting college difficult:

- You will be part of a more diverse student body.

- You may not feel as unique or special if you attend a larger college.

- Managing your time will be more complex because of classes meeting on various days and commitments including work, family, activities, and sports.

- There will be more people to be friends with—but more difficulty choosing those you want to build a lasting relationship with.

- Your college classes may have a lot more students in them and meet for longer periods.

- College tests are given less frequently.

- You will do more writing in college.

- Your teacher rarely will monitor your progress. You're on your own.

- You will have to choose from many more types of courses.

- While peer pressure keeps many high school students from interacting with faculty, in college it's the *norm* to ask a teacher for advice or guidance.
- You and your teachers will have more freedom to express different views.
- College teachers usually have private offices and keep regular office hours.
- High school is more "textbook focused," while college is more "lecture focused."
- In college you will be encouraged to do original research and to investigate differing points of view on a topic.
- College students have more work to do, both in and out of class.
- College students often live far from home.

Returning Students versus Traditional Students

Returning students also must deal with major life changes when they begin college:

- Returning students whose grown children have moved away may find college a liberating experience, a new beginning, a stimulating challenge, a path to a career, or all of these things.
- Working full-time and attending college at night, on weekends, or both can produce added stress, especially with a family at home.
- Returning students tend to work harder than younger students because they realize how important an education can be. Consequently, they also tend to earn higher grades even though many believe they won't be able to keep up with their younger classmates.
- Returning students, generally speaking, take their studies more seriously than younger students.
- Age brings with it a wealth of wisdom that, properly used, can help returning students achieve or exceed their goals.

TURNING POINT

I went from being in the military one day to stepping into college the next. This is no exaggeration. Classes started on Monday and I flew in on Saturday. It took me a week and a half just to find the cafeteria that was two hundred yards from my dorm. Eventually I learned who to go to for help with math and that professors really do want you to come and see them. I assisted in captaining a flag football team that went on to win the championship. My fellow residents suggested that I run for Residential Assistant, so I did, and got the job. Although it was a rocky start, I would do it all over again.

Lance A.
Northern Kentucky University

Those Who Start and Those Who Finish

In 1900 fewer than 2 percent of Americans of traditional college age attended college. Today, new technologies and the information explosion are changing the workplace so drastically that few people can support themselves and their families adequately without some education beyond high school.

Today, more than 60 percent of high school graduates go on to college, with over 4,100 colleges serving more than 15 million students. Nearly half of those enrolling in college begin in two-year institutions. Adult students are also enrolling in record numbers. In the first decade of the new millennium, over one-third of college students are over age 25.

See Exercise 1.2: With or Without

According to the Carnegie Commission on Higher Education, as a college graduate you will have a less erratic job history, will earn more promotions, and will likely be happier with your work. You will be less likely than a non-graduate to become unemployed. As the saying goes, "If you think education is expensive, try ignorance."

As the statistics in Table 1.1 indicate, it pays to go to college—in more ways than one. Not only does income go up, as a rule, with each degree earned, but the unemployment rate goes down. You not only will earn more with a college degree, you also will find it easier to get a job and hold on to it.

In a healthy economy, the highest unemployment rate by educational attainment belongs to those with less than a high school diploma, while the lowest rate belongs to those with professional degrees or doctorates, with bachelor's and master's degrees rates only slightly higher. Education pays.

Hidden Advantages of a College Education

Of course, college will affect you in other ways. A well-rounded college education will expand life's possibilities for you by steeping you in the richness of how our world, our nation, our society, and its people came to be.

As a result of your college education, you will understand how to accumulate knowledge. You will encounter and learn more about how to appreciate the cultural, artistic, and spiritual dimensions of life. You will be more likely to seek appropriate information before making a decision. Such information also will help you realize how our lives are shaped by global as well as local political, social, psychological, economic, environmental, and physical forces. You

TABLE 1.1   Median* Earnings by Educational Attainment for Year-Round, Full-Time Workers Age 25+

Professional degree	$100,000
Doctorate	96,880
Master's degree	78,541
Bachelor's degree	68,728
Associate degree	51,970
Some college, no degree	45,854
High school graduate	36,835
Less than high school diploma	22,718

* These are *median* earnings, meaning half the group earned less and half the group earned more.
Source: Bureau of the Census, 2003.

will grow intellectually through interaction with cultures, languages, ethnic groups, religions, nationalities, and socioeconomic groups other than your own.

You also will:

- Know more, have more intellectual interests, be more tolerant of others, and continue to learn throughout life.

- Have greater self-esteem and self-confidence, which will help you realize how you might make a difference in the world.

- Be more flexible in your views, more future oriented, more willing to appreciate differences of opinion, more interested in political and public affairs, and less prone to criminal activity.

See Working Together: The Many Reasons for College

- Tend to have children with greater learning potential who will achieve more in life.

- Be an efficient consumer, save more money, make better investments, and spend more on home, intellectual, and cultural interests as well as on your children.

- Be able to deal with bureaucracies, the legal system, tax laws, and advertising claims.

- Spend more time and money on education, hobbies, and civic and community affairs.

- Be more concerned with wellness and preventive health care and consequently—through diet, exercise, stress management, a positive attitude, and other factors—live longer and suffer fewer disabilities.

Where to Go for Help

ON CAMPUS

To find the college support services you need, ask your academic advisor or counselor; consult your college catalog, phone book, and home page on the Internet. Or call or visit student services (or student affairs). Most of these services are free. In subsequent chapters, we will include a "Where to Go for Help" feature keyed to the chapter topic.

Academic Advisement Center: Help in choosing courses, information on degree requirements.

Academic Skills Center: Tutoring, help in study and memory skills, help in studying for exams.

Adult Reentry Center: Programs for returning students, supportive contacts with other adult students, information about services such as child care.

Career Center: Career library, interest assessments, counseling, help in finding a major, job and internship listings, co-op listings, interviews with prospective employers, help with résumés and interview skills.

Chaplains: Worship services, fellowship, personal counseling.

Commuter Services: List of off-campus housing, roommate lists, orientation to community. Maps, information on public transportation, child care, and so forth.

Computer Center: Minicourses, handouts on campus and other computer resources.

Counseling Center: Confidential counseling on personal concerns. Stress management programs.

Disabled Student Services: Assistance in overcoming physical barriers or learning disabilities.

Financial Aid and Scholarship Office: Information on financial aid programs, scholarships, and grants.

Health Center: Help in personal nutrition, weight control, exercise, and sexuality. Information on substance abuse programs and other health issues. Often includes pharmacy.

Housing Office: Help in locating on- or off-campus housing.

Legal Services: Legal aid for students. If your campus has a law school, it may offer assistance by senior students.

Math Center: Help with math skills.

Physical Education Center: Facilities and equipment for exercise and recreational sports.

Writing Center: Help with writing assignments.

ACHIEVE IT! Setting Goals for Success

College is an ideal time to begin setting and fulfilling short- and long-term goals. A short-term goal might be to read twenty pages from your history text twice a week, anticipating the exam that will cover the first hundred pages of the book. A long-term goal might be to begin predicting which college courses will help you fulfill your career goals. It's okay if you don't know which career to pursue; more than 60 percent of college students change majors at least once. In every chapter of this book, you'll find opportunities to set some short- and long-term goals. Here's how to do that:

Go back to the self-assessment at the beginning of this chapter and select one to three unchecked items from the list. Use these to formulate short-term goals for yourself. Be specific about what you want to achieve and when (for example, not "practice critical thinking," but "focus on the four steps of the critical thinking process and be comfortable with them by October 15"). Remember to choose goals that are realistic and important to you. Think about what obstacles could get in the way of achieving your goals, and make your plan. In the event you checked all items in the self-assessment, come up with one or more additional goals for this exercise.

Be Realistic. Be sure that the goal is achievable. Have you allowed enough time to pursue it? Do you have the necessary skills, strengths, and resources? If not, modify the goal to make it achievable.

Examine Your Values. Be certain you really want to achieve this goal. Don't set out to work toward something only because you feel you should. Be certain your goals are consistent with your values.

Overcome Obstacles. Identify and plan for difficulties you might encounter. Find ways to overcome them.

Make a Plan. Devise strategies for achieving the goal. How will you begin? What comes next? What should you avoid? Create steps for achieving your goal and set a timetable for the steps.[2]

Depending on how well you've mastered the topics in this chapter, you may want to set one, two, or three goals for yourself. Write them in the boxes provided here.

	GOAL 1	GOAL 2	GOAL 3
My short-term goal is . . .			
I want to achieve this goal by . . . (date)			
This goal matters because . . .			
I may encounter the following obstacles . . .			
My method for for accomplishing this goal will be to . . .			

Set a Date. Put your deadline for achieving your goal(s) in your calendar. Count back ten days from your deadline and write a reminder for yourself.

Reassess. After your deadline passes, ask yourself: Did I meet this goal on time? What change has it made in my life? If I did not meet it, what am I planning to do about it?

[2] Adapted from *Human Potential Seminars* by James D. McHolland and Roy W. Trueblood, Evanston, IL.: 1972. Used by permission of the authors.

TRY IT! *Exercises*

The exercises at the end of each chapter will help you sharpen what we believe are the critical skills for college success: writing, critical thinking, learning in groups, planning, reflecting, and taking action. You can further explore the topic of each chapter by completing the exercises on the website for this text: **http://success.wadsworth.com/gardner7e/**. For this, you will need a Personal Identification Number (PIN).

WORKING TOGETHER: The Many Reasons for College

In a small group, discuss the reasons in this chapter for attending college. Share with the group the ones that seem most relevant to you. Compile a group list of the most important reasons, and discuss them with your instructor. What did you learn about yourself and your classmates?

EXERCISE 1.1: Solving a Problem

What has been your biggest unresolved problem to date in college? What steps have you attempted to solve it? Discuss this with your instructor in a note or e-mail. Read your instructor's response and see if it's of any help to you. If you still have questions, ask to meet with your instructor.

EXERCISE 1.2: With or Without

This chapter has stressed the differences between a high school and college education. Imagine you are still trying to decide whether or not to attend college. Drawing on the material in this chapter as well as your own ideas, make a list of reasons to earn a college degree. Then make a list of reasons not to go to college. For example, pipe fitters earn impressive salaries, while librarians earn much less. How do you justify a college education on those terms?

EXERCISE 1.3: Focusing on Your Concerns

Browse the table of contents of this book. Find one or more chapters that address your most important concerns. Take a brief look at each chapter you have chosen. If a chapter appears to be helpful, read it before your instructor assigns it and try to follow its advice.

WRITE ABOUT IT! My Personal Journal

This is your place to sound off, to ask your teacher to clarify part of the lesson or to write him or her about a minor or major crisis you're experiencing. Find out if your teacher wishes you to turn in your journals. Ask if they will remain confidential. Even if the journal isn't used in your course, you can still use the format to write about and reflect on issues regarding the class, yourself, or both.

1. *What was the one major lesson you learned from reading this chapter and/or from class lecture and discussion?*

2. *What are some other important lessons about this topic?*

3. *If you believe some parts of this chapter are unimportant, spell them out here and tell why you think so. (You even might want to discuss this point with your classmates to see if they came up with a similar list.)*

4. *If anything is keeping you from performing at your peak level academically, describe what it is. Your instructor may be able to help, or refer you to someone else on campus who can help.*

5. *What behaviors are you planning to change after reading this chapter? Why?*

Time Management

In This Chapter YOU WILL LEARN

- How to take control of your time and your life
- How to use goals and objectives to guide your planning
- How to prioritize your use of time
- How to combat procrastination
- How to use a daily planner and other tools
- How to organize your day, your week, your school term
- The value of a "to-do" list
- How to avoid distractions
- The importance of civility
- How to make all of this work

How do you finish everything in your day?

Jeanne L. Higbee of the University of Minnesota Twin Cities contributed her valuable and considerable expertise to the writing of this chapter.

SELF-ASSESSMENT
TIME MANAGEMENT

Check the items below that apply to you.

1. ___ It is important to feel that I am in control of my time.

2. ___ I am aware of how my background (family, culture, lifestyle, commitments, gender, age, and other factors) influences my approach to time management.

3. ___ I set academic and personal goals every term to guide how I prioritize my time.

4. ___ I am able to focus on the task at hand instead of getting distracted or procrastinating.

5. ___ I know my most productive times of the day.

6. ___ I use a daily or weekly planner or some other type of planning device (a PDA, for example) to keep track of my commitments.

7. ___ I maintain a "to-do" list to keep track of the tasks I must complete.

8. ___ I am able to balance my social life and my need for personal time with my academic requirements.

9. ___ I am able to say "no" to requests so that I do not become overextended.

10. ___ I am punctual and almost never turn in an assignment late, skip class, or miss an appointment.

If you checked seven or fewer of the items, find someone who can help you understand why all ten items are critical. At the end of this chapter, you will be asked to set personal goals for one or more of your unchecked items. If you checked all items, you will be asked to set other goals.

How do you approach time? Because people have different personalities and come from different cultures, they may also view time in different ways. Some of these differences may have to do with your preferred style of learning. For example, if you're a natural organizer, you probably enter on your calendar or hand-held personal digital assistant (PDA) all due dates for assignments, exams, and quizzes as soon as you receive each course syllabus, and you may be good at adhering to a strict schedule. On the other hand, if you take a more laid-back approach to life, you may prefer to be more flexible, able to "go with the flow," rather than following a daily or weekly schedule. You may be good at dealing with the unexpected, but you may also be a procrastinator.

Time management involves:

- Knowing what your goals are
- Setting priorities to meet your goals
- Anticipating the unexpected
- Placing yourself in control of your time
- Making a commitment to being punctual
- Carrying out your plans

Taking Control of Your Time

The first step to effective time management is recognizing that *you* can be in control. How often do you find yourself saying, "I don't have time"? Once a week? Once a day? Several times per day? The next time you find yourself saying this, stop and ask yourself whether it is really true. Is it really that you do not have time, or have you made a choice, whether consciously or unconsciously, not to make time for that particular task or activity? When we say that we don't have time, we imply that we do not have a choice. But we *do* have a choice. We *do* have control over how we use our time. We *do* have control over many of the commitments we choose to make.

Being in control means that you make your own decisions. Two of the most often cited differences between high school and college are increased **autonomy**, or independence, and greater responsibility. If you are not a recent high school graduate, you have most likely already experienced a higher level of independence, but returning to school creates additional responsibilities above and beyond those you already have, whether those include employment, family, community service, or other activities.

Whether you are beginning college immediately after high school, or are continuing your education after a hiatus, now is the time to establish new priorities for how you spend your time. To take control of your life and your time, and to guide your decisions, it is wise to begin by setting some goals for the future.

Time Management and Goal Setting

Where do you see yourself five years from now? Ten years from now? What are some of your goals for the coming decade? One goal is probably to earn a two-year or four-year degree or technical certificate. You already may have decided on the career that you want to pursue. Or perhaps you plan to go on to graduate or professional school. As you look to the future, you may see yourself buying a new car, or owning a home, or starting a family. Maybe you dream of owning your own business someday, want time off to travel every year, or plan to retire early. Time management is one of the most effective tools to assist you in meeting these goals.

Take a few minutes to complete Exercise 2.1. List five goals for yourself for the coming decade. Your goals can be lofty, but they should also be attainable. You do not want to establish such high goals that you are setting yourself up for failure. Then determine at least two objectives for achieving each goal. The difference between a goal and an objective is that a goal is what you want to achieve, while an objective is a tangible, measurable method for getting there.

See Exercise 2.1: Goal Setting

Some goals may also be measurable, such as completing a degree program or earning a 3.0 or higher **grade point average (GPA)**. But other goals, for example "to be happy" or "to be successful," may mean different things to different people. No matter how you define success, you should be able to identify some specific steps you can take to achieve your goals. Perhaps one of the goals you will set is to find a good job upon completion of your degree, or one that is significantly better than the job you currently have. Now, at the beginning of your college experience, is an important time to think about what that means.

You can start by deciding what is a "good" job and how you can make yourself a more competitive candidate in a job search. You might also want to consider setting objectives like "complete an internship in a related field" (your college or university's Career Center can help you arrange for an internship, co-op, or other hands-on experience) or "engage in community service to gain experience" (your Student Affairs or Student Activities Office can probably provide contact information) in order to meet your goals.

A college degree and good grades may not be enough. When setting goals and objectives and thinking about how you will allocate your time, you may want to consider the importance of:

- Having a well-rounded résumé when you graduate

- Being well-informed about the world around you

- Setting aside time to participate in extracurricular activities

- Gaining leadership experience

- Engaging in community service

- Taking advantage of internship or co-op opportunities

- Developing job-related skills

- Keeping abreast of technological advances

- Participating in a study abroad program

- Pursuing relevant part- or full-time employment while you are also attending classes

When it is time to look for a permanent job, you want to be able to demonstrate that you have used your college years wisely, and that requires planning and effective time management, which in themselves are skills that employers value very highly.

Setting Priorities

Once you have established goals and objectives, decide how you want to prioritize your time. Which goals and objectives are most important to you? Which are the most urgent? For example, studying in order to get a good grade on a test tomorrow may have to take priority over attending a job fair today. However, don't ignore long-term goals in order to meet short-term goals. Using good time management, you can study during the week prior to the test so that you can attend the job fair the day before. One way that skilled time managers establish priorities is to maintain a "to-do" list (discussed in more detail later in this chapter) and then rank-order the items on that list, determining schedules and deadlines for each task.

TURNING POINT

I found little "shortcuts" in my college success textbook that showed how to better schedule my time and leave enough for a social life. One of them was to prioritize and analyze. Prioritize those that are of the utmost importance and then analyze them so that they don't seem so daunting of a task.

Celestino M. R.
Westwood College of O'Hare

Another aspect of setting priorities while in college is finding an appropriate way to balance an academic schedule, social life, and time alone. It is true that "all work and no play" can make you a "dull" or uninteresting person, and can also undermine your academic motivation. Similarly, never having time alone or time to think can leave you feeling out of control. Of course, for many students the greatest challenge of prioritizing will be balancing school with work and family obligations that are equally important and not "optional." But social activities are also an important part of the college experience, and being involved in campus life has been found to enhance student satisfaction, achievement, and retention.

Staying Focused

Many of the decisions you make today are reversible. You may change your major, and your career and life goals may change as well. But the decision to take control of your life—to establish your own goals for the future, set your priorities, and manage your time accordingly—is an important one. Most first-year students, especially recent high school graduates, temporarily lose sight of their goals and enjoy their first term of college by opening themselves up to a wide array of new experiences. While we encourage you to do this, within limits, we recognize that some students will spend the next four or five years trying to make up for poor decisions made early in their college careers, decisions that led to plummeting GPAs and the threat of academic probation or worse, academic dismissal.

Most adults reentering college question the decision to go back to school and may feel temporarily overwhelmed by the additional responsibilities on top of their other commitments. Prioritizing, rethinking some commitments, letting some things go, and weighing the advantages and disadvantages of attending school part-time versus full-time can help you work through this adjustment period. Again, keep your long-term goals in mind and find ways to manage your stress, rather than react to it (see Chapter 16 for help with stress).

While this book is full of suggestions for enhancing academic success, the bottom line is keep your eyes on the prize and take control of your time and your life. This is known as "staying focused," which is what successful people frequently indicate is a key to their success. To help you stay focused, make a plan. Begin with your priorities: attending classes, studying, working, spending time with the people who are important to you. Then think about the necessities of life: sleeping, eating, bathing, exercising, and relaxing. Leave time for fun things like talking with friends, watching TV, going out for the evening, and so forth; you deserve them. But finish what *needs* to be done before you move from work to pleasure. And don't forget about personal time. Depending on your personality and cultural background, you may require more or less time to be alone.

If you live in a residence hall or share an apartment with other college students, communicate with your roommate(s) about how you can coordinate your class schedules so that you each have some privacy. If you live at home with your family, particularly if you are a parent, work together to create special family times as well as quiet study times.

Overcoming Procrastination

Procrastination is a serious problem that can trip up many otherwise capable people. There are many reasons why people procrastinate. Psychological studies have found that even students who are highly motivated may fear failure, and some students even fear success. Some students procrastinate because they are perfectionists; not doing a task may be easier than having to live up to expectations—either your own or those of your parents, teachers, or peers. Others procrastinate because they find an assigned task boring or irrelevant, or consider it "busy work" and believe that they can learn the material just as effectively without doing the homework.

Simply not enjoying an assignment is not a good excuse to put it off. Throughout life you'll be faced with boring, distasteful, or irrelevant tasks; in most cases, you won't have the option to not do them. However, procrastinating may be a signal to you that it's time to reassess your goals and objectives; maybe at this point in your life you are not ready to make a commitment to academic priorities. Only you can decide, but a counselor or academic advisor can help you sort it out.

Regardless of its source, procrastination may be your single greatest enemy. Getting started requires self-discipline and self-control. Here are some ways to beat procrastination:

- Say to yourself, "I need to do this now, and I am going to do this now. I will pay a price if I do not do this now." Remind yourself of the possible consequences if you do not get down to work. Then get started.

- Create a to-do list. Check off things as you get them done. Use the list to focus on the things that aren't getting done. Move them to the top of your next day's list, and make up your mind to do them. Working from a list will give you a feeling of accomplishment and lead you to do more.

- Break down big jobs into smaller steps. Tackle short, easy-to-accomplish tasks first. Take things one step at a time.

- Before you begin to work, promise yourself a reward for finishing the task. Then, even if completing the task itself is not rewarding, you will not need to feel that your work was in vain. Do not allow yourself to have the reward if you do not complete the task. For more substantial tasks, give yourself bigger and better rewards.

- Take control of your study environment. Eliminate distractions—including the ones you love! Say no to friends and family who want your attention. Agree to spend time with them at a specific time later. Let them be your reward for doing what you must do now.

- Don't make or take phone calls during planned study sessions. Close your door.

If these ideas fail to motivate you to get to work, it may be time to reexamine your values and priorities. What is really important to you? Are these values important enough to forgo some temporary fun or laziness in order to get down to work? Are your academic goals really your own, or were they imposed on you by family members, your employer, or societal expectations? If you are not willing to make yourself stop procrastinating and get to work on the tasks at hand, you may want to reconsider why you are in school and if this is the right time for you to pursue higher education.

Recent research indicates that college students who procrastinate in their studies also avoid confronting other tasks and problems and are more likely to develop unhealthy habits like higher alcohol consumption, smoking, insomnia, poor diet, and lack of exercise. If you cannot get procrastination under control, it is in your best interest to seek help at your campus counseling service before you begin to feel as if you are losing control over other aspects of your life as well.

Creating a Workable Class Schedule

As a first-year student, you may not have had much flexibility in determining your course schedule; by the time you were allowed to register for classes, some sections of the courses you needed may already have been closed. You also may not have known whether you would prefer taking classes back to back or giving yourself a break between classes.

How might you use time between classes wisely? This may have been your first opportunity to take classes that do not meet five days a week. Do you prefer spreading your classes over five or six days of the week, or would you like to go to class just two or three days a week, or even once a week for a longer class period? Your decision may be influenced by your attention span as well as by your other commitments. In the future, you may have more control over how you schedule your classes.

Before you register, think about how to make your class schedule work for you—how you can create a schedule that allows you to use your time more efficiently. Also consider your own **biorhythms** by recognizing what part of the day or evening you are most alert and engaged.

See Exercise 2.2: The Ideal Class Schedule and Working Together: Comparing Class Schedules

TURNING POINT

I use a planner that my school gives all students at the beginning of the year. In it, I keep my schedule, class locations, and homework assignments. Thus, I have everything I need for classes in one book. But I am also careful to not let that be my only copy of my schedule. I keep an extra copy of my schedule and homework in my desk.

Adam W.
Taylor University

Using a Daily Planner

In college, as in life, you will quickly learn that managing time is an important key not only to success, but to survival. A good way to start is to look at the big picture. Use the *term assignment preview* (Figure 2.2) on pages 28–29 to give yourself an idea of what's ahead. You should complete your term assignment preview by the beginning of the second week of classes so that you can continue to use your time effectively. Then purchase a "week-at-a-glance" organizer for the current year. Your campus bookstore may sell one designed just for your school, with important dates and deadlines already provided. If you prefer to use an electronic planner, that's fine, your PC, laptop, or PDA will come equipped with a calendar.

Regardless of the format you prefer (electronic or hard copy), enter the notes from your preview sheets into your planner, and continue to enter all due dates as soon as you know them. Write in meeting times and locations, scheduled social events (jot down phone numbers, too, in case something comes up and you need to cancel), study time for each class you're taking, and so forth. Carry your planner with you in a convenient place.

Now is the time to get into the habit of using a planner to help you keep track of commitments and maintain control of your schedule. This practice will become invaluable to you in the world of work. Check your notes daily for the current week and the coming week. Choose a specific time of day to do this, perhaps just before you begin studying, before you go to bed, or at a set time on weekends. But check it daily, and at the same time of day. It takes just a moment to be certain that you aren't forgetting something important, and it helps relieve stress!

Maintaining a "To-Do" List

Keeping a to-do list can also help you avoid feeling stressed or out of control. Some people start a new list every day or once a week. Others keep a running list, and only throw a page away when everything on the list is done. Use your to-do list to keep track of all the tasks you need to remember, not just academics. You might include errands you need to run, appointments you need to make, e-mail messages you need to send, and so on. Develop a system for prioritizing the items on your list: highlight; use colored ink; or mark with one, two, or three stars, or A, B, C. You can use your to-do list in conjunction with your planner. See Figure 2.1.

As you complete each task, cross it off your list. You may be surprised at how much you have accomplished, and how good you feel about it.

Guidelines for Scheduling Week by Week

- Begin by entering all of your commitments for the week—classes, work hours, family commitments, and so on—on your schedule.

- Examine your toughest weeks on your term assignment preview sheet (see Figure 2.2). If paper deadlines and test dates fall during the same week, find time to finish some assignments early to free up study time for tests. Note this in your planner.

See Exercise 2.3: Tracking "Actual Time"
- Try to reserve at least two hours of study time for each hour spent in class. This "two-for-one" rule is universally accepted and reflects faculty members' expectations for how much work you should be doing to earn a good grade in their classes.

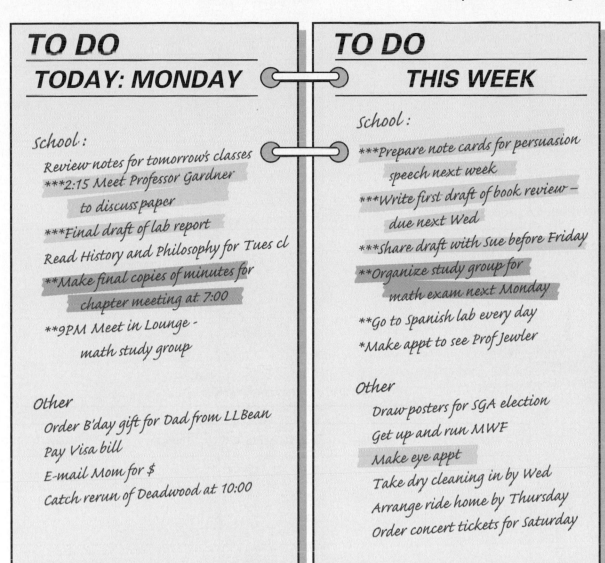

FIGURE 2.1
This to-do list won't allow you to forget!

This means that if you are taking a typical full-time class load of fifteen credits, for example, you should be planning to study an additional thirty hours per week. Think of this 45-hour-per-week commitment as comparable to a full-time job. Then if you are also working, reconsider how many hours per week it will be reasonable for you to be employed above and beyond this commitment, or consider reducing your credit load. At many institutions you need to carry a minimum of twelve or thirteen credits to be considered a full-time student, which can be important for financial aid and various forms of insurance.

- Depending on your biorhythms, obligations, and potential distractions, decide whether you will study more effectively in the day or in the evening, or a combination of both. Determine whether you are capable of getting up very early in the morning to study, or how late you can stay up at night and still wake up for morning classes.

	Monday	Tuesday	Wednesday	Thursday	Friday
Week 1					
Week 2					
Week 3					
Week 4					

	Monday	Tuesday	Wednesday	Thursday	Friday
Week 5					
Week 6					
Week 7					
Week 8					

FIGURE 2.2 **Term Assignment Preview**

Using the course syllabi provided by your instructors, enter all due dates on this term calendar. For longer assignments, such as term papers, divide the task into smaller parts and establish your own deadline for each part of the assignment, such as deadlines for choosing a topic, completing your library research, developing an outline of the paper, writing a first draft, and so on.

	Monday	Tuesday	Wednesday	Thursday	Friday
Week 9					
Week 10					
Week 11					
Week 12					

	Monday	Tuesday	Wednesday	Thursday	Friday
Week 13					
Week 14					
Week 15					
Week 16					

FIGURE 2.2 **Term Assignment Preview** *(continued)*

- Break large assignments such as term papers into smaller steps such as choosing a topic, doing research, creating a mind map (a technique we will describe in Chapter 9) or an outline, writing a first draft, and so on. Add deadlines in your schedule for each of the smaller portions of the project.

- All assignments are not equal. Estimate how much time you will need for each one, and begin your work early. A good time manager frequently finishes assignments before actual due dates to allow for emergencies.

- Keep track of how much time it takes you to complete different kinds of tasks. For example, depending on your skills and interests, it may take longer to read a chapter in a biology text than one in a literature text. Keeping track of your time will help you estimate how much time to allocate for similar tasks in the future. How long does it really take you to complete a set of twenty math problems or to write up a chemistry lab? Using a schedule form like that provided in Figure 2.2, or by entering all your activities in your planner (see Figure 2.3), actually track how you spend your time for an entire week.

- Set aside time for research and other preparatory tasks. Though instructors may expect you to be computer literate, they usually don't have time to explain how to use a word processor, spreadsheet, or statistical computer program. Most campuses have learning centers or computer centers that offer tutoring, walk-in assistance, or workshops to assist you with computer programs, e-mail, or searching the Internet. Your library may offer sessions on how to search for information using a variety of computer databases. Such services will save you time and usually are free.

- Schedule at least three aerobic workouts per week. (Walking to and from classes doesn't count!) You need to maintain an elevated heart rate for 30 minutes, plus allow time for warming up, stretching, and cooling down.

Use Figure 2.3 to tentatively plan how you will spend your hours in a typical week.

Where to Go for Help

ON CAMPUS

Academic Skills Center: Along with assistance on studying for exams, reading textbooks, and taking notes, your campus academic skills center has specialists in time management who can offer advice for your specific problems.

Counseling Center: This is another source to consider if your problems with time management involve emotional issues you are unable to resolve.

Your Academic Advisor/Counselor: If you have a good relationship with this person, he or she may be able to offer advice or to refer you to another person on campus, including those in the offices mentioned above.

A Fellow Student: A friend and good student who is willing to help you with time management can be one of your most valuable resources in this area.

ONLINE

Dartmouth College Academic Skills Center: http://www.dartmouth.edu/~acskills/success/time.html This website offers tips and resources for managing your time. Under "Time Management Resources," click to view the Time Management Video. You will need QuickTime® for this; it can be downloaded free from the QuickTime website.

	Sunday	Monday	Tuesday	Wednesday	Thursday	Friday	Saturday
6:00							
7:00							
8:00							
9:00							
10:00							
11:00							
12:00							
1:00							
2:00							
3:00							
4:00							
5:00							
6:00							
7:00							
8:00							
9:00							
10:00							
11:00							

FIGURE 2.3 Weekly Timetable
This chart may be used for several purposes: Using the suggestions in this chapter, create your perfect schedule for next term. Do you want your classes back-to-back or with breaks in between? How early in the morning are you willing to start classes? Do you prefer—or do work or family commitments require you—to take evening classes? Are there times of day when you are more alert? Less alert? How many days per week do you want to attend classes? At some institutions you can go to school full-time by attending classes on Saturday only. Plan how you will spend your time for the coming week. Track all of your activities for a full week by entering into this schedule form *everything* you do and how much time each task requires. Use this record to help you estimate the time needed for similar activities in the future.

Organizing Your Day

Being a good student does not necessarily mean studying day and night and doing little else. Keep the following points in mind as you organize your day:

See Exercise 2.4: Your Daily Plan

- Set realistic goals for your study time. Assess how long it takes to read a chapter in different types of texts and how long it takes you to review your notes from different instructors, and schedule your time accordingly. Give yourself adequate time to review and then test your knowledge when preparing for exams.

- Use waiting time (on the bus, before class, waiting for appointments) to review.

- Prevent forgetting what you have learned by allowing time to review as soon as reasonable after class. (Immediately after class may be possible, but not reasonable if you are too burned out to concentrate!)

- Know your best times of day to study. Schedule other activities, like doing laundry, responding to e-mail, or spending time with friends, for times when it will be difficult to concentrate.

- Schedule time right before and after meals for leisure activities; it's hard to study on an empty or full stomach.

- Use the same study area regularly. Have everything you may need, such as dictionary, thesaurus, writing utensils, highlighter, and note cards, readily available. Make sure you have adequate lighting, a chair with sufficient back support, and enough desk space to spread out everything you need. When working at a computer, make sure that the keyboard is at an appropriate height and that you adjust monitor settings to avoid eye strain.

- Assess your attention level. Make sure that you are studying actively, that you can recite what you have learned.

- Study difficult or boring subjects first, when you are fresh. (*Exception:* If you are having trouble getting started, it might be easier to get started with your favorite subject.)

- Avoid studying similar subjects back-to-back if you might confuse the material presented in each.

- Divide study time into fifty-minute blocks. Study for fifty minutes, then take a ten- or fifteen-minute break, then study for another fifty-minute block. Try not to study for more than three fifty-minute blocks in a row, or you will find that you are not accomplishing fifty minutes' worth of work. (In economics, this is known as the *law of diminishing returns*.)

- Break extended study sessions into a variety of activities, each with a specific objective. For example, begin by reading, then develop "flash cards" by writing key terms and their definitions or formulas on note cards, and finally test yourself on what you have read. You cannot expect yourself to concentrate on reading in the same text for three consecutive hours.

- Restrict repetitive, distracting, and time-consuming tasks like checking your e-mail to a certain time, not every hour.

- Avoid **multitasking.** Even though you may actually be quite good at it, or at least think that you are, the reality is that you will be able to study more effectively and retain more if you concentrate on one task at a time.

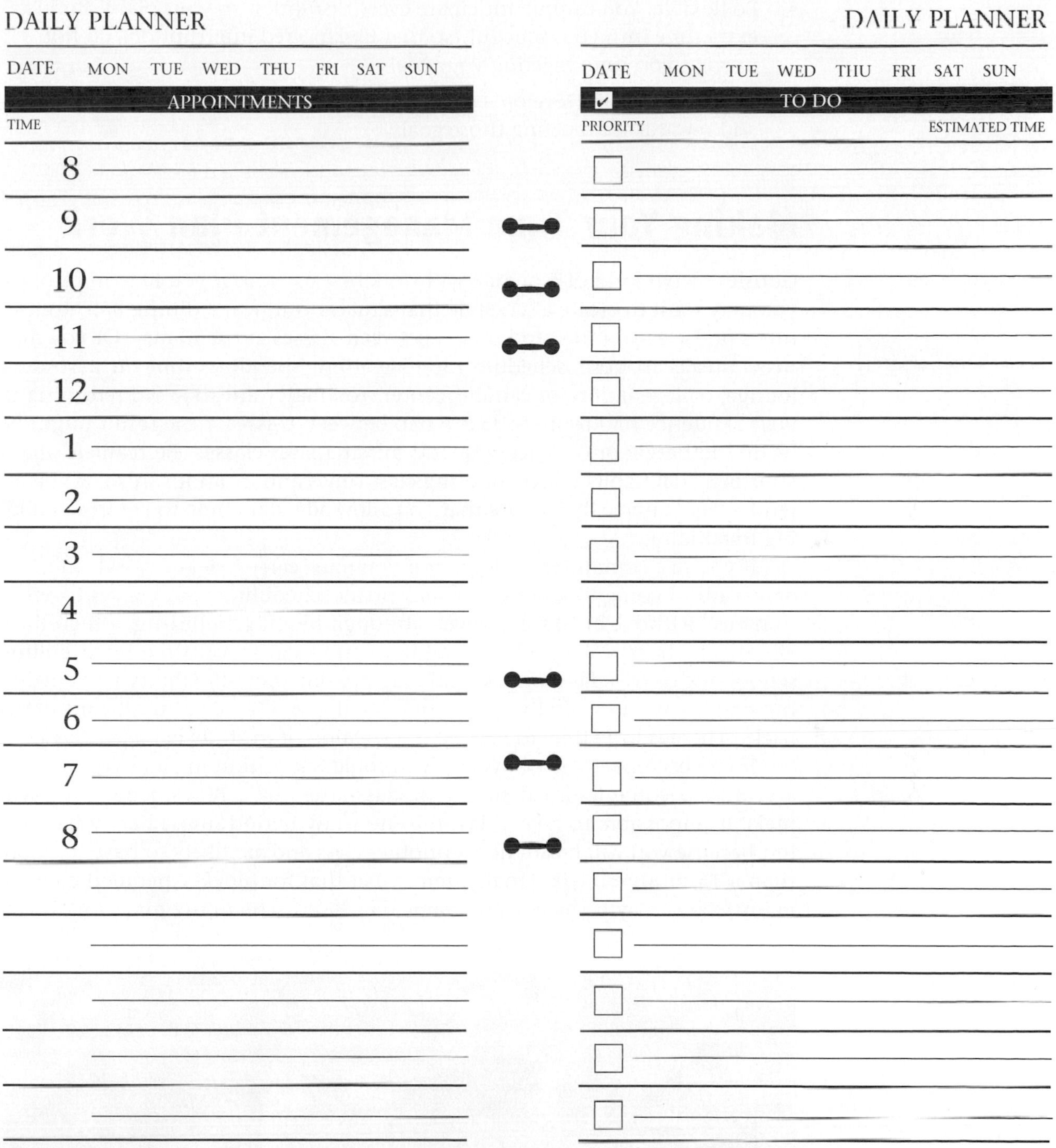

DAILY PLANNER

DATE   MON   TUE   WED   THU   FRI   SAT   SUN

APPOINTMENTS

TIME

8 ——————————————————

9 ——————————————————

10 —————————————————

11 —————————————————

12 —————————————————

1 ——————————————————

2 ——————————————————

3 ——————————————————

4 ——————————————————

5 ——————————————————

6 ——————————————————

7 ——————————————————

8 ——————————————————

DAILY PLANNER

DATE   MON   TUE   WED   THU   FRI   SAT   SUN

☑   **TO DO**

PRIORITY   ESTIMATED TIME

☐ ————————————————

☐ ————————————————

☐ ————————————————

☐ ————————————————

☐ ————————————————

☐ ————————————————

☐ ————————————————

☐ ————————————————

☐ ————————————————

☐ ————————————————

☐ ————————————————

☐ ————————————————

☐ ————————————————

☐ ————————————————

☐ ————————————————

☐ ————————————————

☐ ————————————————

FIGURE 2.4   **Sample Daily Planner**

List all of your classes and appointments for the day on the left side. Enter your to-do list for the day on the opposite page. In the boxes provided, indicate A for top priority, B for a lower level of priority, etc. Then return to the left-hand page to schedule times to complete your highest priority tasks.

- Be flexible! You cannot anticipate every disruption to your plans. Build extra time into your schedule so that unexpected interruptions do not prevent you from meeting your goals.

- Reward yourself! Develop a system of short- and long-term study goals and rewards for meeting those goals.

Making Your Time Management Plan Work

Consider what kind of schedule will work best for you. If you live on campus, you may want to create a schedule that situates you near a dining hall at mealtimes or forces you to spend breaks between classes at the library. Or you may need breaks in your schedule for relaxation, spending time in a student lounge, college union, or campus center. You may want to avoid returning to your residence hall room to take a nap between classes if the result might be feeling lethargic or oversleeping and missing later classes. Be realistic about your personal habits when choosing class times and locations. Also, if you attend a large university, be sure that you allow adequate time to get from building to building.

If you're a commuter student, or if you must carry a heavy workload in order to afford going to school, you may prefer scheduling your classes together in blocks without breaks. However, although **block scheduling**, which literally means back-to-back classes, allows you to cut travel time by attending school one or two days a week, and may provide more flexibility for scheduling employment or family commitments, it can also have significant drawbacks. There is little time to process information or to study between classes.

If you become ill on a class day, you could fall behind in all of your classes. You may become fatigued sitting in class after class. Block scheduling will make it impossible to have a last-minute study period immediately before a test because you will be attending another class and are likely to have no more than a 15-minute break. Finally, remember that for block-scheduled courses, many exams may be held on the same day. Block scheduling may work better

Avoid multitasking.

if you can attend lectures at an alternative time in case you are absent, if you alternate classes with free periods, and if you seek out instructors who allow you flexibility in completing assignments.

Don't Overextend Yourself

Being overextended is a primary source of stress for college students. Determine what is a realistic workload for you; this can vary significantly from person to person. Do not take on more than you can handle. Learn to say no. Do not feel obligated to provide a reason; you have the right to decline requests that will prevent you from getting your own work done.

With the best intentions, some students using a time management plan allow themselves to become overextended. If there is not enough time to carry your course load and meet your commitments, drop a course before the **drop date** so you won't have a low grade on your permanent record. If you are on financial aid, keep in mind that you must be registered for a minimum number of credit hours to be considered a full-time student and thereby maintain your current level of financial aid.

If dropping a course is not feasible, or if other activities are lower on your list of priorities, which is likely for most college students, assess your other time commitments and let go of one or more. Doing so can be very difficult, especially if you think that you are letting other people down. However, it is far preferable to excuse yourself from an activity in a way that is respectful to others than to fail to come through at the last minute because you have committed to more than you can possibly achieve.

Reduce Distractions

Where should you study? Do not study in places associated with leisure, such as the kitchen table, the living room, or in front of the TV, because they lend themselves to interruptions by others and other distractions. Also, your association with social activities in these locations can distract you even when others are not there. Similarly, it is unwise to study on your bed. You may find yourself drifting off when you need to study, or you may learn to associate your bed with studying and not be able to go to sleep when you need to. Instead, find quiet places, both on campus and at home, where you can concentrate and develop a study mind-set each time you sit down to do your work.

Try to stick to a routine as you study. The more firmly you have established a specific time and a quiet place to study, the more effective you will be in keeping up with your schedule. If you have larger blocks of time available on the weekend, for example, take advantage of that time to review or catch up on major projects, such as term papers, that can't be completed effectively in fifty-minute blocks. Break down large tasks and take one thing at a time; then you will make more progress toward your ultimate academic goals.

Here are some more tips to help you deal with distractions:

- Don't eat while you study. Ever wonder where that whole bag of chips went? You want your body to be focused on thinking, not digesting, and you want to avoid gaining that "freshman fifteen." (*Note:* This can happen regardless of your age when you begin college.)

- Leave the TV, CD player, DVD, iPod, and radio off, unless the background noise or music really helps you concentrate on your studies or drowns out more distracting noises (people laughing or talking in other rooms or hall-ways, for instance).

- Don't let personal concerns interfere with studying. If necessary, call a friend or write in a journal before you start to study, and then put your worries away. You might actually put your journal in a drawer and consider that synonymous with putting your problems away.

- Develop an agreement with your roommate(s)/family about "quiet" hours.

Time Management and "Civility"

Civility refers to basic politeness or good manners in the classroom, as well as how we communicate with one another. "Civility" really is all about extending respect to others. During the past decade college educators have begun to focus much more on this issue because many believe that levels of fundamental civility have been declining. Many of the types of disrespectful behaviors frequently mentioned by faculty members are in some way related to time management, most notably the practices of repeatedly arriving late for class and leaving before class periods have officially ended.

At times what instructors perceive as inappropriate or disrespectful behavior may be the result of a cultural misunderstanding. All cultures view time differently. In American academic culture, punctuality is a virtue. This may be a difficult adjustment for you if you were raised in a culture that is more flexible in its approach to time, but it is important to recognize the values of the new culture you have entered. Although you should not have to alter your cultural identity in order to be successful in college, you need to be aware of the expectations faculty members typically place on students.

- Be in class on time. Arrive early enough to shed outerwear, shuffle through your backpack, and have your assignments, notebooks, and writing utensils ready to go.

- Be on time for scheduled appointments. Avoid behaviors that show a lack of respect for both the instructor and other students, including walking out in the middle of class to plug a parking meter or answer your cell phone; returning five or ten minutes later and disrupting class twice; doing homework for another class; falling asleep; or whispering or talking.

- Make adequate transportation plans in advance, get enough sleep at night, wake up early enough to be on time for class, and complete assignments prior to class.

Time management is a lifelong skill. The better the job you have after college, the more likely it is that you will be managing your own time and possibly that of other people you supervise. It is critical to understand the importance of demonstrating respect for others through your approach to managing your own time.

ACHIEVE IT!   *Setting Goals for Success*

Go back to the self-assessment at the beginning of this chapter and select one to three unchecked items from the list. Use these to formulate short-term goals for yourself. Be specific about what you want to achieve and when (for example, not "become an active learner," but "find an excuse to meet with at least one of my teachers sometime next week"). Remember to choose goals that are realistic and important to you. Think about what obstacles could get in the way of achieving your goals, and make your plan. In the event you checked all items in the self-assessment, come up with one or more additional goals for this exercise.

	Goal 1	Goal 2	Goal 3
My short-term goal is . . .			
I want to achieve this goal by . . . (date)			
This goal matters because . . .			
I may encounter the following obstacles . . .			
My method for accomplishing this goal will be to . . .			

Set a Date. Put your deadline for achieving your goal(s) in your calendar. Count back ten days from your deadline and write a reminder for yourself.

Reassess. After your deadline passes, ask yourself: Did I meet this goal on time? What change has it made in my life? If I did not meet it, what am I planning to do about it?

TRY IT! *Exercises*

The exercises at the end of each chapter will help you sharpen what we believe are the critical skills for college success: writing, critical thinking, learning in groups, planning, reflecting, and taking action. You can further explore the topic of each chapter by using your PIN to complete the exercises on the website for this text: **http://success.wadsworth.com/gardner7e/.**

WORKING TOGETHER: Comparing Class Schedules

In a small group, share your current class schedules with the other students. Exchange ideas on how to effectively handle time management problems and the challenges you see in others' schedules. Discuss how you would arrange your schedule differently for the next term.

EXERCISE 2.1: Goal Setting

A. Name five goals you would like to set for yourself for the coming decade.

1. _____

2. _____

3. _____

4. _____

5. _____

B. List two measurable objectives for achieving each of the goals set above.

1. a. _____

   b. _____

2. a. _____

   b. _____

3. a. _____

   b. _____

4. a. _____

   b. _____

5. a. _____

   b. _____

EXERCISE 2.2: The Ideal Class Schedule

After you have participated in the Working Together exercise, use the weekly timetable (see Figure 2.3, page 31) to create your ideal class schedule. Then look in your school's schedule of courses for next term, and see if you can find courses you need that fit your ideal schedule. Complete this activity before you meet with your advisor to talk about registration for next term.

EXERCISE 2.3: Tracking "Actual Time"

Using the weekly timetable (see Figure 2.3) or your planner or handheld PDA, keep track of how you spend your time every hour for an entire week. Fill in every time slot. Then count how many hours you spent on various activities. How many hours did you spend studying? With family? Socializing? By yourself/personal time? Exercising? Relaxing? Working? Sleeping? Doing household chores like laundry or dishes? Watching television? Eating? Shopping? Reading for pleasure? Talking on the phone? What activities merit more time? On which activities should you be spending less time? In what ways did you waste time?

EXERCISE 2.4: Your Daily Plan

Using one day from this week's schedule, make a daily plan by filling in the daily planner in Figure 2.4. Circle the day of the week. List the day's appointments on the page with hours of the day. On the opposite page, list your to-do activities. Using a simple priority system, label them with an A, B, or C, with A's deserving the most attention. By tackling these first, you may not finish your list but you probably will be more satisfied with your accomplishments.

Check out the different calendar and personal planner formats at your bookstore and buy one that works for you. Make a commitment to use it. You may want to purchase an electronic planner or put your schedule on your personal computer. Writing and revising the schedule, however, should not become a goal in itself. The important thing is not how you write the schedule, but how easily you can keep track of it and adhere to it.

WRITE ABOUT IT! My Personal Journal

This is your place to sound off, to ask your teacher to clarify part of the lesson, or to write him or her about a minor on major crisis you're experiencing. Find out if your teacher wishes you to turn in your journals. Ask if they will remain confidential. Even if the journal isn't used in your course, you can still use the format to write about and reflect on issues regarding the class, yourself, or both.

1. What was the one major lesson you learned from reading this chapter and/or from class lecture and discussion?

2. What are some other important lessons about this topic?

3. If you believe some parts of this chapter are unimportant, spell them out here and tell why you think so. (You even might want to discuss this point with your classmates to see if they came up with a similar list.)

4. If anything is keeping you from performing at your peak level academically, describe what it is. Your instructor may be able to help or refer you to someone else on campus who can help.

5. What behaviors are you planning to change after reading this chapter? Why?

How We Learn

In this chapter YOU WILL LEARN

- Many approaches to understanding your learning styles or preferences
- How learning styles and teaching styles may differ
- How to optimize your learning style in any classroom setting
- How to understand and recognize a learning disability

There are many ways to learn. What strategies do you use?

Tom Carskadon of Mississippi State University contributed his valuable and considerable expertise to the writing of this chapter.

SELF-ASSESSMENT
HOW WE LEARN

Check the items below that apply to you.

1. ___ I think that there are many ways to learn beyond listening and reading.

2. ___ I know which of my senses I use most frequently in learning.

3. ___ I understand what is meant by the theory of multiple intelligences.

4. ___ I know something about the Myers-Briggs Type Indicator®.

5. ___ I can identify which of my classes are taught in ways that allow me to use my preferred style of learning.

6. ___ I know where on my campus to get help with a learning problem.

7. ___ I have developed ways to use all my strengths in the learning process.

8. ___ I understand which of my current courses ask me to learn in different ways.

9. ___ I can identify students in each of my classes, or at least some of my classes, who learn the same way I do, or in different ways.

10. ___ I understand the meaning of the term *dyslexia*.

If you checked seven or fewer of the items, find someone who can help you understand why all ten items are critical. At the end of this chapter, you will be asked to set personal goals for one or more of your unchecked items. If you checked all items, you will be asked to set other goals.

People learn differently. This is hardly a novel idea, but in order for you to do well in college it is important that you become aware of your preferred way or "style" of learning. Experts agree that there is no one best way to learn. You may have trouble paying attention to a long lecture, or listening may be the way you learn best. You may love classroom discussion, or you may consider hearing what other students have to say in class a big waste of time.

You've probably already discovered that college instructors and even courses have their own inherent styles. Many instructors rely almost solely on lecturing, and others use lots of visual aids such as PowerPoint outlines, charts, graphs, and pictures. In science courses, you will conduct experiments or go on field trips where you can observe or touch what you are studying; and in dance, theater, or physical education, learning takes place in both your body and your mind. And in almost all courses, you'll also learn by reading both textbooks and other materials. Some instructors are friendly and warm; others seem to want little interaction with students. It's safe to say that in at least some of your college courses, you won't find a close match between the way you learn most effectively and the way you're being taught. This chapter will help you first to understand how you learn best, and then to think of ways you can create a link between your style of learning and the expectations of each course and each instructor.

There are many ways of thinking about and describing **learning styles**. Some of these will make a lot of sense to you; others may initially seem confusing or counterintuitive. Some learning styles theories are very simple, with only two or three components, and others are far more complex. One of the simplest descriptions of learning styles is the division of all learners into **splitters** and **lumpers**. You are a splitter if you tend to analyze information logically and break it down into small parts and a lumper if you tend to watch for patterns and relationships in order to get the big picture.[1] Differences in splitters and lumpers are often played out in the biological sciences. In biology, lumpers are researchers who prefer to take a broad view and assume that differences between species are not as important as their similarities. Splitters, on the other hand, use very precise definitions, and create new categories and subcategories to account for every difference.

In addition to its focus on learning styles, this chapter will also explore **learning disabilities**. You may know someone who has been diagnosed with a learning disability such as dyslexia or attention deficit disorder. By reading this chapter you will learn more about common types of learning disabilities, how to recognize them, and what to do if you or someone you know has a learning disability.

Learning about Learning Styles

Of the dozens of learning styles models, we will review five that are perhaps best known and most relevant to your learning. You will notice some overlap between the different models, but using several of them may help you do a more precise job of discovering your learning style. If you are interested in reading more about learning styles, your library and your learning center will have many resources available to you.

Field Dependence/Independence

Let's begin by describing a simple learning styles model called **Field Dependence/Independence**. This is a concept that defines whether and to what degree learners are influenced by the surrounding environment and relationships within the classroom setting. *Field-independent learners* tend to be highly autonomous. They require little interaction with instructors or other students and tend to favor areas of study that call for analytic skills, such as mathematics, engineering, and science. *Field-dependent students* tend to learn more effectively in a classroom where there is frequent interaction with others, and they tend to choose majors that include interpersonal relationships, such as clinical psychology, humanities, counseling, and teaching.[2]

Think about your classes this term. Which of them would you describe as favoring field-independent or field-dependent students? If you believe you are "field-dependent," you may feel lonely and alienated in some of your classes if there is only "one-way" interaction—that is, the instructor is talking "at" you. And if you are "field-independent," you may become annoyed if the instructor spends time in creating ways for you to interact with your classmates.

Research has found that field dependence is more common in women and in students from some racial or ethnic groups. And because the word *dependence*

[1] P. Kirby, "Cognitive Style, Learning Style and Transfer Skill Acquisition," Information Series No. 195. (Columbus, OH: Ohio State University, National Center for Research in Vocational Education, 1979).
[2] Herman A. Witkin, "Cognitive Style in Academic Performance and in Teacher-Student Relations," in *Individuality in Learning,* ed. Samuel Messick & Associates (San Francisco: Jossey-Bass, 1976).

has negative connotations, some educators have suggested that the term *field-sensitive* be substituted. But whatever term you use, you can work to make the classroom more conducive to your learning. If you are taking a large lecture class and find that you want to interact with other students or with the instructor, arrange study sessions with other students, have conversations before and after class with the persons sitting next to you, and take advantage of your instructor's office hours. If there is too much interaction to suit your taste, realize that some students in your class really need that interaction in order to learn effectively. It may not be your "cup of tea," but interacting with others in the classroom may, in fact, enhance your learning also. Bottom line: It is important that, whatever the prevailing classroom environment, you not allow that to be an excuse for doing less than your best.

Kolb Inventory of Learning Styles

A more complex learning model that is widely used and referenced by researchers and educators is the *Kolb Inventory of Learning Styles*, developed in the 1980s by David Kolb. This inventory is based on a four-stage cycle of learning (see Figure 3.1)

According to Kolb, effective learners need four different kinds of abilities: **concrete experience** abilities, which allow them to involve themselves fully in new experiences; **reflective observation** abilities, which help them to reflect on their experiences from many perspectives; **abstract conceptualization**

Figure 3.1 The Experiential Learning Model

Adapted from Kolb, 1981

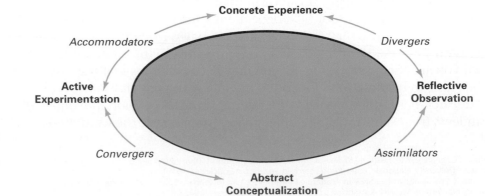

abilities, which help them integrate observations into logically sound theories; and **active experimentation** abilities, which enable them to make decisions, solve problems, and test what they have learned in new situations.

Kolb's inventory of learning styles measures differences along the two basic dimensions of **abstract-concrete** and **active-reflective** and divides learners into four discrete groups: **divergers, assimilators, convergers,** and **accommodators** (see Figure 3.1).

If you are a *diverger,* you are good at reflecting on situations from many viewpoints. You excel at brainstorming, and you're imaginative, people oriented, and sometimes emotional. On the downside, you sometimes have difficulty making decisions. Divergers tend to major in the humanities or social sciences.

If you are an *assimilator,* you like to think about abstract concepts. You are comfortable in classes where the instructor lectures about theoretical ideas without relating the lectures to real-world situations. Assimilators often major in math, physics, or chemistry.

If you are a *converger,* you like the world of ideas and theories, but you also are good at thinking about how to apply those theories to real-world, practical situations. You differ from divergers by your preference for tasks and problems rather than social and interpersonal issues. Convergers tend to choose health-related and engineering majors.

If you are an *accommodator,* you prefer hands-on learning. You are good at making things happen, you rely on your intuition, and you like people. However, sometimes you may be pushy, and impatient, and may use trial and error, rather than logical analysis, to solve problems. Accommodators often major in business, especially in marketing or sales.[3]

Doing well in college will require that you adopt some behaviors characteristic of each of these four styles. Some of them may be uncomfortable for you, but that discomfort will indicate that you're growing, stretching, and not relying on the learning style that may be easiest or most natural (Kolb, 1981). In your classes, you will need to develop the strengths of convergers—imagination, brainstorming, and listening with an open mind. The abilities that are characteristic of assimilators, developing theories and concepts, are of value for all students, especially those in the sciences. If you major in the health sciences or in engineering, you'll routinely practice the skills of convergers—experimenting with new ideas and choosing the best solution, and finally, whatever your major and ultimate career, you'll need to get things done, take some risks, and become a leader—skills characteristic of accommodators.

The Myers-Briggs Type Indicator

One of the best known and most widely used personality inventories that can also be used to describe learning styles is the *Myers-Briggs Type Indicator*® or MBTI. The MBTI was created by Isabel Briggs Myers and her mother, Katharine Cook Briggs. The inventory identifies and measures psychological type as developed in the personality theory of Carl Gustav Jung, the great twentieth-century psychoanalyst. The MBTI is given to several million people around the world each year. In fact, many first-year seminar or college success courses include a focus on the MBTI because it provides a good way to begin a dialogue about how students learn. All the psychological types described by

[3] Adapted from David A. Kolb, "Learning Styles and Disciplinary Differences," in *The Modern American College,* ed. Arthur W. Chickering, 232–55 (San Francisco: Jossey Bass, 1981).

the MBTI are normal and healthy; there is no good or bad or right or wrong—people are simply different. When you complete the Myers-Briggs survey instrument, your score is your "psychological type"—the combination of your preferences on four different scales. These scales measure how you take in information and how you then make decisions or come to conclusions about that information. Each preference has a one-letter abbreviation. The four letters together make up your "type."

Extraversion (E) vs. Introversion (I): The Inner or Outer World

The E-I preference indicates whether you direct your energy and attention primarily toward the outer world of people, events, and things or the inner world of thoughts, feelings, and reflections.

Extraverts tend to be outgoing, gregarious, and talkative. They often "think with the volume on," saying out loud what is going through their minds. They are energized by people and activity, and they seek this in both work and play. They are people of action, who like to spend more time doing things than thinking about them. At their best, they are good communicators who are quick to act and lead. At their worst, they talk too much and too loudly, drowning out others, and they act before they think. (Note that when using the term in the context of psychological type and the MBTI, "extravert" is spelled with an "a" and not an "o," even though the latter is the more common spelling elsewhere.)

Introverts prefer to reflect carefully on things and think them through before taking action. They think a lot, but if you want to know what's on their minds, you may have to ask them. They are refreshed by quiet and privacy. At their best, introverts are good, careful listeners whose thoughts are deep and whose actions are well considered. At their worst, they may be too shy and not aware enough of the people and situations around them, and they may think about things so long that they neglect to actually start doing them.

Sensing (S) vs. Intuition (N): Facts or Ideas

The S-N preference indicates how you perceive the world and take in information: directly, through your five senses; or indirectly, using your intuition. (This preference is similar to the notion, mentioned earlier, of "splitters" and "lumpers.")

Sensing types are interested above all in the facts, what is known and what they can be sure of. Typically they are practical, factual, realistic, and down-to-earth. They can be very accurate, steady, precise, and patient and effective with routine and details. They are often relatively traditional and conventional. They dislike unnecessary complication, and they prefer to practice skills they already know. At their best, sensing types can be counted on to do things right, with every detail well taken care of. At their worst, they can plod along while missing the point of why they are doing what they do, not seeing the forest (the whole picture) for the trees (the details).

Intuitive types are fascinated by possibilities—not so much the facts themselves, but what those facts mean, what concepts might describe those facts, how those might relate to other concepts, and what the implications of the facts would be. Intuitive types are less tied to the here and now and tend to look further into the future and the past. They need inspiration and meaning for what they do, and they tend to work in bursts of energy and enthusiasm. Often they are original, creative, and nontraditional. They may have trouble with routine and details, however, and they would rather learn a new skill than keep practicing the one they have already mastered. They can be bad at facts and may exaggerate without realizing it. At their best, intuitive types are bright, innovative people who thrive in academic settings and the world of invention and ideas. At their worst, they can be impractical dreamers whose visions fall short because of inattention to detail.

Thinking (T) vs. Feeling (F): Logic or Values

The T-F preference indicates how you prefer to make your decisions: through logical, rational analysis or through your subjective values, likes, and dislikes.

Thinking types are usually logical, rational, analytical, and critical. They pride themselves on reasoning their way to the best possible decisions. They tend to decide things relatively impersonally and objectively, and they are less swayed by feelings and emotions—both their own and other people's. Other people's feelings sometimes puzzle or surprise them. They can deal with interpersonal disharmony and can be firm and assertive when they need to be. In all their dealings, they need and value fairness. At their best, thinking types are firm, fair, logical, and just. At their worst, they may be cold, insensitive to other people's feelings, and overly blunt and hurtful in their criticisms.

Feeling types are typically warm, empathic, sympathetic, and interested in the happiness of others as well as themselves. They need and value harmony, and they may be distressed and distracted by argument and conflict. They sometimes have trouble being assertive when it would be appropriate to do so. Above all, they need and value kindness. At their best, feeling types are warm and affirming and facilitate cooperation and goodwill among those around them while pursuing the best human values. At their worst, feeling types can be illogical, emotionally demanding, reluctant to tackle unpleasant tasks, and unaffected by objective reason and evidence.

Judging (J) vs. Perceiving (P): Organization or Adaptability

The J-P preference indicates how you characteristically approach the outside world: making decisions and judgments, or observing and perceiving instead.

Judging types approach the world in a planned, orderly, organized way; as much as possible, they try to order and control their part of it. They make their decisions relatively quickly and easily. They like to make and follow plans. They are usually punctual and tidy, and they appreciate those traits in others. At their best, judging types are natural organizers who get things done and done on time. At their worst, judging types may jump to conclusions prematurely, be too judgmental of people, make decisions too hastily without enough information, and have trouble changing their plans even when those plans are not working.

Perceiving types don't try to control their world, as much as adapt to it. Theirs is a flexible, wait-and-see approach. They deal comfortably and well with changes, unexpected developments, and emergencies, adjusting their plans and behaviors as needed. They tend to delay decisions so that they can keep their options open and gather more information. They may procrastinate to a serious degree, however, and they may try to carry on too many things at once, without finishing any of them. At their best, perceiving types are spontaneous, flexible individuals who roll with the punches and find ways to take the proverbial lemons in life and turn them into lemonade. At their worst, perceiving types may become messy, disorganized procrastinators.

Because there are two possible choices for each of four different prefer-ences, there are sixteen possible psychological types. No matter what your Myers-Briggs type, all components of personality have value in the learning process. The key to success in college, therefore, is to use all the attitudes and functions (E, I, S, N, T, F, J, and P) in their most positive sense. As you go about your studies, here is a system we recommend:

1. **Sensing: Get the facts.** Use sensing to find and learn the facts. What are the facts? How do we know them? What is the factual evidence for what is being said?
2. **Intuition: Get the ideas.** Now use intuition to consider what those facts mean. Why are those facts being presented? What concepts and ideas are being supported by those facts? What are the implications? What is the "big picture"?
3. **Thinking: Critically analyze.** Use thinking to analyze the pros and cons of what is being presented. Are there gaps in the evidence? What more do we need to know? Do the facts really support the conclusions? Are there

alternative explanations? How well does what is presented hang together logically? How could our knowledge of it be improved?

4. **Feeling: Make informed value judgments.** Why is this material important? What does it contribute to people's good? Why might it be important to you personally? What is your personal opinion about it?

5. **Introversion: Think it through.** Before you take any action, carefully go over in your mind everything you have encountered so far.

6. **Judging: Organize and plan.** Don't just dive in! Now is the time to organize and plan your studying so you will learn and remember everything you need to. Don't just plan in your head, either; write your plan down, in detail.

7. **Extraversion: Take action.** Now that you have a plan, act on it. Do whatever it takes. Create note cards, study outlines, study groups, and so on. If you are working on a paper instead of a test, then now is the time to start writing.

8. **Perceiving: Change your plan as needed.** Be flexible enough to change your plan if it isn't working. Expect the unexpected and deal with the unforeseen. Don't give up the whole effort the minute your original plan stops working; figure out what's wrong, and come up with another, better plan and start following that.[4]

See Exercise 3.1: Myers-Briggs Exploration

There are many paths and directions to learning. Explore them all!

Multiple Intelligences

Another way of measuring how we learn is the theory of multiple intelligences, developed in 1983 by Dr. Howard Gardner, a professor of education at Harvard University. Gardner's theory is based on the premise that the traditional notion of human intelligence is very limited. He proposes eight different intelligences to describe how humans learn.

As you might imagine, Gardner's work is very controversial as it calls into question our historic definitions of intelligence. But Gardner argues that students should be encouraged to develop the abilities they have and that evaluation should measure all forms of intelligence, not just linguistic and logical-mathematical.

As you think of yourself and your friends, what kinds of intelligences do you have? Do college courses measure all the ways that you are intelligent? Here is a short inventory that will help you recognize your multiple intelligences.

[4] Isabel Briggs Myers, *Introduction to Type*, 6th ed. (Palo Alto, CA: CPP, Inc., 1998).

Multiple Intelligences Inventory

Research shows that all human beings have at least eight different types of intelligence. Depending on your background and age, some intelligences are likely to be more developed than others. This activity will help you find out what your intelligences are. Knowing this, you can work to strengthen the other intelligences that you do not use as often.

Put a check mark next to the items that apply to you.

Verbal/Linguistic Intelligence

____ I enjoy telling stories and jokes

____ I have a good memory for trivia

____ I enjoy word games (for example, Scrabble and puzzles)

____ I read books just for fun

____ I am a good speller (most of the time)

____ In an argument, I tend to use put-downs or sarcasm

____ I like talking and writing about my ideas

____ If I have to memorize something, I create a rhyme or saying to help me remember

____ If something breaks and won't work, I read the instruction book before I try to fix it

____ When I work with others in a group presentation I prefer to do the writing and library research

Logical/Mathematical Intelligence

____ I really enjoy my math class

____ I like logical math puzzles or brain teasers

____ I find solving math problems to be fun

____ If I have to memorize something, I tend to place events in a logical order

____ I like to find out how things work

____ I enjoy computer and math games

____ I love playing chess, checkers, or Monopoly

____ In an argument, I try to find a fair and logical solution

____ If something breaks and won't work, I look at the pieces and try to figure out how it works

____ When I work with others in a group presentation, I prefer to create the charts and graphs

Visual/Spatial Intelligence

____ I prefer a map to written directions

____ I daydream a lot

____ I enjoy hobbies such as photography

____ I like to draw and create

____ If I have to memorize something, I draw a diagram to help me remember

____ I like to doodle on paper whenever I can

____ In a magazine, I prefer looking at the pictures rather than reading the text

____ In an argument, I try to keep my distance, keep silent, or visualize some solution

____ If something breaks and won't work, I tend to study the diagram of how it works

____ When I work with others in a group presentation, I prefer to draw all the pictures

Bodily/Kinesthetic Intelligence

____ My favorite class is gym since I like sports

____ I enjoy activities such as woodworking, sewing, and building models

____ When looking at things, I like touching them

____ I have trouble sitting still for any length of time

____ I use a lot of body movements when talking

____ If I have to memorize something, I write it out a number of times until I know it

____ I tend to tap my fingers or play with my pencil during class

____ In an argument, I tend to strike out and hit or run away

____ If something breaks and won't work, I tend to play with the pieces to try to fit them together

____ When I work with others in a group presentation, I prefer to move the props around, hold things up, or build a model

Musical/Rhythmic Intelligence

____ I enjoy listening to CDs and the radio

____ I tend to hum to myself when working

____ I like to sing

____ I play a musical instrument quite well

____ I like to have music playing when doing homework or studying

____ If I have to memorize something, I try to create a rhyme about the event

____ In an argument, I tend to shout or punch, or move in some sort of rhythm

____ I can remember the melodies of many songs

____ If something breaks and won't work, I tend to tap my fingers to a beat while I figure it out

____ When I work with others in a group presentation, I prefer to put new words to a popular tune or use music

Interpersonal Intelligence

____ I get along well with others

____ I like to belong to clubs and organizations

____ I have several very close friends

____ I like helping teach other students

____ I like working with others in groups

____ Friends ask my advice because I seem to be a natural leader

____ If I have to memorize something, I ask someone to quiz me to see if I know it

____ In an argument, I tend to ask a friend or some person in authority for help

____ If something breaks and won't work, I try to find someone who can help me

____ When I work with others, I like to help organize the group's efforts

(From http://www.ldrc.ca/projects/miinventory/mitest.html)

Intrapersonal Intelligence

___ I like to work alone without anyone bothering me

___ I like to keep a diary

___ I like myself (most of the time)

___ I don't like crowds

___ I know my own strengths and weaknesses

___ I find that I am strong-willed, independent, and don't follow the crowd

___ If I have to memorize something, I tend to close my eyes and feel the situation

___ In an argument, I will usually walk away until I calm down

___ If something breaks and won't work, I wonder if it's worth fixing

___ When I work with others in a group presentation, I like to contribute something that is uniquely mine, often based on how I feel

Naturalist Intelligence

___ I am keenly aware of my surroundings and of what goes on around me

___ I love to go walking in the woods and looking at the trees and flowers

___ I enjoy gardening

___ I like to collect things like rocks, sports cards, and stamps

___ I like to get away from the city and enjoy nature

___ If I have to memorize something, I tend to organize it into categories

___ I enjoy learning the names of living things in our environment, such as flowers and trees

___ In an argument, I tend to compare my opponent to someone or something I have read or heard about and react accordingly

___ If something breaks down, I look around me to try and see what I can find to fix the problem

___ When I work with others in a group presentation, I prefer to organize and classify the information into categories so it makes sense

A *verbal/linguistic learner* likes to read, write, and tell stories, and is good at memorizing information.

A *logical/mathematical learner* likes to work with numbers, and is good at problem solving and logical processes.

A *visual/spatial learner* likes to draw and play with machines, and is good at puzzles and reading maps and charts.

A *bodily/kinesthetic learner* likes to move around and is good at sports, dance, and acting.

A *musical learner* likes to sing and play an instrument, and is good at remembering melodies and noticing pitches and rhythms.

An *interpersonal learner* likes to have many friends and is good at understanding people, leading others, and mediating conflicts.

An *intrapersonal learner* likes to work alone and is good at understanding his/her self and being original.

A *naturalistic learner* likes to be outside and is good at preservation, conservation, and organizing a living area.

You can use your intelligences to help you make decisions about a major, choose activities, and investigate career options. Which of these eight intelligences best describes you?

TOTAL SCORE

_____ Verbal/Linguistic

_____ Logical/Mathematical

_____ Visual/Spatial

_____ Bodily/Kinesthetic

_____ Musical/Rhythmic

_____ Interpersonal

_____ Intrapersonal

_____ Naturalist

Add the number of check marks you made in each section. Your score for each intelligence will be a number between 1 and 10. Note especially your "high" (7 or more) scores in order to get a sense of your own multiple intelligences.

See Working Together:
Multiple Intelligences

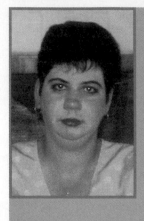

TURNING POINT

I learn best hands on. I need to do it for myself before I can learn something. Sometimes, it is easy for me to learn visually. For example, reading the text or a handout is beneficial. I find it hard to learn in auditory mode, but certain strategies, like reading the assignment after it has been discussed in class, help. Discussing the assignment with other students with different learning styles helps to give me a better perspective on the material.

Laurie T.
Jackson State Community College

The VARK (Visual, Aural, Read/Write, and Kinesthetic) Learning Styles Inventory

The VARK is different from the four previously described learning styles theories because it relies less on basic personality or intelligence and more on *how learners prefer to use their senses to learn.* The acronym VARK stands for "Visual," "Aural," "Read/Write," and "Kinesthetic." Visual learners prefer to learn information through charts, graphs, symbols, and other visual means. Aural learners prefer to hear information. Read/Write learners prefer to learn information that is displayed as words, and Kinesthetic learners prefer to learn through experience and practice, whether simulated or real. To determine your learning style according to the VARK Inventory, respond to the questionnaire below.

The VARK Questionnaire

Revised version - January 2005

This questionnaire is designed to tell you something about your preferences for the way you work with information. Choose the answer that best explains your preference. Check the box next to that item. Please select as many boxes as apply to you. If none of the response options to apply to you, leave the item blank.

1. You are about to give directions to a person who is staying in a hotel in town and wants to visit your house later. She has a rental car. You would:
   ☐ draw or provide a map on paper. (a)
   ☐ tell her the directions. (b)
   ☐ write down the directions (without a map). (c)
   ☐ collect her from the hotel in a car. (d)

2. You are not sure whether a word should be spelled *dependent* or *dependant*. You would:
   ☐ look it up in the dictionary. (c)
   ☐ see the word in your mind and choose by the way it looks. (a)
   ☐ sound it out in your mind. (b)
   ☐ write both versions down on paper and choose one. (d)

3. You have just received a copy of your itinerary for a world trip. This is of interest to some friends. You would:
   ☐ phone, text message, or e-mail them and tell them about it. (b)
   ☐ send them a copy of the printed itinerary. (c)
   ☐ show them on a map of the world. (a)
   ☐ describe what you plan to do at each place on the itinerary. (d)

4. You are going to cook something as a special treat for your family. You would:
   ☐ cook something familiar without the need for instructions. (d)
   ☐ thumb through the cookbook looking at the pictures to get ideas. (a)
   ☐ refer to a specific cookbook where there is a good recipe. (c)

5. A group of tourists has been assigned to you to find out about wildlife reserves or parks. You would:
   - [ ] drive them to a wildlife reserve or park. (d)
   - [ ] show them slides and photographs. (a)
   - [ ] give them pamphlets or a book on wildlife reserves or parks. (c)
   - [ ] give them a talk on wildlife reserves or parks. (b)

6. You are about to purchase a new CD player. Other than price, what would most influence your decision?
   - [ ] what the salesperson tells you. (b)
   - [ ] reading the details about it. (c)
   - [ ] playing with the controls and listening to it. (d)
   - [ ] the way it looks. (a)

7. Recall a time in your life when you learned how to do something like playing a new board game. Try to avoid choosing a very physical skill, such as riding a bike. You learned best by:
   - [ ] visual clues—pictures, diagrams and charts. (a)
   - [ ] written instructions. (c)
   - [ ] listening to somebody explain it. (b)
   - [ ] doing it or trying it. (d)

8. You have a knee problem. You would prefer that the doctor:
   - [ ] tell you what was wrong. (b)
   - [ ] show you a diagram of what was wrong. (a)
   - [ ] use a model of a knee to show you what was wrong. (d)

9. You are about to learn to use a new program on a computer. You would:
   - [ ] sit down at the keyboard and experiment with the program. (d)
   - [ ] read the manual that came with the program. (c)
   - [ ] telephone or text message a friend and ask questions about the program. (b)

10. You are staying in a hotel and have a rental car. You would like to visit friends whose address/location you do not know. You would like them to:
    - [ ] draw you a map on paper or provide a map from the Internet. (a)
    - [ ] tell you the directions. (b)
    - [ ] write down the directions (without a map). (c)
    - [ ] collect you from the hotel in a car. (d)

11. Apart from the price, what would most influence your decision to buy a particular textbook?
    - [ ] You have used a copy before. (d)
    - [ ] A friend talks about it. (b)
    - [ ] You quickly read parts of it. (c)
    - [ ] The way it looks is appealing. (a)

12. A new movie has arrived in town. What would most influence your decision to go (or not go)?
    - [ ] You heard a review about it on the radio. (b)
    - [ ] You read a review about it. (c)
    - [ ] You saw a preview of it. (a)

13. Do you prefer a teacher who likes to use:
    - [ ] a textbook, handouts, and readings (c)
    - [ ] flow diagrams, charts, and graphs. (a)
    - [ ] field trips, models, laboratories, and practical sessions. (d)
    - [ ] class or e-mail discussion, online chat groups, and guest speakers. (b)

Source: http://www.vark-learn.com/english/index.asp

Scoring the VARK

To score the VARK, first count your responses for each letter. Then total your responses.

Responses marked letter a = _____ (Visual)

Responses marked letter b = _____ (Aural)

Responses marked letter c = _____ (Read/Write)

Responses marked letter d = _____ (Kinesthetic)

Total responses   = _____

If your total number of responses is 31 or more, a strong learning preference is indicated by a difference of 6 or more between the highest number and other numbers, and a mild preference by a difference of 5. If differences are less than 5, you are multimodal.

If your total is 23–30, a strong learning preference is indicated by a difference of 5 or more between the highest number and other numbers, and a mild preference by a difference of 4. If differences are less than 4, you are multimodal.

If your total is 17–22, a strong learning preference is indicated by a difference of 3 or more between the highest number and other numbers, and a mild preference by a difference of 2. If differences are less than 2, you are multimodal.

If your total is no more than 16, a strong learning preference is indicated by a difference of 3 or more between the highest number and other numbers, and a mild preference by a difference of 2. If differences are less than 2, you are multimodal.

Here is a sample chart to help you with scoring:

	V	A	R	K	TOTAL
Betsy	10	0	2	1	13
Randy	8	7	3	5	23
John	7	4	6	3	17
Jerry	3	3	5	3	14

Betsy has a very strong visual preference ($10 - 2 = 8$) so A, R, and K are eliminated.

Randy is multimodal VAK, so R is eliminated ($8 - 3 = 5$).

John is multimodal VR, so A and K are eliminated ($7 - 4 = 3$; $7 - 3 = 4$).

Jerry has a mild preference for read/write ($5 - 3 = 2$).

Using VARK Results to Study More Effectively

How can knowing your VARK score help you do better in your college classes? Here are ways of using learning styles to develop your own study strategies.

If you have a **visual learning preference**, underline or highlight your notes, use symbols, charts, or graphs to display your notes, use different arrangements of words on the page, and redraw your pages from memory.

If you are an **aural learner**, talk with others to verify the accuracy of your lecture notes. Put your notes on tape and listen or tape class lectures. Read your notes out loud; ask yourself questions and speak your answers.

If you have a **read/write learning preference**, write and rewrite your notes, and read your notes silently. Organize diagrams or flow charts into statements, and write imaginary exam questions and respond in writing.

If you are a **kinesthetic learner**, you will need to use all your senses in learning—sight, touch, taste, smell, and hearing. Supplement your notes with real-world examples; move and gesture while you are reading or speaking your notes.

When Learning Styles and Teaching Styles Are in Conflict

See Exercise 3.2: Learning Styles Models

Researchers have found that college instructors tend to teach in ways that conform to their own particular style of learning. So if you have an instructor who is field-independent, introverted, prefers abstract concepts and reflection (an assimilator according to Kolb), and learns best in a read/write mode or aural mode, it is probable that her class will be primarily a lecture-only experience with little opportunity for either interaction or visual and kinesthetic learning. Conversely, an instructor who himself needs a more interactive, hands-on classroom environment will likely involve students in classroom discussion and learning through experience.

When you recognize a mismatch between how you learn best and how you are being taught, it is important that you take more control over your learning process. Don't depend on the instructor or the classroom environment to give you everything you need to maximize your learning. Employ your own unique preferences, talents, and abilities in developing ways to study and retain information. Look back through this chapter to remind yourself of the ways that you can use your own learning styles to be more successful in any class you take.

Learning with a Learning Disability

While everyone has a learning style, a portion of the population has what is characterized as a learning disability. Learning disabilities are usually recognized and diagnosed in grade school. But occasionally students are very successful at compensating for a learning problem and reach college never having been properly diagnosed or assisted.

What Is a Learning Disability (LD)?

LD is a disorder that affects people's ability either to interpret what they see and hear or to link information from different parts of the brain. These limitations can show up as specific difficulties with spoken and written language, coordination, self-control, or attention. Such difficulties can impede learning to read, write, or do math. LD is a broad term that covers a pool of possible causes, symptoms, treatments, and outcomes. Because of this it is difficult to diagnose or to pinpoint the causes. The types of LD that most commonly affect college students are academic skills disorders, including developmental reading, writing, and mathematics disorders.

Dyslexia, a developmental reading disorder, is quite widespread. A person can have problems with any of the tasks involved in reading. However, scientists have found that a significant number of people with dyslexia share an inability to distinguish or separate the sounds in spoken words. For instance, dyslexic individuals sometimes have difficulty assigning the appropriate sounds to letters either by themselves or when letters are combined to form words. However, there is more to reading than recognizing words. If the brain is unable to form images or relate new ideas to those stored in memory, the reader can't understand or remember the new concepts. So other types of reading disabilities can appear when the focus of reading shifts from word identification to comprehension.

Writing, too, involves several brain areas and functions. The brain networks for vocabulary, grammar, hand movement, and memory must all be in good working order. So a **developmental writing disorder** may result from problems in any of these areas. Someone who can't distinguish the sequence of sounds in a word will often have problems with spelling. Persons with writing disabilities, particularly **expressive language disorders** (the inability to express oneself using accurate language or sentence structure), are often unable to compose complete, grammatical sentences.

A student with a **developmental arithmetic disorder** will have difficulty recognizing numbers and symbols, memorizing facts such as the multiplication table, aligning numbers, and understanding abstract concepts like place value and fractions.

Another common type of learning disability is an **attention disorder**. Some students who have attention disorders appear to daydream excessively.

And once you get their attention, they may be easily distracted. Individuals with either attention deficit disorder (ADD) or attention deficit hyperactivity disorder (ADHD) often have trouble organizing tasks or completing their work. They don't seem to listen to or follow directions. Their work may be messy and appear careless. Attention disorders, with or without hyperactivity, are not considered learning disabilities in themselves. However, because attention problems can seriously interfere with academic performance, they often accompany academic skills disorders.

Here are some additional warning signs that will help you determine whether you or someone you know has a learning disability.

- Do you perform poorly on tests even when you feel you have studied and are capable of performing better?

- Do you have trouble spelling words?

- Do you work harder than your fellow classmates at basic reading and writing?

- Do your instructors tell you that your performance in class is "inconsistent"? For example, do you answer questions correctly in class but have trouble writing your answers?

- Do you have a really short attention span, or do your parents or instructors say that you do things "without thinking"?

While responding "yes" to any of the above questions *does not* mean that you have a learning disability, if you are concerned, you can use the resources of your campus's learning center, office of "special needs," or student disabilities office to help you respond to any problem you might have and devise ways to learn more effectively. And anyone who is diagnosed with a learning disability is in very good company. Magic Johnson, Jay Leno, Whoopi Goldberg, Tom Cruise, Cher, and Danny Glover are just a few of the famous and successful people who have diagnosed learning disabilities. A final word: A learning disability is a "learning difference," but is in no way related to intelligence. Having a learning disability is not a sign that you are "dumb." Far from it! Some of the most intelligent individuals in human history have had a learning disability.

See Exercise 3.3: Learning More about Learning Disabilities

Anyone can have a learning disability.

Where to Go for Help

ON CAMPUS

To learn more about learning styles and learning disabilities, talk to your first-year seminar instructor about campus resources. Most campuses will have a learning center, or center for students with disabilities. You may also find that instructors within the area of education or psychology have a strong interest in the processes of learning. Finally, don't forget your library or the Internet. A great deal of published information is available to describe how we learn.

BOOKS

Learning Outside the Lines: Two Ivy League Students with Learning Disabilities and ADHD Give You the Tools for Academic Success and Educational Revolution, by Edward M. Hallowell (Foreword), Jonathan Mooney, and David Cole. New York: Fireside, 2000.

Survival Guide for College Students with ADD or LD, by Kathleen G. Nadeau. Washington, DC: Magination Press, 1994.

ADD and the College Student: A Guide for High School and College Students with Attention Deficit Disorder, by Patricia O. Quinn, MD, ed. Washington, DC: Magination Press, 2001.

ONLINE

LD Pride: http://www.ldpride.net/learningstyles.MI.htm. This site was developed in 1998 by Liz Bogod, an adult with learning disabilities. It provides general information about learning styles and learning disabilities and offers an interactive diagnostic tool to determine your learning style.

Support 4 Learning: http://www.support4learning.org.uk/education/lstyles.htm. This site is supported by HERO, Higher Education and Research Opportunities, which is the official online gateway to UK universities, colleges, and research organizations. The site provides learning styles inventories and helpful hints about how to use your learning style to do well in college courses.

National Center for Learning Disabilities: http://www.ncld.org. This is the official website for the National Center for Learning Disabilities. The site provides a variety of resources on diagnosing and understanding learning disabilities.

ACHIEVE IT! *Setting Goals for Success*

Go back to the self-assessment at the beginning of this chapter and select one to three unchecked items from the list. Use these to formulate short-term goals for yourself. Be specific about what you want to achieve and when. Remember to choose goals that are realistic and important to you. Think about what obstacles could get in the way of achieving your goals, and make your plan. In the event you checked all items in the self-assessment, come up with one or more additional goals for this exercise.

	Goal 1	Goal 2	Goal 3
My short-term goal is . . .			
I want to achieve this goal by . . . (date)			
This goal matters because . . .			
I may encounter the following obstacles . . .			
My method for accomplishing this goal will be to . . .			

Set a Date. Put your deadline for achieving your goal(s) in your calendar. Count back ten days from your deadline and write a reminder for yourself.

Reassess. After your deadline passes, ask yourself: Did I meet this goal on time? What change has it made in my life? If I did not meet it, what am I planning to do about it?

TRY IT!   *Exercises*

The exercises at the end of each chapter will help you sharpen what we believe are the critical skills for college success: writing, critical thinking, learning in groups, planning, reflecting, and taking action. You can further explore the topic of each chapter by using your PIN to complete the exercises on the website for this text: **http://success.wadsworth.com/gardner7e/**.

WORKING TOGETHER: Multiple Intelligences

After completing the Multiple Intelligences Inventory, ask all students to determine their highest point score, and break the class into groups according to those scores. Ask group members to discuss the classes they're now taking, out-of-class activities in which they're involved, and intended majors. Each group should then describe their conversation to the whole class.

EXERCISE 3.1: Myers-Briggs Exploration

(For classes using the Myers-Briggs Type Indicator). Have all class members learn their own types. Form three groups of three to five students each. All members of Group 1 should be extraverted/sensing types; all members of Group 2 should be introverted/intuitive types; for Group 3, include as many of the different preferences represented as possible. Have each group outline or write a brief recruiting brochure aimed at convincing prospective students to come to your college or university. After the groups have finished, ask all three groups to share their results with the rest of the class. Do you notice any differences in the approach of each group? Which group do you think produced the best plan for a brochure and why?

EXERCISE 3.2: Learning Styles Models

In a small group, discuss the five learning styles models presented by this chapter. Which was the easiest or the most difficult to understand? Which of the models did group members like best and why? Each group should report on their opinions to the whole class.

EXERCISE 3.3: Learning More about Learning Disabilities

Using your library or the Internet, find the names of three famous people not mentioned in this chapter who have learning disabilities and how they have dealt with or overcome that disability. Working in small groups, share what you learned in your research.

WRITE ABOUT IT! My Personal Journal

This is your place to sound off, to ask your teacher to clarify part of the lesson, or to write him or her about a minor or major crisis you're experiencing. Find out if your teacher wishes you to turn in your journals. Ask if they will remain confidential. Even if the journal isn't used in your course, you can still use the format to write about and reflect on issues regarding the class, yourself, or both.

1. *What was the one major lesson you learned from reading this chapter and/or from class lecture and discussion?*

2. *What are some other important lessons about this topic?*

3. *If you believe some parts of this chapter are unimportant, spell them out here and tell why you think so. (You even might want to discuss this point with your classmates to see if they came up with a similar list.)*

4. *If anything is keeping you from performing at your peak level academically, describe what it is. Your instructor may be able to help or refer you to someone else on campus who can help.*

5. *What behaviors are you planning to change after reading this chapter?*

Engagement with Learning

● ●

In this chapter YOU WILL LEARN

- What *engagement* means and why it is important
- Differences between high school and college
- How engagement with learning can improve your learning curve
- The value of study groups
- How to establish an academic relationship with your teachers
- What to do if things go wrong between you and your teacher

Learning in action. What would you like to discover?

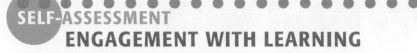

ENGAGEMENT WITH LEARNING

Check the items below that apply to you:

1. ____ I'm usually comfortable asking a question in class.

2. ____ Whether the class has 15 students or 150, I should ask about something I don't understand.

3. ____ I plan to participate in a study group to help me improve my grades.

4. ____ I plan to sit as close to the front as possible in every class so I can focus on the topic, the instructor, and the board.

5. ____ I believe that most college teachers are eager to discuss my progress. I will be sure to make an appointment if I'm having difficulty.

6. ____ I have no problem understanding my instructors.

7. ____ I feel just as comfortable in class participation as I do in a lecture class, where only the teacher is talking.

8. ____ I believe that if I can find a good mentor, that person can help me with many phases of my life.

9. ____ It's okay with me if college teachers digress from their lesson plans if worthwhile discussions arise in class.

10. ____ If I disagree with the teacher, I should raise my hand and politely tell him or her why I disagree.

If you checked seven or fewer of the items, find someone who can help you understand why all ten items are critical. At the end of this chapter, you will be asked to set personal goals for one or more of your unchecked items. If you checked all items, you will be asked to set other goals.

● ●

Research reveals that students who become thoroughly *engaged* in their college experience stand a greater chance of success than those who do not. **Engagement** means active involvement in every aspect of life. It means approaching every challenge with determination, whether it be learning, activities, friendships, community work, or teacher-student relationships. The more engagement, the more connections. The more connections, the richer the experience. If you are on a campus that encourages engagement, you're doubly lucky.

"Engagement is a critical factor in the educational process because the more time and energy students devote to desired activities, the more likely they are to develop the habits of the mind that are key to success after college, including participating in civic affairs," reports George Kuh, director of the National Survey of Student Engagement. According to that survey, students who engage more frequently in "deep" learning activities report greater educational and personal gains from college, participate in more enriching educational experiences, perceive their campus to be more supportive, and are more satisfied overall with college. In 2004, this survey found that since 2000 more seniors:

- Participate in service learning (+7%).

- Have serious conversations with students with different social, political, and religious views (+10%).

- Perceive their campus administration to be responsive, flexible, and supportive (+15%).

  All of these are forms of engagement. But the findings were not all positive.

- Only 10 percent of students rely on newspapers or magazines as their primary source of local, national, or international news; more than 50 percent say television is their primary source.

- 40 percent of first-year students and 25 percent of seniors never discuss ideas from their classes or readings with a faculty member outside of class.

- About a fifth of all students spend no time on physical fitness.

- More than a quarter of first-year (26%) and senior students (31%) never attended an art exhibit, gallery, play, dance, or other theater performance during the current school year.[1]

As you can see, you have almost unlimited choices to become engaged with your campus and with the world. One way to begin is to become acquainted with your college teachers, especially those who offer you the chance to learn *actively* rather than to be taught *passively*. Whenever your teacher asks you a question in class, puts you in groups to solve a problem, requires you to make an oral presentation to the class, or does anything else that gives you and other students a voice in the learning process, you're all the more engaged in learning. As a result, learning should not only be easier, but also more productive.

Benefits of Engagement

In addition to placing you "center stage," engagement with learning helps you acquire many of the skills employers want most: thinking, written and oral communication, goal setting, time management, relationship building, problem solving, ethical reasoning, leadership, and so forth.

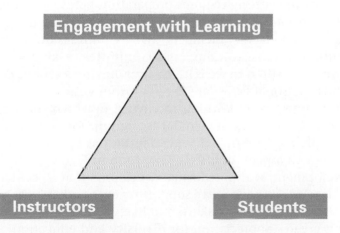

FIGURE 4.1
When all three of these parts work in harmony, learning tends to improve.

---

[1] George Kuh. NSSE director of the National Survey of Student Engagement and Chancellor's Professor of Higher Education, Indiana University, Bloomington. From "Student Engagement: Pathways to Collegiate Success," *Viewpoint*, a publication of NSSE. Bloomington, IN: NSSE, November 2004.

Although you may acquire knowledge listening to a lecture, you may not be motivated to think about what that knowledge means. By being actively engaged in learning, you will learn not only the material in your notes and textbooks, but also how to:

- Work with others.
- Improve your critical thinking, listening, writing, and speaking skills.
- Function independently and teach yourself.
- Manage your time.
- Gain sensitivity to cultural differences.

TURNING POINT

Since I go to a college that uses the Socratic (that is, discussion) method, participating in class is essential both to true understanding and to my grade. I've learned that saying something helpful requires that I read the assignment carefully and well. I've learned that you have to do your homework until you're sure you understand the material. If you are no longer sure you get it, ask someone who does. When that doesn't work, ask the professor. College is about expanding your understanding, not just getting the degree.

Damon R.
Thomas Aquinas College

Engagement in learning requires preparation before and after every class, not just before exams. It might include researching in the library, making appointments to talk to faculty members, making outlines from your class notes, going to cultural events, working on a committee, asking someone to read something you've written to see if it's clear, or having a serious discussion with students whose personal values are different from yours.

This active approach to learning and living, in which you are connected to organizations, study with other students, sign up for classes offering service learning, complete an internship, and so forth, has the potential to make you well rounded in all aspects of life. The hexagon in Figure 4.2 depicts seven aspects of development, with intellectual development at its center. Optimal development depends on each area's supporting every other area.

With good active-learning skills, you likely will feel more comfortable socially, gain a greater appreciation for diversity and education, and be better able to clarify your major and future career. Staying physically active can reduce stress and keep your mind alert as you study. Developing a sense of values can help you choose your friends more carefully and decide how to manage your time.

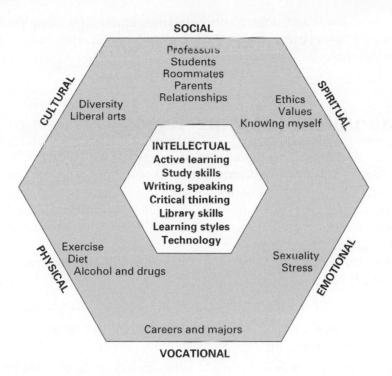

FIGURE 4.2
Aspects of Student
Development

The One-Minute Paper and Other Tips for Engagement

Another simple way to become engaged in learning is through a process called the "one-minute paper." In a major study of teaching at Harvard University, one of many suggestions for improving learning was a simple feedback exercise. At the end of each class, students were asked to write what they thought was the main issue of that class and what their unanswered questions were for the next class. Using the one-minute paper helps your instructor to determine if he or she provided a clear presentation and to use your unanswered questions for the next class. Even if your instructors don't require it, try writing a one-minute paper each day at the end of class. Use it to think about the main issues discussed that day, and save it so that you will be prepared to ask good questions at the next class meeting. If you're in a study group, compare answers and questions; you may learn something!

Here are some additional things you can do to become engaged in learning:

- Ask friends which teachers employ active learning before you choose a class.

- Even in a large class, sit as close to the front as you can, and never hesitate to raise your hand if you don't understand something. Chances are, the others didn't understand it either. Even reasonable "wrong" answers or questions are better than none at all.

- Put notes into your own words instead of just memorizing the book or the lecture.

- If you disagree with what your instructor says, politely challenge him or her. Good teachers will listen and may still disagree with you, but they may think more of you for showing you can think.

See Working Together: Ways to Be Engaged

- Stay in touch with teachers, other students, and your academic advisor. One easy way is through e-mail. Or call and leave a voice mail if the person is out.

Collaborative Learning Teams

More than likely, you'll be working with others after college, so now is a good time to learn how—to **collaborate**. Students who engage in learning through study groups not only learn better but enjoy their learning experiences more. Whether in groups or by themselves, engaged learners are willing to try new ideas and discover new knowledge by exploring the world around them instead of just memorizing facts.

Joseph Cuseo of Marymount College, an expert on collaborative learning, points to these advantages of learning groups:

- Learners learn from one another as well as from the instructor.

- Collaborative learning is by its very nature active learning, and so it tends to increase learning through engagement.

- "Two heads are better than one." Collaboration can lead to more ideas, alternative approaches, new perspectives, and better solutions.

- If you're not comfortable speaking out in larger classes, you will tend to be more comfortable speaking in smaller groups, resulting in better communication and better ideas.

- You will develop stronger bonds with other students in the class, which may increase everyone's interest in attending.

- "Positive competition" among groups happens when several groups are asked to solve the same problem—with the instructor clarifying that the purpose is for the good of all.

See Exercise 4.1: To Collaborate or Not?

- Working in groups may help you develop leadership skills.

Making Learning Teams Productive

Not all learning groups are equally effective. Sometimes teamwork is unsuccessful or fails to reach its potential because no thought was given to how the group was formed or how it should function. Use the following strategies to develop high-quality learning teams that maximize the power of peer collaboration:

1. Remember that learning teams are more than study groups. Effective student learning teams collaborate regularly for other academic tasks besides test review sessions.
2. In forming teams, seek students who will contribute quality and diversity to the group. Resist the urge to include people just like you. Look for students who are motivated, attend class regularly, are attentive and participate actively while in class, and complete assignments. Include teammates from different ethnic, racial, or cultural backgrounds; different age groups; and different personality types and learning styles. Include males and females.
3. Keep the group small (four to six teammates). Smaller groups allow for more face-to-face interaction and eye contact and less opportunity for any one individual to shirk responsibility to the team.

4. Hold individual team members personally accountable for contributing to the learning of their teammates. One way to ensure accountability is to have each member come to group meetings with specific information or answers to share with teammates as well as questions to ask the group.

TURNING POINT

Clubs, study groups, and different organizations can keep you involved with what you are studying. I find that studying in groups is the best way to achieve a good grade.

Alex M.
Sinclair Community College

The Many Uses of Learning Teams

- **Note-taking teams.** Team up with other students immediately after class to share and compare notes so that your group may still have a chance to consult with the instructor about any missing or confusing information.

- **Reading teams.** After completing reading assignments, team with other students to compare your highlighting and margin notes. See if all agree.

- **Library research teams.** This an effective way to develop a support group for reducing "library anxiety" and for locating and sharing sources of information. This does not constitute cheating or plagiarizing as long as the final product you turn in represents your own work.

- **Team/instructor conferences.** Have your learning team visit the instructor during office hours to seek additional assistance as needed.

- **Team test results review.** After receiving test results, members of a learning team can review their individual tests together to help one another identify the sources of their mistakes and to review any answers that received high scores.

If you are a returning student, you and other returnees may wish to form your own group and discuss the differences between your lives before college and now; or you may prefer to join a group of recent high school graduates to hear and provide a different point of view.

See Exercise 4.2: Forming Your Ideal Learning Team

Using Study Groups in Mathematics and Science

In his groundbreaking study of the factors that predict success in calculus, Professor Uri Treisman of the University of Texas at Austin determined that the most effective strategy for success in calculus turned out to be active participation in a study group! It is now widely accepted that, by working together, a group of students can significantly enhance each other's performance, especially in problem-solving courses; this is even more so when one member of the group is an advanced math student.

It seems that the larger the class, and the more complex the material, the more valuable the study group. Treisman-style workshops in calculus, chemistry, physics, and other subjects have been established by schools across the country, but most study groups are informal and organized by students themselves. Study groups work best when members are serious about their commitment to each other, make faithful attendance a priority, and set specific goals for each session.

Besides persisting to find the solution to difficult problems, what else can a math or science study group do for you?

Compare Lecture Notes Look at the level of detail in each other's notes, and adopt the best of each other's styles. Discuss places where you got lost in an example problem. Talk about technical terms or symbols you didn't understand or couldn't decipher on the board and questions asked in class that you weren't able to hear.

Teach Each Other Split up the difficult topics and assign them to various members to prepare and present to the group. Remember that the best way to really learn something is to explain it to someone else.

Prepare for Tests Group members can divide the job of making a study outline. Each person brings his or her section. The members discuss and modify the outlines, and a final version is created for all. Group members can quiz one another, focusing on facts and specific pieces of information for an objective test, and on how those pieces relate to one another for an essay exam. Members then can write practice questions for each other, or the group might create an entire sample exam, and take it together under timed conditions. As you conclude each group study session, make a specific plan for the next meeting: "On Tuesday we'll use flash cards to be sure we understand the nervous system."

Provide Makeup Notes Of course you should aim for perfect class attendance in all your courses. But if you absolutely have to miss a math or science class, your study group is a source for notes and the assignment. If you do have to miss a class, it's important to get the notes from a study partner and catch up *before the next class.* Otherwise you have effectively missed two classes.

Ask the Right Questions Never criticize a question in your study group; respond cheerfully and express appreciation: "I'm glad you asked that." If you notice someone is lost, give them an opportunity to ask a question by reviewing the work: "Let's see if we all understand what we've done so far. . . ." If you are explaining your solution to a problem, try leading the others through it by asking a series of simple questions. Above all, come to the group meeting prepared—not with all the answers, but knowing what specific questions you have.

Working with Your College Teachers

One of your greatest opportunities for learning in college will come from one-on-one instruction with a teacher outside of class. Instructors are required to keep office hours; make an appointment to see them during that time. Don't feel as if you're bothering them. It's part of their job to make time for you.

Good instructors may be so enthusiastic about their fields of study that they speed up their lectures because they want to tell you the whole story. If you just can't keep up, raise your hand and politely ask them to slow down.

You can do a few simple things to improve relations between you and your teachers:

- Come to class regularly and be on time.
- Take advantage of office hours and see instructors when appropriate.
- Realize that instructors are not people to be avoided at all costs, and that you will not be criticized by your peers if you're seen talking with them.
- Use their office hours to get to know your instructors.
- Read the assigned material before class.
- Ask questions.
- Sit near the front of the class. A number of studies have shown that students who do so tend to make better grades.
- Never talk or whisper while instructors are lecturing. They may interpret this as an uncaring or even rude gesture.
- Don't hand your instructors "phony baloney" excuses. They've been hearing it for years, and may spot a lie a mile away. If you're sincere and give honest reasons for missing class or work, they're more likely to try and work around some rules for you.

Instructors may do things your high school teachers never did, such as:

- Supplementing textbook assignments with other information
- Giving exams covering both assigned readings and lectures
- Questioning conclusions of other scholars
- Accepting several different student opinions on a question
- Never checking to see if you are taking notes or reading the text
- Demanding more reading of you in a shorter period of time
- Giving fewer quizzes or many more quizzes

- Expecting you to be familiar with topics related to their field

See Exercise 4.3:
Differences between High
School and College

- Being sympathetic to difficulties you may have while holding firm to high standards of grading. You may be on friendly terms with your instructor and find you have received a low grade.

A Good Teacher Wants You to Succeed

Whether you know it or not, many of your college teachers are seriously interested in your well-being, and may work you hard in hopes you'll earn high grades in their classes. However, these same individuals also may be quick to disagree with your ideas, ready to correct you when you answer a question in class, and be extremely demanding about the amount of work they expect from you. Yet establishing a positive relationship with your college instructors can be one of the most rewarding experiences of your life.

"Great teachers know their subjects well. But they also know their students well," says Dr. Eliot Engel of North Carolina State University. "In fact," he continues, "great teaching fundamentally consists of constructing a bridge from the subject taught to the student learning it. Both sides of that bridge must be surveyed with equal care if the subject matter of the teacher is to connect with the gray matter of the student. But great teachers transcend simply knowing their subjects and students well. They also admire both deeply."[2]

To find out what kind of people instructors are, you might begin by studying their offices. Usually, you will find them decorated to reflect the interests and personality of each teacher. Instructors read and like to talk about what they have read. Some may speak of travels abroad, or to other parts of the United States, where they have lived, taught, or attended college.

You might be surprised to learn that most of your college instructors never have taken a course in teaching. Instead, they chose courses in their fields of study to acquire and understand new knowledge. Some instructors have left

[2] From a column in the *Dickens Dispatch,* the newsletter of the North Carolina Dickens Club, January 1989.

careers to teach their professions to college students: you'll find lawyers teaching law, physicians teaching medicine, newspaper editors teaching journalism, and executives teaching business management.

See Exercise 4.4: Sizing Up Your College Teachers

Faculty and Academic Freedom

Academic freedom is a right most college faculty enjoy at the majority of private and state-supported institutions. The concept of academic freedom allows instructors to raise controversial issues without risk of losing their jobs. It doesn't give them total immunity, but it does allow them more latitude than teachers you knew in high school.

Academic freedom is a long-established tradition in American higher education. Colleges and universities have found it desirable to promote the advancement of research and knowledge by giving their scholars and instructors virtually unlimited freedom of inquiry, as long as human lives, rights, and privacy are not violated. This allows an instructor to open the door to less conventional thoughts and actions that may surprise and even anger you at times. Certainly you needn't agree with them in order to get good grades. On the other hand, you should try to understand their views and be prepared to defend yours as well.

On the flip side, when conservative activist David Horowitz founded Students for Academic Freedom in 2003, his goal was to empower students to speak out when they disagreed with their instructors without fear of reprisal.[3] For example, a student should not tolerate being ridiculed in front of the class because he smokes and his instructor champions making smoking a federal offense. A member of ROTC who shows up for class in uniform should not be embarrassed before the class by an instructor who opposes war.

The question is, no matter what an instructor believes—good or bad—does he or she have the right to campaign in the classroom? (We warned you that college was not going to be cut and dried!)

Finding a Mentor

In his study of the aging process in men, the late Yale psychiatrist Daniel J. Levinson discovered several things about those who tended to be successful in life:

- They had developed a "dream" in adolescence, an idealized conception of what they wanted to become.

- They went on to find a **mentor**—an older, successful individual—who personified that dream.

- They also enjoyed friendships with a few other people who encouraged, nurtured, and supported them in their pursuit of their dream.

A mentor is a person who is now, in some respect, what you hope to be in the future. What mentors have you had? What specific qualities have you tried to emulate? What are you seeking in a college mentor? If you have a mentor now, what might you do to make more use of this person? If you don't have a mentor, consider whether you might find one during your first year of college.

---

[3] G. Jeffrey MacDonald, *USA Today*, May 18, 2005.

How do you find a mentor? Look for the person who takes a special interest in you, who encourages you to challenge yourself, who willingly listens to you when you have questions or problems, who offers to meet with you to discuss your work. A mentor may be an academic advisor, instructor, department chair, older student, or anyone else who appears to offer interest, wisdom, and support. Most important, find a person you can trust, who will deal with you confidentially, and who is genuinely interested in your well-being but asks little or nothing in return.[4]

If Things Go Wrong between You and a Teacher

What if you can't tolerate a particular instructor? Arrange a meeting to try to work things out. Getting to know the teacher as a person may help you cope with the way he or she teaches the course. If that fails, check the "drop/add" date, which usually falls at the end of the first week of classes. You may have to drop the course altogether and add a different one. If it's too late to add classes, you may still want to drop by the "drop date" later in the term and avoid a penalty. See your academic advisor or counselor for help with this decision.

If you can't resolve the situation with the instructor and need to stay in the class, see the head of the department. If you are still dissatisfied, move up the administrative ladder until you get a definite answer. Never allow a bad instructor to sour you on college. If all else fails, even the worst course will be over in a matter of weeks.

What if you're not satisfied with your grade? First, make an appointment to see the instructor and discuss the assignment. Your teacher may give you a second chance because you took the time to ask for help. If you get a low grade on an exam, you might ask the instructor to review certain answers with you. Never demand a grade change, as this will most likely backfire.

[4] D. J. Levinson et al., *The Seasons of a Man's Life* (New York: Ballantine, 1978).

Where to Go for Help

ON CAMPUS

Learning (Assistance/Support) Center: Almost every campus has one or more of these. Sometimes they provide help for students in all subjects at all levels; sometimes they are specific to one discipline, such as math or English. The staff will know many, if not all, of your instructors and can provide good advice for using active-learning strategies. These centers typically retain outstanding undergraduate students who serve as tutors. From their experiences, they can teach you how to make active learning easier and more fun. Above all, remember: learning centers are not for poor students— they are for all students who want to improve their learning skills.

Counseling Center: Maybe your relationships with teachers and courses are putting you under excessive stress. This is a fairly common issue among new college students, and there's help right on campus at the Counseling Center, which provides free and confidential support for students. You can get feedback on the sources of your stress and learn some new, healthy coping mechanisms. You already have paid for such services in your basic tuition and fees. And seeking a counselor simply means that, as a new student with concerns, you are quite normal.

Faculty Members: Probably at least one of your instructors has struck you as approachable and sympathetic. Make an appointment to see this person and share your concerns. He or she may have had similar concerns when beginning college. Certainly the authors of this book did.

Academic Advisor/Counselor: Make a special effort to meet your advisor/counselor, especially if you're having problems in any of your courses or if circumstances are keeping you from earning higher grades. And remember, if you don't feel comfortable with your advisor, you have the right to change advisors. Just ask.

ONLINE

Active Learning: Creating Excitement in the Classroom: http://www.ntlf.com/html/ lib/bib/91-9dig.htm. Check out the authors' interpretation of the active-learning process.

Tools for Teaching: http://teaching.berkeley.edu/bgd/ collaborative.html. Read the information designed for teachers on collaborative learning. According to the author, collaborative learning forces one to learn actively. Do you agree? Explain.

ACHIEVE IT! *Setting Goals for Success*

Go back to the self-assessment at the beginning of this chapter and select one to three unchecked items from the list. Use these to formulate short-term goals for yourself. Be specific about what you want to achieve and when (that is, not "become an active learner," but "find an excuse to meet with at least one of my teachers sometime next week"). Remember to choose goals that are realistic and important to you. Think about what obstacles could get in the way of achieving your goals, and make your plan. In the event you checked all items in the self-assessment, come up with one or more additional goals for this exercise.

	Goal 1	Goal 2	Goal 3
My short-term goal is . . .			
I want to achieve this goal by . . . (date)			
This goal matters because . . .			
I may encounter the following obstacles . . .			
My method for accomplishing this goal will be to . . .			

Set a Date. Put your deadline for achieving your goal(s) in your calendar. Count back ten days from your deadline and write a reminder for yourself.

Reassess. After your deadline passes, ask yourself: Did I meet this goal on time? What change has it made in my life? If I did not meet it, what am I planning to do about it?

TRY IT! *Exercises*

The exercises at the end of each chapter will help you sharpen what we believe are the critical skills for college success: writing, critical thinking, learning in groups, planning, reflecting, and taking action. You can further explore the topic of each chapter by using your PIN to complete the exercises on the website for this text: **http://success.wadsworth.com/gardner7e/**.

WORKING TOGETHER: Ways to Become Engaged

Make your own list of ways you would like to become more engaged with your campus and community. Then, in groups of four to six, share your ideas with others. If others present additional ways that you find interesting, add them to your list. Use your final list as a reminder of what you can do to strengthen your connections with your campus and community.

EXERCISE 4.1: To Collaborate or Not?

Some people may prefer to work alone. This chapter has already listed many benefits of working together. What are some of the benefits of working by yourself? What might influence your decision to work alone as opposed to collaborating? What might influence you to prefer collaboration?

EXERCISE 4.2: Forming Your Ideal Learning Team

If you were to form a group with two or three other students in this class, whom would you choose, and for what characteristics? Write a paper describing your group. Don't reveal their names. Instead, name your collaborators "A," "B," and so forth. If you had to choose one more person, who would that be and why? In what ways do members of this group complement one another's strengths and weaknesses, including yours?

EXERCISE 4.3: Differences between High School and College

This chapter lists just a few of the differences between high school and college that you may encounter. With a small group of other students, brainstorm other differences. Appoint one person in the group to list which differences seem beneficial and which do not. Explain your choices to the rest of the class.

EXERCISE 4.4: Sizing Up Your College Teachers

Draw a line down the middle of a piece of paper. On the left side, write down a list of adjectives that describe the best teachers you've ever had. On the right side, make a list of adjectives describing the worst teachers you've ever had. Now think of a current college teacher and assign as many of the adjectives on the page that seem fitting. Do this with your other college teachers. What did you find out about your learning style, your likes, and your dislikes? Compare lists with other students. What did they learn about their learning styles?

WRITE ABOUT IT! **My Personal Journal**

This is your place to sound off, to ask your teacher to clarify part of the lesson, or to write him or her about a minor or major crisis you're experiencing. Find out if your teacher wishes you to turn in your journals. Ask if they will remain confidential. Even if the journal isn't used in your course, you can still use the format to write about and reflect on issues regarding the class, yourself, or both.

1. *What was the one major lesson you learned from reading this chapter and/or from class lecture and discussion?*

2. *What are some other important lessons about this topic?*

3. *If you believe some parts of this chapter are unimportant, spell them out here and tell why you think so. (You even might want to discuss this point with your classmates to see if they came up with a similar list.)*

4. *If anything is keeping you from performing at your peak level academically, describe what it is. Your instructor may be able to help or refer you to someone else on campus who can help.*

5. *What behaviors are you planning to change after reading this chapter? Why?*

Critical Thinking . . . .

In this chapter YOU WILL LEARN

- Why there are no "right" and "wrong" answers to many important questions
- Four aspects of critical thinking
- How critical arguments differ from emotional arguments
- How college encourages critical thinking
- Why critical thinking is the basis for a liberal education
- The importance of critical thinking beyond college

How do you think through a problem?

SELF-ASSESSMENT
CRITICAL THINKING

Check the items below that apply to you:

1. ____ I try not to allow my emotions to get in the way of making the right decision.

2. ____ Even if I find a person irritating, I try to listen to what he or she has to say while divorcing myself from what I find irritating.

3. ____ Whenever I have a good idea, I let it "sit on the back burner" before deciding to run with it. Meanwhile I do the same with other good ideas.

4. ____ Often I find there is no one "right" answer to some questions.

5. ____ I do my best to ask questions in class and participate in discussion.

6. ____ Teachers can help you choose majors and courses, but I need to research a number of choices before I make an appointment with a teacher.

7. ____ I can recognize when the facts just don't add up, even though they appear to be logical.

8. ____ I am well aware that, as good as a textbook might be, it doesn't give me all the answers I need.

9. ____ I believe that critical thinking is a desired skill with prospective employers.

10. ____ My courses in the liberal arts can help me become a better job prospect in almost any career field.

If you checked seven or fewer of the items, find someone who can help you understand why all ten items are critical. At the end of this chapter, you will be asked to set personal goals for one or more of your unchecked items. If you checked all items, you will be asked to set other goals.

N o doubt you've heard something like this before:

"You're going to sign up for Professor Bligh's astronomy course, aren't you?"

"Actually, I was thinking of taking astronomy with another professor. It fits into my schedule better."

"But Bligh is the most popular astronomy teacher. And not bad looking, either."

"Yeah, but is he a good teacher?"

Would you choose a professor based on good looks and affable personality, the things that may make him or her so popular? Or would you ask your advisor for suggestions? Far too often, people don't think critically (logically) but let their emotions govern their actions. In college, that can lead to trouble!

College has been described as "an investment in your future." We like that thought because it suggests that college not only can prepare you for a career, but also can broaden your horizons in other ways. And a main ingredient in a college education is learning how to think critically.

From history classes, you may develop an interest in the French Revolution and other things *français*. From music appreciation, you may become a regular concert-goer. A literature course may help you discover the authors you will be reading long after you've said goodbye to campus. From other courses, you may develop interests in world travel, native crafts, or theater.

And if you believe that college is a path to a high-paying job, remember that a good critical thinker is a good job candidate.

College Helps You Develop Critical Thinking Skills

Theodora Kalikow, president of the University of Maine at Farmington, describes what characteristics students should have in order to receive a good college education—which demands above all else **critical thinking**:

- A lithe mind, able to move rapidly in new directions

- The ability to analyze a problem

- The ability to imagine solutions, weigh them by rational **criteria**, or standards, and commit to one of them

- An understanding of the investigative approaches of various disciplines or subject areas to acquire the ability to become one's own best lifelong teacher

- A skepticism of facile arguments and easy solutions and a distrust of simplistic analysis

- A tolerance for ambiguity and complexity

- An ability to imagine and share the perceptions of different individuals, cultures, and times

- An appreciation of the community and one's place in it—the need to contribute to society through public and private service[1]

On the flip side, prizewinning author John Updike told a group of college students that he isn't particularly fond of higher education. "I'm not a great romantic of the college experience," he said. "I enjoyed my four years of college. But I didn't feel the need to extend them. I always kind of resented being educated. It takes away the self you brought to college," he concluded.

Updike's views obviously conflict with what most people believe about the value of college. What do you suppose is going through the mind of this successful writer who did complete college and claims he enjoyed it? Can you provide arguments for *and* against his statement? Is "enjoyment" one goal of college? What are others?

Imagine that one of your instructors tells you on the first day of class:

> I'm going to fill your minds with lots of important facts, and I expect you to take extensive notes and to know those facts in detail when you take your quizzes. The important thing in my class *is how well you learn the material and how frequently you choose the right answers*. And remember, while there are lots of wrong answers, there is only one answer that always is correct.

In another class, the instructor introduces the course quite differently:

> Although I've taught this course many times, it's never quite the same. Each time a new group of students begins the course, they bring their own values, ideas, and past knowledge to the material. The important thing in my class is that you use your heads. You certainly will need to read the assignments and take notes on the lectures and discussions in class. But what's most important is that you learn to analyze facts, decide which facts are supportable by evidence, and know how to convince others of your beliefs. And remember, while there are lots of wrong conclusions, there also may be more than one right conclusion.

When you earn your college degree and land a job, chances are your employer is going to be more interested in how well you think than in how well you can memorize minute bits of information. The second instructor quoted above seems to be moving in that direction. She admits that many possibilities may exist. She realizes that the class may come up with a better answer—or answers—if each student gathers his or her own information on the topic, if students discuss it in small groups, and if they share what they have learned with the teacher, who may then react to what she hears.

---

[1] Theodora J. Kalikow, "Misconceptions about the Word 'Liberal' in Liberal Arts Education," *Higher Education and National Affairs*, June 8, 1998.

The first instructor will *tell you what you should know*; the second instructor wants you—through class discussion, small group sessions, problem solving, research, and other methods—*to discover the truths yourself*. If you do, you will probably have more faith in your conclusions and remember the information much more easily. Most importantly, you will surely learn something!

Going from Certainty to Healthy Uncertainty

If you have just completed high school, you may be experiencing an awakening as you enter college. (Even if you're an older returning student, discovering that your instructor trusts you to find valid answers may be somewhat surprising and stressful.) In high school you may have been conditioned to believe that things are either right or wrong. If your high school teacher asked, "What are the three branches of the U.S. government?" you had only one choice: "legislative, executive, and judicial." You might have learned the names of the three branches, but knowing names doesn't necessarily help you understand what the branches do, or how they do it.

Uncertainty can be healthy; it makes you try harder.

A college instructor might ask instead, "Under what circumstances might conflicts arise among the three branches of government, and what does this reveal about the democratic process?" Certainly, there is no simple—or single—answer. Most likely, your instructor is attempting not to embarrass you for giving a wrong answer but to engage you in the process of critical thinking.

A Higher-Order Thinking Process

Critical thinking is a process of choosing alternatives, weighing them, and considering what they suggest. It involves understanding why some people believe one thing rather than another—whether you agree with those reasons or not. Critical thinking is learning to ask pertinent questions and testing your assumptions against hard evidence.

If you lack critical thinking capabilities, you might exhibit behaviors similar to these:

- You try to reach a classmate on the phone to ask a question about tomorrow's quiz. When you can't reach him, you become so anxious that you can't study or sleep.

- You are asked to read two news articles about the 2000 presidential election between George W. Bush and Al Gore. One article claims the electoral college system is outdated; the other defends that system. After reading them, you can't see how both sides can be right. You don't even know which one is wrong.

- On the day an important paper is due, a heavy snowstorm rolls in. You brave the cold to get to class. When you arrive, no one—including the teacher—is there. You take a seat and wait for class to begin.

Now let's transform you into a critical thinker and look at what the outcomes might be:

- When you can't reach a classmate on the phone to ask a question about tomorrow's quiz, you review the material once more, then call one or more other classmates. Then you consider their views against your textbook and class. Instead of deciding on one point of view for each important topic, you decide to keep in mind all of those that make sense, leaving your final decision until you have the quiz in your hand.

- You compare the representation afforded by the electoral college system with the representation afforded by the popular vote, using library or Internet sources to find at least three articles defending each side of the issue. You look further to see if any article supports the system as it now stands. Now you have a number of things to write about. You find there isn't a clear-cut answer. That's okay. It's what you learned that counts.

- On the day an important paper is due, a heavy snowstorm rolls in. You check the college website first thing that morning and discover that classes have been canceled. You stay at home.

Collaboration Fosters Critical Thinking

A study by Professor Anuradha A. Gokhale at Western Illinois University, published in the fall 1995 issue of the *Journal of Technology Education*, found that students who participated in collaborative learning performed significantly better on a test requiring critical thinking than students who studied individually. The study also found that both groups did equally well on a test requiring only memorization.[2]

One can easily understand why, especially after reading Chapter 4 on engagement with learning. The simple fact that more than one student is involved in the learning processes generates a number of thoughts instead of just one. As a group learns to agree on the most reliable thoughts, it moves closer to a surer solution.

[2] Anuradha Gokhale, "Collaborative Learning Enhances Critical Thinking," *Journal of Technology Education* 7.1 (1995).

A Skill to Carry You through Life

Employers hiring college graduates often say they want an individual who can find information, analyze it, organize it, draw conclusions from it, and present it convincingly to others. One executive said she looked for superior communication skills "because they are in such short supply these days." These skills are the basic ingredients of critical thinking, which includes the ability to:

- Manage and interpret information in a reliable way.

- Examine existing ideas and develop new ones.

- Pose logical arguments that further the absorption of knowledge. In college, the term **argument** refers not to an emotional confrontation but to reasons and information brought together in logical support of some idea.

- Recognize reliable evidence and form well-reasoned conclusions.

Walking through the Process

When thinking about an argument, a good critical thinker considers questions like the following:

- Is the information given in support of the argument true? For example, could it be possible that both the electoral college system and the popular vote system might be equally representative?

- Does the information really support the conclusion? If you determine that each system has its merits (the electoral college gives more voting power to the less populated states, whereas the popular vote represents how the majority of voters feel), can you conclude that there may be a more judicious way to employ both systems in presidential elections?

- Do you need to withhold judgment until better evidence is available? Maybe you haven't any proof that a system that counted both the electoral vote and the popular vote would be more equitable because it has never been tried.

- Is the argument really based on good reasoning, or does it appeal mainly to your emotions? You may think the electoral vote can alter the results of elections in a way that undermines the intentions of the voters, as evidenced in the 2000 presidential election. But you need to come to terms with your emotions and ask if they are guiding you to this conclusion instead of relevant information that supports the argument.

- Based on the available evidence, are other conclusions equally likely (or even more likely)? Is there more than one right or possible answer? Perhaps there is a third or fourth way to count the vote by replacing the electoral college concept with something else.

See Exercise 5.1: Reflecting on Arguments

- What more needs to be done to reach a good conclusion? You may need to do more reading about the election process and find some evidence that the system didn't work as planned in earlier presidential elections. Then you might try to find out how people felt about the voting system. Since you are far from an expert on this, perhaps you should hold a forum with local voters to gain more views on the pros and cons of the electoral college system.

Good critical thinking also involves thinking creatively about what assumptions may have been left out or what alternative conclusions may not have been considered. When communicating an argument or idea to others, a good critical thinker knows how to organize it in an understandable, convincing way in speech or in writing.

This appears to be anything but a logical argument!

Critical Thinking and a Liberal Education

Critical thinking is at the core of a liberal education. A **liberal education** provides the foundation to define and pursue goals. In a liberal education, students are taught to investigate all sides of a question and all possible solutions to a problem before reaching a conclusion or planning a course of action.

See Exercise 5.2: Learning about a Liberal Education

The word *liberal* as used here has no political connotation, but is a direct reference to the ability of education to free your mind. The word itself comes from the Latin *libero*, a verb meaning "to free." The goal of a liberal education is to free you from the biases, superstitions, prejudices, and lack of knowledge that may have characterized you before you came to college. Next time you wonder why you are required to take courses outside your major, remember how important they can be.

Four Aspects of Critical Thinking

Critical thinking cannot be learned overnight. Yet as interpreted by William T. Daly, teacher of political science at The Richard Stockton College of New Jersey, the critical thinking process can be divided into four basic steps. Practicing these basic ideas can help you become a more effective thinker.

1. Abstract Thinking: Using Details to Discover Some Bigger Idea

From large numbers of facts, seek the bigger ideas or the **abstractions** behind the facts. What are the key ideas? Even fields like medicine, which involve countless facts, culminate in general ideas such as the principles of circulation or the basic mechanisms of cell division.

Ask yourself what larger concepts the details suggest. For example, you read an article that describes how many people are using the Internet now, how much consumer information it provides, what kinds of goods you can buy cheaply over the Internet, and also that many low-income families are still without computers. Think carefully about these facts, and you might arrive at several different important generalizations.

One might be that as the Internet becomes more important for shopping, the lack of computers in low-income households will put poor families at an even greater disadvantage. Or your general idea might be that because the Internet is becoming important for selling things, companies will probably find a way to put a computer in every home.

2. Creative Thinking: Seeking Connections, Finding New Possibilities, Rejecting Nothing

Use the general idea you have found to see what further ideas it suggests. The important thing at this stage is not to reject any of your ideas. Write them all down. You'll narrow this list in the next step.

The creative phase of thinking can lead in many directions. It might involve searching for ways to make the Internet more available to low-income households. Or it might involve searching out more detailed information on how much interest big companies really have in marketing various goods to low-income families. In essence, the creative thinking stage involves extending the general idea—finding new ways to apply it or identifying other ideas it might suggest.

Remember that most creative ideas start with two stages—brainstorming and refinement—and work best when two or more heads contribute ideas. In **brainstorming**, the goal is to get everyone's creative juices flowing and to come up with as many related ideas as possible, saving judgment for the refinement stage. During a brainstorming exercise, everyone's ideas get written down, and no one is allowed to comment on them, either positively or negatively. The concept behind the technique is to create a fertile environment in which each team member builds on the thoughts of others without getting sidetracked by prematurely evaluating the practicality of the ideas.

If brainstorming is about quantity and options, the emphasis in the refinement stage is on making decisions. Refinement involves taking all of those ideas and winnowing them down, ultimately selecting the one(s) the team intends to pursue. This process isn't necessarily a matter of figuring out the "best" idea. Depending on the goals of the activity, it may simply be the one that the group thinks is most fun or practical. For a business decision, it might involve a cost/benefit analysis to decide which computer equipment to purchase for your lab. With kids in a learning center, it might be a matter of helping them decide on a plot for a video or on a topic for an inquiry-based learning project.

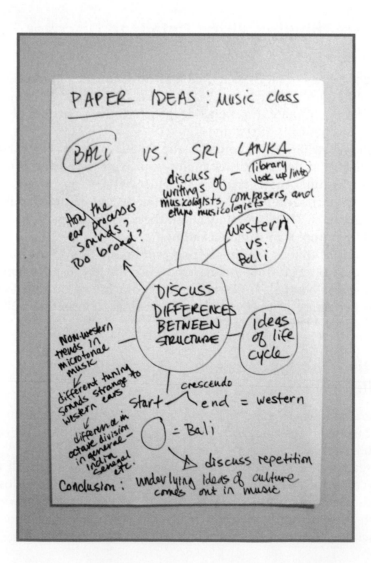

Some famous writers and artists say their ideas come to them while they're taking a shower or a long walk. Others get ideas while driving or through talking about a topic with a friend. Advertising professional Terrence Poltrack, in "Stalking the Big Idea," claims "the process is one part reason, one part heart, and big part pure, simple intuition."[3]

In fact, the process for generating ideas practically parallels the critical thinking process:

1. **Immersion.** Totally immerse yourself in background research.
2. **Digestion.** Play with the information. Look at it from different perspectives. Jot down phrases. Exercise your mind.
3. **Incubation.** Put your notes aside. Go for a walk. Catch a movie. Shoot some hoops. Do whatever will relax your mind, and let your mind review the material while you have fun.
4. **Illumination.** Chances are your mind will spurt out an idea or two. Be ready to write the idea down, because ideas don't stay with the mind very long.
5. **Reality Testing.** Is the idea really good? Does it solve the problem?[4]

3. Systematic Thinking: Organizing the Possibilities, Tossing Out the Rubbish

Systematic thinking involves looking at the outcome of the second phase in a more demanding, critical way. This is where you narrow that list from step 2. If you are looking for solutions to a problem, which ones really seem most promising after you have conducted an exhaustive search for materials? Do some answers conflict with others? Which ones can be achieved? If you have found new evidence to refine or further test your generalization, what does that new evidence show? Does your original generalization still hold up? Does it need to be modified? What further conclusions do good reasoning and evidence support? Which notions should be abandoned?

4. Precise Communication: Being Prepared to Present Your Ideas Convincingly to Others

Intelligent conclusions aren't very useful if you cannot share them with others. Consider what your audience will need to know to follow your reasoning and be persuaded. Remember to have "facts in hand" as you attempt to convince others of the truth of your argument. Don't be defensive; instead, just be logical.

Avoiding Logical Fallacies

You may believe you've solved a problem logically, but later you find yourself a victim of **faulty reasoning**. The following arguments, will not help you think critically or correctly. Avoid using any of these **fallacies:**

Attack the Argument, Not the Person When you attack other people's positions, make sure it's their arguments you're attacking and not

---

[3] Terrence Poltrack, "Stalking the Big Idea," *Agency*, May/June 1991.
[4] A. Jerome Jewler and Bonnie Drewniany. *Creative Strategy in Advertising*, 8th ed. (Belmont, CA: Wadsworth, 2005).

the individuals themselves. When very controversial or emotional questions, such as the legalization of abortion, are at issue, people often get caught up with the character or reputation of their opponent rather than with the content and meaning of the opponent's argument.

Don't Threaten in Order to Win an Argument Your parents may make you admit they were right on some issue by suggesting that, unless you did, you might not receive your allowance for the month. Students use such arguments against teachers when they threaten to give them a poor evaluation. Teachers use the argument on students when they threaten to fail them for not agreeing with them.

Don't Beg "Please, officer, don't give me a ticket because if you do I'll lose my license, and I don't deserve to lose my license because I have five little children to feed and won't be able to feed them if I can't drive my truck." None of the driver's statements offer any evidence, in any legal sense, as to why he or she shouldn't be given a ticket. The driver is making an *appeal* to pity.

Avoid Appealing to Authority If you base your claim on the authority of someone who may or may not be an authority on the topic, you're relying on the appearance of authority rather than real evidence to make your argument. We see this all the time in advertising. Sports stars who are not doctors, dieticians, or nutritionists urge us to eat a certain cereal for breakfast. Glamorous women who aren't mechanics tell us that a certain transmission will help our cars run better. Students frequently fall into the authority trap by putting great weight on what other students say about teachers or courses or by consulting a friend about proper answers for a class assignment. Don't let this trap prevent you from getting good advice from the right advisors.

It's Not a Popularity Contest Studies by psychologists indicate that people generally listen more to popular people than to others. In other words, we believe more what we're told by successful and attractive people than what we're told by those who aren't so successful or attractive. One of the worst kinds of reasoning you can follow is to imitate commercials and base your arguments on a person's popularity. Students frequently choose their classes on the basis of such irrelevant things as a teacher's looks or popularity.

It Isn't True Simply Because It Hasn't Been Proved False Go to a bookstore and you'll find dozens of books detailing close encounters with flying saucers and beings from outer space. All of these books describe the person who has had the "close encounter" as beyond reproach in integrity and sanity. Because critics could not disprove the claims of the witnesses, the events "really occurred." Even in science, few things are ever proved completely false, but evidence can be discredited.

Don't Fall Victim to False Cause Frequently, we think that just because one event was followed by another, the first event must have caused the second. This reasoning is the basis for many superstitions. The ancient Chinese once believed that by striking a large gong, they could make the sun reappear after an eclipse. They knew that on one such occasion the sun reappeared after a large gong had been struck. You go shopping and an inconsiderate person sneezes on you in an elevator. You become ill that evening and place the blame on the sneezer.

All too often, students tend to put the blame for their failure on the teacher, yet students often cause their own failures. Blaming your instructor when you don't take notes in class, don't review them, and don't take notes as you read, is an example of the *fallacy of false cause*.

Avoid Hasty Generalizations If someone selected one green marble from a barrel containing 100 marbles, you wouldn't assume that the next marble would be green. After all, there are still ninety-nine marbles in the barrel, and you know nothing about the colors of those marbles. Given fifty draws from the barrel, however, each of which produced a green marble after the barrel had been shaken thoroughly, you would be more willing to conclude that the next marble drawn would be green, too. Likewise, reaching a conclusion in a research paper based on the opinion of one source is like figuring all the marbles in the barrel are green after pulling out one marble. So don't jump into hasty generalizations in your courses. Don't assume, either, that just because one course you took in sociology or biology was boring, all courses in those subjects will be boring.

To test your reasoning, ask this of your arguments: If the conclusion inferred from my premises is false, isn't it likely that one or more of my premises is also false? If you're convinced the answer is yes, you probably have a proper argument. If your answer is no, try another argument, for the chances are you've committed a fallacy in your reasoning. Above all, never forget that correct reasoning is a key factor for success in college and in life.

How College Encourages Critical Thinking

Many college students believe that their teachers will have all the answers. Unfortunately, most important questions do not have simple answers, and you discover numerous ways to look at important issues. In any event, you must be willing to challenge assumptions and conclusions, even those presented by experts.

To challenge how you think, a good college teacher may insist that how you solve a problem is as important as the solution, and even may ask you to describe that problem-solving process.

Because critical thinking depends on discovering and testing connections between ideas, your instructor may ask open-ended questions that have no clear-cut answers, questions of "Why?" "How?" or "What if?" For example: "In these essays we have two conflicting ideas about whether bilingual education is effective in helping children learn English. What now?" Your instructor may ask you to break a larger question into smaller ones: "Let's take the first point. What evidence does the author offer for his idea that language immersion programs get better results?"

She or he may insist that more than one valid point of view exists: "So, for some types of students, you agree that bilingual education might be best? What other types of students should we consider?" Your instructor may require you to explain concretely the reason for any point you reject: "You think this essay is flawed. Well, what are your reasons?" Or he or she may challenge the authority of experts: "Dr. Fleming's theory sounds impressive. But here are some facts he doesn't account for . . ." You may discover that often your instructor reinforces the legitimacy of your personal views and experiences: "So something like this happened to you once, and you felt exactly the same way. Can you tell us why?" And you also will discover that you can change your mind.

See Exercise 5.3: The Challenge of Classroom Thinking

It is natural for new college students to find this mode of thinking difficult and to discover that answers are seldom entirely wrong or right but more often somewhere in between. Yet the questions that lack simple answers usually are the ones most worthy of study.

If you hang on to these rules, we can't promise your classes will be easier, but we can promise they certainly will be more interesting, for now you know how to use logic to figure things out instead of depending purely on how you feel or what you've heard about something.

Better than any other Diet pill you may have tried.
The new and improved SlimTab is now available in stores near you!

Eat what you want! Stop watching every bite you take. With new SlimTab, all you have to do is take one tablet before each meal, and just watch the pounds fall off!! Feel at ease attending those holiday parties. Finally, something that really works and is better than the rest!

No more diet food!

Weight Loss-
Instant and Lasting!

Guaranteed

How true can this claim be? What is the definition of "better"? Does the headline mean that other brands are just as good—but not better—than the one this ad is promoting?

A good class becomes a critical thinking experience. As you listen to the instructor, try to predict where the lecture is heading and why. When other students raise issues, ask yourself whether they have enough information to justify what they have said. And when you raise *your* hand to participate, remember that asking a sensible question may be more important than trying to find the elusive "right" answer.

See Exercise 5.4: Hard or Easy?

The best way to learn, practice, and develop critical thinking skills is to take demanding college courses that provide lots of opportunities to think out loud, discuss and interact in class, and especially to do research and write, write, write. Take courses that use essay examinations as opposed to multiple choice, true/false, short answer; the latter three are much less likely to develop your critical thinking skills.

Critically Evaluating Information on the Internet

Anyone can put anything on the Internet. An academic researcher found a movie review on the Internet, printed it, and discussed it in his seminar, only to realize later that it was written by an adoring fan, not an authoritative critic.

It is often difficult to tell where something on the Internet came from, how it got there, or who wrote it. In other words, the lack of a proper **citation** makes it difficult to judge the credibility of the information. So the first thing to do is to look for a citation. Then, using the citation, do a search for the original source and evaluate its authenticity. If there is no citation, chances are you should avoid the site. Ask yourself other questions, too.

Is It Credible? Is it the original? Is it quoted out of context? Plagiarized? Altered—intentionally or unintentionally—from the original? Has the material been reviewed by experts?

Who Is the Author? What can you find out about her or him? Is she or he qualified to write this article? If you can't find information on the author, think twice before using the information. Beware of sites that have no date on the document, make sweeping generalizations, and use information that is biased and does not acknowledge opposing views.

Does It Reflect Mainstream Opinions? Whether you're looking for a fact, an opinion, or some advice, it is a good idea to find at least three sources that agree. If the sources do not agree, do further research to find out the range of opinion or disagreement before you draw your conclusions. If the site is sponsored by an **advocacy group**, be aware of the group's agenda or cause; it will affect the reliability of the information [5]

How and Where to Check

Check online directory sources for affiliations and biographical information. Look for other works by the author. Read a few of them. How accurate and unbiased do they sound?

Most print matter (books, articles, and so forth) has been reviewed (vetted) by an editorial board. Frequently it's difficult to confirm that the same is true for information on an Internet source, with some exceptions. If you are searching through a database, such as the Human Genome Database, the Civil War Database, or Eldis: the Gateway to Development Information (a poverty database), it is highly likely that sources from these collections have been reviewed.

---

[5] Excerpt from VirtualSalt.com, www.virtualsalt.com. Reprinted by permission.

Of course, you may use the search engines, too; but you should compare the information you find with information from print sources or at least two other vetted electronic databases.

Nine C's for Evaluating Internet Sources

See Exercise 5.5: Handling It Emotionally or Logically?

See Working Together: Gathering Information for Decision Making

The library at the University of Wisconsin at Eau Claire offers these additional suggestions for checking Internet sources:

Content What is the intent of the content? Are the title and author identified? Is the content "juried"? Is the content "popular" or "scholarly," satiric or serious? What is the date of the document or article? Is the "edition" current? Do you have the latest version? (Is this important?) How do you know?

Credibility Is the author identifiable and reliable? Is the content credible? Authoritative? Should it be? What is the purpose of the information? Is it serious, satiric, humorous? Is the URL extension .edu, .com, .gov, or .org? What does this tell you about the "publisher"?

Critical Thinking How can you apply critical thinking skills, including previous knowledge and experience, to evaluate Internet resources? Can you identify the author, publisher, edition, and so on as you would with a "traditionally" published resource? What criteria do you use to evaluate Internet resources?

Copyright Even if the copyright notice does not appear prominently, someone wrote, or is responsible for, the creation of a document, graphic, sound, or image, and the material falls under the copyright conventions. "Fair use" applies to short, cited excerpts, usually as an example for commentary or research. Materials are in the "public domain" if this is explicitly stated. Internet users, as users of print media, must respect copyright.

Citation Internet resources should be cited to identify sources used, both to give credit to the author and to provide the reader with avenues for further research. Standard style manuals (print and online) provide some examples of how to cite Internet documents, although these standards are not uniform.

Continuity Will the Internet site be maintained and updated? Is it now and will it continue to be free? Can you rely on this source over time to provide up-to-date information? Some good .edu sites have moved to .com, with possible cost implications. Other sites offer partial use for free, and charge fees for continued or in-depth use.

Censorship Has your discussion list "been evaluated"? Messages posted to a "moderated list" are reviewed by a "moderator" before they are distributed to the entire list. Does your search engine or index look for all words or are some words excluded? Is this censorship? Does your institution, based on its mission, parent organization, or space limitations, apply some restrictions to Internet use? Consider censorship and privacy issues when using the Internet.

Comparability Does the Internet resource have an identified comparable print or CD-ROM data set or source? Does the Internet site contain comparable and complete information? (For example, some newspapers have partial but not full text information on the Internet.) Do you need to compare data or statistics over time? Can you identify sources for comparable earlier or later data? Comparability of data may or may not be important, depending on your project.

Context What is the **context** (frame of reference) for your research? Can you find commentary, opinion, narrative, statistics, and so forth? Are you looking for current or historical information? Definitions? Research studies or articles? How does Internet information fit in the overall information context of your subject? Before you start searching, define the research context and research needs, and decide what sources might be best to use to successfully fill information needs without data overload.

Where to Go for Help

ON CAMPUS

Logic Courses: Check out your Philosophy Department's course in "Introduction to Logic." This may be the single best course designed to teach you critical thinking skills. Virtually every college offers such a course.

Argument Courses and Critical Thinking Courses: These are usually offered in the English Department. They will help you develop the ability to formulate logical arguments and avoid such pitfalls as "logical fallacies."

Debating Skills: Some of the very best critical thinkers are those who developed debating skills during college. Go to either your Student Activities Office or your Department of Speech/Drama and find out if your campus has a Debate Club/Society or a Debate Team. Debating can be fun and chances are you would meet some interesting student thinkers.

ONLINE

Check the following website for a critical review of a book titled *The Encyclopedia of Stupidity:* **http://enjoyment.independent.co.uk/books/reviews/story.jsp?story=390625**.

ACHIEVE IT! *Setting Goals for Success*

Go back to the self-assessment at the beginning of this chapter and select one to three unchecked items from the list. Use these to formulate short-term goals for yourself. Be specific about what you want to achieve and when (for example, not "become an active learner," but "find an excuse to meet with at least one of my teachers sometime next week"). Remember to choose goals that are realistic and important to you. Think about what obstacles could get in the way of achieving your goals, and make your plan. In the event you checked all items in the self-assessment, come up with one or more additional goals for this exercise.

	Goal 1	Goal 2	Goal 3
My short-term goal is . . .			
I want to achieve this goal by . . . (date)			
This goal matters because . . .			
I may encounter the following obstacles . . .			
My method for accomplishing this goal will be to . . .			

Set a Date. Put your deadline for achieving your goal(s) in your calendar. Count back ten days from your deadline and write a reminder for yourself.

Reassess. After your deadline passes, ask yourself: Did I meet this goal on time? What change has it made in my life? If I did not meet it, what am I planning to do about it?

TRY IT! *Exercises*

The exercises at the end of each chapter will help you sharpen what we believe are the critical skills for college success: writing, critical thinking, learning in groups, planning, reflecting, and taking action. You can further explore the topic of each chapter by using your PIN to complete the exercises on the website for this text: **http://success.wadsworth.com/gardner7e/**.

WORKING TOGETHER: Gathering Information for Decision Making

In groups of four to six, choose a major problem on campus, such as binge drinking, cheating, date rape, parking, safety, class size, or lack of student participation in organizations.

Between this class and the next, seek information about this problem and possible solutions by interviewing a campus authority on the topic, searching campus library holdings, and/or conducting a survey of students. When you regroup during the next class, share your findings, citing your sources, with other members of the group. Try to reach consensus in the group on the best way to solve the problem. If any members of the group are using emotional rather than logical arguments, point it out to them.

EXERCISE 5.1: Reflecting on Arguments

Review the list of questions on pages 85–86 of this chapter. Are they the kinds of questions that you tend to ask when you read, listen to, or take part in discussions? Each evening for the next week, revisit the list and think about whether you have asked such questions that day. Also try to notice whether people are stating their assumptions or conclusions.

EXERCISE 5.2: Learning about a Liberal Education

Choose one of your teachers whose field is in the humanities (art, literature, writing, history, government, etc.), in mathematics, or in the sciences (social, biological, or physical). Make an appointment to interview her or him, and ask for an explanation of how a liberal education and the instructor's particular field of study contribute to a fuller life, no matter what a student's major is.

EXERCISE 5.3: The Challenge of Classroom Thinking

Think about your experiences in each of your classes so far this term.

- Have your instructors pointed out any conflicts or contradictions in the ideas they have presented? Or have you noted any contradictions that they have not acknowledged?
- Have they asked questions for which they sometimes don't seem to have the answers?
- Have they challenged you or other members of the class to explain yourselves more fully?

- Have they challenged the arguments of other experts? Have they called on students in the class to question or challenge certain ideas?
- How have you reacted to their words? Do your responses reflect critical thinking?

Write down your thoughts for possible discussion in class. Consider sharing them with your instructors.

EXERCISE 5.4: Hard or Easy?

In your opinion, is it harder to think critically than to base your arguments on how you feel about a topic? What are the advantages of finding answers based on your feelings? Based on critical thinking? How might you use both approaches in seeking an answer?

EXERCISE 5.5: Handling It Emotionally or Logically?

Your best friend tells you that your favorite teacher, the one who's been so helpful to you, is a first-class jerk. Write a script in which your reaction to her is purely emotional ("Don't say that to me," for example). Write a second script that shows you've examined the situation logically, using the critical thinking process ("I wish you'd tell me why you think so," and so forth). Compare the two scripts. Which one would most people use? Which one gets to the heart of the matter and allows room for correcting misperceptions? Are they the same scripts or not?

WRITE ABOUT IT: My Personal Journal

This is your place to sound off, to ask your teacher to clarify part of the lesson, or to write him or her about a minor or major crisis you're experiencing. Find out if your teacher wishes you to turn in your journals. Ask if they will remain confidential. Even if the journal isn't used in your course, you can still use the format to write about and reflect on issues regarding the class, yourself, or both.

1. *What was the one major lesson you learned from reading this chapter and/or from class lecture and discussion?*

2. *What are some other important lessons about this topic?*

3. *If you believe some parts of this chapter are unimportant, spell them out here and tell why you think so. (You even might want to discuss this point with your classmates to see if they came up with a similar list.)*

4. *If anything is keeping you from performing at your peak level academically, describe what it is. Your instructor may be able to help or refer you to someone else on campus who can help.*

5. *What behaviors are you planning to change after reading this chapter? Why?*

Sharpen Your Skills!

Listening, Note-Taking, and Participating

In this chapter YOU WILL LEARN

- How to assess your note-taking skills and how to improve them
- Why it's important to review your notes as soon as reasonable after class
- How your five senses can assist in learning and remembering
- How to prepare before class
- How to listen critically and take good notes in class
- Why you should speak up in class
- How to review class and textbook materials after class

What would you ask if you were there? What would you want to know?

Jeanne L. Higbee of the University of Minnesota Twin Cities contributed her valuable and considerable expertise to the writing of this chapter.

● ●

SELF-ASSESSMENT
LISTENING, NOTE-TAKING, AND PARTICIPATING

Check the items below that apply to you:

1. ___ Before class I read the assignment and, if applicable, download any information posted on the teacher's website.

2. ___ If I arrive at class early, I spend the time before class begins reviewing the reading or my notes from the previous lecture.

3. ___ If the instructor puts an outline on the board or overhead projector, I copy each part as we come to it in the lecture.

4. ___ During the lecture I try to determine what information is most important.

5. ___ During class I try to write down all key points in my notes.

6. ___ If I realize that I have missed something important in my notes, I ask the teacher or a classmate for the information.

7. ___ If I do not understand something, I do not hesitate to ask questions in class, even in large lecture sections.

8. ___ I take notes on class discussion as well as on the lecture.

9. ___ When I have to miss class, I contact the instructor immediately, preferably before class begins.

10. ___ I belong to a study group for each of my classes, and we meet often to go over our notes and prepare for exams.

If you checked seven or fewer of the items, find someone who can help you understand why all ten items are critical. At the end of this chapter, you will be asked to set personal goals for one or more of your unchecked items. If you checked all items, you will be asked to set other goals.

● ●

In virtually every college class you take, you'll need to master two skills to earn high grades: listening and note-taking. Taking an active role in your classes—asking questions, contributing to discussions, or providing answers—will help you listen better and take more meaningful notes. That in turn will enhance your ability to learn: to understand abstract ideas, find new possibilities, organize those ideas, and recall the material once the class is over.

Listening and note-taking are critical to your academic success because your college instructors are likely to introduce new material in class that your texts don't cover, and chances are that much of this material will resurface on quizzes and exams.

Here are some helpful tips for assuring that you will retain what is important from class:

1. Instead of chatting with friends before class begins, review your study notes for the previous class.

2. If you would like to tape-record a lecture, be sure to ask the instructor's permission first. But keep in mind that it will be difficult to make a high-

quality recording in an environment with so much extraneous noise. And even though you're recording, take notes. Also consider asking the instructor to speak more slowly or to repeat key points. You also may find it is helpful to meet with a study group to compare notes on the lecture content.

3. Choose the note-taking system that works for you. If a formal outline works for you, fine. If it doesn't, consider other suggestions provided in this chapter for organizing your notes so you can come back to them later and understand them.

4. Be aware that what the instructor says in class may not always be in the textbook, and vice versa. And the instructor often thinks that what he or she said in class is more important than what is in the text; therefore, you are more likely to see that material on a test.

5. Don't copy an outline from the board or screen until the instructor covers each point in sequence. Write down the first point and listen. Take notes. When the next point is covered, do the same, and so on. If you attempt to copy the whole outline initially, you will not be able to concentrate on the instructor's explanation.

6. Since writing down everything the instructor says is probably not possible and you cannot be sure that you have written down everything that is important, ask questions in class. This will ensure that you more clearly understand what you are writing down. Going over your notes with a tutor or someone from your campus learning center, or comparing your notes with a friend's may also help you.

7. Take notes on the discussion. Your instructors may be taking notes on what is said and could use them on exams. You should be participating as well as taking notes.

8. If something is not clear, ask the instructor either in class or after class. Your friends may not have "gotten it" either or may have misunderstood the point the instructor was making. Remember that the teacher, if accessible, is always the best source.

9. Make it a habit to review notes with other students.

10. Speak up! People tend to remember what they have said more than what others are saying to them.

Pay attention to the suggestions in this chapter, decide which ones work best for you, and practice them regularly until they become part of your study routine.

Listening and Forgetting

Have you ever noticed how easy it is to learn the words of a song? We remember songs more easily than other kinds of information or communication because they follow a tune and have a beat, because we may repeat them—sometimes unconsciously—over and over in our heads, and because they often have a personal meaning for us: we relate them to something in our everyday lives. We remember prose less easily unless we make an effort to relate it to what we already know. And, because gibberish or nonsense words are the most unstructured form of communication, and virtually impossible to relate to previous knowledge, we can hardly remember them.

When preparing for tests or for the next lecture, you may sometimes labor over your class notes, trying to figure out exactly what you wrote, what the notes mean, and what the central idea is. That's because most forgetting takes place within the first twenty-four hours after you see or hear something. So, if you do not review almost immediately after class, it may be difficult to retrieve the material later. In two weeks, you will have forgotten up to 70 percent of the material! Forgetting can be a serious problem when you are expected to learn and remember a mass of different facts, figures, concepts, and relationships. Once you understand how to improve your ability to remember, you will retain information more easily and completely. Many instructors draw a significant proportion of their test items from their lectures; therefore, remembering what is presented in class is crucial to doing well on exams.

Using Your Senses in the Learning Process

You can enhance memory by using as many of your senses as possible while learning. How do you believe you learn most effectively?

See Exercise 6.1: Using Your Five Senses to Learn

1. **Aural:** Are you an **auditory learner?** Do you learn by listening to other people talk, or does your mind begin to wander when listening passively for more than a few minutes?
2. **Visual:** Do you like reading? Do you learn best when you can see the words on the printed page? During a test, can you actually visualize where the information appears in your text? Can you remember data best when it's presented in the form of a picture, graph, chart, map, or video?
3. **Interactive:** Do you enjoy discussing course work with friends, classmates, or the teacher? Does talking about information from the lecture or the text help you remember it?
4. **Tactile:** Do you learn through your sense of touch? Does typing your notes help you remember them?
5. **Kinesthetic:** Can you learn better when your body is in motion? When participating in sports, dancing, or working out, do you know immediately if a movement feels right? Do you learn more effectively by doing it than by listening or reading about it?
6. **Olfactory:** Does your sense of taste or smell contribute to your learning process? Do you cook using a recipe or by tasting and adding ingredients? Are you sensitive to odors?

Two or three of these modes probably describe your preferred ways of learning better than the others. At the college level, many faculty members share information primarily via lecture and the textbook. However, many students like to learn best through visual and interactive means, creating a mismatch between learning and teaching styles. Is this a problem? Not necessarily. It is only a problem if you do not learn how to adapt material conveyed by means of lecture and text to your preferred modes of learning.

The following system will help you remember and understand lecture material better and relate information to other things you already know. It consists of three major parts:

- Preparing to listen before class
- Listening and taking notes during class
- Reviewing and recalling information after class

Before Class: Prepare to Remember

Even if lectures don't allow for active participation, you can take a number of **active learning** steps to make your listening and note-taking more efficient. Remember that your goals are:

- Improved learning in the classroom
- A better understanding of what the instructor considers important
- A longer attention span
- Enhanced retention of information
- Clear, well-organized notes for when it's time to study for exams
- Better grades

Because many lectures are a challenge to understand, you need to be prepared before class begins. You would not want to walk in unprepared to give a speech, interview for a job, plead a case in court, or compete in sports. For each of these situations, you would want to prepare in some way. For the same reasons, you should begin active listening, learning, and remembering before the lecture.

1. **Do the assigned reading.** Unless you do, you may find the lecturer's comments disjointed, and you may not understand some terms used. Some instructors refer to assigned readings for each class session; others may hand out a **syllabus** and assume you are keeping up with the assigned readings. Completing the assigned readings on time will help you listen better and pick out what information is most important when taking notes. Read carefully and take good notes. In books that you own, **annotate** (add critical or explanatory margin notes), highlight, or underline the text. In books that you do not own, such as library books, make a photocopy of the pages and then annotate or highlight.

2. **Pay careful attention to your course syllabus.** Syllabi are formal statements of course expectations, requirements, and procedures. Instructors assume that once a student has received the syllabus, he or she will understand and follow course requirements with few or even no reminders.

3. **Make use of auxiliary materials provided by the instructor.** Many teachers post lecture outlines or notes to a website prior to class. Download and print these materials for easy reference during class. These materials often provide hints regarding what the instructor considers most important; they also can create an organizational structure for note-taking.

4. **Warm up for class.** Before class begins warm up or "preview" by reviewing chapter introductions and summaries and by referring to related sections in your text and to your notes from the previous class period. This prepares you to pay attention, understand, and remember.

5. **Keep an open mind.** Every class holds the promise of discovering new ideas and uncovering different perspectives. Some teachers may intentionally present information that challenges your value system. One of the purposes of college is to teach you to think in new and different ways and to learn to provide support for your own beliefs. Instructors want you to think for yourself, and do not necessarily expect you to agree with everything they or your classmates say. However, if you want people to respect *your* values and ideas, you must show respect for *them* as well by listening to what they have to say with an open mind.

6. **Get organized.** Develop an organizational system. Decide what type of notebook will work best for you. Many study skills experts suggest using three-ring binders because you can punch holes in syllabi and other course handouts and keep them with class notes. If you prefer using spiral notebooks, consider buying multisubject notebooks that have pocket dividers for handouts, or be sure to maintain a folder for each course. Consider purchasing notebook paper that has a larger left-hand margin (this is sometimes called "legal-ruled") for ease in annotating your lecture notes.

7. **Prepare to track your progress.** Create a recording system to keep track of grades on all assignments, quizzes, and tests. Retain any papers that are returned to you until the term is over and your grades are posted on your transcript. That way, if you need to appeal a grade because an error occurs, you will have the documentation you need to support your appeal. If you keep your papers, notes, and other course materials organized throughout the term, you will be aware of exactly where you stand going into final

exams and can prioritize how you spend your study time to review most efficiently for each course.

TURNING POINT

College life truly represents the differing opinions found in the world. Learning about types of learners, learning styles, types of listeners, and where I fit in this process is absolutely crucial and necessary for emotional development. I have been able to apply this knowledge at my job with impressive results.

Eddie R.
Westwood College, O'Hare Campus

During Class: Listen Critically

Listening in class is not like listening to a TV program, listening to a friend, or even listening to a speaker at a meeting. Knowing how to listen in class can help you get more out of what you hear, understand better what you have heard, and save time. Here are some suggestions:

1. **Be ready for the message.** Prepare yourself to hear, to listen, and to receive the message. If you have done the assigned reading, you will know what details are already in the text so that you can focus your notes on key concepts during the lecture. You will also know what information is not covered in the text, and you will be prepared to pay closer attention when the instructor is presenting unfamiliar material.

2. **Listen to the main concepts and central ideas, not just to fragmented facts and figures.** Although facts are important, they will be easier to remember and will make more sense when you can place them in a context of concepts, themes, and ideas. You want to understand the material, and only memorizing it won't help you understand it.

3. **Listen for new ideas.** Even if you are an expert on a topic, you can still learn something new. Do not assume that college instructors will present the same information you learned in a similar course in high school.

4. **Really hear what is said.** Hearing sounds is not the same as hearing the intended message. Listening involves hearing what the speaker wants you to understand. Don't give in to distractions, and try not to pass quick judgment on what is being said. As a critical thinker, make a note of questions that arise in your mind as you listen, but save the judgments for later.

5. **Repeat mentally.** Words can go in one ear and out the other unless you make an effort to retain them. Think about what you hear and restate it silently in your own words. If you cannot translate the information into your own words, ask for further clarification.

6. **Decide whether what you have heard is not important, somewhat important, or very important.** If it's really not important, let it go. If it's very important, make it a major point in your notes by highlighting or underscoring it, or use it as a major topic in your outline if that is the

method you use for note-taking. If it's somewhat important, try to relate it to a very important topic by writing it down as a subset of that topic.

7. **Ask questions.** Early in the term, determine whether the instructor is open to responding to questions during lecture. Some teachers prefer to save questions for the end or to have students ask questions during separate discussion sections or office hours. To some extent, this may depend on the nature of the class, such as large lecture versus small seminar. If your teacher is open to answering questions as they arise, do not hesitate to ask if you did not hear or understand what was said. It is best to clarify things immediately, if possible, and other students are likely to have the same questions. If you can't hear another student's question or response, ask that it be repeated.

8. **Listen to the entire message.** Concentrate on "the big picture," but also pay attention to specific details and examples that can assist you in understanding and retaining the information.

9. **Respect your own ideas and those of others.** You already know a lot of things. Your own thoughts and ideas are valuable, and you need not discard them just because someone else's views conflict with your own. At the same time, you should not reject the ideas of others too casually.

10. **Sort, organize, and categorize.** When you listen, try to match what you are hearing with what you already know. Take an active role in deciding how best to recall what you are learning.

During Class: Take Effective Notes

You can make class time more productive by using your listening skills to take effective notes, but first you have to decide on a system.

Cornell Format

One method for organizing notes is called the **Cornell format,** in which you create a "recall" column on each page of your notebook by drawing a vertical line about 2 to 3 inches from the left border. (See Figure 6.1.) You can use the Cornell format in combination with each of the other formats mentioned next. As you take notes during lecture—whether just writing down ideas, making lists, or using an outline or paragraph format or some other type of system—write only in the wider column on the right and leave the recall column on the left blank. (If you have large handwriting and this method seems unwieldy, consider using the back of the previous notebook page for your recall column.) We'll return to the recall column later.

	Psychology 101, 1/31/05
	Theories of Personality
Personality trait: define	Personality trait ="durable disposition to behave in a particular way in a variety of situations"
Big 5: Name + describe them	Big 5-McCrae + Costa- (1)extroversion, (or positive emotionality)=outgoing, sociable, friendly, upbeat, assertive,; (2) neuroticism=anxious, hostile, self-conscious, insecure, vulnerable; (3)openness to experience=curiosity, flexibility, imaginative,; (4) agreeableness=sympathetic, trusting, cooperative, modest; (5)conscientousness=diligent, disciplined, well organized, punctual, dependable
Psychodynamic Theories: Who?	Psychodynamic Theories focus on unconscious forces Freud-psychoanalysis-3 components of personality- (1)id=primitive, instinctive,
3 components of personality: name and describe	operates according to pleasure principle (immediate gratification); (2)ego=decision-making component, operates according to reality principle (delay gratification until appropriate); (3)superego=moral component, social standards, right + wrong
3 levels of awareness: name and describe	3 levels of awareness-(1) conscious=what one is aware of at a particular moment; (2)preconscious=material just below surface, easily retrieved; (3)unconscious=thoughts, memories, + desires well below surface, but have great influence on behavior

Figure 6.1
Note-taking in the Cornell Format

Outline Format

Outline notes are widely used. You are probably already acquainted with what a formal outline looks like, with key ideas represented by Roman numerals, and other ideas relating to each key idea represented in order by uppercase letters, numbers, and lowercase letters. If you use this approach, try to determine the instructor's outline and recreate it in your notes. Add details, definitions, examples, applications, and explanations. (See Figure 6.2.)

Paragraph Format

Writing detailed paragraphs, with each containing a summary of a topic, may work better for summarizing what you have read than for class notes, because

Psychology 101, 1/31/05: Theories of Personality

I. Personality trait = "durable disposition to behave in a particular way in a variety of situations"
II. Big 5-McCrae + Costa
   A. Extroversion, (or positive emotionality) = outgoing, sociable, friendly, upbeat, assertive
   B. Neuroticism = anxious, hostile, self-conscious, insecure, vulnerable
   C. Openness to experience = curiosity, flexibility, imaginative
   D. Agreeableness = sympathetic, trusting, cooperative, modest
   E. Conscientousness = diligent, disciplined, well organized, punctual, dependable
III. Psychodynamic Theories-focus on unconscious forces-- Freud—psychoanalysis
   A. 3 components of personality
      1. Id = primitive, instinctive, operates according to pleasure principle (immediate gratification)
      2. Ego = decision-making component, operates according to reality principle (delay gratification until appropriate)
      3. Superego = moral component, social standards, right + wrong
   B. 3 levels of awareness
      1. Conscious = what one is aware of at a particular moment
      2. Preconscious = material just below surface, easily retrieved
      3. Unconscious = thoughts, memories, + desires well below surface, but have great influence on behavior

Figure 6.2
Note-taking in the Outline Format

it may be difficult to summarize the topic until your teacher has covered it completely. By that time, it may be too late to recall critical information. (See Figure 6.3.)

List Format

This format can be effective when taking notes on lists of terms and definitions, facts, or sequences, such as the body's pulmonary system. It is easy to use lists in combination with the Cornell format, with key terms on the left and their definitions and explanations on the right. (See Figure 6.4.)

Once you have decided on a format for taking notes, you may also want to develop your own system of abbreviations. For example, you might write

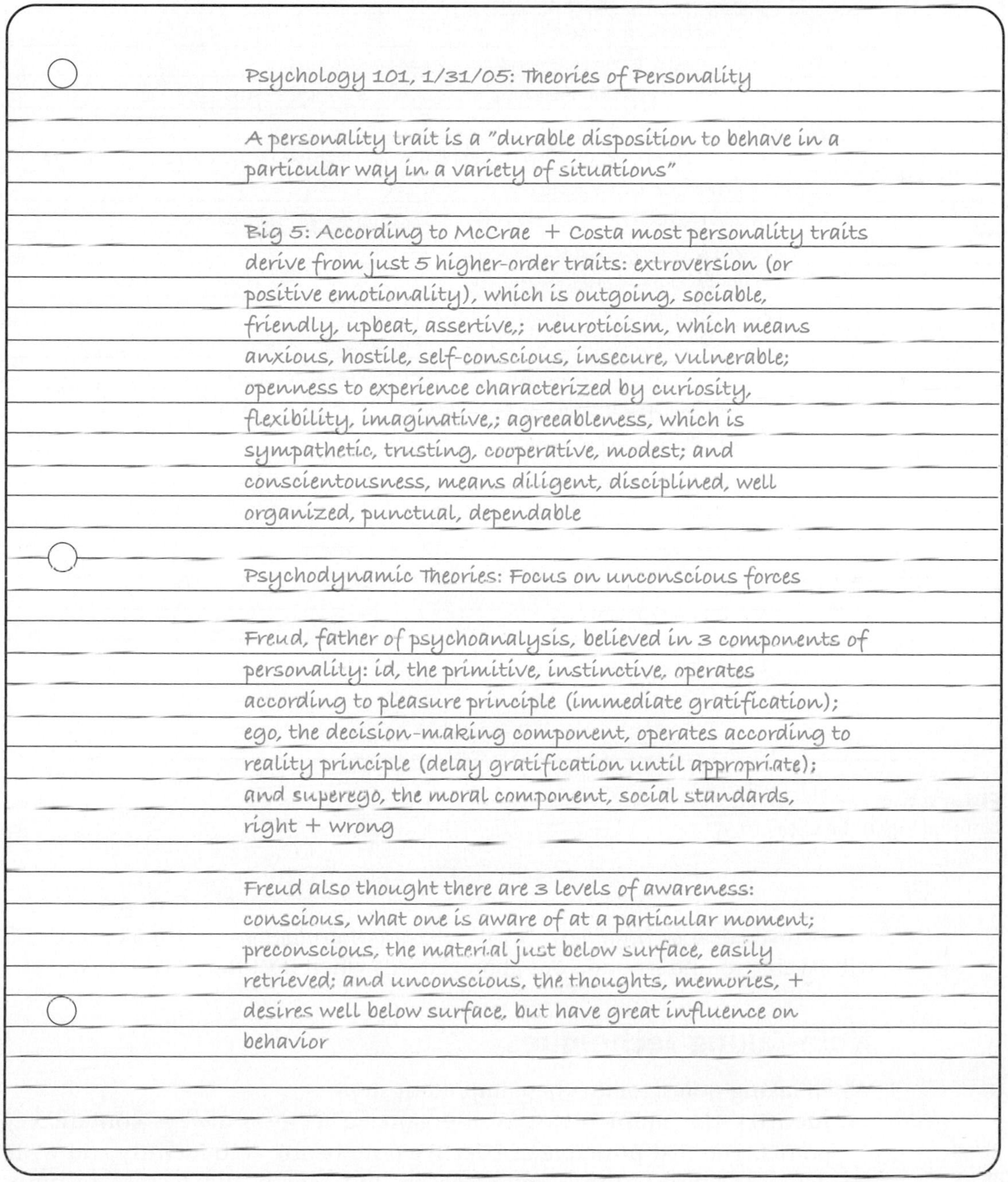

Psychology 101, 1/31/05: Theories of Personality

A personality trait is a "durable disposition to behave in a particular way in a variety of situations"

Big 5: According to McCrae + Costa most personality traits derive from just 5 higher-order traits: extroversion (or positive emotionality), which is outgoing, sociable, friendly, upbeat, assertive,; neuroticism, which means anxious, hostile, self-conscious, insecure, vulnerable; openness to experience characterized by curiosity, flexibility, imaginative,; agreeableness, which is sympathetic, trusting, cooperative, modest; and conscientousness, means diligent, disciplined, well organized, punctual, dependable

Psychodynamic Theories: Focus on unconscious forces

Freud, father of psychoanalysis, believed in 3 components of personality: id, the primitive, instinctive, operates according to pleasure principle (immediate gratification); ego, the decision-making component, operates according to reality principle (delay gratification until appropriate); and superego, the moral component, social standards, right + wrong

Freud also thought there are 3 levels of awareness: conscious, what one is aware of at a particular moment; preconscious, the material just below surface, easily retrieved; and unconscious, the thoughts, memories, + desires well below surface, but have great influence on behavior

Figure 6.3
Note-taking in the Paragraph Format

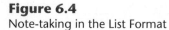

Psychology 101, 1/31/05: Theories of Personality

- A personality trait is a "durable disposition to behave in a particular way in a variety of situations"
- Big 5: According to McCrae + Costa most personality traits derive from just 5 higher-order traits
    - extroversion, (or positive emotionality)=outgoing, sociable, friendly, upbeat, assertive
    - neuroticism=anxious, hostile, self-conscious, insecure, vulnerable
    - openness to experience=curiosity, flexibility, imaginative
    - agreeableness=sympathetic, trusting, cooperative, modest
    - conscientousness=diligent, disciplined, well organized, punctual, dependable
- Psychodynamic Theories: Focus on unconscious forces
- Freud, father of psychoanalysis, believed in 3 components of personality
    - id=primitive, instinctive, operates according to pleasure principle (immediate gratification)
    - ego=decision-making component, operates according to reality principle (delay gratification until appropriate)
    - superego=moral component, social standards, right + wrong
- Freud also thought there are 3 levels of awareness
    - conscious=what one is aware of at a particular moment
    - preconscious=material just below surface, easily retrieved
    - unconscious=thoughts, memories, + desires well below surface, but have great influence on behavior

Figure 6.4
Note-taking in the List Format

"inst" instead of *institution* or "eval" instead of *evaluation*. Just make sure you will be able to understand your abbreviations when it's time to review.

Note-Taking Techniques

When taking notes, follow these important steps:

1. **Identify the main ideas.** Well-organized lectures always contain key points. The first principle of effective note-taking is to identify and write down the most important ideas around which the lecture is built. Although supporting details are important as well, focus your note-taking

See Exercise 6.2: What System of Note-Taking Works for You?

Personality trait	I. Personality trait ="durable disposition to behave in a particular way in a variety of situations"
	II. Big 5 McCrae + Costa
Big 5: Who?	A. Extroversion, (or positive emotionality)=outgoing, sociable, friendly, upbeat, assertive
Name + describe them	B. Neuroticism=anxious, hostile, self-conscious, insecure, vulnerable
	C. Openness to experience=curiosity, flexibility, imaginative
	D. Agreeableness=sympathetic, trusting, cooperative, modest
	E. Conscientousness=diligent, disciplined, well organized, punctual, dependable
	III. Psychodynamic Theories-focus on unconscious forces-- Freud-psychoanalysis
Psychodynamic Theories: Who?	A. 3 components of personality
3 components.	1. Id=primitive, instinctive, operates according to pleasure principle (immediate gratification)
Name, define, relate each to a	2. Ego=decision-making component, operates according to reality principle (delay
principle	gratification until appropriate)
	3. Superego=moral component, social standards, right + wrong
	B. 3 levels of awareness
	1. conscious=what one is aware of at a particular
3 levels of	moment
awareness: name	2. preconscious=material just below surface, easily
and describe	retrieved
	3. unconscious=thoughts, memories, + desires well below surface, but have great influence on behavior

Figure 6.5
Cornell Format combined with Outline Format

on the main ideas. Such ideas may be buried in details, statistics, anecdotes, or problems, but you will need to identify and record them for further study.

Some instructors announce the purpose of a lecture or offer an outline, thus providing you with the skeleton of main ideas, followed by the details. Others develop overhead transparencies or PowerPoint presentations, and may make these materials available on a class website before the lecture. If so, you can enlarge them, print them out, and take notes on the teacher's outline or next to the PowerPoint slides.

Some lecturers change their tone of voice or repeat themselves for each key idea. Some ask questions or promote discussion. If a lecturer says something more than once, chances are it's important. Ask yourself, "What does my instructor want me to know at the end of today's class?"

2. **Don't try to write down everything.** Some first-year students try to do just that. They stop being thinkers and become stenographers. Learn to avoid that trap. If you're an active listener, you will ultimately have shorter but more useful notes. (See an exception in the section on taking notes in math and science courses on pages 117–118.)

As you take notes, leave spaces so that later you can fill in additional details that you might have missed during class. But remember to do it as soon after class as possible; remember the "forgetting curve," how quickly you forget what you didn't write down.

4. **Don't be thrown by a disorganized lecturer.** When a lecture is disorganized, it's your job to try to organize what is said into general and specific frameworks. When the order is not apparent, you'll need to indicate in your notes where the gaps lie. After the lecture, you will need to consult your reading material or classmates to fill in these gaps.

You might also consult your instructor. Most instructors have regular office hours for student appointments, yet it is amazing how few students use these opportunities for one-on-one instruction. You can also raise questions in class. Asking questions may help your instructor discover which parts of the lecture need more attention and clarification.

5. **When using the Cornell format, return to your recall column.** The recall column is essentially the place where you write down the main ideas and important details for tests and examinations as you sift through your notes as soon after class as feasible, preferably within an hour or two. It can be a critical part of effective note-taking and becomes an important study device for tests and examinations. In anticipation of using your notes later, treat each page of your notes as part of an exam-preparation system.

If you are a visual learner, dividing the page creates a visual image that makes it easier to picture key concepts. If you are an interactive learner, study in pairs or with a group. Test one another on the key words or phrases you have jotted down in the recall column to see how much of the material presented in lecture you can remember. If you are an aural learner, look at the recall column while you cover the rest of the page, and recite out loud, in your own words, what you remember from your notes. Keep in mind that you want to use as many of your five senses as possible to enhance memory. The recall column is a powerful study device that reduces forgetting, helps you warm up for the next class, promotes understanding during class, and provides you with an easy means of testing yourself when preparing for exams.

Taking Notes in Nonlecture Courses

Always be ready to adapt your note-taking methods to match the situation. Group discussion is becoming a popular way to teach in college because it involves active learning. On your campus you may also have **Supplemental Instruction (SI)** classes that provide further opportunity to discuss the information presented in lectures.

How do you keep a record of what's happening in such classes? Assume you are taking notes in a problem-solving group assignment. You would begin your notes by asking yourself "What is the problem?" and writing down the answer.

As the discussion progresses, you would list the solutions offered. These would be your main ideas. The important details might include the positive and negative aspects of each view or solution. The important thing to remember when taking notes in nonlecture courses is that you need to record the information presented by your classmates as well as by the instructor, and to consider all reasonable ideas, even though they may differ from your own.

When a course has separate lecture and discussion sessions, you will need to understand how the discussion sessions relate to and augment the lectures. If different material is covered in lecture or discussion, you may need to ask for guidance in organizing your notes. When similar topics are covered, you can combine your notes so that you have comprehensive, unified coverage of each topic.

How to organize the notes you take in a class discussion depends on the purpose or form of the discussion. But it usually makes good sense to begin with the list of issues or topics that the discussion leader announces. Another approach is to list the questions that the participants raise for discussion. If the discussion is exploring reasons for and against a particular argument, it makes sense to divide your notes into columns or sections for pros and cons. When conflicting views are presented in discussion, it is important to record different perspectives and the rationales behind them. Your teacher may ask you to defend your own opinions in light of those of others.

Taking Notes in Science and Mathematics Courses

Many mathematics and science courses often build on each other from term to term and year to year. When you take notes in these courses, you are likely to need to refer to back to them in future terms. For example, when taking organic chemistry, you may need to refer to notes taken in earlier chemistry courses. This can be particularly important when time has elapsed since your last course, like after a summer break. Here are some ideas for getting organized:

- Keep your notes and supplementary materials (such as teachers' handouts) for each course in a separate three-ring binder labeled with the course number and name. If the binders are too bulky to carry around all day in your backpack, create a separate folder for each class, stocked with loose-leaf notebook paper. Before class, label and date the paper you will be using for taking notes. Then, as soon after class as possible, move your notes from the folder to the binder.

- Download any notes, outlines, or diagrams, charts, graphs, and other visual representations of the material that are provided on the instructor's website prior to class and bring them with you. You may be able to save yourself considerable time during the lecture if you do not have to try to copy complicated graphs and diagrams while the instructor is talking; instead you can focus on the ideas being presented, meanwhile adding your own labels and notes to the visual image.

- Take notes only on the front of each piece of loose-leaf paper. Then later you can use the back of each sheet to add further details, annotations, corrections, comments, questions, and a summary of each lecture. Or, once placed in the binder, you can use what have now become the left-hand pages the same way that you would use the recall column in the Cornell format, noting key ideas to be used for testing yourself when preparing for exams. You may find that this approach works better than enlarging the left-hand margin when you need the full page for recording complicated formulas, equations, charts, or graphs.

- Consider taking your notes in pencil or erasable pen. When copying long equations while also trying to pay attention to what the instructor is saying, or when copying problems that students are solving at the board, it is not unusual to need to erase or make changes as you go along. You want to keep your notes as neat as possible. You can then use colored ink to add other details later.

- Organize your notes in your binder chronologically. Then create separate tabbed sections for homework, lab assignments, returned tests, and other materials.

- If handouts are distributed in class, label them and place them in your binder either immediately before or immediately after the notes for that day. Purchase a portable three-ring hole punch that can be kept in your binder. Do not let handouts accumulate in your folders; each day as you are reviewing your notes also add any handouts to your binders.

- Keep your binders for math and science courses until you graduate (or even longer if there is any chance that you will attend graduate school at some point in the future). They will serve as beneficial review materials for later classes in math and science sequences and for preparing for standardized tests like the Graduate Record Exam (GRE) or Medical College Admission Test (MCAT). In some cases, these notes can also prove helpful in the workplace.

Suggestions for taking notes in math and science courses can be different from suggestions for other types of classes, where it is not a good idea to try to write down every word the instructor says. Here are some tips to keep in mind specifically when taking notes in quantitative and scientific classes:

- Write down any equations, formulas, diagrams, charts, graphs, and definitions that the instructor puts on the board or screen.

- Quote the instructor's words precisely to the extent possible. Technical terms often have exact meanings and cannot be paraphrased.

- Use standard symbols, abbreviations, and scientific notation.

- Write down all worked problems and examples, step-by-step. They often provide the template for exam questions. Actively engage in solving the problem yourself as it is solved at the front of the class. Be sure that you can follow the logic and understand the sequence of steps. If you have questions that you cannot ask during lecture, write them down in your notes so that you can ask them in discussion, lab, or during the instructor's office hours.

- Listen carefully to other students' questions and the instructor's answers. Take notes on the discussion and during question-and-answer periods.

- Use asterisks, exclamation points, question marks, or symbols of your own to highlight important points in your notes or questions that you need to come back to when you review.

- Refer back to the textbook after class; the text may contain more accurate diagrams and other visual representations than you are able to draw while taking notes in class. If they are not provided in handouts or on the instructor's website, you may even want to photocopy diagrams from the text and include them with your notes in your binder.

Using Technology to Take Notes

Laptops are often poor tools for taking notes during class. Computers are not conducive to making marginal notes, circling important items, or copying complex equations or diagrams while they are being presented in class. Entering notes on a computer *after* class for review purposes may be helpful, especially if you are a tactile learner. After class you can also cut and paste diagrams and other visual representations into your notes. Then you can print out your notes and highlight or annotate just as you would handwritten notes. However, for many students, time will be better spent reviewing notes than typing or copying them. Similarly, some students think it will be advantageous to tape lectures, but it is then too easy to become a passive nonparticipant in class rather than listening actively, because you know that you have the tape as a fallback. In actuality, if you tape lectures you are then doubling your time requirement; you will then have to listen to the whole lecture again.

There are some notable exceptions to these rules of thumb, and students with specific types of disabilities may be urged to tape lectures, or may have note-takers who type at a laptop while the student views the notes on a separate screen. However, for the vast majority of learners, listening and taking notes by hand is still the most effective means of learning.

After Class: Respond, Recite, Review

Don't let the forgetting curve take its toll on you. As soon after class as possible, review your notes and fill in the details you still remember, but missed writing down, in those spaces you left in the right-hand column.

Relate new information to other things you already know. Organize your information. Make a conscious effort to remember. One way is to recite important data to yourself every few minutes. If you are an aural learner, repeat it out loud. Another is to tie one idea to another idea, concept, or name, so that thinking of one will prompt recall of the other. Or you may want to create your own poem, song, or slogan using the information.

For interactive learners, the best way to learn something may be to teach it to someone else. You will understand something better and remember it longer if you try to explain it. This helps you discover your own reactions and uncover gaps in your comprehension of the material. (Asking and answering questions in class also provides you with the feedback you need to make certain your understanding is accurate.) Now you're ready to embed the major points from your notes into your memory. Use these three important steps for remembering the key points in the lecture:

1. **Write the main ideas in the recall column**. For five or ten minutes, quickly review your notes and select key words or phrases that will act as labels or tags for main ideas and key information in the notes. Highlight the main ideas and write them in the recall column next to the material they represent.
2. **Use the recall column to recite your ideas.** Cover the notes on the right and use the prompts from the recall column to help you recite *out loud* a brief version of what you understand from the class in which you have just participated.

If you don't have a few minutes after class when you can concentrate on reviewing your notes, find some other time during that same day to review what you have written. You might also want to ask your teacher to glance at your recall column to determine whether you have noted the major ideas.

3. **Review the previous day's notes just before the next class session.** As you sit in class the next day waiting for the lecture to begin, use the time to quickly review the notes from the previous day. This will put you in tune with the lecture that is about to begin and also prompt you to ask questions about material from the previous lecture that may not have been clear to you.

These three ways to engage with the material will pay off later, when you begin to study for your exams.

What if you have three classes in a row and no time for recall columns or recitations between them? Recall and recite as soon after class as possible. Review the most recent class first. Never delay recall and recitation longer than one day; if you do, it will take you longer to review, make a recall column, and recite. With practice, you can complete your recall column quickly, perhaps between classes, during lunch, or while riding the bus.

Comparing and Recopying Notes

You may be able to improve your notes by comparing notes with another student or in a study group, Supplemental Instruction session, or a learning community, if one is available to you. Knowing that your notes will be seen by someone else will prompt you to make your notes well organized, clear, and accurate. Compare your notes: Are they as clear and concise as other students'? Do you agree on the important points that should be included in the recall column? Share with each other how you take and organize your notes. You may get new ideas for using abbreviations. Take turns testing each other on what you have learned. By doing this, you are predicting exam questions and determining whether you can answer them.

Incidentally, comparing notes is not the same as copying somebody else's notes. You simply cannot learn as well from someone else's notes, no matter how good they are, if you have not attended class.

If your campus has a note-taking service, check with your instructor about making use of this for-pay service, but keep in mind that such notes are intended to supplement the ones you take, not to substitute for them. Some students choose to copy their own notes as a means of review, or because they think their notes are too messy and that they will not be able to understand them later. Unless you are a tactile learner, copying or typing your notes may not help you learn the material. A more profitable approach might be to summarize your notes in your own words.

Finally, have a backup plan in case you do need to be absent due to illness or a family emergency. Exchange phone numbers and e-mail addresses with other students so that you can contact one of them to learn what you missed and get a copy of their notes. Also contact your instructor to explain your absence and set up an appointment during office hours to make sure you understand the work you missed.

See Working Together: Comparing Notes

Class Notes and Homework

Good class notes can help you complete homework assignments. Follow these steps:

1. **Take ten minutes to review your notes.** Skim the notes and put a question mark next to anything you do not understand at first reading. Draw

stars next to topics that warrant special emphasis. Try to place the material in context: What has been going on in the course for the past few weeks? How does today's class fit in?

2. **Do a warm-up for your homework.** Before doing the assignment, look through your notes again. Use a separate sheet of paper to rework examples, problems, or exercises. If there is related assigned material in the textbook, review it. Go back to the examples. Cover the solution and attempt to answer each question or complete each problem. Look at the author's work only after you have made a serious personal effort to remember it.

   Keep in mind that it can help to go back through your course notes, reorganize them, highlight the essential items, and thus create new notes that let you connect with the material one more time and that are better than the originals.

3. **Do any assigned problems and answer any assigned questions.** When you start doing your homework, read each question or problem and ask: What am I supposed to find or find out? What is essential and what is extraneous? Read each problem several times and state it in your own words. Work the problem without referring to your notes or the text, as though you were taking a test. In this way, you will test your knowledge and know when you are prepared for exams.

4. **Persevere.** Don't give up too soon. When you encounter a problem or question that you cannot readily handle, move on only after a reasonable effort. After you have completed the entire assignment, come back to those items that stumped you. Try once more, then take a break. You may need to mull over a particularly difficult problem for several days. Let your unconscious mind have a chance. Inspiration may come when you are waiting for a stoplight or just before you fall asleep.

5. **Complete your work.** When you finish an assignment, talk to yourself about what you learned from this particular assignment. Think about how the problems and questions were different from one another, which strategies were successful, and what form the answers took. Be sure to review any material you have not mastered. Seek assistance from the teacher, a classmate, study group, learning center, or tutor to learn how to answer any questions that stumped you.

You may be thinking, "That all sounds good, but who has the time to do all that extra work?" In reality, this approach does work and can actually save you time. Try it for a few weeks. You will find that you can diminish the frustration that comes when you tackle your homework cold, and that you will be more confident going into exams.

Participating in Class: Speak Up!

Learning is not a spectator sport. To really learn, you must talk about what you are learning, write about it, relate it to past experiences, and make what you learn part of yourself. Participation is the heart of active learning. When we say something in class, we are more likely to remember it than when someone else does. So when a teacher tosses a question your way, or when you have a question to ask, you're actually making it easier to remember the day's lesson.

Naturally, you will be more likely to participate in a class where the teacher emphasizes discussion, calls on students by name, shows students signs of approval and interest, and avoids criticizing you for an incorrect answer.

See Exercise 6.3: Memory Using a Recall Column

Where to Go for Help

ON CAMPUS

Learning Assistance Center: Almost every campus has one of these, and this chapter's topic is one of their specialties. More and more the best students, and good students who want to be the best students, use Learning Centers as much as students who are having academic difficulties. These services are offered by both full-time professionals and highly skilled student tutors, all of whom are available at times convenient for you.

Fellow College Students: Often the best help we can get is the closest to us: fellow students. But, of course, not just any student. Keep an eye out in your classes, residence hall, cocurricular groups, and other places for the most serious, purposeful, and directed students. Those are the ones to seek out. Find a tutor. Join a study group. Students who do these things are much more likely to stay in college and be successful. It does not diminish you in any way to seek assistance from your peers.

ONLINE

Mary Helen Callarman Center for Academic Excellence at the University of Central Florida: **http://www.sarc.sdes.ucf.edu/learningskills.html.** This excellent web link gives note-taking tips.

See guidelines for speaking in class at: **http://www.utm.edu/stafflinks/ccenter/counseling/publicspeaking anxiety.html** and **http://www.school-for-champions.com/grades/speaking.htm.**

Often, answers you and others offer that are not quite correct can lead to new perspectives on a topic.

Unfortunately, large classes often cause instructors to use the lecture method. And large classes can be intimidating. If you speak up in a class of 100 and think you've made a fool of yourself, you also think that 99 other people

will know it. Of course, that's somewhat unrealistic, since you've probably asked a question that they were too timid to ask, and they'll silently thank you for doing so. If you're lucky, you might even find that the instructor of such a class takes time out to ask or answer questions. To take full advantage of these opportunities in all classes, try using these techniques:

1. **Take a seat as close to the front as possible.** If you're seated by name and your name is Zitch, plead bad eyesight or hearing—anything to get moved up front.

2. **Keep your eyes trained on the teacher.** Sitting up front will make this easier for you to do.

3. **Focus on the lecture.** Do not let yourself be distracted. It might be wise not to sit near friends who can be distracting without meaning to be.

4. **Raise your hand when you don't understand something.** The instructor may answer you immediately, ask you to wait until later in the class, or throw your question to the rest of the class. In each case, you benefit in several ways. The instructor gets to know you, other students get to know you, and you learn from both the instructor and your classmates. But don't overdo it. Both the instructor and your peers will tire of too many questions that disrupt the flow of the class.

5. **Speak up in class.** Ask a question or volunteer to answer a question or make a comment. It becomes easier every time you do this.

6. **Never feel that you're asking a "stupid" question.** If you don't understand something, you have a right to ask for an explanation.

7. **When the instructor calls on you to answer a question, don't bluff.** If you know the answer, give it. If you're not certain, begin with, "I think . . . , but I'm not sure I have it all correct." If you don't know, just say so.

8. **If you've recently read a book or article that is relevant to the class topic, bring it in.** Use it either to ask questions about the piece or to provide information from it that was not covered in class. Next time you have the opportunity, speak up. Class will go by faster, you and your fellow students will get to know one another, your instructor will get to know you, and he or she will, in all likelihood, be grateful to have your participation.

ACHIEVE IT! *Setting Goals for Success*

Go back to the self-assessment at the beginning of this chapter and select one to three unchecked items from the list. Use these to formulate short-term goals for yourself. Be specific about what you want to achieve and when (for example, not "become an active learner," but "find an excuse to meet with at least one of my teachers sometime next week"). Remember to choose goals that are realistic and important to you. Think about what obstacles could get in the way of achieving your goals, and make your plan. In the event you checked all items in the self-assessment, come up with one or more additional goals for this exercise.

	Goal 1	Goal 2	Goal 3
My short-term goal is . . .			
I want to achieve this goal by . . . (date)			
This goal matters because . . .			
I may encounter the following obstacles . . .			
My method for accomplishing this goal will be to . . .			

Set a Date. Put your deadline for achieving your goal(s) in your calendar. Count back ten days from your deadline and write a reminder for yourself.

Reassess. After your deadline passes, ask yourself: Did I meet this goal on time? What change has it made in my life? If I did not meet it, what am I planning to do about it?

TRY IT! *Exercises*

The exercises at the end of each chapter will help you sharpen what we believe are the critical skills for college success: writing, critical thinking, learning in groups, planning, reflecting, and taking action. You can further explore the topic of each chapter by using your PIN to complete the exercises on the website for this text: **http://success.wadsworth.com/gardner7e/**.

WORKING TOGETHER: Comparing Notes

Pair up with another student and compare your class notes for this course. Are your notes clear? Do you agree on what is important? Take a few minutes to explain to each other your note-taking systems. Agree to use a recall column during the next class meeting. Afterward, share your notes again and check on how each of you used the recall column. Again, compare your notes and what each of you deemed important.

EXERCISE 6.1: Using Your Five Senses to Learn

Refer back to page 107 in this chapter and decide which two modes of learning seem to work best for you: aural, visual, interactive, tactile, kinesthetic, or olfactory. If you are not an aural learner, how can you use *your* preferred ways of learning to master information presented in lecture-style courses? Brainstorm ways to convert lecture material into a format that is a better match for how you best use your five senses in the learning process. See if other students also have creative ideas for doing this.

EXERCISE 6.2: What System of Note-Taking Works for You?

Pick one of your lecture courses and over the next four or five class periods try out each of the methods of note-taking described in this chapter: Cornell format, outline, paragraph, and list formats, or a combination. Then find a time within a couple of hours after a lecture to review your notes. Which method seems to work best for you? Which method will be easiest to refer back to when studying for tests? Are there any advantages to using a combination of methods (such as using an outline in conjunction with the Cornell format for taking the notes in class, and then using the recall column for testing yourself on the contents of your outline using the outline)?

EXERCISE 6.3: Memory Using a Recall Column

Refer to Figure 6.1 and study the material provided in the right-hand column until you think you know it well enough to take a test on it. Then cover the right-hand column. Using the recall column, try reciting in your own words the main ideas from these sample notes. Uncover the right-hand column when you need to refer to it. If you can phrase the main ideas from the recall column in your own words, you are well on your way to mastering this note-taking system for dealing with lectures. Does this system seem to work? If not, why not?

WRITE ABOUT IT! My Personal Journal

This is your place to sound off, to ask your teacher to clarify part of the lesson or to write him or her about a minor or major crisis you're experiencing. Find out if your teacher wishes you to turn in your journals. Ask if they will remain confidential. Even if the journal isn't used in your course, you can still use the format to write about and reflect on issues regarding the class, yourself, or both.

1. *What was the one major lesson you learned from reading this chapter and/or from class lecture and discussion?*

2. *What are some other important lessons about this topic?*

3. *If you believe some parts of this chapter are unimportant, spell them out here and tell why you think so. (You even might want to discuss this point with your classmates to see if they came up with a similar list.)*

4. *If anything is keeping you from performing at your peak level academically, describe what it is. Your instructor may be able to help or refer you to someone else on campus who can help.*

5. *What behaviors are you planning to change after reading this chapter? Why?*

Reading Strategies

Chapter 7

In this chapter YOU WILL LEARN

- How to "prepare to read"
- How to preview reading material
- How to read your textbooks efficiently
- How to mark your textbooks
- How to review your reading
- How to adjust your reading style to the material
- How to develop a more extensive vocabulary

If you were reading this, where would you start?

Jeanne L. Higbee of the University of Minnesota Twin Cities and Mary Ellen O'Leary of the University of South Carolina at Columbia contributed their valuable and considerable expertise to the writing of this chapter.

SELF-ASSESSMENT
READING STRATEGIES

Check the items below that apply to you:

1. ____ I skim or "preview" a chapter before I begin to read.

2. ____ I concentrate while reading a text.

3. ____ I wait to underline, highlight, or annotate the text until *after* I read a page or section.

4. ____ I take notes while I read.

5. ____ I pause at the end of each section or page to review what I have read.

6. ____ After reading, I recite key ideas to myself or with a study partner.

7. ____ I review everything I have read for a class at least once a week.

8. ____ I know the difference between a textbook and primary source material.

9. ____ I look for connections between the text and class lectures or discussions.

10. ____ I set reading goals for each study period and take a short break when I have reached my goal.

If you checked seven or fewer of the items, find someone who can help you understand why all ten items are critical. At the end of this chapter, you will be asked to set personal goals for one or more of your unchecked items. If you checked all items, you will be asked to set other goals.

Why is reading college textbooks more challenging than reading high school texts or reading for pleasure? College texts are loaded with concepts, terms, and complex information that you are expected to learn on your own in a short period of time. To do this, you will need to learn and use a reading method such as the one in this chapter.

The following plan for textbook reading can pay off. It is designed to increase your focus and concentration, promote greater understanding of what you read, and prepare you to study for tests and exams. This system is based on four steps:

Previewing

Reading

Marking

Reviewing

Previewing

The purpose of previewing is to get the "big picture," to understand how what you are about to read is connected to what you already know and to the material the instructor is covering in class. Begin by reading the title of the chapter. Ask yourself, "What do I already know about this subject?" Next, quickly read through the introductory paragraphs, then read the summary at the beginning or end of the chapter (if one is there). Finally, take a few minutes to skim through the chapter headings and subheadings. Note any study exercises at the end of the chapter.

As part of your preview, note how many pages the chapter contains. It's a good idea to decide in advance how many pages you can reasonably expect to cover in your first fifty-minute study period. This can help build your concentration as you work toward your goal of reading a specific number of pages. Before long, you'll know how many pages are practical for you.

Keep in mind that different types of textbooks may require more or less time to read. For example, depending on your interests and previous knowledge, you may be able to read a psychology text more quickly than a logic text that presents a whole new symbol system.

Mapping

Mapping the chapter as you preview it provides a visual guide to how different chapter ideas fit together. Because about 75 percent of students identify themselves as visual learners, visual mapping is an excellent learning tool for test preparation as well as reading (see Chapter 3: How We Learn). How do you map a chapter? While you are previewing, use either a wheel or a branching structure. In the wheel structure, place the central idea of the chapter in the circle. The central idea should be found in the introduction to the chapter and may also be apparent in the chapter title. Place secondary ideas on the spokes emanating from the circle, and place offshoots of those ideas on the lines attached to the spokes. In the branching map, the main idea goes at the top, followed by supporting ideas on the second tier, and so forth. Fill in the title first. Then, as you skim through the rest of the chapter, use the headings and subheadings to fill in the key ideas.

Wheel Map

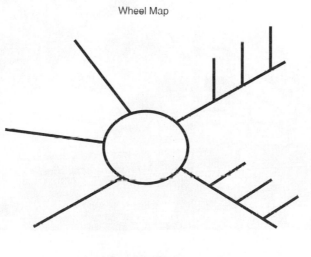

Branching Map

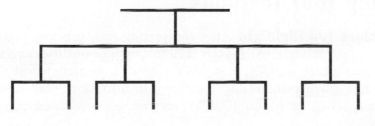

Figure 7.1
Wheel and Branching Maps

See Exercise 7.1: Previewing and Creating a Visual Map

Alternatives to Mapping

Perhaps you prefer a more linear visual image. If so, consider making an outline of the headings and subheadings in the chapter. You can fill in the outline after you read. Or make a list. Making a list can be particularly effective when dealing with a text that introduces lots of new terms and their definitions. Set up the list with the terms in the left column and fill in definitions, descriptions, and examples on the right after you read. Divide the terms on your list into groups of five, seven, or nine, and leave white space between the clusters so that you can visualize each group in your mind. This practice is known as **"chunking."** Research indicates that we learn material better in chunks of five, seven, or nine.

If you are an interactive learner, make lists or create a flash card for each heading and subheading. Then fill in the back of each card after reading each section in the text. Use the lists or flash cards to review with a partner, or to recite the material to yourself.

Previewing, combined with mapping, outlining, or flash cards, may require more time up front, but it will save you time later because you have created an excellent review tool for quizzes and tests. You will be using your visual learning skills as you create "advance organizers" to help you associate details of the chapter with the larger ideas. Such associations will come in handy later.

As you preview the text material, look for connections between the text and the related lecture material. Call to mind the related terms and concepts that you recorded in the lecture. Use these strategies to warm up. Ask yourself, "Why am I reading this? What do I want to know?"

Reading Your Textbook

Read Before You Highlight After completing your preview, you are ready to read the text actively. With your skeleton map or outline, you should be able to read more quickly and with greater comprehension. To avoid marking too much or marking the wrong information, read first without using your pencil or highlighter. When you have reached the end of a

TURNING POINT

Reading can definitely be a challenge for me, especially when the material is very difficult or I have a lot of it due on the same day. When I feel overwhelmed with my reading, I usually try to write up a schedule for myself. I'll plan out how many pages I can realistically get done in an hour. If I'm able to achieve that goal, I'll reward myself by taking a quick break to get a snack or just rest.

Jennifer S.
New York University

section, stop and ask yourself, "What are the key ideas in this section? What do I think I'll see on the test?" Then, and only then, decide what to underline or highlight.

Annotate You may want to try a strategy known as annotating the text. In your own words, write key ideas in the margins of the text.

Learn to Concentrate Two common problems students have with reading textbooks are trouble concentrating and not understanding the content. Many factors may affect your ability to concentrate and understand texts: the time of day, your energy level, your interest in the material, and your study location.

Consider these suggestions, and decide which would help you improve your reading ability:

- Find a study location, preferably in the library if you are on campus, that is removed from traffic and distracting noises.

- Read in fifty-minute blocks of time, with short breaks in between. By reading for fifty minutes more frequently during the day instead of cramming all your reading in at the end of the day, you should be able to process material more easily.

- Set goals for your study period, such as "I will read twenty pages of my psychology text in the next fifty minutes." Reward yourself with a ten-minute break after each fifty-minute study period.

- If you are having trouble concentrating or staying awake, take a quick walk around the library or down the hall. Stretch or take some deep breaths and think positively about your study goals. Then go back and resume studying.

- Jot study questions in the margin, take notes, or recite key ideas. Reread confusing parts of the text, and make a note to ask your instructor for clarification.

- Experiment with your reading rate. Try to move your eyes more quickly over the material by focusing on phrases, not individual words. If that doesn't work, go back to the method that does.

- Focus on the important portions of the text. Pay attention to the first and last sentences of paragraphs and to words in italics or bold print.

- Use the glossary in the text to define unfamiliar terms.

See Exercise 7.2: Doing What It Takes to Understand

As you begin reading, be sure to learn more about the textbook and its author by reading the front matter in the book, the preface, foreword, introduction, and author's biographical sketch. The preface is usually written by the author(s) and will tell you why the book was written and what material is covered. Textbooks often have a preface written to the instructor and a separate preface for the students. The foreword is often an endorsement of the book written by someone other than the author. Some books will have an additional introduction that reviews the book's overall organization and its contents chapter-by-chapter. Books will also include biographical information about each author that will give you important details about his or her background. Many textbooks will have questions at the end of each chapter that can be used as a study guide or quick check to see if you understand the chapter's main points. Take time to read and respond to these questions, whether or not you are required to do so by your instructor.

Textbooks by their very nature are trying to cover a lot of material in a fairly limited space. Although many of them seem detailed, they won't necessarily provide all the things *you* want to know about a topic—those things that can make your reading more interesting. If you find yourself fascinated by a particular topic, go to the **"primary sources"**—the original research or document. You'll find those referenced in many textbooks, either at the end of the chapters or in the back of the book. We've included more information about primary sources on page 135.

Because some textbooks are sold with "test banks," your instructors may draw their examinations directly from the text, or they may consider the textbook just "supplementary" to the lectures. Ask the instructor, if he or she has not made it very clear in class, what will be covered on the test and the types of questions used. In addition, try to find a student who has taken a course with your instructor so that you can get a better idea of how tests are designed. Some instructors expect that you will learn the kinds of detail that you can only get through the textbook. Others are much more concerned that you be able to understand broad concepts that come from lectures in addition to texts and other readings.

Finally, not all textbooks are equal. Some are simply better designed and written than others. If your textbook is exceptionally hard to understand or seems disorganized, let your instructor know your opinion. Based on what you say, your instructor may decide to do a better job of explaining the text and how it's organized or to use a different text for future classes. And, by the way, you should be applying these same principles to this text and this course.

Reading Math Texts

Traditional textbooks in mathematics tend to have lots of symbols and very few words. Each statement and every line in the solution of a problem needs to be considered and digested slowly. Typically, the material is presented through definitions, theorems, and sample problems. As you read, pay special attention to definitions. Learning all the terms in a new topic is the first step toward understanding.

Derivations of formulas and proofs of theorems are usually included to maintain mathematical rigor. You must understand and be able to apply the formulas and theorems, but unless your course has a particularly theoretical emphasis, you are less likely to be responsible for all the proofs. Thus, if you get lost in the proof of a theorem, go on to the next item in the section. When you come to a sample problem, it's time to get busy. Pick up pencil and paper and work through the problem with the author. Then cover the solution and think through the problem on your own. Of course, the exercises that follow each text section form the heart of any math book. A large portion of the time you devote to the course will be spent completing assigned textbook exercises. It is absolutely vital that you do this homework in a timely manner, *whether or not your instructor collects it.*

After you complete the assignment, skim through the other exercises in the problem set. Just reading the unassigned problems will deepen your understanding of the topic and its scope. Finally, "talk it through to yourself." As you do, be sure your focus is on understanding the problem and its solution, and not on memorization. Memorizing something may help you remember how to work through one problem, but it does not help you understand the steps involved so that you can employ them on other problems.

Reading Science Texts

Your approach to your science textbook will depend somewhat on whether you are studying a math-based science, such as physics, or a text-based science, such as biology. In either case, you need to become acquainted with the overall format of the book. Review the table of contents and the glossary and check the material in the appendices. There you will find lists of physical constants, unit conversions, and various charts and tables. Many physics and chemistry books also include a mini-review of the math you will need in science courses.

Notice the organization of each chapter and pay special attention to graphs, charts, and boxes. The amount of technical detail may seem overwhelming, but—believe it or not—the authors have sincerely tried to present the material in an easy-to-follow format. Each chapter may begin with chapter objectives and conclude with a short summary, sections you may wish to study both before and after reading the chapter. You will usually find answers to selected problems in the back of the book. Use the answer key and/or the student solutions manual in a responsible way to promote your mastery of each chapter.

As you begin an assigned section in a science text, skim the material quickly to gain a general idea of the topic. Begin to absorb the new vocabulary and technical symbols. Then skim the end-of-chapter problems so you'll know what to look for in your detailed reading of the chapter. State a *specific goal:* "I'm going to learn about recent developments in plate tectonics," "I'm going to distinguish between mitosis and meiosis," "I'm going to learn about valence bond theory," or "Tonight I'm going to focus on the topics in this chapter that were stressed in class."

Should you underline and highlight, or should you outline the material in your science textbooks? You may decide to underline or highlight in a subject such as anatomy, which involves a lot of memorization. But use that highlighter with restraint; it should pull your eye only to important terms and facts. If highlighting is actually a form of procrastination for you (you are reading through the material but planning to learn it at a later date) or if you are highlighting nearly everything you read, your colorful pages of yellow, pink, or orange may be doing you more harm than good. You won't be able to quickly identify important concepts if they're lost in a sea of color.

In most sciences, it is best to outline the text chapters. You can usually identify main topics, subtopics, and specific terms under each subtopic in your text by the size of the print. For instance, in each chapter of this textbook, the main topics (or level-1 headings) are in large red letters. Following each major

topic heading, you will find subtopics, or level-2 headings, printed in green letters. The level-3 headings, which tell more about the subtopics, are in bold, blue letters. To save time when you are outlining, you won't write full sentences, but will include clear explanations of new technical terms and symbols. Pay special attention to topics that were covered in class. If you aren't sure whether your outlines contain too much or too little detail, compare them with those of members of your study group. In preparing for a test, it's a good idea to make condensed versions of your chapter outlines so that you can see how everything fits together.

Reading Social Science and Humanities Texts

Many of the suggestions that apply to science textbooks also apply to reading in the **social sciences** (sociology, psychology, anthropology, economics, political science, and history). Social science texts are filled with special terms or **"jargon"** unique to the field of study. They also describe research and theory building and will have references to many primary sources. Your social science texts may also describe differences in opinions or perspectives. Not all social scientists agree about any one issue, and you may be introduced to a number of ongoing debates about particular issues. In fact, your reading can become more interesting if you seek out different opinions about a common issue. You may have to go beyond your particular textbook, but your library will be a good source of various viewpoints about ongoing controversies.

Textbooks in the **humanities** (philosophy, religion, literature, music, and art) provide facts, examples, opinions, and original material such as stories or essays. You will often be asked to react to your reading by identifying central themes or characters.

Some instructors believe that the way we structure courses and majors artificially divides human knowledge and experience. For instance, they argue that subjects such as history, political science, and philosophy are closely linked, and studying each subject separately will result in only partial understanding They will stress the linkages between courses and encourage you to think in an "interdisciplinary" manner. You might be asked to consider how the book or story you're reading or the music you're studying reflects the political atmosphere or the prevailing culture of the period. Your art instructor may direct you to think about how a particular painting gives you a window on the painter's psychological make-up or religious beliefs.

Reading Primary Source Material

Whether or not your instructor requires you to read material in addition to the textbook, your reading will be enriched if you go to some of the "primary sources" that are referenced in each chapter of your text. These sources may take the form of journal articles, research papers, dissertations (the major research papers that students write to earn a doctoral degree), or original essays, and can be found in your library and, increasingly, on the Internet. Reading primary source material gives you a depth of detail that few textbooks accomplish.

Many primary sources were originally written for other instructors or researchers. Therefore they often use language and refer to concepts that are familiar to other scholars but not necessarily to first-year college students. If you are reading a journal article that describes a theory or research study, one technique for easier understanding is to read from the end to the beginning. Read the article's conclusion and the "discussion" section and then go back to see how the experiment was done or the ideas were formulated. If you aren't concerned about the specific method used to collect the data, you can skip

over the "methodology" section. In almost all scholarly journals, articles are introduced by an **"abstract,"** a paragraph-length summary of the methods and major findings. Reading the abstract is a quick way to get the gist of a research article before you dive in. As you're reading research articles, always ask yourself, "So what?" Was the research important to what we know about the topic, or, in your opinion, was it unnecessary?

Marking Your Textbook

Think a moment about your goals for making marks in your own texts. Some students report that *marking* is an active reading strategy that helps them focus and concentrate on the material as they read. In addition, most students expect to use their text notations when studying for tests. To meet these goals, some students like to underline, some prefer to highlight, and others use margin notes or annotations. Figure 7.2 provides an example of each method. No matter what method you prefer, remember these two important guidelines:

1. **Read before you mark.** Finish reading a section before you decide which are the most important ideas and concepts. Mark only those ideas, using your preferred methods (highlighting, underlining, circling key terms, annotating).
2. **Think before you mark.** When you read a text for the first time, everything may seem important. Only after you have completed a section and reflected on it will you be ready to identify the key ideas. Ask yourself, "What are the most important ideas? What will I see on the test?" This can help you avoid marking too much material.

Two other considerations may affect your decisions regarding textbook marking. First, if you just make notes or underline directly on the pages of your textbook, you are committing yourself to at least one more viewing of all the pages that you have already read—all 400 pages of your anatomy or art history textbook. A more productive use of your time might be taking notes, creating flash cards, making lists, or outlining textbook chapters. These methods are also more practical if you intend to review with a friend or study group.

Second, sometimes highlighting or underlining can provide you with a false sense of security. You may have determined what is most important, but you have not necessarily tested yourself on your understanding of the material. When you force yourself to put something in your own words while taking notes, you are not only predicting exam questions but assessing whether you can answer them. Although these active reading strategies take more time initially, they can save you time in the long run because they not only promote concentration as you read but also make it easy to review. So you probably won't have to pull an all-nighter before an exam.

See Exercise 7.3: Preparing to Read, Think, and Mark

Reading to Question, to Interpret, to Understand

Monitor Your Comprehension

An important step in textbook reading is to monitor your comprehension. As you read, ask yourself, "Do I understand this?" If not, stop and reread the material. Look up words that are not clear. Try to clarify the main points and how they relate to one another.

7. Some students who read a chapter slowly get very good grades; others get poor grades. Why?

8. Most actors and public speakers who have to memorize lengthy passages spend little time simply repeating the words and more time thinking about them. Why? (Check your answers on page 288.)

People need to monitor their understanding of a text to decide whether to keep studying or whether they already understand it well enough. Most readers have trouble making that judgment correctly.

SELF-MONITORING OF UNDERSTANDING

Whenever you are studying a text, you periodically have to decide, "Should I keep on studying this section, or do I already understand it well enough?" Most students have trouble monitoring their own understanding. In one study, psychology instructors asked their students before each test to guess whether they would do better or worse on that test than they usually do. Students also guessed after each test whether they had done better or worse than usual. Most students' guesses were no more accurate than chance (Sjostrom & Marks, 1994). Such inaccuracy represents a problem: Students who do not know how well they understand the material will make bad judgments about when to keep on studying and when to quit.

Even when you are reading a single sentence, you have to decide whether you understand the sentence or whether you should stop and reread it. Here is a sentence once published in the student newspaper at North Carolina State University:

He said Harris told him she and Brothers told French that grades had been changed.

Ordinarily, when good readers come to such a confusing sentence, they notice their own confusion and reread the sentence or, if necessary, the whole paragraph. Poor readers tend to read at their same speed for both easy and difficult materials; they are less likely than good readers to slow down when they come to difficult sentences.

Although monitoring one's own understanding is difficult and often inaccurate, it is not impossible. For example, suppose I tell you that you are to read three chapters dealing with, say, thermodynamics, the history of volleyball, and the Japanese stock market.

Later you will take tests on each chapter. Before you start reading, predict your approximate scores on the three tests. Most people make a guess based on how much they already know about the three topics. If we let them read the three chapters and again make a guess about their test performances, they do in fact make more accurate predictions than they did before reading (Maki & Serra, 1992). That improvement indicates some ability to monitor one's own understanding of a text.

A systematic way to monitor your own understanding of a text is the SPAR method: *S*urvey, *P*rocess meaningfully, *A*sk questions, and *R*eview and test yourself. Start with an overview of what a passage is about, read it carefully, and then see whether you can answer questions about the passage or explain it to others. If not, go back and reread.

THE TIMING OF STUDY

Other things being equal, people tend to remember recent experiences better than earlier experiences. For example, suppose someone reads you a list of 20 words and asks you to recall as many of them as possible. The list is far too long for you to recite from your phonological loop; however, you should be able to remember at least a few. Typically, people remember items at the beginning and end of the list better than they remember those in the middle.

That tendency, known as the **serial-order effect**, includes two aspects: The *primacy effect* is the tendency to remember the first items; the *recency effect* refers to the tendency to remember the last items. One explanation for the primacy effect is that the listener gets to rehearse the first few items for a few moments alone with no interference from the others. One explanation for the recency effect is that the last items are still in

SPAR
Survey
Process
Ask
Review

why

How

Also decide about larger units?

Cause of primacy effect

MEMORY IMPROVEMENT

283

Pages adapted with permission from James W. Kalat. *Introduction To Psychology*, 4th ed. (Pacific Grove, CA: Brooks/Cole, 1996).

Figure 7.2
Sample Marked Pages

the listener's phonological loop at the time of the test.

Cause of recency effect

The phonological loop cannot be the whole explanation for the recency effect, however. In one study, British rugby players were asked to name the teams they had played against in the current season. Players were most likely to remember the last couple of teams they had played against, thus showing a clear recency effect even though they were recalling events that occurred weeks apart (Baddeley & Hitch, 1977). (The phonological loop holds information only for a matter of seconds.)

So, studying material—or, rather, *reviewing* material—shortly before a test is likely to improve recall. Now let's consider the opposite: Suppose you studied something years ago and have not reviewed it since then. For example, suppose you studied a foreign language in high school several years ago. Now you are considering taking a college course in the language, but you are hesitant because you are sure you have forgotten it all. Have you?

Harry Bahrick (1984) tested people who had studied Spanish in school 1 to 50 years previously. Nearly all agreed that they had rarely used Spanish and had not refreshed their memories at all since their school days. (That is a disturbing comment, but beside the point.) Their retention of Spanish dropped noticeably in the first 3 to 6 years, but remained fairly stable from then on (Fig-

ure 7.18). In other words, we do not completely forget even very old memories that we seldom use.

In a later study, Bahrick and members of his family studied foreign-language vocabulary either on a moderately frequent basis (practicing once every 2 weeks) or on a less frequent basis (as seldom as once every 8 weeks), and tested their knowledge years later. The result: More frequent study led to faster learning; however, less frequent study led to better long-term retention, measured years later (Bahrick, Bahrick, Bahrick, & Bahrick, 1993).

The principle here is far more general than just the study of foreign languages. *If you want to remember something well for a test,* your best strategy is to study it as close as possible to the time of the test, in order to take advantage of the recency effect and decrease the effects of retroactive interference. Obviously, I do not mean that you should wait until the night before the test to start studying, but you might rely on an extensive review at that time. You should also, ideally, study under conditions similar to the conditions of the test. For example, you might study in the same room where the test will be given, or at the same time of day.

However, *if you want to remember something long after the test is over,* then the advice I have just given you is all wrong. To be able to remember something whenever you want, wherever you are, and whatever you are doing, you should study it under as varied circumstances as possible. Study and review at various times and places with long, irregular intervals between study sessions. Studying under such inconsistent conditions will slow down your original learning, but it will improve your ability to recall it long afterwards (Schmidt & Bjork, 1992).

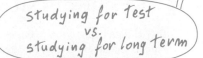

studying for Test vs. studying for long term

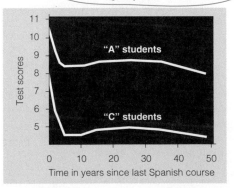

FIGURE 7.18
(Left) Spanish vocabulary as measured by a recognition test shows a rapid decline in the first few years but then long-term stability. (From Bahrick, 1984.) (Right) Within a few years after taking your last foreign-language course, you may think you have forgotten it all. You have not, and even the part you have forgotten will come back (through relearning) if you visit a country where you can practice the language.

Figure 7.2
Sample Marked Pages *(continued)*

Another way to check comprehension is to try to recite the material aloud to yourself or your study partner. Using a study group to monitor your comprehension gives you immediate feedback and is highly motivating. One way that group members can work together is to divide up a chapter for previewing and studying and get together later to teach the material to one another.

Recycle Your Reading

After you have read and marked or taken notes on key ideas from the first section of the chapter, proceed to each subsequent section until you have finished the chapter.

After you have completed each section—and *before* you move on to the next section—ask again, "What are the key ideas? What will I see on the test?" At the end of each section, try to guess what information the author will present in the next section.

Good reading should lead you from one section to the next, with each new section adding to your understanding.

Reviewing

The final step in effective textbook reading is reviewing. Many students expect the improbable—that they will read through their text material one time and be able to remember the ideas four, six, or even twelve weeks later at test time. More realistically, you will need to include regular reviews in your study process. Here is where your notes, study questions, annotations, flash cards, visual maps, or outlines will be most useful. Your study goal should be to review the material from each chapter every week.

Consider ways to use your many senses to review. Recite aloud. Tick off each item in a list on each of your fingertips. Post diagrams, maps, or outlines around your living space so that you will see them often and will likely be able to visualize them while taking the test.

Where to Go for Help

ON CAMPUS

Learning Assistance Center: Most campuses have one of these, and reading assistance is one of their specialties. The best students, good students who want to be the best students, and students with academic difficulties all use Learning Centers. These services are offered by both full-time professionals and highly skilled student tutors.

Fellow College Students: Often the best help we can get is the closest to us. Keep an eye out in your classes, residence hall, cocurricular groups, and so forth for the best students—those who appear to be the most serious, purposeful, and directed. Hire a tutor. Join a study group. Students who do these things are much more likely to be successful.

ONLINE

Middle Tennessee State University: http://www.mtsu.edu/~sudskl/Txtbook.html. The "Study Skills Help" web page has a link to "Advice for Getting the Most from Reading Textbooks."

Niagara University's Office for Academic Support: http://www.niagara.edu/oas/lc/ Study & Reading Strategies/ 21_tips_for_better_textbook_read.htm. Read these "21 Tips for Better Textbook Reading."

Adjusting Your Reading Style

With effort, you can improve your reading dramatically, but remember to be flexible. How you read should depend on the material. Assess the relative importance and difficulty of the assigned readings, and adjust your reading style and the time you allot accordingly. Connect one important idea to another by asking yourself, "Why am I reading this? Where does this fit in?" When the textbook material is virtually identical to the lecture material, you can save time by concentrating mainly on one or the other. It takes a planned approach to read textbook materials and other assigned readings with good understanding and recall.

Developing Your Vocabulary

Textbooks are full of new terminology. In fact, one could argue that learning chemistry is largely a matter of learning the language of chemists and that mastering philosophy or history or sociology requires a mastery of the terminology of each particular **discipline**.

If words are such a basic and essential component of our knowledge, what is the best way to learn them? Follow these basic vocabulary-building strategies:

- During your overview of the chapter, notice and jot down unfamiliar terms. Consider making a flash card for each term, or making a list.

- When you encounter challenging words, consider the context. See if you can predict the meaning of an unfamiliar term using the surrounding words.

- If context by itself is not enough, try analyzing the term to discover the root, or base part, or other meaningful parts of the word. For example, *emissary* has the root "to emit" or "to send forth," so we can guess that an emissary is someone sent forth with a message. Similarly, note prefixes and suffixes. For example, *anti-* means "against" and *pro-* means "for."

- Use the glossary of this text, a dictionary, or **http://www.m-w.com/netdict.htm** (*The Merriam-Webster Dictionary Online*) to locate the definition. Note any multiple definitions and search for the meaning that fits this usage.

- Take every opportunity to use these new terms in your writing and speaking. If you use a new term, then you'll know it! In addition, studying new terms on flash cards or study sheets can be handy at exam time.

No room for argument: Listening, note-taking, and reading are the essentials for success in each of your classes. You can perform these tasks without a plan, or you can practice some of the ideas presented in this chapter. If your notes are already working, great. If not, now you know what to do.

If English Is Not Your First Language

See Working Together: Thinking Back to High School

The English language is one of the most difficult languages to learn. Words are often spelled differently than the way they sound, and the language is full of **idioms**—phrases that are peculiar and cannot be understood from the individual meanings of the words. If you are a non-native English speaker and are having trouble reading your texts, don't give up. Reading slowly and reading more than once can help you improve your comprehension. Make sure that

you have two good dictionaries—one in English and one that links English with your primary language—and look up every word that you don't know. Be sure to practice thinking, writing, and speaking in English, and take advantage of your college's helping services. Your campus may have ESL (English as a Second Language) tutoring and workshops. Ask your advisor or your first-year seminar instructor to help you locate those services.

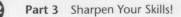

ACHIEVE IT! *Setting Goals for Success*

Go back to the self-assessment at the beginning of this chapter and select one to three unchecked items from the list. Use these to formulate short-term goals for yourself. Be specific about what you want to achieve and when. Remember to choose goals that are realistic and important to you. Think about what obstacles could get in the way of achieving your goals, and make your plan. In the event you checked all items in the self-assessment, come up with one or more additional goals for this exercise.

	Goal 1	Goal 2	Goal 3
My short-term goal is . . .			
I want to achieve this goal by . . . (date)			
This goal matters because . . .			
I may encounter the following obstacles . . .			
My method for accomplishing this goal will be to . . .			

Set a Date. Put your deadline for achieving your goal(s) in your calendar. Count back ten days from your deadline and write a reminder for yourself.

Reassess. After your deadline passes, ask yourself: Did I meet this goal on time? What change has it made in my life? If I did not meet it, what am I planning to do about it?

TRY IT!   *Exercises*

The exercises at the end of each chapter will help you sharpen what we believe are the critical skills for college success: writing, critical thinking, learning in groups, planning, reflecting, and taking action. You can further explore the topic of each chapter by using your PIN to complete the exercises on the website for this text: **http://success.wadsworth.com/gardner7e/**.

WORKING TOGETHER: Thinking Back to High School

Write down the reading methods that worked best for you in high school. Share these with others in the class as a lead-in to discussing how reading in college differs from reading in high school.

EXERCISE 7.1: Previewing and Creating a Visual Map

Preview this chapter and create a visual map, noting the following information: title, key points from the introduction, any graphics (maps, charts, tables, diagrams), study questions, or exercises built into or at the end of the chapter, introduction, and summary paragraphs. Create either a wheel or a branching map, as shown in Figure 7.1. Add spokes or tiers as necessary. In a small group, compare your work. Now, arrange the same information in outline form. Which seems to work better for you? Why?

EXERCISE 7.2: Doing What It Takes to Understand

How far must you go to understand the material in a textbook? Here is one way to find out. If you need to go through all the steps, don't panic. Most people would probably have to do the same.

1. Read a brief chapter in your book as if you were reading for pleasure.

2. Read it a second time, but pause at the end of each section to mentally review what you just read.

3. Read it a third time, pause at the end of each section for review, then go back and highlight important words or sentences.

4. Read it a fourth time and do all of the above. This time ask a friend to read with you and discuss each passage in the chapter before going on to the next. Also stop and take notes, write in the margins, highlight, and so forth.

EXERCISE 7.3: Preparing to Read, Think, and Mark

Choose a reading assignment for one of your classes. After previewing the material as described earlier in this chapter, begin reading until you reach a major heading or until you have read at least a page or two. Now stop and write down what you remember from the material. Now go back to the same material and mark what you believe are the main ideas.

Don't fall into the trap of marking too much. Now, list four of the main ideas from the reading:

1. _____

2. _____

3. _____

4. _____

WRITE ABOUT IT! My Personal Journal

This is your place to sound off, to ask your teacher to clarify part of the lesson, or to write him or her about a minor or major crisis you're experiencing. Find out if your teacher wishes you to turn in your journals. Ask if they will remain confidential. Even if the journal isn't used in your course, you can still use the format to write about and reflect on issues regarding the class, yourself, or both.

1. What was the one major lesson you learned from reading this chapter and/or from class lecture and discussion?

2. What are some other important lessons about this topic?

3. If you believe some parts of this chapter are unimportant, spell them out here and tell why you think so. (You even might want to discuss this point with your classmates to see if they came up with a similar list.)

4. If anything is keeping you from performing at your peak level academically, describe what it is. Your instructor may be able to help or refer you to someone else on campus who can help.

5. What behaviors are you planning to change after reading this chapter? Why?

Improving Your Memory.

In this chapter, YOU WILL LEARN

- How experts describe memory and its functions
- Common myths about memory
- How to improve your ability to memorize
- How commonsense study methods can produce greater learning and greater memory
- Why a good memory can be an asset, but isn't all you need to do well in college

Spend five seconds looking at this photo and then close the book. How many things in the photo can you remember?

SELF-ASSESSMENT
IMPROVING YOUR MEMORY

Check the items below that apply to you:

1. ___ I usually don't have any trouble remembering information that I'm tested on.

2. ___ I always pay close attention to my instructors when they lecture and explain course material in class.

3. ___ I prepare for exams in advance so that I don't have to pull all-nighters.

4. ___ I have a pretty good idea of the kinds of study and memory techniques that work best for me.

5. ___ I regularly study in a quiet place.

6. ___ I think that almost anyone can improve the ability to remember.

7. ___ I use strategies for organizing information that help me remember it better.

8. ___ I know the definition of *mnemonics*.

9. ___ I've used a mnemonic strategy as a memory aid.

10. ___ I realize that memorizing something isn't always the same as understanding it.

If you checked seven or fewer of the items, find someone who can help you understand why all ten items are critical. At the end of this chapter, you will be asked to set personal goals for one or more of your unchecked items. If you checked all items, you will be asked to set other goals.

Throughout history, human memory has been a topic of great interest and fascination for scientists and the general public. In recent years, Hollywood has capitalized on our fascination with memory. In the movies *50 First Dates* (2004) and *Memento* (2000) the central characters have serious memory deficiencies that are the result of head injuries. *Memento*'s protagonist is Leonard (played by Guy Pearce), a man who is trying to solve a murder mystery but can remember information for only about fifteen minutes. Because Leonard has only "short-term memory," he records clues all over his body so that they will be with him at all times. His arms, legs, and torso are covered with notes. In *50 First Dates,* Lucy (played by Drew Barrymore) can remember each day's events until she goes to sleep. In this bittersweet comedy, Lucy essentially "starts over" every morning, making the development of a romantic relationship with Henry (Adam Sandler) almost impossible.

Although severe memory disorders such as Leonard's and Lucy's are extremely rare, you're in good company if you find that occasionally your memory lets you down, especially if you're nervous or stressed or when grades depend on immediate recall of what you have read, heard, or written.

So how can you increase your ability to store information in your brain for future use? Psychologists and learning specialists have conducted research on memory and have developed a number of strategies that you can use as part of a study skills regimen. This chapter will review these strategies. Some of them may be new to you, but others will be simple commonsense notions for ways to maximize your learning—ideas that you've heard before, but perhaps not in the context of increasing your memory.

Memory and Learning

It's easy for many of us to blame a poor memory on the way we live; "multi-tasking" has become the norm for college students and instructors. Admittedly, it's hard to focus on anything for very long if your life is full of daily distractions and competing responsibilities, or if you're not getting the sleep you need. Have you ever had the experience of walking into a room with a particular task in mind and immediately forgetting what that task was? You were probably interrupted either by your own thoughts or by someone or something else. Or have you ever felt the panic that comes from blanking on a test, even though you studied hard and thought you knew the material? It may have been that you pulled an all-nighter studying and that exhaustion raised your stress level and caused your mind to go blank. Such experiences are common and happen to everyone at one time or another. But obviously, to do well in college—and in life—it's important that you improve your ability to remember what you're reading, hearing, and experiencing. As one writer says, "there is no learning without memory."[1] On the other hand, not all memory involves real learning.

Is a good memory all you need to do well in college? Most memory strategies tend to focus on helping you remember names, dates, numbers, vocabulary, graphic materials, formulas—the bits and pieces of knowledge. While it's important to be able to remember specific bits of information, it is even more important to develop a deep understanding of course material. If you know the date the Civil War began and the fort where the first shots were fired, but you don't really know *why* the Civil War was fought, you're missing the point of a college education. College is about **deep learning**, understanding the "why" and "how" behind the details. So don't forget that while recall of specific facts is certainly *necessary*, it isn't *sufficient*. In order to do well in college courses you

---

[1] Harry Lorayne, *Super Memory, Super Student: How to Raise Your Grades in 30 Days*, (Boston: Little, Brown and Company, 1990).

will need to understand major themes and ideas. And you will also need to hone your ability to think critically about what you're learning—a topic that is discussed in depth in Chapter 5 of this book.

How Memory Works

Kenneth Higbee (1988) describes two different processes involved in memory. The first is **short-term memory**, defined as how many items you are able to perceive at one time. Higbee writes that information stored in short-term memory is forgotten in less than thirty seconds (and sometimes much faster) unless you take action to either keep that information in short-term memory or move it to **long-term memory**.

While short-term memory is significantly limited, it has a number of uses. It serves as an immediate but temporary holding tank for information. It helps you maintain a reasonable attention span so that you can keep track of topics mentioned in conversation, and it enables you to stay on task with the goals you are pursuing at any moment. But even these simple functions of short-term memory fail on occasion. If the telephone rings, if someone asks you a question, if you're interrupted in any way, you may find that your attention suffers and that you essentially have to start over in reconstructing short-term memory.

The second memory process is **long-term memory**, and this is the type of memory that you will need to improve in order to remember what you're learning in college. Long-term memory can be described in three ways: "procedural," remembering how to do something such as solving a mathematical problem or playing a musical instrument; "semantic," remembering facts and meanings without remembering where and when you learned those things; and "episodic," remembering particular events, their time and place.[2] You are using your procedural memory when you get on a bicycle you haven't ridden in years, when you can recall the first piece you learned to play on the piano, or when you effortlessly type a letter or class report. Your semantic memory is used continuously to recall word meanings or important dates, such as your mother's or father's birthday. Episodic memory allows you to remember events in which you were involved: a vacation, your first day in school, the moment you opened your acceptance letter from your college or university. Some people can recall not only the event but also the very date and time the event happened. For others, although the event stands out, the dates and times are harder to remember immediately.

Myths about Memory

Although scientific knowledge about how our brains function increases all the time, Kenneth Higbee suggests that there are some myths about memory that you may have heard or may even believe yourself. Here are five of these memory myths, and what experts say about them.

1. **The myth:** Some people are stuck with bad memories.
   The reality: Although there are probably some differences among people in innate memory (the memory ability you are born with), what really give

---

[2] W. F. Brewer & J. R. Pani, The Structure of Human Memory. In *The Psychology of Learning and Motivation: Advances in Research and Theory*, ed. G. H. Bower, vol. 17, 1–38 (New York: Academic Press, 1983).

you the edge are your learned memory skills. The capacity of your memory is a function of the memory techniques you use. Virtually anyone can improve the ability to remember and recall.

2. **The myth:** Some people have photographic memories.

The reality: Although there are a few individuals with truly exceptional memories, most research has found that these abilities are more often the function of learned memory strategies, interest, and practice rather than some innate ability. Even though you may not have what psychologists would classify as an "exceptional" memory, by applying memory strategies you can improve it.

3. **The myth:** Memory benefits from "exercise."
The reality: Practicing memorizing can help improve memory. If you have ever served as a waitperson in a restaurant, you may have been required to "memorize the menu." You may have even surprised yourself at your ability to memorize not only the main entrees, but sauces and side dishes. Experts acknowledge that practice often improves memory, but they argue that the way you practice, such as using special creative strategies called *mnemonics*, is more important than how long you practice. There is more information about mnemonics later in this chapter.

4. **The myth:** Remembering too much can clutter your mind.
The reality: For all practical purposes, the storage capacity of your memory is unlimited. In fact, the more you learn about a particular topic, the easier it is to learn even more.

5. **The myth:** People only use 10 percent of their brain power.
The reality: No scientific research is available to measure accurately how much of our brain we actually use. However, most psychologists and learning specialists believe that we all have far more mental ability than we actually tap.

Strategies for Improving Your Memory

The benefits of having a good memory are obvious. In college, your memory will help you retain information and ace tests. After college, the ability to recall names, procedures, presentations, and appointments will save you energy, time, and a lot of embarrassment.

There are many ways to go about remembering. Have you ever had to memorize a speech or lines from a play? How you approach committing the lines to memory may depend on your learning style (see Chapter 3). If you're an "aural" learner, you might choose to record your lines as well as lines of other characters and listen to them on tape. If you're a "visual" learner, you might remember best by visualizing where your lines appear on the page in the script. If you learn best by reading, you might simply read and reread the script over and over, and if you're a kinesthetic learner, you may need to walk or move across an imaginary stage while you're reading the script.

Can you apply similar approaches to remembering material for an exam? Perhaps you can. But although knowing specific words will help, remembering concepts and ideas may be much more important. To embed such ideas in your mind, ask yourself these questions as you review your notes and books:

See Exercise 8.1: Getting the Big Picture

1. What is the essence of the idea?
2. Why does the idea make sense—what is the logic behind it?
3. How does this idea connect to other ideas in the material?
4. What might be arguments against the idea?

TURNING POINT

Flashcards have been the most effective way for me to avoid forgetting things. You can study them almost anywhere. When it comes to memorization, repetition is the key.

Nadia A.
University of California, Berkeley

Specific Aids to Memory

The human mind has discovered ingenious ways to remember information. Here are some additional methods that may be useful to you as you're trying to nail down the causes of World War I, trying to remember the steps in a chemistry problem, or absorbing a mathematical formula.

1. **Pay attention to what you're hearing or reading.** This suggestion is perhaps the most basic and the most important. If you're sitting in class thinking about everything except what the professor is saying, your memory doesn't have a chance. If you're reading and you find that your mind is wandering, you're wasting your study time. So force yourself to focus.
2. **Don't rely on studying just once before an exam.** Read and review class material many times starting just after each class. The more often you review, the more likely the material will be "imprinted" on your brain.

3. **Overlearn the material.** After you know and think you understand the material you're studying, go over it again to make sure that you'll retain it for a long time. Test yourself or ask someone else to test you. Recite what you're trying to remember aloud in your own words.

4. **Check out the Internet.** If you're having trouble remembering what you have learned, Google a keyword and try to find interesting details that will engage you in learning more, not less, about the subject. Many first-year courses cover such a large amount of material that you'll miss the more interesting details—unless you seek them out for yourself. But as your interest increases, so will your memory.

5. **Study in groups.** Although group study has far broader applications than improving your memory, working with others on difficult material is a great way to remember more of the content. Group members can test each other and challenge each other's interpretation of the material. Group members can think together about creative or even silly ways to remember.

6. **Be sure you have the "big picture."** Whenever you begin a course, make sure that you're clear on what the course will cover. You can talk with someone who has already taken the course or you can take a brief look at all the reading assignments. Having the big picture will help you fit in and remember the details of what you're learning.

7. **Look for connections between your life and what's going on in your courses.** College courses may seem irrelevant to you, but actually, if you look, you'll find many connections between course material and your daily life. Seeing those connections will make your course work more interesting and will help you remember what you're learning. For example, if you're taking a music theory course and studying chord patterns, listen for those patterns in contemporary music. Many pop songs are built around a "1–4–5–1" chord sequence. Can you recognize them?

8. **Analyze how you study and remember best.** How are you more likely to remember what you hear, what you read, what you sing, or what you do? If you learn best by listening, tape class lectures and replay them. If it's easy for you to remember songs, put your class notes to music. If you need to be *doing* something in order to remember, stand up or sit on the edge of your chair, walk around, or gesture with your arms while you read and recite. Exerting energy while you study will keep you alert.

9. **Work around what you are trying to remember.** If your memory is stuck, try to remember words or concepts that are related. Brainstorm with yourself everything you know about that concept or person, and it is likely that you'll be able to remember the specific information you've temporarily forgotten.

10. **Take notes on your notes.** Some people find they study best by writing and rewriting. Rewriting the most important themes in your notes and taking additional notes on your reading material will help you remember what's most important.

11. **Get organized.** If your desk or your computer is organized, you'll spend less time remembering a file name or where you put a particular document. And as you rewrite your notes, putting them in a logical order (either chronological or thematic) that makes sense to you will help you remember them.

12. **Find the right atmosphere for studying and remembering.** Where do you concentrate most effectively—at your home, in your residence hall, in the library? Whatever the space, you need a quiet location where you will not be distracted. Some people concentrate best in absolute quiet; others seem to benefit from some soft background music (instrumental). But

don't fool yourself. Studying in bed, in front of the TV, or while listening to loud music (or loud friends) may be a waste of your study time.

13. **Avoid pre-exam all-nighters.** You may hear your friends bragging about pulling an all-nighter before an exam. But last-minute cramming, especially when it deprives you of sleep, is probably the worst thing you can do if you want to remember what you've read.

14. **Say it over and over.** Probably the most time-tested memory technique is reciting whatever you're trying to remember over and over out loud. Talking out loud is particularly important and is more effective than reciting "in your head." This may mean that you'll need occasionally to find a study location where you're alone and won't bother others when you're talking to yourself.

15. **Reduce stressors in your life.** Although there's no way to determine how much worry or stress causes you to forget, most people will agree that stress can be a distraction. Healthy, stress-reducing behaviors, such as meditation, exercise, and sleep, are especially important for college students. Many campuses have counseling or health centers that can provide resources to help you deal with whatever might be causing stress in your daily life. (See Chapter 16 for more tips on reducing the stress in your life.)

Mnemonics

Mnemonics (pronounced "ne MON iks") are various methods or techniques to aid the memory. More specifically, mnemonics are unusual and somewhat artificial strategies for remembering information. These memory tricks tend to fall into four basic categories.

1. *Acronyms* or new words created from beginning letters of several words. The Great Lakes can be more easily recalled by remembering the word HOMES for Huron, Ontario, Michigan, Erie, and Superior.

2. *Acrostics.* An acrostic is a verse in which certain letters of each word or line form a message. Many piano students were taught the order of sharps by remembering the acrostic "Francis Can Go Down And Eat Bread" – F, C, D, A, E, B.

See Working Together: Creating an Acrostic

3. *Rhymes* that can be said or sung. Do you remember learning "Thirty days hath September, April, June, and November. All the rest have thirty-one, excepting February alone. It has twenty-eight days time, but in leap years it has twenty-nine"? You were using a mnemonic rhyming technique to remember the days in each month.

4. *Visual methods.* You use visualization to associate words or concepts or stories with visual images. The more ridiculous the image, the more likely you are to remember it. So use your imagination to create mental images when you're studying important words or concepts. For example, as you're driving to campus, choose some landmarks along the way to help you remember material for your history test. The next day, as you pass those landmarks, relate them to something from your class notes or readings. A white picket fence might remind you of the British army's eighteenth-century approach to warfare, with its official uniforms and straight lines of infantry, while a stand of trees of various shapes and sizes might remind you of the Continental army's more rustic approach.

See Exercise 8.2: Using Memory Strategies

Mnemonics work because they make information meaningful through the use of rhymes, patterns, and associations. They impose meaning where meaning may be hard to recognize. Mnemonics provide a way of organizing material—a sort of mental filing system. That's why mnemonics probably aren't needed if what you are studying is very logical and organized.

However, although mnemonics are a time-tested way of remembering, there are some limitations to this method. The first is time. Thinking up rhymes, associations, or visual images may take longer than simply learning the words themselves through repetition. Also, it is often difficult to convert abstract concepts into concrete words or images, and it's possible that you may be able to remember an image without recalling the underlying concept. Finally, memory specialists debate whether learning through mnemonics actually helps with long-term knowledge retention and whether this technique helps or interferes with deeper understanding.

See Exercise 8.3: How Accurate Is Your Memory?

See Exercise 8.4: The Name Game

Where to Go for Help

ON CAMPUS

Your campus probably has a study skills center or learning center that can help you develop effective memory strategies. Other students and faculty can also give you tips on how they remember course material. And your college library will have many books on the topic of memory. Some are written by researchers for the research community, but others are written for people just like you who are trying to improve their memory.

Check out these resources:

BOOKS

Kenneth L. Higbee, Ph.D., *Your Memory: How It Works and How to Improve It,* 2nd rev. ed. New York: Marlowe & Co., 2001.

Tony Buzan, *Use Your Perfect Memory,* 3rd rev. ed. New York: Penguin Books, 1991.

Harry Lorayne, *Super Memory, Super Student: How to Raise Your Grades in 30 Days.* Boston: Little, Brown and Company, 1990.

ONLINE

Review of the Research on Memory and College Student Learning: http://www.ferris.edu/ HTMLS/academics/center/ Teaching_and_Learning_Tips/Memory/ ResearchonMemoryandCollegeStudentLearning. htm. This website is designed for instructors; however, it includes lots of interesting information for students as well.

Memorization Techniques: http://www.accd.edu/ sac/history/keller/ACCDitg/SSMT.htm. This excellent website is maintained by the Alamo Community College District.

Technology—A Help or a Hindrance to Memory?

Do you have a PDA (personal digital assistant), a computer calendar, or a watch that beeps when you have an appointment? These are just a few of the devices that can help you remember names, dates, telephone numbers, addresses, and your daily schedule. But there may be a danger in becoming too dependent on technology and losing trust in your own memory. While technological devices are valuable as memory aids, be careful not to rely on them exclusively. Work to move important numbers, names, dates, and information from your short-term to your long-term memory, and use that memory bank first. A PDA or some other computerized device can be a handy backup.

When You're Tempted to Aid Your Memory through Cheating

This chapter began by describing some fictional movie characters. One maintained short-term memory by writing all over his body. Unfortunately, this behavior is not unlike that of many college students who write crib sheets on their arms, hands, bills of baseball caps, and other handy but hidden locations. When you decide to cheat, however you accomplish it, you are doing something that is ethically wrong and unfair to yourself and to other students, that shortchanges your own ability to learn, and that may result in serious penalties, including course failure and expulsion. And cheating easily can become a habit, one that will likely catch up with you at some critical point in your life. So trust your ability to learn and devote the time and energy necessary to do your own work. In the long run, you'll be a wiser person.

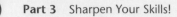

ACHIEVE IT! *Setting Goals for Success*

Go back to the self-assessment at the beginning of this chapter and select one to three unchecked items from the list. Use these to formulate short-term goals for yourself. Be specific about what you want to achieve and when. Remember to choose goals that are realistic and important to you. Think about what obstacles could get in the way of achieving your goals, and make your plan. In the event you checked all items in the self-assessment, come up with one or more additional goals for improving or using your memory for this exercise.

	Goal 1	Goal 2	Goal 3
My short-term goal is . . .			
I want to achieve this goal by . . . (date)			
This goal matters because . . .			
I may encounter the following obstacles . . .			
My method for accomplishing this goal will be to . . .			

Set a Date. Put your deadline for achieving your goal(s) in your calendar. Count back ten days from your deadline and write a reminder for yourself.

Reassess. After your deadline passes, ask yourself: Did I meet this goal on time? What change has it made in my life? If I did not meet it, what am I planning to do about it?

TRY IT!   *Exercises*

The exercises at the end of each chapter will help you sharpen what we believe are the critical skills for college success: writing, critical thinking, learning in groups, planning, reflecting, and taking action. You can further explore the topic of each chapter by using your PIN to complete the exercises on the website for this text: **http://success.wadsworth.com/gardner7e/**.

WORKING TOGETHER: Creating an Acrostic

Working in a small group, select a list of words that someone in the group needs to remember. For instance, you might select the original thirteen colonies in the United States or famous composers of the Romantic period. Using the first letters of each word, create a sentence that everyone can remember. (For instance, the composers Liszt, Chopin, Berlioz, Weber, Schumann, and Wagner could be remembered by remembering the sentence <u>L</u>et's <u>C</u>all <u>B</u>rother <u>W</u>hile <u>S</u>ister <u>W</u>aits.)

EXERCISE 8.1: Getting the Big Picture

Select a concept from this book and respond to the four questions listed on page 150, Strategies for Improving Your Memory. Share your work with a small group of students in your class.

EXERCISE 8.2: Using Memory Strategies

Practice using association, visualization, and flash cards to improve your memory. Try this with a week's lessons from one of your courses.

1. **Visualization.** Close your eyes and "see" your notes or textbook assignments in action. Break your notes into chunks and create a visual image for each chunk.

2. **Association.** Associate a chunk of information to something familiar. If you want to remember that *always* usually signifies a wrong answer on multiple choice or true/false quizzes, associate the word *always* with a concept such as "always wrong."

3. **Flash cards.** Write a key word from the material on one side, and put the details on the reverse. Review often, looking at only five to nine cards at a time. An example might be: Write the words "Ways to Remember" on one side, and on the other write "Go over it again. Use all senses. Organize it. Mnemonics. Association. Visualization. Flash cards." Which of the methods worked best for you?

EXERCISE 8.3: How Accurate Is Your Memory?

This exercise should demonstrate how difficult it can be to remember things accurately. One student whispers the name of an object (lamp, bike, hamburger) to the other. Then the second student whispers the word(s) to the third student and adds a second word or phrase. The third student whispers both words, adding still another word, and so forth. Each student who adds a word should write it down. When the final student recites the list, students whose words were left out or changed should speak up. The class should then discuss what strategies they were using to remember the list and why they forgot certain items.

EXERCISE 8.4: The Name Game

Seated in a circle, each student states his or her first name preceded by a descriptive adjective. For example, Sophisticated Susan, Tall Tom, Jolly Jennifer. Moving around the circle, all students state their name first followed by the names (and descriptors) of all preceding students. Students can help each other when someone's memory fails.

WRITE ABOUT IT! My Personal Journal

This is your place to sound off, to ask your teacher to clarify part of the lesson, or to write him or her about a minor or major crisis you're experiencing. Find out if your teacher wishes you to turn in your journals. Ask if they will remain confidential. Even if the journal isn't used in your course, you can still use the format to write about and reflect on issues regarding the class, yourself, or both.

1. What was the one major lesson you learned from reading this chapter and/or from class lecture and discussion?

2. What are some other important lessons about this topic?

3. If you believe some parts of this chapter are unimportant, spell them out here and tell why you think so. (You even might want to discuss this point with your classmates to see if they came up with a similar list.)

4. If anything is keeping you from performing at your peak level academically, describe what it is. Your instructor may be able to help or refer you to someone else on campus who can help.

5. What behaviors are you planning to change after reading this chapter? Why?

Taking Exams and Tests

● ●

In this chapter YOU WILL LEARN

- ● Ways to prepare yourself for exams physically, emotionally, and academically

- ● How study groups can help you prepare

- ● How to devise a study plan for an exam

- ● How to reduce test anxiety

- ● What to do during the exam

- ● How to take different types of tests

- ● How cheating hurts you, your friends, and your college or university

How would you describe what is happening in this photo?

Jeanne L. Higbee of the University of Minnesota Twin Cities contributed her valuable and considerable expertise to the writing of this chapter.

SELF-ASSESSMENT
TAKING EXAMS AND TESTS

Check the items below that apply to you:

1. ___ I always begin studying for an exam at least a week in advance.

2. ___ I usually find that my class notes are very helpful when I'm preparing for an exam.

3. ___ I usually study for an exam with at least one other person.

4. ___ I usually know what to expect on a test before I go into the exam.

5. ___ I study for tests by predicting possible questions and seeing if I am prepared to answer them.

6. ___ I predict essay questions and develop outlines of the answers.

7. ___ I am careful to maintain good eating, sleeping, and exercise habits before exams.

8. ___ If I finish an exam early or on time, I recheck my paper.

9. ___ I usually know that I have done well on an exam when I finish.

10. ___ I seldom feel overly nervous when studying for or taking exams.

If you checked seven or fewer of the items, find someone who can help you understand why all ten items are critical. At the end of this chapter, you will be asked to set personal goals for one or more of your unchecked items. If you checked all items, you will be asked to set other goals.

You can prepare for exams in many ways, and certain methods are more effective depending on your preferred learning style.

In college, most instructors expect you to use higher-level thinking skills like *analysis, synthesis,* and *evaluation.* On tests and exams they expect you to be able to provide the reasons, arguments, and assumptions on which a given position is based, and the evidence that confirms or discounts it. They want you to be able to support your opinions, to see *how* you think. They are not looking for answers that merely prove that you can memorize the material presented in lecture and the text.

Exams: The Long View

You actually began preparing for a test on the first day of the term. All of your lecture notes, assigned readings, and homework are part of that preparation. As the test day nears, you should know how much additional time you will need to review, what material the test will cover, and what format the test will take. It is very important to analyze your syllabi exam dates, as in Figure 9.1, and to incorporate these into your overall plans for time management, for example, in your daily and weekly "to-do" lists.

Three things will help you study well:

1. **Ask your instructor.** Find out the purpose, types of questions, conditions (how much time you will have to complete the exam), and content to be

History 111, US History to 1865
Fall 2006

Examinations
Note: In this course, most of your exams will be on Fridays, except for the Wednesday before Thanksgiving and the final. This is to ensure you put in a full week and will permit me to grade them over the weekend and return the exams to you on Monday. I believe in using a variety of types of measurements. In addition to those scheduled below, I reserve the right to give you unannounced quizzes on daily reading assignments. Also, current events are fair game on any exam! Midterm and final exams will be cumulative (on all material since beginning of the course). Other exams cover all classroom material and all readings covered since the prior exam. The schedule is as follows:

Friday, 9/1: Objective type

Friday, 9/15: Essay type

Friday, 10/13: Midterm: essay and objective

Friday, 10/27: Objective

Friday, 11/10: Open-book type

Wednesday, 11/22: Essay

Tuesday, 12/12: Essay and objective

FIGURE 9.1 A Sample Course Syllabus

covered on the exam. Talk with your instructor to clarify any misunderstandings you may have about the content of the course.
2. **Manage your time wisely.** Create a schedule that will give you time to review effectively for the exam without waiting until the night before. Is your schedule flexible, allowing for unexpected distractions?
3. **Sharpen your study habits.** Figure out what you can effectively review that is likely to be on the exam. If you are an interactive learner, have you collaborated with other students in a study group or as study partners to share information? If you are a visual learner, have you created maps, lists, diagrams, flash cards, tables, or other visual aids that will enhance memory?

Planning Your Approach

Doing well on exams can depend upon your physical and emotional preparation as well as your knowledge of the content.

Prepare Physically

- **Maintain your regular sleep routine.** Don't cut back on your sleep in order to cram in additional study hours. Remember that most tests will require you to be able to think clearly about the concepts that you have studied. Especially during final-exam weeks, it is important to be well rested in order to remain alert for extended periods of time. This is no time for partying.

- **Follow your regular exercise program.** Walking, jogging, swimming, or other aerobic activities are effective stress reducers that may help you think more clearly and provide positive—and needed—breaks from studying.

- **Eat right.** You really are what you eat. Avoid drinking more than one or two caffeinated drinks a day or eating foods that are high in sugar or fat. Eat a light breakfast before a morning exam and avoid greasy or acidic foods that might upset your stomach. Choose fruits, vegetables, and other foods that are high in energy-rich complex carbohydrates. Ask the instructor if you can bring a bottle of water with you to the exam.

Prepare Emotionally

- **Know your material.** If you have given yourself adequate time to review, you will enter the classroom confident that you are in control. Study by testing yourself or quizzing each other in a study group or learning community so you will be sure you really know the material.

- **Practice relaxing.** Some students experience upset stomachs, sweaty palms, racing hearts, or other unpleasant physical symptoms of test anxiety before an exam. See your counseling center about relaxation techniques. Some campus learning centers also provide workshops on reducing test anxiety. If this is a problem you experience, read the section on test anxiety later in this chapter.

- **Use positive self-talk.** Instead of telling yourself "I never do well on math tests" or "I'll never be able to learn all the information for my history essay exam," make positive statements, such as "I have attended all the lectures, done my homework, and passed the quizzes. Now I'm ready to pass the test!"

Prepare for Test Taking

- **Find out about the test.** Ask your instructor whether the test will be essay, multiple choice, true/false, fill-in-the-blank, short-answer, or another format. Ask how long the test will last and how it will be graded. Ask whether all questions will have the same point value.

Some instructors may let you see copies of old exams, so you can see the types of questions they use. Never miss the last class before an exam, because your instructor may summarize valuable information.

- **Design an exam plan.** Use the information about the test as you design a plan for preparing. Build that preparation into a schedule of review dates. Develop a to-do list of the major steps you need to take in order to be ready. The week before the exam, set aside a schedule of one-hour blocks of time for review, and make notes on what you specifically plan to accomplish during each hour.

- **Join a study group.** Numerous research studies have shown that joining a study group is one of the most effective strategies for preparing for exams. Study groups can help you develop better study techniques. In addition, you can benefit from different views of your instructors' goals, objectives, and emphasis; have partners quiz you on facts and concepts; and gain the enthusiasm and friendship of others to help sustain your motivation.

  Some instructors will provide time in class for the formation of study groups. Otherwise, ask your teacher, advisor, or campus tutoring or learning center to help you identify interested students and decide on guidelines for the group. Study groups can meet throughout the term, or they can review for midterms or final exams. Group members should complete their assignments before the group meets and prepare study questions or points of discussion ahead of time. If your study group decides to meet just before exams, allow enough time to share notes and ideas.

See Exercise 9.1: Designing an Exam Plan

See Working Together: Forming a Study Group

- **Get a tutor.** If you think tutoring is just for failing students, you're wrong! Often the very best students seek tutorial assistance to ensure their A's. In the typical large lecture classes for first-year students, you have limited opportunity to ask instructors questions. Many tutors are students

who excelled when taking the same courses. They know the highlights and pitfalls of the course.

Many campus tutoring services are free. Ask your academic advisor or counselor or campus learning center. Most academic support centers or learning centers have computer labs that can provide assistance for course work. Some offer walk-in assistance for help in using word processing, spreadsheet, or statistical computer programs. Often computer tutorials are available to help you refresh basic skills. Math and English grammar programs may also be available, as well as access to the Internet.

TURNING POINT

In high school, I didn't care what I would score on tests. It's different now. I took English, a lot of different computer classes, and a study skills class before I started my degree because I felt it would help me prepare for college.

Michael F.
Des Moines Area Community College

Studying for Tests

Through the consistent use of proven study techniques, you will already have processed and learned most of what you need to know. Now you can focus your study efforts on the most challenging concepts, practice recalling information, and familiarize yourself with details.

Review Sheets, Mind Maps, and Other Tools

To prepare for an exam covering large amounts of material, you need to condense the volume of notes and text pages into manageable study units. Review your materials with these questions in mind: Is this one of the key ideas in the chapter or unit? Will I see this on the test? As indicated in Chapter 6, you may prefer to highlight, underline, or annotate the most important ideas, or you may create outlines, lists, or visual maps containing the key ideas.

Use your notes to develop review sheets. Make lists of key terms and ideas (from the recall column, if you've used the Cornell method) that you need to remember. Also, do not underestimate the value of using the recall column from your lecture notes to test yourself or others on information presented in class.

A **mind map** is essentially a review sheet with a visual element. Its word and visual patterns provide you with highly charged clues to jog your memory. Because they are visual, mind maps help many students recall information more easily.

Figure 9.2 shows what a mind map might look like for a chapter on listening and learning in the classroom. See if you can reconstruct the ideas in the chapter by following the connections in the map. Then make a visual mind map for this chapter, and see how much more you can remember after studying it a number of times.

In addition to review sheets and mind maps, you may want to create flash cards. One of the advantages of flash cards is that you can keep them in an outside pocket of your backpack and pull them out to study anywhere, even when you might not think that you have enough time to pull out your notebook to study. Also, you always know where you left off. Flash cards can assist you in making good use of time that otherwise might be wasted, like time spent on the bus or waiting for a friend.

Summaries

Writing summaries of class topics can be helpful in preparing for essay and short-answer exams. By condensing the main ideas into a concise written summary, you store information in your long-term memory so you can retrieve it to answer an essay question. Here's how:

1. **Predict a test question from your lecture notes or other resources.**
2. **Read the chapter, supplemental articles, notes, or other resources.** Underline or mark main ideas as you go, make notations, or outline on a separate sheet of paper.
3. **Analyze and abstract.** What is the purpose of the material? Does it compare, define a concept, or prove an idea? What are the main ideas? How would you explain the material to someone else?

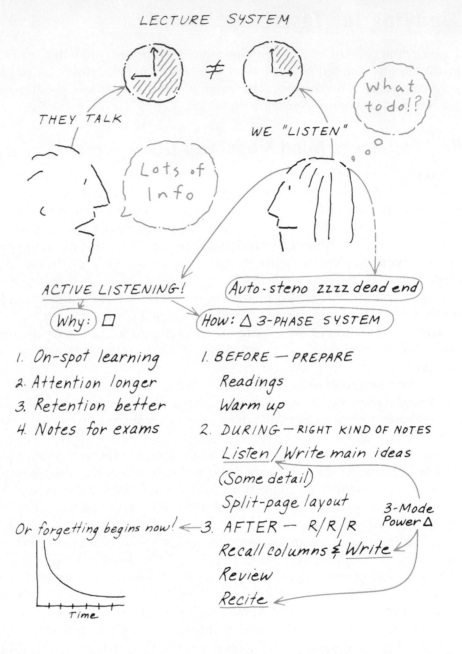

FIGURE 9.2

Sample Mind Map on Listening and Learning in the Classroom

4. **Make connections between main points and key supporting details.** Reread to identify each main point and supporting evidence. Create an outline to assist you in this process.

5. **Select, condense, order.** Review underlined material and begin putting the ideas into your own words. Number what you underlined or highlighted in a logical order.

6. **Write your ideas precisely in a draft.** In the first sentence, state the purpose of your summary. Follow with each main point and its supporting ideas. See how much of the draft you can develop from memory without relying on your notes.

7. **Review your draft.** Read it over, adding missing transitions or insufficient information. Check the logic of your summary. Annotate with the material you used for later reference.

8. **Test your memory.** Put your draft away and try to recite the contents of the summary to yourself out loud, or explain it to a study partner who can provide feedback on the information you have omitted.

9. **Schedule time to review summaries, and double-check your memory shortly before the test.** You may want to do this with a partner, but some students prefer to review alone. Some faculty members will also be open to assisting you in this process and providing feedback on your summaries.

Overcoming Test Anxiety

Test anxiety takes many different forms. Part of combatting test anxiety is understanding its sources and identifying its symptoms.

Test anxiety has many sources. It can be the result of the pressure that students put on themselves to succeed. Without any pressure, students would not be motivated to study; some stress connected with taking exams is natural and can enhance performance. However, when students put too much pressure on themselves or set unrealistic goals for themselves, the result is stress that is no longer motivating, but debilitating.

The expectations of parents, a spouse, friends, and other people who are close to you can also induce test anxiety. Sometimes, for example, students who are the first in their families to attend college bear on their shoulders the weight of generations before them who have not had this opportunity. The pressure can be overwhelming! Finally, some test anxiety is caused by lack of preparation, by not keeping up with assigned reading, homework, and other academic commitments leading up to the test. Procrastination can begin a downward spiral, because after you do poorly on the first test in a course, there is even more pressure to do well on subsequent tests in order to pull up your course grade. This situation becomes even more dire if the units of the course build on one another, like in math and foreign languages, or if the final exam is cumulative. While you are trying to master the new material after the test, you are still trying to catch up on the old material as well.

Types of Test Anxiety

Students who experience test anxiety under some circumstances do not necessarily feel it in all testing situations. For example, you may do fine on classroom tests, but feel anxious during standardized examinations like the SAT and ACT. One reason standardized tests are so anxiety provoking is the belief that they determine your future. Believing that the stakes are so high can create unbearable pressure. One way of dealing with this type of test anxiety is to ask yourself, "What is the worst that can happen?" Remember that it is not the "end of the world." How you do on standardized tests may limit some of your options, but going into these tests with a negative attitude will certainly not improve your chances. Attending preparation workshops and taking practice exams not only can better prepare you for standardized tests, but also can assist you in overcoming your anxiety.

Some students are only anxious about some types of classroom tests. Practice always helps in overcoming test anxiety; if you fear essay exams, try predicting exam questions and writing sample essays as a means of reducing your anxiety.

Some students have difficulty taking tests at a computer terminal. Some of this anxiety may be related to lack of computer experience. On the other hand, not all computerized tests are user-friendly. You may only be allowed to see one item at a time. Often, you do not have the option of going back and checking over all your answers before submitting them. In preparation for computerized tests, ask the instructor questions about how the test will be structured. Also, make sure you take any opportunities to take practice tests at a learning center or lab.

For some students test anxiety is discipline-specific. For example, some students have math test anxiety even if they do not suffer from test anxiety in other courses. It is important to distinguish the anxiety that arises from the subject matter itself from more generalized test anxiety.

Symptoms of Test Anxiety

Test anxiety can manifest itself in many ways. Some students feel it on the very first day of class. Other students begin showing symptoms of test anxiety when it is time to start studying for a test. Others do not get nervous until the night before the test or the morning of an exam day. And some students only experience symptoms while actually taking a test.

Symptoms of test anxiety can include "butterflies" in the stomach, feeling queasy or nauseous, severe headaches, a faster heartbeat, hyperventilating, shaking, sweating, or muscle cramps. During the exam itself, students overcome by test anxiety can experience the sensation of "going blank," unable to remember what they *know* they know. At this point students may undermine both their emotional and academic preparation for the test and convince themselves that they cannot succeed.

Test anxiety can impede the success of *any* college student, no matter how intelligent, motivated, and prepared. That is why it is critical to seek help from your college or university's counseling service or another professional if you think that you have test anxiety. If you are not sure where to go for help, ask your advisor, but seek help promptly! If your symptoms are so severe that you become physically ill (with migraine headaches, hyperventilating, vomiting), you should also consult your physician or campus health service.

Strategies for Combating Test Anxiety

In addition to studying hard, eating right, and getting plenty of sleep, there are a number of simple strategies that you can employ to overcome the physical and emotional impact of test anxiety. First, any time that you begin to feel nervous or upset, take a long, deep breath and slowly exhale to restore your breathing to a normal level. This is the quickest and easiest relaxation device, and no one needs to know that you are doing it!

Before you go into the test room, especially prior to multihour final exams or sitting through several exams on the same day, it can help to stretch your muscles just as you would when preparing to exercise. Stretch your calf and hamstring muscles and roll your ankles. Stretch your arms; roll your shoulders. Tilt your head to the right, front, and left (but, to avoid injury, not to the back) to stretch your neck muscles.

Then when you sit down to take the test, pay attention to how you are sitting. Sit with your shoulders back and relaxed, rather than shrugged forward, and with your feet on the floor. Smooth out your facial muscles rather than wrinkling your forehead or frowning. Resist the temptation to clench your pencil or pen too tightly in your fist; take a break and stretch your fingers now and then.

Anxiety-reducing techniques that may be available through your campus counseling center include systematic desensitization, progressive muscle relaxation, and visualization. One of the most popular is creating your own peaceful scene and mentally taking yourself there when you need to relax. Try to use all five senses to recreate your peaceful scene in your mind: What would you see, hear, feel, taste, or smell?

See Exercise 9.2: Create Your Own Peaceful Scene

These strategies can assist you in relaxing physically, but meanwhile you must also pay attention to the mental messages that you are sending yourself. Focus on the positive! If you are telling yourself that you are not smart enough, that you did not study the right material, or that you are going to fail, you need to turn those messages around. This technique is called **cognitive restructuring.** We all talk to ourselves. Think about what you are saying. Make sure that your self-messages are encouraging rather than stress provoking. When you are studying, practice sending yourself positive messages: "I really know this stuff. I am going to ace this test!"

Similarly, do not allow others, including classmates, your spouse, parents, or friends, to undermine your confidence. If you belong to a study group, discuss the need to stay positive. Sometimes by getting to the test room early you expose yourself to other students asking questions or making comments that are only going to make you nervous. Get to the building early, but wait until just a few minutes before the exam begins to approach the classroom itself.

See Exercise 9.3: Positive Self-Messages

If at any point during a test you begin to feel like you cannot think clearly, or you have trouble remembering, or you come to a question you cannot answer, stop for a brief moment and take another long, deep breath and slowly exhale. Then remind yourself of the positive self-messages you have been practicing.

Tips for Successful Test Taking

The following tips apply to any test situation:

1. **Write your name on the test** (unless directed not to) and answer sheet.
2. **Analyze, ask, and stay calm.** Take a long, deep breath and slowly exhale before you begin. Read all the directions so that you understand what to do. Ask the instructor or exam monitor for clarification if you don't understand something. Be confident. Don't panic. Answer one question at a time.
3. **Make the best use of your time.** Quickly survey the entire test and decide how much time you will spend on each section. Be aware of the point values of different sections of the test. Are some questions worth more points than others?
4. **Answer the easy questions first.** Expect that you'll be puzzled by some questions. Make a note to come back to them later. If different sections consist of different types of questions (such as multiple-choice, short-answer, and essay), complete the types of question you are most comfortable with first. Be sure to leave enough time for any essays.
5. **If you feel yourself starting to panic or go blank, stop whatever you are doing.** Take a long, deep breath and slowly exhale. Remind yourself you will be okay and that you do know your stuff and can do well on this test. Then take another deep breath. If necessary, go to another section of the test and come back later to the item that triggered your anxiety.
6. **If you finish early, don't leave.** Stay and check your work for errors. Reread the directions one last time. If using a Scantron answer sheet, make sure that all answers are bubbled accurately and completely.

Essay Questions

Many college teachers have a strong preference for the essay exam for a simple reason: It promotes higher-order critical thinking, whereas other types of exams tend to be exercises in memorization. Generally, the closer you are to graduation, the more essay exams you'll take. To be successful on essay exams, follow these guidelines:

1. **Budget your exam time.** Quickly survey the entire exam, and note the questions that are the easiest for you, along with their point values. Take a moment to weigh their values, estimate the approximate time you should allot to each question, and write the time beside each item number. Be sure you know whether you must answer all the questions or choose among

questions. Remember, it can be a costly error to write profusely on easy questions of low value, taking up precious time you may need on more important questions. Wear a watch so you can monitor your time, including time at the end for a quick review.

2. **Develop a very brief outline of your answer before you begin to write.** Start working on the questions that are easiest for you, and jot down a few ideas before you begin to write. First, make sure that your outline responds to all parts of the question. Then use your first paragraph to introduce the main points, and subsequent paragraphs to describe each point in more depth. If you begin to lose your concentration, you will be glad to have the outline to help you regain your focus. If you find that you are running out of time and cannot complete an essay, at the very least provide an outline of key ideas. Instructors usually assign points based on your coverage of the main topics from the material. Thus, you will usually earn more points by responding to all parts of the question briefly than by addressing just one aspect of the question in detail.

3. **Write concise, organized answers.** Many well-prepared students write fine answers to questions that may not have been asked because they did not read a question carefully or did not respond to all parts of the question. Others hastily write down everything they know on a topic. Answers that are vague and tend to ramble will be downgraded by instructors.

4. **Know the key task words in essay questions.** Being familiar with the **key word** in an essay question will help you answer it more specifically. The following key task words appear frequently on essay tests. Take time to learn them, so that you can answer essay questions more accurately and precisely.

Analyze To divide something into its parts in order to understand it better. To show how the parts work together to produce the overall pattern.

Compare To look at the characteristics or qualities of several things and identify their similarities or differences. Do not just describe the traits; define how the things are alike and how they are different.

Contrast To identify the differences between things.

Criticize/Critique To analyze and judge something. Criticism can be positive, negative, or both. A criticism should generally contain your own judgments (supported by evidence) and those of other authorities who can support your point.

Define To give the meaning of a word or expression. Giving an example sometimes helps to clarify a definition, but an example by itself is not a definition.

Describe To give a general verbal sketch of something, in narrative or other form.

Discuss To examine or analyze something in a broad and detailed way. Discussion often includes identifying the important questions related to an issue and attempting to answer these questions. A good discussion explores all relevant evidence and information.

Evaluate To discuss the strengths and weaknesses of something. Evaluation is similar to criticism, but the word *evaluate* places more stress on the idea of how well something meets a certain standard or fulfills some specific purpose.

Explain To clarify something. Explanations generally focus on why or how something has come about.

Interpret To explain the meaning of something. In science, you might explain what an experiment shows and what conclusions can be drawn from it. In a literature course, you might explain—or interpret—what a poem means beyond the literal meaning of the words.

Justify To argue in support of some decision or conclusion by showing sufficient evidence or reasons in its favor. Try to support your argument with both logical and concrete examples.

Narrate To relate a series of events in the order in which they occurred. Generally, you will also be asked to explain something about the events you are narrating.

Outline To present a series of main points in appropriate order. Some instructors want an outline with Roman numerals for main points followed by letters for supporting details. If in doubt, clarify with the instructor whether he or she wants a formal outline.

Prove To give a convincing logical argument and evidence in support of some statement.

Review To summarize and comment on the main parts of a problem or a series of statements. A review question usually also asks you to evaluate or criticize.

Summarize To give information in brief form, omitting examples and details. A summary is short yet covers all important points.

Trace To narrate a course of events. Where possible, you should show connections from one event to the next.

Multiple-Choice Questions

Preparing for multiple-choice tests requires you to actively review all of the material covered in the course. Reciting from flash cards, summary sheets, mind maps, or the recall column in your lecture notes is a good way to review these large amounts of material.

Take advantage of the many cues that multiple-choice questions contain. Careful reading of each item may uncover the correct answer. Always question choices that use absolute words such as *always, never,* and *only.* These choices are often (but not always) incorrect. Also, read carefully for terms such as *not, except,* and *but* that are introduced before the choices. Often the answer that is the most inclusive is correct. Generally, options that do not agree grammatically with the first part of the item are incorrect, but this is not always the case.

Some students are easily confused by multiple-choice answers that sound alike. The best way to respond to a multiple-choice question is to read the first part of the item and then predict your own answer before reading the options. Choose the letter that corresponds with the option that best matches your prediction.

If you are totally confused by a question, leave it and come back later, but always double-check that you are filling in the answer for the right question. Sometimes another question will provide a clue for a question you are unsure about. If you have absolutely no idea, look for an answer that at least contains some shred of information. If there is no penalty for guessing, fill in an answer for every question, even if it is just a guess.

Fill-in-the-Blank Questions

In many ways preparing for fill-in-the-blank questions is similar to getting ready for multiple-choice items, but fill-in-the blank is harder because you do not have a choice of possible answers right in front of you. Not all fill-in-the-blank questions are constructed the same. Some teachers will provide a series of blanks to give you a clue regarding the number of words in the answer, but if just one long blank is provided you cannot assume that the answer is just one word. If possible, ask the teacher whether the answer is supposed to be a single word per blank or can be a longer phrase.

True/False Questions

Remember, for the question to be true, every detail of the question must be true. Questions containing words such as *always, never,* and *only* are usually false, whereas less definite terms such as *often* and *frequently* suggest the statement may be true. Read through the entire exam to see if information in one question will help you answer another. Do not begin to second-guess what you know or doubt your answers because a sequence of questions appears to be all true or all false.

Matching Questions

The matching question is the hardest to answer by guessing. In one column you will find the term, in the other the description of it. Before answering any question, review all of the terms and descriptions. Match those terms you are sure of first. As you do so, cross out both the term and its description, and then use the process of elimination to assist you in answering the remaining items. Flash cards and lists that can be created from the recall column in your notes are excellent ways to prepare for matching questions.

Types of Tests

Problem-Solving Tests

In the physical and biological sciences, mathematics, engineering, statistics, and symbolic logic, some tests will require that you solve problems showing *all* steps. Even if you know a "shortcut," it is important to document how you got from Step A to Step B. On other tests all that will matter is whether you have the correct solution to the problem, but doing all the steps will still help ensure that you get the right answer. For these tests you must also be very careful that you have made no errors in your scientific notation. A misplaced sign, parenthesis, bracket, or exponent can make all the difference.

Be sure that you read all directions carefully. Are you required to reduce the answer to simplest terms? Are you supposed to graph the solution? Be careful when "canceling terms," cross-multiplying, distributing terms, and combining fractions. Whenever possible, after you complete the problem, work it "backwards" to check your solution, or plug your solution back into the equation and make sure it adds up. Also check to make sure that your solution makes sense. You cannot have negative bushels of apples, for example, or a fraction of a person, or a correlation less than negative 1 or greater than 1.

Machine-Scored Tests

It is important to follow the directions for machine-scored tests carefully. Be sure that in addition to your name you provide all the information sought on the answer sheet, such as the instructor's name, the number for the class section, or your student ID number. Each time you fill in an answer, make sure that the number on the answer sheet corresponds with the number of the item on the test. If you have questions that you want to come back to, if you are allowed to do so, mark them on the test itself rather than on the answer sheet.

Although scoring machines have become more sophisticated over time, stray marks on your answer sheet can still be misread and throw off the scoring. When a machine-scored test is returned to you, check your answer sheet against the scoring key, if provided, to make sure that you receive credit for all the questions you answered correctly.

Computerized Tests

Your comfort with taking computerized tests may depend upon how computer literate you are in general for objective tests, as well as your keyboarding skills for essay exams. If your instructor provides the opportunity for "practice" tests, be sure to take advantage of this chance to get a better sense of how the tests will be structured. There can be significant variations depending on the kind of test, the academic subject, and whether the test was constructed by the teacher or by a textbook company or other source.

For multiple-choice and other objective forms of computerized tests, you may be allowed to scroll down and back through the entire test, but this is not always the case. Sometimes you are only allowed to see one question at a time, and after you complete that question you may not be allowed to go back to it. In this situation you cannot skip questions that are hard and come back to them later, so be sure that you try to answer every question.

For computerized tests in math and other subjects that require you to solve each problem, record an answer, and then move to the next problem. Be sure to check each answer before you submit it. Also know in advance what materials you are allowed to have on hand, including a calculator and scratch paper for working the problems.

Laboratory Tests

In many science courses and in some other academic disciplines, you will be required to take lab tests during which you rotate from one lab station to the next and solve problems, identify parts of models or specimens, explain chemical reactions, and complete other tasks similar to those that you have been performing in lab. At some colleges and universities, lab tests are now administered at computer terminals via simulations. To prepare for lab tests, always attend lab, take good notes, including diagrams and other visual representations as necessary, and be sure to study your lab notebook carefully prior to the test. If possible, create your own diagrams or models, and then see if you can label them without looking at your book.

You may also have to take lab tests in foreign language courses. These tests can have both oral and written components. Work with a partner or study group to prepare for oral exams. Ask one another questions that require using key vocabulary words. Try taping your answers to work on your pronunciation. Particularly in foreign languages that use a different symbol system, such as Chinese, you may also have computerized lab tests that require you to identify syllables or words and indicate the order and direction of the strokes required to create them. The best way to prepare for these tests is to learn the meaning and parts of the symbols and practice writing them regularly.

Open-Book and Open-Note Tests

If you never had open-book or open-note tests in high school, you may be tempted to study less thoroughly, thinking that you will have access to all the information you need during the test. This is a common misjudgment on the part of first-year students. Open-book and open-note tests are usually *harder* than other exams, not easier.

Most students do not really have time to spend looking things up during this type of exam. The best way to prepare is to begin the same way you would study for a test in which you cannot refer to your notes or text. But as you do so, develop a list of topics and the page numbers where they are covered in your text. You may want to use the same strategy in organizing your lecture notes. Number the pages in your notebook. Later type a three-column grid (or use an Excel spreadsheet) with your list of topics in alphabetical order in the first column and corresponding pages from your text and notebook in the second and third columns so that you can refer to them quickly if necessary. Or you may want to paste colored tabs onto your textbook or notebook pages for different topics. But whatever you do, study as completely as you would for any other test, and do not be fooled into thinking that you do not need to know the material thoroughly.

During the test, monitor your time carefully. Do not waste time unnecessarily looking up information in your text or notes to double-check yourself if you are confident of your answers. Instead, wait until you have finished the test, and then, if you have extra time, go back and look up answers and make any necessary changes. But if you have really studied you probably will not find this necessary.

Sometimes the only reason a teacher allows open books or open notes is so that students can properly reference their sources when responding to essay or short-answer tests. Make sure that you are aware whether you are expected to document your answers and provide a reference or "works cited" list.

Take-Home Tests

Like open-book and open-note tests, take-home tests are usually more difficult than in-class tests. Many take-home tests are essay tests, though some teachers will give take-home objective tests as well. Be sure to allow plenty of time to complete a take-home test. Read the directions and questions as soon as you receive the test in order to gauge how much time you will need. If the test is all essays, consider how much time you might allocate to writing several papers of the same length. Remember, your teacher will expect your essay answers to look more like assigned out-of-class papers than like the essays you would write during an in-class test.

Unfortunately, academic honesty issues can arise for take-home tests. If you are accustomed to working with a study group or in a learning community for the course, check with the teacher in advance to determine the extent to which collaboration is allowed on the test. One thing that can be very confusing for students is to be encouraged to work together throughout the academic term and then to be told that there should be no communication outside of class about a take-home test.

Academic Honesty

Imagine where society would be if researchers reported fraudulent results that were then used to develop new machines or medical treatments. Integrity is a cornerstone of higher education, and activities that compromise that integrity damage everyone: your country, your community, your college or university, your classmates, and yourself.

Types of Misconduct

Institutions vary widely in how they define broad terms such as lying or cheating. One university defines cheating as "intentionally using or attempting to use unauthorized materials, information, notes, study aids, or other devices . . . [including] unauthorized communication of information during an academic exercise." This would apply to looking over a classmate's shoulder for an answer, using a calculator when it is not authorized, procuring or discussing an exam (or individual questions from an exam) without permission, copying lab notes, purchasing term papers over the Internet, watching the video instead of reading the book, and duplicating computer files.

Plagiarism, or taking another person's ideas or work and presenting them as your own, is especially intolerable in academic culture. Just as taking someone else's property constitutes physical theft, taking credit for someone else's ideas constitutes intellectual theft.

On most tests, you do not have to credit specific individuals. (But some instructors do require this; when in doubt, ask!) In written reports and papers, however, you must give credit any time you use (a) another person's actual words, (b) another person's ideas or theories—even if you don't quote them directly, and (c) any other information not considered common knowledge.

Many schools prohibit other activities, besides lying, cheating, unauthorized assistance, and plagiarism. Examples of prohibited behaviors include intentionally inventing information or results, earning credit more than once for the same piece of academic work without permission, giving your work or exam answers to another student to copy during the actual exam or before the exam is given to another section, and bribing in exchange for any kind of academic advantage. Most schools also outlaw helping or attempting to help another student commit a dishonest act.

Reducing the Likelihood of Problems

To avoid becoming intentionally or unintentionally involved in academic misconduct, consider the reasons it could happen.

- **Ignorance.** In a survey at the University of South Carolina, 20 percent of students incorrectly thought that buying a term paper wasn't cheating. Forty percent thought using a test file (a collection of actual tests from previous terms) was fair behavior. Sixty percent thought it was all right to get answers from someone who had taken an exam earlier in the same or in a prior semester. What do you think?

- **Cultural and campus differences.** In other countries and on some U.S. campuses, students are encouraged to review past exams as practice exercises. Some student government associations maintain test files for use by students. Some campuses permit sharing answers and information for homework and other assignments with friends.

- **Different policies among instructors.** Because there is no universal code that dictates such behaviors, ask your instructors for clarification. When a student is caught violating the academic code of a particular school or teacher, pleading ignorance of the rules is a weak defense.

- **A belief that grades—not learning—are everything**, when actually the reverse is true. This may reflect our society's competitive atmosphere. It also may be the result of pressure from parents, peers, or teachers. In truth, grades are nothing if one has cheated to earn them.

- **Lack of preparation or inability to manage time and activities.** Before you consider cheating, ask an instructor to extend a deadline so that a project can be done well.

Here are some steps you can take to reduce the likelihood of problems:

1. **Know the rules.** Learn the academic code for your school. Study course syllabi. If a teacher does not clarify standards and expectations, ask exactly what they are.
2. **Set clear boundaries.** Refuse to "help" others who ask you to help them cheat. This may be hard to do, but you've got to say no. In test settings, keep your answers covered and your eyes down, and put all extraneous materials away, including cell phones. Now that many cell phones enable text messaging, instructors are rightfully suspicious when they see students playing with their cell phones during an exam.
3. **Improve time management.** Be well prepared for all quizzes, exams, projects, and papers. This may mean unlearning habits such as procrastination (see Chapter 2, Time Management).
4. **Seek help.** Find out where you can obtain assistance with study skills, time management, and test taking. If your methods are in good shape but the

content of the course is too difficult, see your instructor, join a study group, or visit your campus learning center or tutorial service.

5. **Withdraw from the course.** Your school has a policy about dropping courses and a last day to drop without penalty. You may decide only to drop the course that's giving you trouble. Some students may choose to withdraw from all classes and take time off before returning to school if they find themselves in over their heads or if a long illness, a family crisis, or some other unexpected occurrence has caused them to fall behind. Before you withdraw, you should ask about campus policies as well as ramifications in terms of federal financial aid and other scholarship programs. See your advisor or counselor.

6. **Reexamine goals.** Stick to your own realistic goals instead of giving in to pressure from family or friends to achieve impossibly high standards. You may also feel pressure to enter a particular career or profession of little or no interest to you. If so, sit down with counseling or career services professionals or your academic advisor and explore alternatives.

Where to Go for Help

ON CAMPUS

Learning Assistance Support Center: Almost every campus has one of these, and studying for tests is one of their specialties. The best students, good students who want to be the best students, and students with academic difficulties use learning centers and tutoring services. These services are offered by both full-time professionals and highly skilled student tutors.

Counseling Services: College and university counseling centers offer a wide array of services, often including workshops and individual or group counseling for test anxiety. Sometimes these services are also offered by the campus health center.

Fellow College Students: Often the best help we can get is the closest to us. Keep an eye out in your classes, residence hall, extracurricular activities, and so forth for the best students, those who appear to be the most serious, purposeful, and directed. Hire a tutor. Join a study group. Students who do these things are much more likely to be successful.

ONLINE

Read the following two websites. Take notes. Write a summary of what you believe to be the important facts.

The Academic Center for Excellence, University of Illinois at Chicago: http://www.uic.edu/depts/counselctr/ace/examprep.htm

Learning Centre of the University of New South Wales in Sydney, Australia: http://www.lc.unsw.edu.au/onlib/exam.html Includes the popular SQ3R method.

ACHIEVE IT! *Setting Goals for Success*

Go back to the self-assessment at the beginning of this chapter and select one to three unchecked items from the list. Use these to formulate short-term goals for yourself. Be specific about what you want to achieve and when (for example, not "become an active learner," but "find an excuse to meet with at least one of my teachers sometime next week"). Remember to choose goals that are realistic and important to you. Think about what obstacles could get in the way of achieving your goals, and make your plan. In the event you checked all items in the self-assessment, come up with one or more additional goals for this exercise.

	Goal 1	Goal 2	Goal 3
My short-term goal is . . .			
I want to achieve this goal by . . . (date)			
This goal matters because . . .			
I may encounter the following obstacles . . .			
My method for accomplishing this goal will be to . . .			

Set a Date. Put your deadline for achieving your goal(s) in your calendar. Count back ten days from your deadline and write a reminder for yourself.

Reassess. After your deadline passes, ask yourself: Did I meet this goal on time? What change has it made in my life? If I did not meet it, what am I planning to do about it?

TRY IT! *Exercises*

The exercises at the end of each chapter will help you sharpen what we believe are the critical skills for college success: writing, critical thinking, learning in groups, planning, reflecting, and taking action. You can further explore the topic of each chapter by using your PIN to complete the exercises on the website for this text: **http://success.wadsworth.com/gardner7e/**.

WORKING TOGETHER: Forming a Study Group

Use the goal-setting process from Chapter 1 to form a study group for at least one of your courses. Think about your strengths and weaknesses in a learning or studying situation. For instance, do you excel at memorizing facts but find it difficult to comprehend theories? Do you learn best by repeatedly reading the information or by applying the knowledge to a real situation? Do you prefer to learn by processing information in your head or by participating in a hands-on demonstration? Make some notes about your learning and studying strengths and weaknesses here.

Strengths:

_____

_____

_____

_____

_____

Weaknesses:

_____

_____

_____

_____

_____

Now in your study group brainstorm how each of your strengths can help others. What strengths will each of you look for in others that will help you?

How you can help others:

_____

_____

_____

_____

_____

How others can help you:

_____

_____

_____

_____

Create a study plan for your study group. Review the test schedule for the course and set times for future meetings.

What will each member of the group do in preparation for your next meeting?

EXERCISE 9.1: Designing an Exam Plan

Use the following guidelines to design an exam plan for one of your courses:

1. What type of exam will be used?

2. What material will be covered?

3. What type of questions will it contain?

4. How many questions do you think there will be?

5. What approach will you use to study for the exam?

6. How many study sessions—and how much time—will you need?

Now list all material to be covered and create a study schedule for the week prior to the exam, allowing as many one-hour blocks as you will need.

EXERCISE 9.2: Create Your Own Peaceful Scene

Think about the most peaceful place you can imagine. It can be real or imaginary. It may be a place you remember fondly from your childhood, like taking a nap in your grandmother's feather bed, or a special family vacation spot or a place where you always felt safe. Or it can be a place that you enjoy visiting now: the beach, the mountains, a cabin in the woods, or sitting in a comfortable chair near a fireplace on a cold day. Now think about what you would hear, see, smell, taste, and feel if you were there right now. Do not just think about *how* you would feel (hopefully relaxed), but *what* you would feel: the warmth of a fire, a gentle breeze, the sand between your toes. Now use all five senses to take yourself to your peaceful place. Just let yourself relax there for a while and get rid of any tension in your body. Practice this technique regularly, and you will be able to recreate your peaceful scene with ease when you need to relax.

EXERCISE 9.3: Positive Self-Messages

Some people have a "mantra"—something they say to themselves to keep focused. Adopt a mantra of your own, a phrase or sentence to say to yourself whenever you begin to doubt your ability to succeed academically or when you start to feel anxious about a test. It can be something as simple as "I know I can do it!" or "I will succeed!" Or you can quote a favorite song lyric or make it special to fit your unique personality.

WRITE ABOUT IT! My Personal Journal

This is your place to sound off, to ask your teacher to clarify part of the lesson, or to write him or her about a minor or major crisis you're experiencing. Find out if your teacher wishes you to turn in your journals. Ask if they will remain confidential. Even if the journal isn't used in your course, you can still use the format to write about and reflect on issues regarding the class, yourself, or both.

1. *What was the one major lesson you learned from reading this chapter and/or from class lecture and discussion?*

2. *What are some other important lessons about this topic?*

3. *If you believe some parts of this chapter are unimportant, spell them out here and tell why you think so. (You even might want to discuss this point with your classmates to see if they came up with a similar list.)*

4. *If anything is keeping you from performing at your peak level academically, describe what it is. Your instructor may be able to help or refer you to someone else on campus who can help.*

5. *What behaviors are you planning to change after reading this chapter? Why?*

Effective Writing and Speaking

In this chapter YOU WILL LEARN

- That writing is a process leading to a product
- Why writing e-mail and other forms of electronic communication is not the same as writing a college paper
- How to use reviews and revisions to strengthen your writing
- Six steps to success in preparing a speech
- How best to use your voice and body language
- How to sound organized when speaking on the spot

What is this speaker doing to communicate effectively?

Constance Staley, University of Colorado at Colorado Springs, and R. Stephen Staley, Colorado Technical University, contributed their valuable and considerable expertise to the speaking portion of this chapter.

● ●

SELF-ASSESSMENT
EFFECTIVE WRITING AND SPEAKING

Check the items below that apply to you:

1. ____ I understand that spoken English, "e-mail English," and formal written English are very different from each other.

2. ____ I need to spend more than just one night working on a paper in order to earn a good grade.

3. ____ The more I revise my paper, the better it gets.

4. ____ I am careful to attribute material to the proper sources.

5. ____ I often include my opinions in a paper, but I make sure the reader knows they are my opinions, not some facts I looked up.

6. ____ The more I narrow a topic for a paper, the easier it is to come up with ideas.

7. ____ The best way for me to prepare for an oral presentation is to begin gathering facts early, allow ample time for rehearsal, and have the speech down pat when it's time to present.

8. ____ I feel comfortable and sound competent speaking in front of a group.

9. ____ When I'm asked an on-the-spot question, I take a deep breath, say, "Let me think about that a moment," then either supply the answer or admit I don't know.

10. ____ When giving a speech, I never try to be someone else. I just act like myself.

If you checked seven or fewer of the items, find someone who can help you understand why all ten items are critical. At the end of this chapter, you will be asked to set personal goals for one or more of your unchecked items. If you checked all items, you will be asked to set other goals.

● ●

Many people can write, but few can write really well. The same is true of speaking. Some people speak with authority while others seem embarrassingly inept—whether they are or not. The ability to write well and speak well makes a tremendous difference in how the rest of the world perceives you and how well you will communicate throughout your life.

Depending on where you went to high school, you may or may not have had much writing practice before you came to college, particularly the kind of essay, report, and analytical writing you will be required to do now. As for speaking in public, most people of any age consider this their number one fear. If you're nervous about turning in a paper or giving a presentation, you are far from alone.

You may wonder, "Why can't more people express themselves effectively?" The answers vary, but all come back to the same theme: Most people do not think of writing and speaking as processes to be mastered step-by-step. Instead, they view writing and speaking as "products"; you knock them out and you're done. Nothing could be further from the truth.

In almost every occupation we can think of, you will be expected to think, create, communicate, manage, and lead. That means you will have to write and speak well. You will have to write reports about your work and the performance of others, internal memos to describe problems and to propose solutions, and position papers to explain and justify to your superiors why the organization must make certain changes. Often the decision makers in your organization will not know you personally. But they will know your writing, all the more reason to do it the right way.

As you lead and manage others, you also will need strong speaking skills in order to explain, report, motivate, direct, encourage, and inspire. You will likely give presentations in meetings to your superiors and their subordinates, and then frequently follow up with a written report or memo. So, as you prepare yourself for a career, you need to start thinking of yourself as a person who participates in the information age by being both a good thinker and a standout communicator.

Most professional writers and speakers would never begin to prepare an assignment only a day or hours before it's time to deliver. For one thing, the mere anxiety such a situation creates would be more than enough to close down any manner of intelligent thinking. Worrying about your grammar and spelling as you write what may be your only draft can be flirting with danger.

When you don't write or speak clearly, this may be all your audience is going to understand.

Proper Communication in Writing and Speech

Writing and speaking are direct representations of who we are. The words we write and speak communicate our innermost thoughts and feelings to others, and therefore call for an acceptable level of usage. But who decides what's acceptable? And how do words and phrases move from small groups to the national vocabulary?

Experts suggest there's no single, universally accepted standard for how to speak or write American English. Even so, school systems, professional communicators, and businesses all have standards and, not surprisingly, the rules do not vary dramatically from place to place. If they did, we'd have a hard time understanding one another, and work would come to a standstill. Our purpose in this chapter is not to teach you grammar and punctuation (save that for your English classes), but to get you to think of writing and speaking as *processes* (how you get there) as well as *products* (the final paper or script) and to help you overcome those "writer's and speaker's blocks" we all encounter from time to time.

Writing guru Peter Elbow[1] says it's impossible to write effectively if you simultaneously try to organize, check grammar and spelling, and offer intelligent thoughts to your readers. He argues that it can't all be done at once, mainly because you use the right, or creative, side of your brain to create thoughts, while you use the left, or logical, side for grammar, spelling, organization, and so forth.

Freewriting

Elbow argues that we can free up our writing and get more energy and "voice" into it by writing more like the way we speak and trying to avoid the heavy overlay of editing in our initial efforts to write. This preliminary step in the writing process is called "freewriting." By **freewriting**, he simply means writing that is temporarily unencumbered with mechanical processes, such as punctuation, grammar, spelling, context, and so forth. Freewriting also is a way to break the habit of trying to write and edit at the same time.

See Exercise 10.1: Engage by Writing

The freewriting process can be difficult because it goes against the grain of how we are accustomed to writing. We normally edit as we write, pausing to collect our thoughts, to recollect the correct spelling of a word, to cross out a sentence that does not belong, to reject a paragraph that doesn't fit with the argument that we are making, or to outline in our mind a structure of the argument that we are trying to make.

To see what freewriting feels like, write, "My writing speaks for me." Put this text down and write for at least ten minutes, nonstop, about that statement. Remind yourself that no one is going to read this. Stop thinking about organization, grammar, punctuation, and spelling, but don't stop writing until time's up. If your classmates have tried this technique, chat with them about how it felt to write this way and what they wrote about.

Using Freewriting to Find What You Want to Write About

In *Zen and the Art of Motorcycle Maintenance,*[2] Robert Pirsig tells a story about his first-year English class. Each week the assignment was to turn in a 500-word essay. One week, a student failed to submit her paper about the town where the college was located, explaining that she had "thought and thought, but couldn't think of anything to write about." Pirsig gave her an additional weekend to complete the assignment. As he said this, an idea flashed through his mind. "I want you to write a 500-word paper just about Main Street, not the whole town," he said.

She gaped at him and stared angrily. How was she to narrow her thinking to just one street when she couldn't think of one thing to write about the en-

---

[1] Peter Elbow, *Writing Without Teachers* (New York: Oxford University Press, 1973).
[2] Robert Pirsig, *Zen and the Art of Motorcycle Maintenance* (New York: Bantam Books, 1984).

tire town? Monday she arrived in tears. "I'll never learn to write." Pirsig's answer: "Write a paper about one building on Main Street. The opera house. And start with the first brick on the lower left side. I want it next class."

The student's eyes opened wide. She walked into class the next time with a 5,000-word paper on the opera house.

"I don't know what happened," she exclaimed. "I sat across the street and wrote about the first brick, then the second, and all of a sudden I couldn't stop."

What had Pirsig done for this person? He had helped her find a focus, a place to begin. And getting started is what blocks most students from approaching writing properly. Had she continued to write about bricks? Of course not. Faced with an ultimatum, she probably began to see for the first time the beauty of the opera house and had gone on to describe it, to find out more about it in the library, to ask others about it, and to comment on its setting among the other buildings on the block.

See Exercise 10.2:
The Power of Focused Observation

Very few writers—even professionally published ones—say what they want to say on their first try. And the sad fact is that really good writers are in the minority. Yet through practice, an understanding of the writing process, and dedication, more people can improve their writing skills. And good writers can make good money.

The Exploratory/Explanatory Process

Exploratory writing helps you first discover what you want to say; *explanatory* writing then allows you to transmit those ideas to others.

Explanatory writing is "published," meaning you have chosen to allow others to read it (your teacher, your friends, other students, the public at large), but it is important that most or all of your exploratory writing be private, to be read only by you as a series of steps toward your published work. Keeping your early drafts under wraps frees you to say what you mean and mean what you say. Later, you will come back and make some adjustments, and each revision will strengthen your message.

Some writers say they gather their best thoughts through exploratory writing—by researching their topic, writing down ideas from their research, and adding their questions and reactions to what they have gathered. As they write, their minds begin to make connections between ideas. They don't attempt to organize, to find exactly the right words, or to think about structure. That might interrupt the thoughts that seem to magically flow onto the paper or computer screen. They frequently chide themselves—in writing—for not being able to find the right words. Of course, when they go from exploratory to explanatory writing, their preparation will help them form crystal-clear sentences, spell properly, and have their thoughts organized so that their material flows naturally from one point to the next.

The Prewriting, Writing, and Rewriting Process

Most writing teachers agree that the writing process consists of these three steps:

1. **Prewriting or rehearsing.** This step includes preparing to write by filling your mind with information from other sources. It is generally considered the first stage of exploratory writing.
2. **Writing or drafting.** This is when exploratory writing becomes a rough explanatory draft.
3. **Rewriting or revision.** This is when you polish your work until you consider it ready for your public.

The reason many students turn in poorly written papers is that they skip the first and last steps and "make do" with the middle one. Perhaps it's a lack of time or putting off things until the night before the paper is due. Whatever the reason, the result is often a poorly written assignment.

Prewriting: The Idea Stage

Many writing experts, such as Donald Murray,[3] believe that, of all the steps, **prewriting** should take the longest. This is when you write down all you think you need to know about a topic and then go digging for the answers.

You might question things that seem illogical. You might recall what you've heard others say. This may lead you to write more, to ask yourself whether your views are more reliable than those of others, whether the topic may be too broad or too narrow, and so forth.

When is a topic appropriate? When is it neither too broad nor too narrow? Test your topic by writing, "The purpose of this paper is to convince my readers that. . ." (but don't use that stilted line in your paper). Pay attention to the assignment. Know the limits of your knowledge, the limitations on your time, and your ability to do enough research.

Writing: The Beginning of Organization

Once you have completed your research and feel you have exhausted all information sources and ideas, it's time to move to the writing, or drafting, stage. It may be a good idea to begin with an outline so that you can put things where they logically belong, build your paper around a coherent topic, and begin

---

[3] Donald Murray, *Learning by Teaching: Selected Articles on Writing and Teaching* (Portsmouth, NH: Boynton/Cook, 1982).

paying attention to the flow of ideas from one sentence to the next and from one paragraph to the next, including subheadings where needed. When you have completed this stage, you will have the first draft of your paper in hand.

Rewriting: The Polishing Stage

Are you finished? Not by a long shot. Here comes the stage where you take a good piece of writing and potentially make it great. The essence of good writing is rewriting. You read. You correct. You add smoother transitions. You slash through wordy sentences or paragraphs that add nothing to your paper. You substitute stronger words for weaker ones. You double-check spelling and grammar. Perhaps you share with others who give you feedback. You continue to revise until you're satisfied. You work hard to stay on deadline. And then you "publish."

William Zinsser,[4] author of several books on writing, says, "The act of writing gives the teacher a window into the mind of the student." In other words, your writing provides tangible evidence of how well you think and how well you understand concepts related to the courses you are taking. Your writing might also reveal a good sense of humor, a compassion for the less fortunate, a respect for family, and many other things. Zinsser reminds us that writing is not merely something that writers do, but a basic skill for getting through life. He claims that far too many Americans are prevented from doing useful work because they never learned to express themselves. You may argue that television personalities are more renowned than writers—until you remember that writers came up with the words for most of them to speak.

The "Write, Read, Observe, Experience, Research, Vocabulary, Grammar, Play, Read Aloud, and Edit" Process

Despite its cumbersome name, the process described by fiction writer and editor Niko Silvester of about.com[5] is very logical and easy to follow.

- **Write.** That's it. Write every day. Write as much as you can. The more you write, the better you'll write.

- **Read.** After you read to understand or enjoy the material, do a second read-through, taking enough time to discover how the writer structured the chapter, book, or article. You won't want to copy his or her style, of course, but you can learn a lot by studying good writing.

- **Observe.** Observe yourself and others. Notice how things look and how their appearance can change.

- **Experience.** Try new things. Do the usual things in unusual ways. Each experience you have gives you more material to write about.

- **Research.** If you can't experience it, look it up. Research what you need, research anything else that appeals to you. You never know when you can use it.

- **Vocabulary.** Learn at least one new word every day. A good resource for accomplishing this is **http://www.wordsmith.org**. You can subscribe at no cost and each day you'll receive an e-mail with a new word and definition.

See Working Together:
Write, Pair, Write, Share

[4] William Zinsser, *On Writing Well* (New York: Harper Resource 25th Anniversary Edition, 2001).
[5] Niko Sylvester, *Top 10 Ways to Become a Better Writer.* (http://teenwriting.about.com/od/thewritingprocess/tp/BetterWriting.htm).

- **Grammar.** Bad grammar is a clue that the writer is less than sharp. Bad grammar can obscure the meaning of a word, a sentence, or a paragraph. Take a grammar course or purchase a grammar book if you're somewhat shaky with grammar. The rules are there for a reason, and it's called "making sense."

- **Play.** Write just for fun, not for an assignment. Your "nonrequired" writing—no pressures attached—will help you make discoveries that will improve your writing assignments.

- **Read aloud.** Read your own writing aloud to hear how it sounds. If you stumble over some words, your readers probably will stumble, too.

- **Edit.** The editing process takes much longer than the writing itself. Editing is the time to slow down and see if what you've written makes sense and is easy to read. It is your "last chance" to get it right. If you've followed all the right steps, you ought to be in good shape.

Allocating Time for Each Writing Stage

When Donald Murray was asked how long a writer should spend on each of the three stages, he offered this thought:

Prewriting: 85 percent (including research and rumination)

Writing: 1 percent (the first draft)

Rewriting: 14 percent (revising till it's right)

If the figures surprise you, here's a true story about a writer who was assigned to create a brochure. He had other jobs to do and kept avoiding that one. But the other work he was doing had a direct bearing on the brochure he was asked to write. So as he was putting this assignment off, he was also "researching" material for it.

After nearly three months, he could stand it no longer. So he sat at his computer and dashed the words off in just under thirty minutes. He felt a rush of ideas, he used words and phrases he'd never used before, and he was afraid to stop until he'd finished. He did some revising, sent it around the office, took some suggestions, and eventually the brochure was published.

He had spent a long time "prewriting" (working with related information without trying to write the brochure). He went through the "writing" stage quickly because his mind was primed for the task. As a result, he had time to polish his work before deciding the job was done.

E-mail: Another Method of Communication

As e-mail communication becomes more common, whether we're using a desktop computer or even the keypad of a mobile phone, many of us are taking more and more shortcuts with standard English. Some e-mail writers use no capital letters. Others use little, if any punctuation. Writer Lynne Truss in her 2003 book, *Eats, Shoots & Leaves*, compares today's e-mail shortcuts—such as "C U later"—with the writing of the child Pip in Charles Dickens's novel, *Great Expectations,* "Mi deer jo I ope u r kr wite well."[6]

In some ways, e-mail communication is a mix of conversation and standard English. Therefore, e-mail, like conversational English, tends to be sloppier than communication on paper. This is not always bad. It makes little sense to slave over a message for hours, making sure that your spelling is faultless, your words eloquent, and your grammar beyond reproach, if the point of the message is to tell your co-worker that you are ready to go to lunch. But you need to be aware of when it's okay to be sloppy and when you have to be meticulous.

E-mail also does not convey emotions nearly as well as face-to-face or even telephone conversations. It lacks vocal inflection, gestures, and a shared environment. Your correspondent may have difficulty telling if you are serious or kidding, happy or sad, frustrated or euphoric. Sarcasm is *particularly* dangerous to use in e-mail.[7] Thus, your e-mail compositions will be different from both your paper compositions and your speech.

Some Final Observations on Becoming a Better Writer and Thinker

First and most important, start writing the day you get the assignment, even if it's only for ten or fifteen minutes. That way, you won't be confronting a blank paper later in the week. Write something every day, because the more you write, the better you'll write. Dig for ideas. Reject nothing at first, then organize and narrow your thoughts later. Read good writing; it will help you find your own writing style. Above all, know that becoming a better thinker and writer takes hard work, but practice—in this case—can make near-perfect.

See Exercise 10.3: Parallels

---

[6] Lynne Truss, *Eats, Shoots & Leaves: The Zero Tolerance Approach to Punctuation* (New York: Gotham Books, 2003).
[7] Kaitlin Duck Sherwood, "A Beginner's Guide to Effective E-mail," (http://www.webfoot.com/advice/email.top.html).

Six Steps to Successful Speaking

Much of what we have written about writing also applies to speaking in public. The major difference, of course, is that you not only have to write; you also have to present your thoughts to others.

Successful speaking involves six fundamental steps:

Step 1: Clarify your objective.
Step 2: Analyze your audience.
Step 3: Collect and organize your information.

See Exercise 10.4: PowerPoint Presentation

TURNING POINT

The first time I was assigned an oral presentation, I was terrified because I had no such experience from my previous education in China. Besides, I always feel nervous talking in front of people. After working hard with other group members and getting help and encouragement from the teacher, I finally went through it smoothly. I also learned how to use PowerPoint.

Ying T.
De Anza College

Step 4: Choose your visual aids.
Step 5: Prepare your notes.
Step 6: Practice your delivery.

Step 1: Clarify Your Objective

Begin by identifying what you want to accomplish. Do you want to persuade your listeners that your campus needs additional student parking? Inform your listeners about student government's accomplishments? What do you want your listeners to know, believe, or do when you are finished?

Step 2: Analyze Your Audience

You need to understand the people you'll be talking to. Ask yourself:

- What do they already know about my topic? If you're going to give a presentation on the health risks of fast food, you'll want to know how much your listeners already know about fast food so you don't risk boring them or wasting their time.

- What do they want or need to know? How much interest do your classmates have in nutrition? Would they be more interested in some other aspect of college life?

- Who are they? What do they have in common with me?

- What are their attitudes toward me, my ideas, and my topic? How are they likely to feel about the ideas I am presenting? What attitudes have they cultivated about fast food?

Step 3: Collect and Organize Your Information

Now comes the critical part of the process: building your presentation by selecting and arranging blocks of information. One useful analogy is to think of yourself as guiding your listeners through the maze of ideas they already have to the new knowledge, attitudes, and beliefs you would like them to have.

Step 4: Choose Your Visual Aids

When visual aids are added to presentations, listeners can absorb 35 percent more information—and over time they can recall 55 percent more. You may choose to prepare a chart, show a video clip, write on the board, or distribute handouts. You may also use your computer to prepare overhead transparencies or dynamic PowerPoint presentations. As you select and use your visual aids, consider these rules of thumb:

- Make visuals easy to follow. Use readable lettering, and don't crowd information.

- Explain each visual clearly.

- Allow your listeners enough time to process visuals.

- Proofread carefully. Misspelled words hurt your credibility as a speaker.

- Maintain eye contact with your listeners while you discuss visuals. Don't turn around and address the screen.

Visual aids help draw your audience into your presentation.

Although a fancy PowerPoint slideshow can't make up for inadequate preparation or poor delivery skills, using quality visual aids can help you organize your material and help your listeners understand what they're hearing. The quality of your visual aids and your skill in using them can contribute to making your presentation as effective as possible.

Step 5: Prepare Your Notes

If you are like most speakers, having an entire written copy of your speech before you may be an irresistible temptation to read much of your presentation. On the other hand, your memory may fail you. And even if it doesn't, your presentation could sound canned. A better strategy is to memorize only the introduction and conclusion so that you can maintain eye contact and therefore build rapport with your listeners.

The best speaking aid is a minimal outline, carefully prepared, from which you can speak extemporaneously. You will rehearse thoroughly in advance. But because you are speaking from brief notes, your choice of words will be slightly different each time you give your presentation, causing you to sound prepared but natural. You may wish to use note cards, because they are unobtrusive. (Make sure you number them, just in case you accidentally drop the stack on your way to the front of the room.) After you become more experienced, you may want to let your visuals serve as notes. A handout or PowerPoint slide listing key points may also serve as your basic outline. Eventually, you may find you no longer need notes.

Step 6: Practice Your Delivery

As you rehearse, form a mental image of success rather than failure. Practice your presentation aloud several times beforehand to harness that energy-producing anxiety.

Begin a few days before your target date, and continue until you're about to go on stage. Make sure you rehearse aloud; thinking through your speech and talking through your speech have very different results. Practice before an audience—your roommate, a friend, your dog, even the mirror. Talking to something or someone helps simulate the distraction listeners cause. Consider audiotaping or videotaping yourself to pinpoint your own mistakes and to re-inforce your strengths. If you ask your practice audience to critique you, you'll have some idea of what changes you might make.

See Working Together: Debate

Using Your Voice and Body Language

Let your hands hang comfortably at your sides, reserving them for natural, spontaneous gestures. Leave your lectern and move around the room. Your speech will be more interesting. Don't lean over or hide behind the lectern. Un-less you must stay close to a fixed microphone, plan to move comfortably about the room, without pacing nervously. Some experts suggest changing positions between major points in order to punctuate your presentation. The unconscious message is, "I've finished with that point; let's shift topics." Face your audience, and move toward them while you're speaking.

Here are some additional suggestions for successful speaking:

- Make eye contact with as many listeners as you can. This helps you read their reactions, demonstrate confidence, and establish command.

- A smile helps to warm up your listeners, although you should avoid smil-ing excessively or inappropriately. Smiling through a presentation on world hunger would send your listeners a mixed message.

- As you practice, pay attention to the pitch of your voice, your rate of speech, and your volume. Project confidence and enthusiasm by varying your pitch. Speak at a rate that mirrors normal conversation—not too fast and not too slow. Consider varying your volume for the same reasons you vary pitch and rate—to engage your listeners and to emphasize important points.

- Pronunciation and word choice are important. A poorly articulated word (such as "gonna" for "going to"), a mispronounced word ("nuculer" for "nuclear"), or a misused word ("anecdote" for "antidote") can quickly erode credibility. Check meanings and pronunciations in the dictionary if you're not sure, and use a thesaurus for word variety. Fillers such as "um," "uh," "like," and "you know" are distracting, too.

- Consider your appearance. Convey a look of competence, preparedness, and success by dressing professionally.

Figure 10.1
The GUIDE Checklist

The GUIDE Checklist

Imagine you've been selected as a guide for next year's prospective first-year students and their families visiting campus. Picture yourself in front of the administration building with a group of people assembled around you. You want to get and keep their attention in order to achieve your objective: raising their interest in your school. Using the GUIDE checklist, shown in Figure 10.1, you would accomplish the following.

Get Your Audience's Attention You can relate the topic to your listeners:

> *"Let me tell you what to expect during your college years here—at the best school in the state."*

Or you can state the significance of the topic:

> *"Deciding on which college to attend is one of the most important decisions you'll ever make."*

Or you can arouse their curiosity:

> *"Do you know the three most important factors students and their families consider when choosing a college?"*

You can also tell a joke (but only if it relates and isn't offensive), startle the audience, tell a story, or ask a "rhetorical" question, a question that is asked solely to produce an effect (especially to make an assertion) rather than to elicit a reply. Regardless of which method you select, remember that a well-designed introduction must not only gain the attention of the audience but also develop rapport with them, motivate them to continue listening, and preview what you are going to say during the rest of your speech.

"You" (U)—Don't Forget Yourself In preparing any speech, don't exclude the most important source of your presentation—you. Even in a formal presentation, you will be most successful if you develop a comfortable style that's easy to listen to. Don't play a role. Instead, be yourself at your best, letting your wit and personality shine through.

Ideas, Ideas, Ideas! Create a list of all the possible points you might want to make. Then write them out as conclusions you want your listeners to accept. For example, imagine that in your campus tour for prospective new students and their parents you want to make the following points:

Tuition is reasonable.

The faculty is composed of good teachers.

The school is committed to student success.

College can prepare you to get a good job.

Student life is awesome.

The library has adequate resources.

The campus is attractive.

The campus is safe.

Faculty members conduct prestigious research.

Our college is the best choice.

For a typical presentation, about five main points are the most that listeners can process. After considering your list for some time, you decide that the following five points are critical:

Tuition is reasonable.

The faculty is composed of good teachers.

The school is committed to student success.

The campus is attractive

The campus is safe.

Try to generate more ideas than you think you'll need so that you can select the best ones. As with writing, don't judge them at first; rather, think up as many possibilities as you can. Then use your critical thinking to decide which are most relevant to your objectives.

As you formulate your main ideas, keep these guidelines in mind:

- **Main points should be parallel, if possible.** Each main point should be a full sentence with a construction similar to the others. A poor, *nonparallel* structure might look like this:

    1. Student life is awesome. (a full-sentence main point)

    2. Tuition. (a one-word main point that doesn't parallel the first point) For a *parallel* second point, try instead:

    2. Tuition is low. (a full-sentence main point)

- **Each main point should include a single idea.** Don't crowd main points with multiple messages, as in the following:

    1. Tuition is reasonable, and the campus is safe.

    2. Faculty are good teachers and researchers.

Ideas rarely stand on their own merit. To ensure that your main ideas work, use a variety of supporting materials. The three most widely used forms of supporting materials are examples, statistics, and testimony.

- **Examples** include stories and illustrations, hypothetical events, and specific cases. They can be powerful, compelling ways to dramatize and clarify main ideas, but make sure they're relevant, representative, and reasonable.

- **Statistics** are widely used as evidence in speeches. Of course, numbers can be manipulated, and unscrupulous speakers sometimes lie with statistics. If you use statistics, make sure they are clear, concise, accurate, and easy to understand.

- **Testimony** includes quoting outside experts, paraphrasing reliable sources, and emphasizing the quality of individuals who agree with your main points. When you use testimony, make sure that it is accurate, expert, and credible.

Finally, because each person in your audience is unique, you are most likely to add interest, clarity, and credibility to your presentation by varying and combining the types of support you provide.

Develop an Organizational Structure For example, you may decide to use a chronological narrative approach, discussing the history of the college from its early years to the present. Or you may wish to use a problem-solution format in which you describe a problem (such as choosing a school), present the pros and cons of several solutions (the strengths and weaknesses of several schools), and finally identify the best solution (your school!).

Begin with your most important ideas. Writing an outline may be the most useful way to begin organizing. List each main point and subpoint separately on a note card. Spread the cards out on a large surface (such as the floor), and arrange, rearrange, add, and delete cards until you find the most effective arrangement. Then simply number the cards, pick them up, and use them to prepare your final outline.

As you organize your presentation, remember that your overall purpose is to guide your listeners. This means you must not neglect *connectors* (or transitions) between your main points. For example:

"Now that we've looked at the library, let's move on to the gymnasium."

"The first half of my presentation has identified our recreational facilities. Now let's look at the academic hubs on campus."

"So much for the academic buildings on campus. What about the campus social scene?"

In speaking, as in writing, transitions make the difference between keeping your audience with you and losing them at an important juncture.

Exit Gracefully and Memorably Plan your ending carefully, realizing that most of the suggestions for introductions also apply to conclusions.

Whatever else you do, go out with style, impact, and dignity. Don't leave your listeners asking, "So that's it?" Subtly signal that the end is in sight (without the overused "So in conclusion"), briefly summarize your major points, and then conclude confidently.

Speaking on the Spot

Most of the speaking you will do in college and after will be on the spot. When your instructor asks your opinion on last night's reading, when a classmate stops you in the hall to find out your position on an issue, or when your best friend asks you to defend your views, you have to give impromptu speeches.

When you must speak on the spot, it helps to use a framework that allows you to sound organized and competent. Suppose your instructor asks, "Do you think the world's governments are working together effectively to ensure a healthy environment?" One of the most popular ways to arrange your thoughts is through the PREP formula.[8] Short for "preparation," this plan requires the following:

See Exercise 10.5: Chiseled-in-Stone Speech

Point of view. Provide an overview—a clear direct statement or generalization: "After listening to yesterday's lecture, yes, I do."

Reasons. Broadly state why you hold this point of view: "I was surprised at the efforts of the United Nations General Assembly to focus on the environment."

Evidence or examples. Present specific facts or data supporting your point of view: "For example, the industrialized nations have set stringent goals on air pollution and greenhouse gases for the year 2010."

Point of view restated. To make sure you are understood clearly, end with a restatement of your position: "So, yes, the world's governments seem to be concerned and working to improve the situation."

[8] Kenneth Wydro, *Think on Your Feet* (Englewood Cliffs, NJ: Prentice-Hall, 1981).

Where to Go for Help

ON CAMPUS

Writing Center: Most campuses have one of these. Frequently it is found within the English Department.

Learning Assistance Center: In addition to help on many other topics, these centers offer help on writing.

Departments of Speech, Theater, and Communications: These offer both resources and specific courses to help you develop your speaking skills.

Student Activities: One of the best ways to learn and practice speaking skills is to become active in student organizations, especially those like the Student Government Association and the Debate Club.

ONLINE

Writing Tips:
http://bss.sfsu.edu/~mpa/skills/writing.htm.
Check out these writing resources from San Francisco State University.

Plain Language: Ever been confused by government gobbledygook? Here's a guide to writing user-friendly documents for federal employees:
http://www.plainlanguage.gov/. Go to the bottom of the page and, under "How to/Tools," click on "Writing Reader-Friendly Documents."

Toastmasters International:
http://www.toastmasters.org.
Click on "10 tips for successful public speaking."

What If All Else Fails?

What if you plan, organize, prepare, and rehearse, but calamity strikes anyway? What if your mind goes completely blank, you drop your note cards, or you say something totally embarrassing? Don't forget that people in your audience have been in your position and empathize with you. Accentuate the positive, rely on your wit, and move back into your speech. Your recovery is what they are most likely to recognize; your success is what they are most likely to remember.

ACHIEVE IT! *Setting Goals for Success*

Go back to the self-assessment at the beginning of this chapter and select one to three unchecked items from the list. Use these to formulate short-term goals for yourself. Be specific about what you want to achieve and when (for example, not "become an active learner," but "find an excuse to meet with at least one of my teachers sometime next week"). Remember to choose goals that are realistic and important to you. Think about what obstacles could get in the way of achieving your goals, and make your plan. In the event you checked all items in the self-assessment, come up with one or more additional goals for this exercise.

	Goal 1	Goal 2	Goal 3
My short-term goal is . . .			
I want to achieve this goal by . . . (date)			
This goal matters because . . .			
I may encounter the following obstacles . . .			
My method for accomplishing this goal will be to . . .			

Set a Date. Put your deadline for achieving your goal(s) in your calendar. Count back ten days from your deadline and write a reminder for yourself.

Reassess. After your deadline passes, ask yourself: Did I meet this goal on time? What change has it made in my life? If I did not meet it, what am I planning to do about it?

RY IT! *Exercises*

The exercises at the end of each chapter will help you sharpen what we believe are the critical skills for college success: writing, critical thinking, learning in groups, planning, reflecting, and taking action. You can further explore the topic of each chapter by using your PIN to complete the exercises on the website for this text: **http://success.wadsworth.com/gardner7e/.**

WORKING TOGETHER: Write, Pair, Write, Share

Do this exercise in small groups of five or six.

1. *Write.* Using the freewriting technique, write for about ten minutes about something that is on your mind. Remember, don't stop to think; just keep writing.

2. *Pair.* When you are told to stop writing, pair off with one or two others in your group, and share what you have written by talking about it with the others. Introduce yourself, and tell where you're from. Listen to what each person in your mini-group has to say about what you told them. Take notes if you wish.

3. *Write.* When you are next told to write, reflect on the interaction in your mini-group, but do it individually, on paper. How has the discussion reinforced, modified, or changed your original thoughts on the subject? Write this down.

4. *Share.* At the given signal, re-form as a small group of five or six. Appoint a leader, a recorder, and a reporter. Share your thoughts with the entire group. Listen to what group members have to say. Present your report to the group at large. Reflect on what learning has taken place and what the next steps should be. How might you apply this process to one of your own classes?

WORKING TOGETHER: Debate

Find a partner, and choose a controversial topic that relates to college life. For example, you might decide to debate about an academic issue such as "doing Internet (versus traditional library) research," a campus issue such as "parking," "athletics," or "cheating," or a national issue such as "student credit card debt." After you decide on a topic, each of you should choose a side to research, either pro or con. Decide how many minutes each side or speaker will be allotted, who will speak first, and so on. After the debate is over, your instructor may call for a "division of the house," requesting that other students in the class go to one side of the room or the other to indicate whether they side with the pro or con argument.

EXERCISE 10.1: Engage by Writing

To practice private writing, summarize in writing a reading assignment you have recently completed. Write down any questions that the reading raised for you. Finally, write down any additional personal responses you may have had to the material. This is private writing, so you don't have to share it with others, but your instructor may ask how going through this process has helped you with the material. Be prepared to answer.

EXERCISE 10.2: The Power of Focused Observation

Remember the student Pirsig wrote about who began with the first brick of the opera house and went on to write a 5000-word paper? Find a favorite spot of yours on campus where you can sit comfortably. Take a good look at the entire area. Now look again, this time noticing specific parts of the area. Choose something; it may be a statue, a building, a tree, or a fence. Now look carefully at just one portion of the object you selected, and start writing about it. See where the writing takes you.

EXERCISE 10.3: Parallels

In what ways are speaking and writing similar? In what ways are they different? How do forms of electronic writing, such as e-mail, instant messaging, and so forth, differ from both speaking and writing?

EXERCISE 10.4: PowerPoint Presentation

Prepare a three- to five-slide PowerPoint presentation to introduce yourself to your classmates. You may create slides about your high school years, your hobbies, your job, your family, and so forth. Use both visuals and text, and be prepared to discuss which PowerPoint features you used to make your presentation as dynamic as possible.

EXERCISE 10.5: Chiseled-in-Stone Speech

Give a one-minute speech to the class on a subject assigned to you by your instructor. During the speech, you must look like a statue. Don't move your arms, legs, or head, and stare at the back wall of the room without looking at your classmates. Note how awkward it feels not to gesture or move about or look at your listeners. Despite having "stage fright," a very common reaction to public speaking, it's also natural to want to connect with your audience and get your ideas across to them. Go with your natural inclinations and capitalize on them to speak at your best.

WRITE ABOUT IT! My Personal Journal

This is your place to sound off, to ask your teacher to clarify part of the lesson, or to write him or her about a minor or major crisis you're experiencing. Find out if your teacher wishes you to turn in your journals. Ask if they will remain confidential. Even if the journal isn't used in your course, you can still use the format to write about and reflect on issues regarding the class, yourself, or both.

1. *What was the one major lesson you learned from reading this chapter and/or from class lecture and discussion?*

2. *What are some other important lessons about this topic?*

3. *If you believe some parts of this chapter are unimportant, spell them out here and tell why you think so. (You might even want to discuss this point with your classmates to see if they came up with a similar list.)*

4. *If anything is keeping you from performing at your peak level academically, describe what it is. Your instructor may be able to refer you to someone else on campus who can help.*

5. *What behaviors are you planning to change after reading this chapter? Why?*

Research and College Libraries

In this chapter YOU WILL LEARN

- The difference between research and simply "finding stuff"
- What membership and participation in the Information Society require of us
- Why Information Literacy is the survival skill for the twenty-first century
- How to employ Information Literacy in the library, in the classroom, and in life
- How to focus upon a topic, narrow it, and shape it
- Specific search strategies
- How to ask librarians for help
- How plagiarism can doom a paper, a course, or a career

What key words could you use to search for more information about this image of Mt. St. Helens volcano, taken from space?

Charles Curran and Rose Parkman Marshall, both of the University of South Carolina, contributed their valuable and considerable expertise to the writing of this chapter.

RESEARCH AND COLLEGE LIBRARIES

Check the items below that apply to you:

1. ___ I have little or no problem navigating a library in search of information.

2. ___ I am always careful to check my sources for accuracy and credit them appropriately.

3. ___ I consider myself to be a literate person.

4. ___ I understand that information drives the world, especially in our time.

5. ___ I understand that "Galloping New Ignorance" refers to being able to capture information from electronic sources so quickly that we often do not take time to verify that information.

6. ___ It's okay if I start my research using encyclopedias if I am looking for other key words or what "the big picture" seems to be. In other words, it's a good start, but only a start.

7. ___ I know the difference between popular magazines and scholarly publications.

8. ___ I understand that in conducting library research I will often have to narrow my topic.

9. ___ Even comparing Subarus to Toyotas can involve research.

10. ___ I know that online catalogs and online periodical databases probably provide more reliable information than "raw" Internet material.

If you checked seven or fewer of the items, find someone who can help you understand why all ten items are critical. At the end of this chapter, you will be asked to set personal goals for one or more of your unchecked items. If you checked all items, you will be asked to set other goals.

Most colleges and universities describe their three major missions as teaching, research, and service. While each of those missions is vital, we know that without the ability to find and evaluate information quickly the world would come to a standstill. Information feeds research, and research produces discoveries that improve our quality of life.

Those who decide not to play, or who play poorly, will lack the ability to keep up, to participate, and to succeed in college, career, and community. "Playing" means more than learning how to operate a computer or visiting the library. It means learning the basic research and critical thinking skills needed to make sense of the vast amount of information at your fingertips. Playing means developing Information Literacy. That holds true whether you plan to be a nurse, engineer, shopkeeper, or builder.

What's Research—and What's Not?

Some of the steps you will go through in the name of research may turn out not to be research after all. See if you can tell the difference:

1. You complete an assignment that requires you to demonstrate how to use a library's electronic book catalog, electronic periodical index, e-mail

Not being able to find the information you need can be frustrating.

delivery system, government documents collection, map depository, and electronic interlibrary loan service.

_____ Research _____ Not Research

2. You are assigned to do a report on ethics; so you go to an encyclopedia, copy selected portions of an article without giving citations, and submit that as your report.

_____ Research _____ Not Research

3. You are assigned to find a definition of ethics, a book on ethics, a journal article on ethics, and one Internet item on ethics.

_____ Research _____ Not Research

4. Your assignment in ethics requires you to use at least five sources; you find five items on the Internet, treat them as equally reliable sources, patch them together without commentary, compose and attach an introduction, and submit your paper.

_____ Research _____ Not Research

5. Assigned to select and report on an ethical issue, you pick ethics in politics, accumulate a dozen sources, interpret them, evaluate, select a few and discard a few, organize the keepers into a coherent arrangement, extract portions that hang together, write a paper that cites your sources, compose an introduction that explains what you have done, draw some conclusions of your own, and submit the results.

_____ Research _____ Not Research

If you were good at #1, you might be well prepared to conduct a research project in a library, but just performing those steps with no specific purpose in mind is not conducting research.

If you were good at #2, chances are you might flunk the paper. Your instructor might teach you a new word: **plagiarism.** Copying information, or using just some of it, even changing the words around, requires that you give credit to the originator. If you were good at #3, that means you are a good retriever. While retrieving and research are not the same, retrieving is an essential research skill.

If you were good at #4, you might be in more trouble than the character in #2. First, there is the plagiarism thing. Second—and much more important a flaw insofar as research is concerned—is the indiscriminate use of sources that may be new or old, useful or dangerously in error, reliable or shaky, research based or anecdotal, or biased beyond credibility.

If you are good at #5, especially in the analysis and drawing of conclusions, then you have experienced the rush that comes with discovery and the righteous joy that accompanies making a statement or taking a stand. The conclusion that you composed is your triumph; it is new information!

The Information Age, the Information Explosion, and the Information Society

See Exercise 11.1: Getting Comfortable in Your Library

During the agricultural age most people farmed. Now only a tiny fraction of us work the land, but our abundance fills our silos and granaries. During the industrial age we made things. We still do, of course, but we have automated industry so that fewer people can produce more goods. In addition, we have shipped much of our manufacturing overseas to cheaper labor markets. Other nations have joined the game and compete strenuously these days. Now we live in the **Information Age**, a name we concocted because it signifies the primacy of information in our everyday lives. Here are some key Information Age observations:

- Information, having overtaken *things*, is the new commodity.

- America's gross national product (GNP) is substantially information based.

- There is more information than ever before. It doubles at ever-shortening intervals. This abundance has not made information easier to get, although the abundance creates that illusion.

- Because abundance and electronic access combine to produce prodigious amounts of retrievable information, people need highly developed sorting skills to cope.

- Most of the American workforce is employed at originating, managing, or transferring information.

- Information has value; you can determine its benefits in dollars, and you can compute the cost of not having it.

- Information Literacy is the survival skill for your generation.

- The information professionals at your library are the world's leading authorities on how to find information.

Making Sense of It All

What is the role of information in our everyday lives? How does one cope with the daily challenge of finding the right information to solve a given problem before it defeats us? Which airline or travel service really offers the cheapest airfare? Is it true that Dr. Smith always asks true/false questions? On third down when State lines up with a slot receiver, do they always pass, and is the slot receiver always the first (and maybe only) target? Which variety of poisonous serpent bit the patient, and which antivenin is required to treat the victim? Which is likely to give me better service, a Subaru or a Toyota? What are the relationships between social class and mental illness? At what stress levels will bridge cables snap? What is iambic pentameter? Who steals most from a chain store, the customers who lift displayed products or the employees who help themselves to inventory? What is the best way to shave time from the manufacture and delivery of tractors?

Each of these questions shares some common factors. Although some of these questions are "academic" and others are down-to-earth questions that people ask as part of their jobs, they share a particular common characteristic. The answers to each are available in information agencies and/or in electronic formats. An inquirer needs instant answers for the question about snake bites because a life hangs in the balance. Other situations may not be so critical.

Information plays a key role in vastly different projects.

Galloping New Ignorance (GNI)

Money confers power, but not if it lies dormant under the mattress. Knowledge contributes to power, but not until someone applies it. Information is power, but not if it just lies there unused. Furthermore, if information is outdated, ignored, misused, or misinterpreted, it can be a source of great *unpower*. An information center with 5 million items has no power at all, but when you retrieve relevant sources from the information center, sort them, interpret them, analyze them, and synthesize them into a well-organized project, you will blow your teacher's socks off. *That's* power! You achieve that power by intelligently managing and presenting timely and useful information that you retrieve from your information place—the four-wall kind and/or the cyber kind.

Galloping New Ignorance (GNI) siphons power. What do we mean by "Galloping New Ignorance"? We mean the assumption that the huge amounts of manageable information available at the press of a button provide knowledge. Put another way, if it is electronic, it is considered gospel. Conversely, if it is in print, it is considered obsolete. The Newly Ignorant rejoice at the discovery of 12,456 hits on fossil fuels. Then *abundance shock* takes hold if and when they realize their discovery is totally unsorted, and they frequently respond by *settling*—using the first five hits, irrespective of quality or authenticity. The reason this Galloping New Ignorance is so commonplace is that it infects smart people—decision makers—people who should know better but

do not and whose decisions suffer as a consequence. Path-of-least-resistance followers, and all who believe that because they are wired they are informed, contribute to the GNI syndrome.

Confusing *information* for *understanding* is a common GNI symptom. People marvel at the information explosion, the paper inflation, and the Internet. They conclude that they are or can easily become informed. Many are unprepared for the blurring of lines between disciplines, the prodigious assault of publications, and the unsorted, unevaluated mass of information that pours down upon them at the press of a button.

What is the antidote for Galloping New Ignorance? How can one become an informed and successful player?

Learning to Be Information Literate

Here are four things to remember about information:

- **Know that information matters.** It helps empower people to make good choices. The choices people make often determine their success in business, their happiness as partners, and their well-being as citizens on this planet. Face it: Information is the key.

- **Know how and where to find it.** If we are sick, we must know whose help to seek. If we are poor, we need to know where to get assistance. If we want to study chemistry, we need to know which schools offer degrees, how much they charge, if there are scholarships, and who will hire us when we graduate.

- **Know how to find and retrieve information.** Once we find where to go and whom to ask, we must possess the skills to ask good questions and to make educated searches of information systems such as the Internet, libraries, and databases. We must cultivate relationships with information professionals—the librarians. We must be able to identify and define our need and to use the kinds of inquiry terminology that will give us hits instead of misses.

- **Learn how to interpret the information you find.** While it is very important to retrieve information, it is even more important to know what to do with it. What does the information *mean*? Have you selected a source you can understand? Is the information accurate? Is the author/provider a reliable source? How can you determine this?

How does the information fit your need?

- **Is it introductory?** Introductory information is very basic and elementary. It does what its name implies: it introduces and provides a first impression. It often neither assumes nor requires prior knowledge about the topic. Example: *A snake is a long-bodied, legless animal.*

- **Is it definitional?** Definitional information provides some descriptive details about a topic. Example: *Snakes are either venomous or nonvenomous. The venom may be of three types: neurotoxic, hemotoxic, or a combination of both.*

- **Is it analytical?** Analytical information supplies data about origins, behaviors, differences, and uses. Example: *While some snakes are shy and prefer to retreat when disturbed, some are aggressive. People often mistake venomous varieties for harmless ones, and they suffer the deadly consequence.*

- **Is it current or dated?** Is it someone's opinion, or is it a rigorously researched document? Can you lay it out in a logical sequence? Can you conclude anything? Use the *"so what?"* test: How important is this discovery?

- **Whom are you going to tell about your discovery, and how?** Will you write a report? What guidelines for construction will you follow? Will you respect the intellectual property of others by giving appropriate credit to sources? Will you give your report orally? If you transfer this information orally, what principles for making presentations will you identify, practice, and master? Or will you just wing your presentation without much forethought?

Information Literacy has many facets, among them:

- **Computer literacy,** the abilities associated with using electronic methods (search language), both for inquiry and for constructing presentations for others of what you have found and analyzed.

- **Media literacy**, which is about facility with various formats: film, tape, CDs, and the machines that operate them.
- **Cultural literacy**, knowing what has gone on and is going on around you. If someone remarks about the Great Bambino or a feat of Ruthian proportion, you have to know about George Herman (Babe) Ruth, or you will not get the point.

You have to know the difference between the Civil War and the Revolution, U2 and Y2K, Eminem and M&Ms, or you will not understand everyday conversation.

Researching and Presenting an Assigned Topic

If you are fortunate to have an instructor who understands that Information Literacy skills are best practiced and learned when an inquirer has a reason for gathering information, that instructor will have given you an assignment to discover, interpret, organize, and present some findings to your classmates. What steps should you take to execute your assignment? If you wanted to forgo the opportunity to improve your Information Literacy skills, you could manage this in your dorm room and pick the first hits you get on the Internet or from *Readers' Guide Abstracts*. But wait!

You have a topic, an inquiry task, and a product to produce:

Topic	Inquiry Task	Product
Political ethics	Definition	Paper and/or oral report
	Introduction	
	Some examples	
	Current	
	Historical	
	Problems, if any	
	Important aspects to report	
	Conclusions to draw	

If you are willing to practice Information Literacy, the survival skill you must acquire if you are to prosper in the Information Society, you must take these steps.

Step 1: Define the Topic in General Terms Since your job is to define and introduce, you will be well served by general and specific dictionaries and encyclopedias. Any respected general dictionary can define *ethics* for you, but it would be a good idea to get your topic defined in context. Since your topic is *political* ethics, consult a political dictionary and an encyclopedia that would consider the political aspects of your ethics topic. For example, you will find a great article on lobbies in the *Encyclopedia of American Political History*.

Step 2: Specify and Narrow Your Topic After you have retrieved a definition that you determine to be complete and understandable, you are ready to search for a good introduction—some basic information that guides you toward a further understanding of the nature of your topic. You have a decision to make. What aspects of political ethics will you pursue? Even if you launch the most general of inquiries, you will very quickly discover that your topic is vast and that there are many related subtopics. Ask your librarians. It's their job to help you.

You are having your first encounter with one of the major Information Literacy opportunities: specifying and narrowing a broad topic so you can focus in and retrieve highly relevant items. Whether you are searching the library or the Internet, narrowing your search is a critical step. Remember those 12,456 hits on fossil fuels? What you want is twelve or so specific, highly relevant hits on an *aspect* of political ethics that you can fashion into a coherent five-minute presentation, or a lucid, well-organized essay or opinion piece.

What *aspect*? Here's where the narrowing comes in, for when you consult political ethics in the *Library of Congress Subject Headings (LCSH)* or when you check political ethics in the library's electronic catalog, you will discover some choices:

See Working Together: Conducting a Group Search of the Library

Civil service, ethics	Judicial ethics
Conflict of interests	Justice
Corporations—Corrupt practices	Legislative ethics
Ethics, modern	Political corruption
Environmental ethics	Political ethics
Fairness	Social ethics
Gifts to politicians	

Note two things. First of all, your topic is broad. Every one of these headings leads to books and articles on political ethics. The good news is there's lots of information; the bad news is there's lots of information. For your sanity's sake, narrow your topic; get specific. In the *Library of Congress Subject Headings (LCSH)* you will encounter some abbreviations that may help you with your *search-and-narrow* mission. In this valuable volume, *BT* means *broader term* and suggests that you can get more specific. *NT* means *narrower term;* you are getting specific. *RT* means *related term* and identifies an additional related topic. *UF* means *used for* and tells you that the subject heading you have found is the standard term used by many finding tools.

See Exercise 11.2: Getting Oriented to Periodicals

Some databases permit keyword searching. Others are very liberal and permit free text or natural language searching. Your library's catalog probably has the keyword option. InfoTrac® College Edition, where available, is a "free text" electronic indexing tool. *Social Science Citation Index* marries the actual words used in the titles of articles in order to permit searchers to inquire, electronically or in print, in everyday language. So be on guard; some indexing tools, such as the *New York Times Index* and *ERIC*, have their own legal subject terms and their own thesauri or lists that you should consult before searching.

Because you may know about the efforts of lobbyists and political action committees (PACS) to influence legislation, and because this subtopic interests you, you may decide upon *gifts to politicians* and *political corruption* as your target topics. Of course, *lobbyists* opens up a new subject area that you may explore if you are interested in the ethical aspects of a legitimate practice that is woven rather tightly into the fabric of our democracy.

Encyclopedic sources will help you craft an Introduction to your three-pronged topic: gifts to politicians, political corruption, and lobbyists. For instance, two editions of the previously cited and very useful specific subject encyclopedia, *The Encyclopedia of American Political History*, can supply some interesting information. It has a good "lobbies and lobbyists" piece, and also a major article on "political corruption." If an encyclopedia has an index, use it. Your chances of finding something useful are increased manyfold if you check the index first.

If you consult your notes and your *topic breakdown,* you will see that you have narrowed your broad topic to a manageable size. From dictionaries and encyclopedias, you have procured definitions, introductory materials, some current and historical examples of political ethics "in action," along with related information on your topic. You are now ready and able to launch a broader search.

Step 3: Launch Your Search It is decision time. Are you going to search print or electronic sources? For best results, decide to do *both.* Where you begin is up to you. Let's say you decide upon periodicals, journals, and magazines first.

Your library may still subscribe to these print indexes: *Readers' Guide, Social Science Index,* and *PAIS (International Political Science Abstracts).* Even if the library has discontinued the current print subscriptions in favor of electronic ones, check out your subject headings in a three- to five-year-old print version. The advantage to this is fourfold:

- You will see full-page displays of multiple listings.

- You will see some retrospective (historical) coverage of your topic.

- You will see titles of some articles that will further inform you.

- You may encounter some useful *see also* subject headings that may help you zero in precisely on your target.

Get the serial *Editorials on File* for some real *point-of-view* observations. Everything you find in *Editorials on File* will be opinion. You will have to search more cleverly in this tool, for the topics you seek will be embedded in more general subject headings. Check the indexes bound at the end of a yearly volume. You may not find *gifts to politicians, political corruption,* or *lobbying,* but under *politics* you can find gems like these: "Bradley/McCain soft money rejection," and "Campaign contributor limit," each of which produces numerous columns of editorial reporting.

In searching articles, you should realize that there may be a heavy dose of bias or point of view in some of them. Although nothing is inherently wrong with point of view, or with having a personal agenda, it is dangerous for an inquirer not to know that the bias is there. A great source for keeping you informed about this is *Magazines for Libraries*[1], which will tell you about a periodical's editorial leanings. Here are some examples:

Periodical Title	Perspective
America	Jesuit/Catholic
Church and State	Historically Protestant
Commentary	American Jewish Committee
Commonweal	Catholic
Time	Major newsweekly; not opinion-free
New Republic	"Even-handed"
National Review	Conservative

[1] Cheryl LaGuardia, Bill Katz, and Linda S. Katz, *Magazines for Libraries,* 13th ed. (New Providence, NJ: RR Bowker LC, 2004.)

Let's Go Electronic

Online periodical databases, online catalogs, and the World Wide Web allow you to quickly locate materials in the vast universe of electronic information. Let's begin with some general information to help you search more effectively.

See Exercise 11.3: Looking Up a Career

First, know the difference between searching online catalogs or periodical databases, and the World Wide Web (WWW). Online catalogs and online periodical databases such as *LexisNexis* are accessed via the Internet; however, the WWW only acts as a "host" to disseminate the information. Information for a database is usually stored in a single location or server that is owned by a company such as Gale Research. Remember, much of the information found in online periodical databases may also be found in print. Human beings, not computers, do the indexing, so you can be fairly sure the information meets certain criteria for inclusion. The indexer may have made a determination as to the accuracy, currency, and authoritativeness of the article he or she is considering. Being careful to search terms relevant to your investigation will help you retrieve material you can use. Hence, searching online catalogs and online periodical databases is a lot like searching the print version of *Readers' Guide*—only much quicker.

Searching the World Wide Web, on the other hand, is a totally different story. You get different results from what you retrieve in a database. The information searched on the WWW is not found in a single location; it is an aggregation of information from the vast universe of servers across the globe. To search the WWW, you need to use a commercial search engine such as Google, Yahoo!, or AltaVista. Anybody and his mama can have a website on the WWW, and a lot of people do! So the information you retrieve from the WWW may be written by anyone—a fifth grader, a distinguished professor, a professional society, or a biased advocate! The super search engines send out little spiders or "bots" to find the words you requested in posted websites, and they may include in their files what their little electronic snoops find in the way of hits. So Joe Blow's uninformed comments on smoking and health could be right next to results from a rigorous scientific study. A critical component of Information Literacy is your ability to determine what you need, what informed people report, what will be useful for your needs, and what is up-to-date. After a few assignments, you will quickly learn when to use a database and when information from the WWW is sufficient.

For example, we chose the subject *political corruption* and got ten pages of hits on Google. The first page yielded these interesting results:

A great collection of links on politics and *political corruption*

A Libertarian Party legislative program on *political corruption*

Two Amazon.com ads

Two sources on *political corruption* in Illinois

A site that offers "research" on gambling and *political corruption*

An article by a political activist on corporate greed and *political corruption*

A university site offering information about *political corruption* in South Africa

An offer to sell you books on *political corruption*

While this is not quite a hodgepodge of suspect and reliable information, it surely demonstrates that one must be alert when examining Internet sources. Mixed in with credible reporting are sales promotions, a piece aimed at making you feel guilty for riding around in your Escalade, some antigambling exhortations, and useful links to other sources. The naïve may be duped.

You should know that an *index* and a *catalog* have completely different uses. A catalog—OPAC (online public access catalog)—tells you what books, magazines, newspapers, videos, and other materials your library owns. An index such as InfoTrac College Edition, *Readers' Guide,* or *America History and Life* allows you to search for articles within periodicals such as newspapers, magazines, journals, or even book chapters. To become a successful and savvy user of electronic resources, you need to establish and follow certain guidelines that work well for you:

1. Write out your topic or problem as a statement or question. "Is it *right* for *politicians* to take *gifts* from *lobbyists*?" "The influence of *lobbyists* or *PACs* has dramatically changed American *political ethics.*" (Keywords are italicized.)

2. Write down several terms or synonyms for your topic so that if one search does not yield any hits, you have some backup terms on hand. Search in a variety of ways. Will you get more hits by using a natural language search—*ethics in politics*—or using Boolean operators—*politics and ethics and gifts*?

3. Understand Boolean operators: *AND, OR*, and *NOT* are the most commonly used. The *OR* operator retrieves all synonyms: PACs, Political Action Committees, and Lobbyists. The *AND* operators retrieves only those records that have *BOTH* sets of terms (A & B) and gives you the intersection (C). (*Hint:* The computer always performs the OR function first.)

4. Know the difference between *subject* and *keyword* searches. **Subject searches** use a controlled vocabulary (one of those *legal* terms) list, and you need to know exact terminology in order to get good results: *political corruption—United States—history.* **Keyword searches** scan the entire record, including the title, notes, table of contents, or perhaps the abstract or the full text as well as the subject field: *political corruption AND United States AND history.* You may use Boolean operators in a keyword search.

5. The first time you use any electronic resource, be sure to consult the Help link provided by the catalog, database, or search engine to learn specific searching techniques. You will get better results if you use the tips and strategies suggested by the database provider.

6. Understand whether you need scholarly publications, popular magazines, or both. Do you know the difference?

Scholarly Journals	Popular Magazines
Long articles	Shorter articles
In-depth information on topic	Broad overview of topic
Written by experts in subject/field	Written by journalists or staff reporters
Graphs, tables, or photographs to support text	Lots of color photos of people and events
Articles "refereed" or reviewed by peers in field	Articles evaluated by editor
Documented by Works Cited or References page	No bibliography provided, but sources credited

7. Select the correct database for your particular subject or topic. Most libraries subdivide their databases by broad general categories such as Humanities, Social Sciences, Science and Technology, Business, Health and Medicine, and Government Information. Each library loads its subscription list onto its electronic resources page. Under "Social Sciences," for example, one might find *International Political Science Abstracts (PAIS)*, *America: History and Life*, and over twenty other databases. Then there are multidisciplinary databases that provide excellent material on most topics you encounter during your first years of college. If you are not sure which database to use, read the "About" feature or check with a librarian.

8. After you scan several entries, decide if (and how) you need to limit your search. You can often limit by date, language, journal name, full-text, refereed, or word(s) in title. If you get too many hits, you may want to add additional search terms. The search *(lobbyists or political action committees) AND gifts* yielded more than 400 hits. Adding *politicians* in a new search reduced the results to a manageable number. (*Hint:* If you get too few hits, omit a search term. It is really better to use a "building blocks" approach to searching: Begin with the general, and add terms to refine and limit search.) For certain current topics, your instructors often prefer information that is no more than five years old, and limiting by date helps you comply with this instruction.

9. Does the database have a thesaurus of terms you may search? Many databases—ERIC and PsychINFO are two that come to mind—have online and print thesauri to help you select the best search terminology and learn related terms.

10. Learn the quirks of databases or search engines you use often. In Google, for example, should you use Boolean operators (*politicians AND lobbyists*)? Can you use natural language to search "ethics in politics" or "gifts to politicians"? You truncate by using an asterisk to replace letters: **Lobby*** gets lobby, lobbying, lobbyist, and lobbyists. (*Hint:* Do not truncate too drastically; otherwise, you will get results you do not need; for example, "Lobb*" will also retrieve lobbed and lobbing.)

11. Check your library's electronic resources page to see what else is available to you online. Most libraries have links to other commonly used electronic reference tools. These include online encyclopedias, dictionaries, almanacs, style guides, biographical and statistical resources, and news sources.

Where to Go for Help

ON CAMPUS

The Library: Libraries offer a variety of forms of help, including library orientation sessions, workshops, and, on some campuses, actual credit-bearing courses to develop your library search and retrieval skills.

Specialized Libraries/Collections: If you are at a large university it will be very common to find multiple libraries that are part of separate "schools" or "colleges." For example, if you are a business administration major, your university will probably have a separate business library that you will need to learn to use in addition to the central library. This is true of many majors.

Technology Support Centers: Many campuses have such units staffed by personnel responsible for the institution's entire technology infrastructure. These units frequently offer noncredit workshops, help sessions, and so on. In addition, in larger universities many of the departments will have their own separate technology labs and centers where you can work and get assistance. It won't surprise you to find that much of the help provided to students comes from fellow students who are often ahead of their faculty in these skills! Some campuses also provide such assistance in residence halls where there may even be a "computing assistant" on a parallel with the "resident assistant."

Discipline-based Courses: Many majors will offer specialized courses in research methods in the particular discipline. You will find these listed in your campus catalog/bulletin. Usually you don't take these in your first year but check them out. And, of course, for those interested in credit-based courses dealing with technology, check out the courses in computer science.

ONLINE

Research and Documenting Sources: http://owl.english.purdue.edu/handouts/research/index.html. Purdue University has an excellent resource on documenting sources, both print and electronic.

If your city has a good library, use it as well as your campus library. You may find a world of additional information sources.

Looking Elsewhere

What if the library does not have the journal or book you really need for your research or project? The interlibrary loan department will be happy to borrow the materials for you. Most libraries allow you to submit your interlibrary loan requests online. Ask about this free service at your reference desk.

Are you a distance education student who cannot come into your college library in person? Libraries provide proxy access to their electronic materials to distance education students. To learn how, e-mail or call the reference desk.

Be sure to use the handouts and guides available in print at the reference desk or online. You will also find online tutorials and virtual tours of the library that enable you to become familiar with the collections, service points, and policies of your library.

Ask a Librarian—Librarians Thrive on Helping You

In your quest for information, you need to begin by assessing what you already know and explore for a while on your own. After ten or twenty minutes, however, you may decide to get some help. Ask a librarian. Librarians are information experts who are trained to assist and guide you to the resources you need. The librarians assigned to reference work or the ones who patrol the computer stations may look busy. That's because they are! But they are busy helping students with projects just like yours. You will not interrupt them when you ask for assistance, and 99 percent of them will help you promptly and ably.

Today, you can contact a reference librarian in several ways. You can e-mail a reference librarian and receive a quick reply. Or you may call the reference desk to ask a question such as, "Do you have a copy of the report *Problems with the Presidential Gifts System*?" Third, you can have a "live chat" online with a library staffer in real time. Fourth, you may come to the reference desk in person. (*Hint:* You will be most successful if you know your assignment and have negotiated it with your instructor. To be on the safe side, bring any written instructions you have to your meeting with the librarian. Tell the librarian what you have already tried—if anything.) If you are not successful in your first attempts at retrieving relevant information, ask for additional help. Finally, you may make an appointment to see a reference librarian. Remember, there are no silly questions. The information staff has heard them all, probably several times today, and a good librarian will treat your inquiry with respect.

See Exercise 11.4: Ethics I

See Exercise 11.5: Ethics II

About Plagiarism

In recent history, a serious candidate for the American presidency was forced to withdraw from the race when opponents discovered he had failed to give proper credit to a source he used in one of his speeches. Over "a little thing like that," he had to drop out. There is a cottage industry of lyrics lurkers just waiting to pounce upon music that is pirated. Everyone is on guard against idea thievery. Have you noticed that they will no longer sing the "real" "Happy Birthday" to you at the all-you-dare-to-eat buffet? Somebody owns the rights to that tune, and that somebody will sue the pants off the waitstaff and owners of the buffet. Do you know that every time Notre Dame scores a touchdown, ex-Beatle Paul McCartney may get a taste? Portions of that storied ND fight song have drifted into the public domain, but MPL Communications and Paul McCartney have secured copyright to parts of it. When ideas are put on paper, film, screens, or tape, they become intellectual property. Using those ideas without permission and/or without saying where you got them, and sometimes without paying for them, can cost you a grade, a course, a degree, maybe even a career. Plagiarism can mess you up big time. And it is so easy to avoid.

Just remember:

- If you use somebody else's exact published words, you have to give that person credit.

- If you use somebody else's published ideas, even if you use *your* words to express his or her ideas, you must give that person credit.

Your instructor will indicate the preferred method for doing this: with footnotes, or parenthetical references embedded in the text of your paper, and/or endnotes of some kind.

Even a novice student can meet the challenge of putting together information about complex topics composed by experts. Remember, part of your mastering Information Literacy includes **sorting**, and you probably have several categories to sort: definition, introduction, examples, problems, and conclusions. You may discard the less relevant. This not only reduces the pile into manageable sections, but is an important step in outlining your project. You may further sort by date (currency), authorship authority, and anecdote-versus-research criteria. This winnows the stock even further, but the best news is that you are practicing a real survival skill, not the false and temporary one of buying your assignment and just changing the name of the author.

Most instructors and most college officials consider plagiarism cheating. They seldom accept "I didn't know" as a defense. They may not acknowledge that plagiarism can be inadvertent or an *oops*! thing. Irony of ironies, the Internet, which can be a tempting repository of ideas to pilfer, now offers programs that help instructors identify plagiarized assignments! Turnitin.com and Plagiarism.org are examples of Internet help available to teachers.

Submitting a term paper purchased from one of the many thriving *term papers 'R' us* electronic mills invites one to:

1. Miss out on the genuine thrill of discovery and analysis that Information Literacy activities provide.
2. Give a false impression that he knows something he does not, a fakery that will catch up with him, in school and certainly on the job.
3. Flunk.
4. Get by, if the ruse is successful, but learn little or nothing.

As a student of English composition, comparative literature, or public relations, your task will be to manage information for projects and presentations, oral and written. In a few years, as a technical writer for IBM, a teacher of English at a school or university, or a campaign manager for a gubernatorial candidate, your task will be the same—to manage information for projects and presentations, oral and written. The Information Literacy skills you learn and employ as a student are the same ones that will serve you well as a successful professional.

ACHIEVE IT! *Setting Goals for Success*

Go back to the self-assessment at the beginning of this chapter and select one to three missed items from the list. Use these to formulate short-term goals for yourself. Be specific about what you want to achieve and when (for example, not "become an active learner," but "find an excuse to meet with at least one of my teachers sometime next week"). Remember to choose goals that are realistic and important to you. Think about what obstacles could get in the way of achieving your goals, and make your plan. In the event you were correct on all items, come up with one or more additional goals for this exercise.

	Goal 1	Goal 2	Goal 3
My short-term goal is . . .			
I want to achieve this goal by . . . (date)			
This goal matters because . . .			
I may encounter the following obstacles . . .			
My method for accomplishing this goal will be to . . .			

Set a Date. Put your deadline for achieving your goal(s) in your calendar. Count back ten days from your deadline and write a reminder for yourself.

Reassess. After your deadline passes, ask yourself: Did I meet this goal on time? What change has it made in my life? If I did not meet it, what am I planning to do about it?

TRY IT! *Exercises*

The exercises at the end of each chapter will help you sharpen what we believe are the critical skills for college success: writing, critical thinking, learning in groups, planning, reflecting, and taking action. You can further explore the topic of each chapter by using your PIN to complete the exercises on the website for this text: **http://success.wadsworth.com/gardner7e/**.

WORKING TOGETHER: Conducting a Group Search of the Library

In groups of three, plan a library visit. Before arriving, one member of the group should call a librarian and ask for a brief meeting.

When you arrive, ask the librarian to show you where to find the following items in the library: reference books, periodicals, and abstracts. Also ask how to use the databases on the library computers to aid and abet your searches.

Then, using three library computers, search for a topic of your choosing, and decide which databases each of you will search. Print out your findings, and share them with the class. What did you learn?

EXERCISE 11.1: Getting Comfortable in Your Library

1. Find out where your library displays current newspapers, and see if the one from your hometown is available.

2. Make an appointment with a librarian so you can really talk about your assignment in some depth.

3. Unobtrusively observe what goes on around the information services or reference area (not the circulation desk where they check out books). Watch at least five transactions. Watch the people who ask questions, and watch the staff people who answer them. Does it appear to you that the "customers" are getting friendly, competent help? Do the staff sit and point, or are they on their feet, and do they sometimes accompany inquirers to stack areas or work with them at the computer stations? How might this influence your strategy for getting help if and when you need it?

EXERCISE 11.2: Getting Oriented to Periodicals

1. Find out how your library arranges periodicals (magazines, journals, newspapers). It probably isn't obvious, so don't hesitate to ask. Why do you think the periodicals are organized this way?

2. Select an important event that was in the news the year you were born. To find out what was happening then, you might want to consult an almanac or ask a reference librarian to recommend a *chronology*. Find a contemporary (written at the time of the event) news report as well as a

scholarly article that analyzes the event in a journal. Describe the event. Why was it significant? Note some of the differences you found between the news report and the scholarly article.

EXERCISE 11.3: Looking Up a Career

1. Go online and find a schedule of courses for people who are getting degrees in library and/or information studies at some university. Here are a few: Michigan, Pittsburgh, North Carolina, South Carolina, Rhode Island, McGill, Emporia, Arizona.

2. Examine those course titles. Would you like to study those areas and topics?

3. Talk to a librarian. Ask him or her where he or she obtained the MLIS degree.

4. Find out if this librarian would recommend a career in information management to you.

5. Ask, "Do you like your job? Why?"

If you do this right, you will make a friend. It is good to have friends in Information Places.

EXERCISE 11.4: Ethics I

Because law school is so competitive, some students have been known to find, and then hide, information needed by a class for a recitation. They will locate an assigned or relevant brief, study it, then hide it by purposely "misshelving" it so only they can find and use it. Then in class, these students can respond to an instructor's question about a case; most of their classmates cannot because they could not access the hidden source. How ethical is this practice in your judgment? Why?

EXERCISE 11.5: Ethics II

The last time a student and his fifty classmates needed an article from a print journal, he discovered that someone had torn the article from the bound periodical. So he went for his second choice. Somebody had ripped off that article, too. "The next time I find some journal article I need, I am razoring it out," he told his classmates. Why do you think this student feels he must respond in this way? How could instructors help prevent such occurrences? How could librarians help students avoid these incidents? *Hint:* Access and pilferage are inversely correlated.

WRITE ABOUT IT! My Personal Journal

This is your place to sound off, to ask your teacher to clarify part of the lesson, or to write him or her about a minor or major crisis you're experiencing. Find out if your teacher wishes you to turn in your journals. Ask if they will remain confidential. Even if the journal isn't used in your course, you can still use the format to write about and reflect on issues regarding the class, yourself, or both.

1. *What was the one major lesson you learned from reading this chapter and/or from class lecture and discussion?*

2. *What are some other important lessons about this topic?*

3. *If you believe some parts of this chapter are unimportant, spell them out here and tell why you think so. (You even might want to discuss this point with your classmates to see if they came up with a similar list.)*

4. *If anything is keeping you from performing at your peak level academically, describe what it is. Your instructor may be able to help or refer you to someone else on campus who can help.*

5. *What behaviors are you planning to change after reading this chapter? Why?*

PART 4
Get Connected!

Majors and Careers: Making the Right Choices

In this chapter YOU WILL LEARN

- Tips for thriving in the current economy
- How majors, interests, and careers are linked—but not always
- How to plan a career itinerary for each year of college
- The skills employers seek in college graduates
- How to search for a job

How many careers can you find in this photo?

Philip Gardner of Michigan State University contributed his valuable and considerable expertise to the writing of this chapter.

Linda Salane of Columbia College, South Carolina, and Stuart Hunter of the University of South Carolina contributed vital material to earlier editions of this chapter.

SELF-ASSESSMENT
MAJORS AND CAREERS

Check the items below that apply to you:

1. ___ I have made contact with my career advisor.

2. ___ I have found useful information about careers on my college website.

3. ___ I have not declared a major, but am working with my academic advisor to make the decision that is right for me.

4. ___ I have declared a major, and I strongly believe I have made the right choice.

5. ___ I believe I have the necessary skills to pursue the major of my choice.

6. ___ I know how to prepare a good résumé.

7. ___ I know how to prepare an effective cover letter to accompany my résumé.

8. ___ I know how to perform well in an interview.

9. ___ I chose my major after careful consideration of market demands.

10. ___ I chose my major because I enjoy this subject.

If you checked seven or fewer of the items, find someone who can help you understand why all ten items are critical. At the end of this chapter, you will be asked to set personal goals for one or more of your unchecked items. If you checked all items, you will be asked to set other goals.

Sara entered college with thoughts of majoring in the sciences because she enjoyed working in the laboratory at her hometown hospital. Her concern for helping others led her to choose nursing as a major; it was a good career path that combined her two primary interests. Sara sailed through the first two years, excelling in her science classes. During her junior year, she began her nursing courses and spent more time observing nursing practice in her university's teaching hospital. After a summer working in various departments of her hometown hospital, Sara made an appointment with a career counselor. She confessed that she did not like being around sick people every day and wanted to change her major but had no idea what she wanted to do.

John explored several majors during his first two years in college by choosing his elective courses with careers in mind and talking to his friends. He settled on business as a major, focusing on finance. John had high aspirations of working for a Fortune 500 company and earning a six-figure salary within five years of graduation. He performed above average in his academic work, although he was occasionally slack with assignments and frequently missed class. He interned with two prominent companies and eventually accepted a position at a Fortune 500 company. To his surprise, he was laid off nine months later because he was frequently late for work and on two occasions missed important deadlines.

Like Sara and John, students planning for careers frequently encounter bumps along the way. Choosing a career is a process of discovery, involving a willingness to remain open to new ideas and experiences. Why begin thinking about your

career now? Because many of the decisions you make during your first year in college will have an impact on where you end up in the workplace.

Careers and the New Economy

In your lifetime, companies have restructured and taken on new shapes to remain competitive. As a result, major changes have taken place in how we work, where we work, and the ways we prepare for work while in college. The following characteristics in many ways define the economy of the early twenty-first century.

- **Global.** Increasingly, national economies have gone multinational, not only moving into overseas markets but seeking cheaper labor, capital, and resources abroad. Factories around the world built to similar standards can turn out essentially the same products. Your career is bound to be affected by the global economy, even if you never leave the United States. For example, when you call an 800 number for customer service, the person who talks to you may be answering your call in Iowa, Ireland, or India.

- **Innovative.** The economy depends on creativity in new products and services to generate consumer interest around the world. We are witnessing an unprecedented expansion of entrepreneurial businesses that have become the foundation for new job growth.

- **Boundaryless.** Teams of workers within an organization need to understand the missions of other teams because they most likely will have to work together. U.S. companies also have partners throughout the world. DaimlerChrysler, the result of a merger of the U.S. Chrysler organization with Germany's Mercedes-Benz group, is one example. Domestically, America Online's purchase of Time Warner created the largest communications group in the country. Crossing boundaries has other implications: You may be an accountant and find yourself working with the public relations division of your company, or you may be a human resources manager who does training for a number of different divisions and in a number of different countries. You might even find yourself moved laterally—to a unit with a different function—as opposed to climbing the proverbial career ladder.

- **Customized.** More and more, consumers are demanding products and services tailored to their specific needs. For example, you surely have noticed the seemingly endless varieties of a single brand of shampoo or cereal crowding your grocer's shelves. Such market segmentation requires constant adaptation of ideas to identify new products and services as new customer demands emerge.

- **Fast.** When computers became popular, people rejoiced because they believed the computer would reduce their workloads. Actually, the reverse happened. Whereas secretaries and other support workers once performed many tasks for executives, now executives are designing their own Power-Point presentations because, as one article put it, "it's more fun to work with a slide show than to write reports." For better or worse, "we want it now" is the cry in the workplace, with product and service delivery time cut to a minimum (the "just-in-time" policy). Being fast requires constant thinking outside the lines to identify new approaches to designing and delivering products.

- **Unstable.** Terrorist attacks, the war in Iraq, and the scandals within the highest ranks of major companies have destabilized the stock market and caused significant layoffs. Consumers are hesitant to travel. Increases in oil prices have a ripple effect through many sectors of the economy. Although things will get better, it's important to follow the economy, especially in times like these.

According to *Fast Company* magazine, the new economy has changed many of the rules about work. Leaders are now expected to teach and encourage others as well as head up their divisions. Careers frequently zigzag into other areas. People who can second-guess the marketplace are in demand. Change has become the norm. Workers are being urged to continue their learning, and companies are volunteering to play a critical role in the welfare of all people through sponsorship of worthy causes. With the lines between work and life blurring, workers need to find healthy balances in their lives. Bringing work home may be inevitable at times, but it shouldn't be the rule.

As you work, you'll be continually enhancing and expanding your skills and competencies. You can accomplish this on your own by taking evening courses or by attending conferences and workshops your employer sends you to. As you prepare over the next few years to begin your career, remember that:

- **You are, more or less, solely responsible for your career.** At one time, organizations provided structured "ladders" that employees could climb in their moves to higher professional levels. In most cases, such ladders have disappeared. Companies may assist you with assessments and information on available positions in the industry, but the ultimate task of engineering a career path is yours.

- **To advance your career, you must accept the risks that accompany employment and plan for the future.** Organizations will continually restructure, merge, and either grow or downsize in response to economic conditions. As a result, positions may be cut. Because you can be unexpectedly unemployed, it will be wise to keep other options in mind.

- **A college degree does not guarantee employment.** Of course, you'll be able to hunt for opportunities that are more rewarding, financially and otherwise, than if you did not have a degree. But just because you want to work for a certain organization doesn't mean there will always be a job for you there.

- **A commitment to lifelong learning will help keep you employable.** In college you have been learning a vital skill: how to learn. *Gradus,* the Latin root of *graduation,* means moving to a higher level of responsibility. Your learning has just begun when you receive your diploma.

Now the good news. Thousands of graduates find jobs every year. Some may have to work longer to get where they want to be, but persistence pays off. If you start now, you'll have time to build a portfolio of academic and **cocurricular experiences** that will begin to add substance to your career profile. Rudyard Kipling's couplet from *The Just So Stories* (1902) is an easy device for remembering how to navigate the fast economy for career success:

> *I keep six honest serving-men;*
>   *(They taught me all I knew);*
> *Their names are What and Why and When*
>   *And How and Where and Who.*

The knowledge to manage your career comes from you (why, who, how) and from an understanding of the career you wish to enter (what, where, when).

- **Why.** Why do you want to be a _____ ? Knowing your goals and values will help you pursue your career with passion and an understanding of what motivates you. When you speak with an interviewer, avoid clichés like " I'm a people person" or " I like to work with people." Sooner or later, most people have to work with people. And your interviewer has heard this much too often.

- **Who. Network** with people who can help you find out what you want to be. Right now, that might be a teacher in your major or an academic advisor or someone at your campus career center. Later, network with others who can help you attain your goal. Someone will always know someone else for you to talk to.

- **How.** Have the technical and communications skills required to work effectively. Become a computer whiz. Learn how to do PowerPoint presentations, build web pages, and create Excel spreadsheets. Take a speech course. Work on improving your writing. Even if you think your future job doesn't require these skills, you'll be more marketable with them.

- **What.** Be aware of the opportunities an employer presents, as well as such "threats" as **outsourcing** jobs. Clearly understand the employment requirements for the career field you have chosen. Know what training you will need to remain in your chosen profession.

- **Where.** Know the points of entry into the field. For example, you can obtain on-the-job experiences through internships, co-ops, or part-time jobs.

- **When.** Know how early you need to start looking. Find out if certain professions hire at certain times of the year.

Connecting Your Major and Your Interests with Your Career

Some students enter college knowing what they want to major in, but many others are at a loss. Either way, it's okay. At some point you'll ask yourself, "Why am I in college?" Although it sounds like an easy question to answer, it's not. Many students would immediately respond, "So I can get a good job or education for a specific career." The problem with this answer is that most majors do not lead into a specific career path or job. Looked at another way, you can enter most career paths from any number of academic majors. Marketing, a common undergraduate business major, is a field that recruits from a wide variety of majors including advertising, communications, and psychology. Sociology majors find jobs in law enforcement, teaching, and public service.

Today English majors are designing web pages, philosophy majors are developing logic codes for operating systems, and history majors are sales representatives and business managers. You do not have to major in science to gain admittance to medical school. Of course, you do have to take the required science and math courses, but medical schools seek applicants with diverse backgrounds. Only a few technical or professional fields, such as accounting, nursing, and engineering, are tied to specific majors.

TURNING POINT

The first time I went to college I was completely clueless about choosing a major. I chose engineering because I was good at math and science. It had nothing to do with what I was actually interested in, which should have been the deciding factor. The second time around I chose history, which was perfect for my interests since I will be pursuing a career in federal law enforcement.

Adam T.
University of Maryland, Baltimore County

Exploring your interests is the best way to choose an academic major. If you're still not sure, take the advice of Patrick Combs, author of *Major in Success,* who recommends that you major in a subject that you are really passionate about. Most advisors would agree.

There is more than one right way to get where you want to go. Before you answer the question, "Why am I in college?" consider these points.

- Am I here to find out who I am and study a subject that I am truly passionate about, regardless of whether it leads to a career?

- Am I here to engage in an academic program that provides an array of possibilities when I graduate?

- Am I here to prepare myself for a graduate program?

- Am I here to obtain specific training in a field that I am committed to?

- Am I here for to gain specific skills for a job I already have?

Do you have to know your goals right now? No, because you can use your first year, and even your second year, to explore your interests and see how they might connect to various academic programs. In the process of your exploration, you may later answer the question differently than you will during the first term on campus.

You can major in almost anything. As this chapter will emphasize, it is how you integrate school with extracurricular engagement and work experience that prepares you for a successful transition into your career. Try a major you think you'll like, and see what develops. But keep an open mind, and don't pin all your hopes on finding a career in that major alone.

Selecting a major and a career ultimately has to fit with your overall life goals, life purposes, values, and beliefs.

See Exercise 12.1: What Are Your Life Goals?

Exploring Your Interests

Dr. John Holland, a psychologist at Johns Hopkins University, has developed a number of tools and concepts that can help you organize the various dimensions of yourself so that you can identify potential career choices.

Holland separates people into six general categories based on differences in their interests, skills, values, and personality characteristics—in short, their preferred approaches to life.[1]

See Exercise 12.2: Finding Your Interests

Realistic (R) These people describe themselves as concrete, down-to-earth, and practical doers. They exhibit competitive/assertive behavior and show interest in activities that require motor coordination, skill, and physical strength. They prefer situations involving action solutions rather than tasks involving verbal or interpersonal skills, and they like to take a concrete approach to problem solving rather than rely on abstract theory. They tend to be interested in scientific or mechanical areas rather than cultural and aesthetic fields.

Investigative (I) These people describe themselves as analytical, rational, and logical problem solvers. They value intellectual stimulation and intellectual achievement and prefer to think rather than to act, to organize and understand rather than to persuade. They usually have a strong interest in physical, biological, or social sciences. They are less apt to be people oriented.

Artistic (A) These people describe themselves as creative, innovative, and independent. They value self-expression and relations with others through artistic expression and are also emotionally expressive. They dislike structure, preferring tasks involving personal or physical skills. They resemble investigative people but are more interested in the cultural or the **aesthetic** than the scientific.

Social (S) These people describe themselves as kind, caring, helpful, and understanding of others. They value helping and making a contribution. They satisfy their needs in one-to-one or small-group interaction using strong speaking skills to teach, counsel, or advise. They are drawn to close interpersonal relationships and are less apt to engage in intellectual or extensive physical activity.

Enterprising (E) These people describe themselves as assertive, risk taking, and persuasive. They value prestige, power, and status and are more inclined than other types to pursue it. They use verbal skills to supervise, lead, direct, and persuade rather than to support or guide. They are interested in people and in achieving organizational goals.

Conventional (C) These people describe themselves as neat, orderly, detail oriented, and persistent. They value order, structure, prestige, and status and possess a high degree of self-control. They are not opposed to rules and regulations. They are skilled in organizing, planning, and scheduling and are interested in data and people.

Holland's system organizes career fields into the same six categories. Career fields are grouped according to what a particular career field requires of a person (skills and personality characteristics most commonly associated with success in those fields) and what rewards those fields provide (interests and values most commonly associated with satisfaction). Here are a few examples:

Realistic (R) Agricultural engineer, electrical contractor, industrial arts teacher, navy officer, fitness director, package engineer, electronics technician, computer graphics technician

---

[1] Adapted from John L. Holland, *Self-Directed Search Manual* (Odessa, FL: Psychological Assessment Resources, 1985).

Investigative (I) Urban planner, chemical engineer, bacteriologist, flight engineer, genealogist, laboratory technician, marine scientist, nuclear medical technologist, obstetrician, quality-control technician, computer programmer, environmentalist, physician, college professor

Artistic (A) Architect, film editor/director, actor, cartoonist, interior decorator, fashion model, graphic communications specialist, journalist, editor, orchestra leader, public relations specialist, sculptor, media specialist, librarian, reporter

Social (S) Nurse, teacher, social worker, genetic counselor, marriage counselor, rehabilitation counselor, school superintendent, geriatric specialist, insurance claims specialist, minister, travel agent, guidance counselor, convention planner

Enterprising (E) Banker, city manager, FBI agent, health administrator, judge, labor arbitrator, salary and wage administrator, insurance salesperson, sales engineer, lawyer, sales representative, marketing specialist

Conventional (C) Accountant, statistician, census enumerator, data processor, hospital administrator, insurance administrator, office manager, underwriter, auditor, personnel specialist, database manager, abstractor/indexer

Your career choices ultimately will involve a complex assessment of the factors that are most important to you. To display the relationship between career fields and the potential conflicts people face as they consider them, Holland's model is commonly presented in a hexagonal shape (Figure 12.1). The closer the types, the closer the relationships among the career fields; the farther apart the types, the more conflict between the career fields.

Holland's model can help you address the problem of career choice in two ways. First, you can begin to identify many career fields that are consistent with what you know about yourself. Once you've identified potential fields, you can use the career library at your college to get more information about those fields, such as daily activities for specific jobs, interests and abilities required, preparation required for entry, working conditions, salary and benefits, and employment outlook. Second, you can begin to identify the harmony or conflicts in your career choices. This will help you analyze the reasons for your career decisions and be more confident as you make choices.

Never feel you have to make a decision simply on the results of one assessment. Career choices are complex and involve many factors; furthermore, these decisions are not irreversible. Take time to talk your interests over with a career counselor. Another helpful approach is to shadow an individual in the occupation that interests you to obtain a better understanding

See Exercise 12.3: Using Your Career Library

See Exercise 12.4: Investigating an Occupation

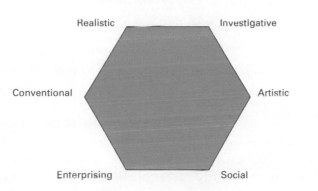

Figure 12.1
Holland's Hexagonal
Model of Career Fields

of what the occupation entails in terms of skills, commitment, and opportunity.

See Working Together:
Work-Shadowing

Factors Affecting Career Choices

Some people have a definite self-image when they enter college, but most of us are still in the process of defining (or redefining) ourselves throughout life. We can look at ourselves in several useful ways with respect to possible careers:

- **Values.** Today, more than ever, knowing your core values (your most important beliefs) will be important in shaping your career path. In a fast economy, having a strong rudder will help you steer through the turbulent times.

- **Interests.** Interests develop from your experiences and beliefs and can continue to develop and change throughout life. You may be interested in writing for the college newspaper because you wrote for your high school paper. It's not unusual to enter Psych 101 with a great interest in psychology and realize halfway through the course that psychology is not what you imagined.

- **Skills.** Skills, or the ability to do something well, can usually be improved with practice.

- **Aptitudes.** Aptitudes, the foundation for skills, are inherent strengths that are often part of your biological heritage or the result of early training. We each have aptitudes we can build on. Build on your strengths.

- **Personality.** Your personality makes you *you* and can't be ignored when you make career decisions. The quiet, orderly, calm, detail-oriented person probably will make a different work choice than the aggressive, outgoing, argumentative person.

- **Life goals and work values.** Each of us defines success and satisfaction in our own way. The process is complex and very personal. Two factors influence our conclusions about success and happiness: (1) knowing that we are achieving the life goals we've set for ourselves, and (2) finding that we gain satisfaction from what we're receiving from our work. If your values are in conflict with the organizational values where you work, you may be in for trouble.

Your Career Planning Timetable

The process of making a career choice begins with

- Understanding your values and motivations
- Identifying your interests
- Linking your personality and learning styles to those interests
- Using this information to decide on an appropriate academic major

This is a process you will begin in your first college year, and you will gradually complete it as you move closer to graduation. So don't worry about finishing this now. Not every student will fall into this pattern. While this is one way to begin investigating career possibilities, circumstances may force you to digress from this plan. Such circumstances might be a change of major, an unforeseen opportunity to intern, etc. You will need to periodically reevaluate your plan to better suit your needs and any special characteristics of your major.

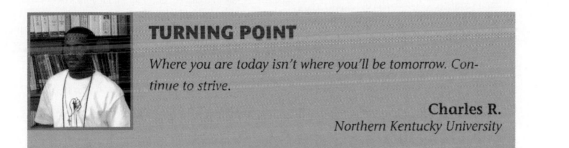

TURNING POINT

Where you are today isn't where you'll be tomorrow. Continue to strive.

Charles R.
Northern Kentucky University

Creating a Plan

A good career plan should eventually include:

- Researching possible occupations that match your skills, your interests, and your academic major

- Building on your strengths and developing your weaker skills

- Preparing a marketing strategy that sells you as a valued member of a professional team

- Writing a convincing résumé and cover letter

Table 12.1 on page 238 provides a guide to what you should be doing during each year of college; if you are in a two-year associate degree program, you will have to do more during your second year than this table suggests.

You may proceed through these steps at a different pace than your friends, and that's okay. What you want is to develop your qualifications, make good choices, and take advantage of any opportunities on campus to learn more about the career search. Keep your goals in mind as you select courses and seek employment, but also keep an eye out for unique opportunities; the route you think you want to take ultimately may not be the best one for you.

Two-Year College Students

If you are a student attending a two-year school and you plan to transfer to a four-year school, your career planning timeline will be compressed. You may find once you get to the four-year school that you have less time to make adjustments in your course work and career opportunities. The major stumbling block is the fact that transfers often arrive on their new campus with enough credits to declare a major; at this point changing your major again can be costly, because it will mean adding time, and therefore expense, until graduation.

Consider these early steps during your first three terms at your two-year school:

- Take a career interest inventory, and begin focusing on the career paths that most interest you.

TABLE 12.1   Your Career Itinerary

A. NO MATTER WHAT YEAR

- Get a job. Even a part-time job will develop your skills and may help you make decisions about what you like—and what you don't—in a work environment. In any job, you can learn vital skills such as teamwork, communication, and interpersonal, computer, and time management skills.

- Register with your college's online job listing system to find listings for part- and full-time, internship, co-op, and seasonal employment.

- Find on-campus interviewing opportunities for internships in your early years and for full-time employment after graduation.

- Network with family, friends, instructors, friends of family, and acquaintances to find contacts in your field(s) of interest so that you can learn more about those areas.

- Volunteer! This can help you explore careers and get some experience in an area that interests you as you help others.

- Conduct occupational and industrial research for your field or area of geographic interest. Look for other options within and beyond those fields.

- Explore career options through informational interviews (interviewing to find out about a career) and job shadowing (getting permission to observe someone as he or she works).

- Prepare a draft of your résumé and have it critiqued by your career counselor and perhaps by a professional in your chosen field.

- Get involved in clubs and organizations; work toward leadership positions.

- Explore overseas study possibilities to gain a global perspective and learn a foreign language.

- Attend career fairs to connect with employers for internships and other career-related opportunities as well as to develop a professional network.

B. FIRST YEAR OF COLLEGE

- Take the Holland Self-Directed Search or a similar interest inventory at your career center.

- Take a variety of classes to get exposure to various skill and knowledge areas.

- Attend your campus's annual job fair to see what is being offered.

- Talk to a career counselor about your skills, aptitudes, and interests. Find out what the career center offers.

C. SECOND YEAR OF COLLEGE

- Attend career fairs to learn more about employers who hire graduates in your major.

- Spend some time talking with your college advisor or career counselor to discuss your career plans.

D. THIRD YEAR OF COLLEGE

- Take an advanced computerized career assessment to discover further career options and to refine your career plans. Visit your career center.

- Take on a leadership role in a club or organization.

- Participate in mock interview activities to improve your interviewing skills.

- Attend workshops to learn more about résumé writing, looking for an internship, interviewing, and other job search skills.

- Explore the option of graduate school.

- Develop a top-ten list of employers of interest.

E. LAST YEAR OF COLLEGE

- Check on-campus interviewing opportunities on a daily basis, beginning in fall term. Interview with organizations recruiting for your major.

- Research organizations of interest to you, interview with those coming to campus, and contact human resources professionals who represent organizations that won't be on campus. Find out if you can interview.

- Attend career fairs to network with employers and set up interviewing opportunities.

- If you're thinking about graduate school, request applications early in the fall, and send them out throughout the fall term.

- Target your geographic areas of interest by contacting local chambers of commerce and using local newspapers, phone books, and Internet resources.

Source: Used by permission of Career Passport, Michigan State University.

- Visit with your career counselor to develop a short-term strategy to test your career interests.

- Enroll in a career-decision-making class.

- **Job shadow** a professional in the occupation(s) that you wish to enter.

- Attend a local job fair (if possible) to learn about potential job opportunities.

During your last term in your two-year school, consider these options:

- Determine what academic majors best match your occupational interests.

- Investigate whether the college or university you will attend next has the majors you need and any prerequisite requirements you will have to meet before you can enroll in your chosen major.

- If you still find you do not have a clear career focus by the time you transfer, meet again with the career advisor at your two-year school.

- Visit the campus you are transferring to prior to registration. Meet with both the career advisor and academic advisor as soon as possible.

Starting Your Search

Some first-year students come to college with a strong sense of self-knowledge and a focus on a specific interest. Others have no idea what their interests might be and are in the process of sorting through their values, interests, and skills in an attempt to define themselves. Such self-definition is an ongoing experience that, for many of us, continues well beyond college. It helps to keep a journal of such thoughts because reviewing these early interests later in life may lead to long-forgotten career paths just when you need them.

As you start examining your aspirations and interests, keep in mind these simple do's and don'ts:

Do's

1. Do explore a number of career possibilities and academic majors.
2. Do get involved through volunteer work, study abroad, and student organizations—especially those linked to your major.
3. Do follow your passion. Learn what you love to do, and go for it.

Don'ts

1. Don't just focus on a major and blindly hope to get a career out of it. That's backward.
2. Don't be motivated primarily by external stimuli, such as salary, prestige, and perks. All the money in the world won't make you happy if you hate what you're doing every day.
3. Don't select a major just because it seems "cool."

4. Don't choose courses simply because your roommate said they were easy. That's wasting your valuable time, not to mention tuition.

Getting Experience

Now that you have a handle on your interests, it's time to test the waters and do some exploring. Your campus has a variety of activities and programs in which you can participate to confirm those interests, check your values, and gain valuable skills. Here are some examples:

- **Volunteer/service learning.** Some instructors build service learning into their courses. Service learning allows you to apply academic theories and ideas to actual practice. Volunteering outside of class is also a valuable way to encounter different life situations and to gain work knowledge in areas such as teaching, health services, counseling, and tax preparation. A little time spent each week can provide immense personal and professional rewards.

- **Study abroad.** Spend at least a term taking courses in another country, and learn about a different culture at the same time. Learn to adapt to new traditions and a different pace of life. Some study abroad programs also include options for both work and service learning experiences.

- **Internships and co-ops.** Many employers now expect these work experiences. They want to see that you have experience in the professional workplace and have gained an understanding of the skills and competencies necessary to succeed. Check with your academic department and your career center on the internships that are available in your major. Many majors offer academic credit for internships. And remember: With an internship on your résumé, you'll be a step ahead of students who ignore this valuable experience.

- **On-campus employment.** On-campus jobs may not provide as much income as off-campus jobs, but on-campus jobs give you a chance to

practice good work habits. On-campus employment also brings you into contact with faculty and other academic professionals whom you can later consult as mentors or ask for references.

- **Student projects/competitions.** In many fields, students engage in competitions based on what they have learned in the classroom. Civil engineers build concrete canoes, and marketing majors develop campaign strategies, for example. They might compete against teams from other schools. In the process, they learn teamwork, communication, and applied problem-solving skills.

- **Research** An excellent way to extend your academic learning is to work with a faculty member on a research project. Research extends your critical thinking skills and provides insight on a subject above and beyond your books and class notes.

Types of Skills

One of the many important purposes and outcomes of your college experience is the acquisition of a combination of knowledge and skills. Two types of skills are essential to employment and to life: *content (mastery) skills* and *transferable skills*.

Content Skills

Content skills, often referred to as cognitive, intellectual, or "hard" skills, are acquired as you gain mastery in your academic field and include writing proficiency, computer literacy, and foreign language skills. Computing knowledge and ability are now perceived as given core skills at the same level of importance as reading, writing, and mathematics. In fact, employer expectations for computer knowledge and application continue to rise.

Content skills are comprised of specific types/sets of information, facts, principles, and rules. For instance, perhaps you have knowledge of the civil engineering of dam construction, or you have extensive experience working with telescopes. Maybe your work in the library and study of library science has trained you in several library databases. Or you may know the most common clinical diagnoses in psychology. We often forget some of the preparation we have gained that augments our mastery of specific academic material, especially statistics, research methods, foreign language aptitude, and computer literacy. You can apply all of this specific knowledge to jobs in a particular field or occupation.

Certain types of employers will expect extensive knowledge in your academic major before they will consider hiring you; for example, to get a job in accounting you must demonstrate knowledge of that field. However, for most college students, it's sufficient to have some fundamental knowledge; you will learn more on the job as you move from entry-level to more advanced positions.

Transferable Skills

Transferable skills are those skills that are general and apply to or transfer to a variety of settings. Examples of transferable skills include excellent public speaking skills, interpersonal understanding, seeing the big picture, grasping the application of a software program to a task, using available software to maintain homepages and transfer information, and providing leadership while working in a team environment. By category, these transferable skills are:

- Communication skills that demonstrate solid oral and listening abilities in addition to a good foundation in the basic content skill of writing.

- Presentation skills, including the ability to justify and persuade as well as to respond to questions and serious critiques of your presentation material.

- Leadership skills, or the ability to take charge or relinquish control according to the needs of the organization.

- Team skills, the ability to work cooperatively and collaboratively with different people while maintaining autonomous control over some assignments.

- Interpersonal abilities that allow you to relate to others, inspire others to participate, or ease conflict between coworkers.

- Personal traits, including showing initiative and motivation, being adaptable to change, having a work ethic, being reliable and honest, possessing integrity, knowing how to plan and organize multiple tasks, and being able to respond positively to customer concerns.

- Critical thinking and problem solving—the ability to identify problems and their solutions by integrating information from a variety of sources and effectively weighing alternatives.

- A willingness to learn quickly and continuously.

Transferable skills are valuable to many kinds of employers and professions. They give you flexibility in your career planning. Acquire as many transferable skills as you can during your college years.

You can gain transferable skills through a variety of activities. For example, volunteer work, study abroad, involvement in a student professional organization or club, and the pursuit of hobbies or interests can all build teamwork, leadership, interpersonal awareness, and effective communication abilities. Internships or career-related work will also be valuable opportunities to practice these skills in a "real world" environment.

Key Competencies

The skills described above and related work experience are what employers expect from today's college graduate. They are the minimum standards. Employers have begun to focus on the following additional key competencies that are critical for success in the new knowledge economy.

- **Integrity.** Being able to act in an ethical manner at work and in the community.

- **Innovation.** Being able to evaluate, synthesize, and create knowledge that will lead to new products and services. Realizing that changing perspective can open new possibilities, employers seek individuals who are willing to take some risks and explore innovative and better ways to deliver products and services.

- **Initiative.** Being able to recognize the need to take action, such as helping a team member, approaching a new client, or taking on assignments without being asked. Employers do not want new employees who will sit passively and wait for a supervisor to provide work assignments; they want people who will see what they have to do and do it.

- **Commitment.** Both employers and graduate schools look for a candidate's commitment to learning. They are looking for an expression of what you really love to study and that you are willing to learn on your own initiative. The best foundation for this competency is to be engaged in an academic program where you wake up every morning and are eager to go to class (test days aside).

Finding a Job

Do you hope to get a job while you are in college? Before you do, be really honest with yourself: is this something I *must* do in order to pay for college or is this something I *want* to do to maintain my life style and acquire the "things" I want? Or is it a combination of both? It is a fact that most students work. There are things you should know about working in college.

Work can support the attainment of your college goals, provide you with the financial means to complete college, and help structure your time so that you are a much better time manager. It can help you meet people who will later serve as important references for graduate school and/or employment. There are other upsides, too, but there are some very significant downsides. Working too much can interfere with your college success, your ability to attend class, do homework, and participate in many other valuable college activities, such as group study, foreign study and travel, and group activities. Take some time to determine how much you need to work, and stay within reasonable limits.

Stated very simply, students who work more than fifteen hours a week have a lower chance of finishing college successfully. And students who work on campus (as opposed to off campus) are also more likely to graduate from college.

On-Campus Jobs

One of the first things you may want to do when you get to campus is find a job on campus. If you have a **work-study award**, check with your student employment office for a listing of possible campus jobs for work-study students. Your career center can tell you how to access your college's online employment system. It probably handles all types of jobs. You may have to register, but that is easy, especially if you have a draft résumé to upload to the web-based form. College employment systems generally channel all jobs collected through faculty, advisors, and career counselors into one database, so it is convenient for you to identify jobs you may want to find.

Many campuses offer an on-campus job fair during the first weeks of the fall term. Even if you might not be interested at the time, a visit to the job fair will give you a great idea of the range and type of jobs available on campus. You will be pleasantly surprised to learn that there are more opportunities than washing dishes in the cafeteria. Job fairs usually include off-campus community employers as well, in part because your institution must spend some of the College Work Study funds it receives supporting off-campus work by students.

Off-Campus Jobs

The best places to start looking are your campus career center and/or your financial aid office. They may well have listings or websites with off-campus employment opportunities. Feel free to speak to a career counselor for suggestions.

- Learn the names of the major employers in your college's geographic area: manufacturers, service industries, resorts, etc. For example, some campuses are near to UPS distribution centers, which are well known for favoring college students for lucrative part-time union-scale wage jobs. Once you know who the major employers are, check them out, visit their websites, and learn more.

- Every state in the country has a state agency to collect and disseminate information about available employment opportunities. Check out the relevant website and see if your state agency has an office in the community where you are attending college.

- Another option is to visit employment agencies, particularly those that seek part-time, temporary workers. This is a convenient, low-risk (for both you and the employer) way to "shop" for a job, and to obtain flexible, short-term, low-commitment employment.

- Visit online job boards, and look at the classified ads in the local newspaper, in print or online. Also, don't forget the classifieds in the national press. Some national firms will have jobs that can be done part-time in your area or even from your own living space!

- Your own campus student newspaper may also be a good source of leads. Employers who favor hiring college students advertise in campus newspapers.

- Most jobs are never posted. Employers find it easier to hire people recommended to them by current employees, friends, or the person vacating the position. Faculty often hire students for their research labs based on performance in the classroom.

See Exercise 12.5: My Current Thinking about Career Choice

- Whom you know is important. Your friends who already work on campus or who have had an internship may be the best people to help you when you are ready to search for your job. Amazing as it sounds, nearly 50 percent of all jobs are found through family and friends.

College students often view the choice of a career as a monumental and irreversible decision. But, in its broadest sense, a career is the sum of the decisions you make over a lifetime. There is no "right occupation" just waiting to be discovered. Rather, there are many career choices you may find fulfilling and satisfying. The question to consider is: What is the best choice for me now?

Building a Résumé

Before you finish college, you'll need a résumé—whether it's for a part-time job, for an internship or co-op position, or for a teacher who agrees to write a letter of recommendation for you. Note the two résumés on the website for this book. One is written in chronological format, and the other is organized by skills. Generally, choose the chronological résumé if you have related job experience, and choose the skills résumé if you can group skills from a number of jobs or projects under several meaningful categories. Try for one page, but if you have a number of outstanding things to say and they run over, add a second page.

Writing a Cover Letter

Sending a cover letter, heed the following suggestions:

- **Find out whom to write to.** It's not the same in all fields. If you were seeking a marketing position at an advertising agency, you would write to the director of account services. If you were approaching General Motors regarding a position in their engineering department, you might write to either the director of human resources for the entire company or to a special human resources director in charge of engineering. Your academic advisor or career counselor can help you here. So can the Internet.

- **Get the most recent name and address.** Advisors or career counselors can guide you to references in your campus or career library. Never write "To whom it may concern."

- **Use proper format for date, address, and salutation,** as shown in the sample cover letter on the website for this book.

See Exercise 12.6: Writing a Résumé and Cover Letter

Interviewing

The first year of college does not seem like a time to be concerned about interviews, certainly not for a job. However, students often find themselves in interview situations shortly after arriving on campus: vying for positions on the student residence governing board, finding an on-campus job, competing for a second-year scholarship, applying for a residence hall assistant position, choosing a summer job opportunity, and being selected for an internship or as a research assistant. Preparing for an interview begins the moment you arrive on campus. Why? Because the interview is about you and how college has changed you. Students who only take a little time to actually reflect on who they are and how they have changed feel lost in an interview.

The purpose of the interview is to exchange information. The interviewer's goal is to evaluate you on your abilities and competencies in terms of what they are looking for. You are looking for a match between your interests and abilities and the position or experience you are seeking.

Here are some important tips as you prepare for an interview:

- Check with your career counselor to see if you can attend a mock interview. Usually designed only for seniors as they prep for their on-campus interviews, mock interviews help students strategize and feel comfortable with an interview. Even if a mock interview session is not available to you, the career center will have tips for handling an interview situation. Check your career center website for sample interview questions so that you can practice before an interview.

- Understand the nature of the "behavioral interview." In a **behavioral interview**, the interviewer assumes that your past experiences are good predictors of your future abilities and performance. They want to hear stories about things that you have done that can help them assess your skills and behaviors. Often there is not a right or wrong answer. Answering a behavioral question can be hard. A method used at Michigan State University and other campus to help students think through possible answers is the PARK method. The PARK method helps focus in on the most relevant aspects of your experience.

  P: The problem or situation (What happened?)

  A: The actions you took (What did you do?)

  R: The results or outcomes (What was the result of the actions you took?)

  K: The knowledge you gained and applied through the experience (What did you learn? How did you apply it?)

- Dress appropriately. Dress codes vary depending on the location of the interview, and the type of interview (professional, student focused). First impressions matter, so as a rule of thumb always dress neatly. You can be somewhat casual for some types of employers, but remember that professional attire is common. It is better to dress too professionally (in a dress suit and polished shoes) than too informally.

Where to Go for Help

ON CAMPUS

Your College Website: Search your campus career resources. Larger campuses may have specialized career service centers for specific professional schools and clusters of majors. Often student professional organizations, academic advisors, and departments will provide relevant career information on their websites.

Career Center: Almost every college campus has a career center where you can obtain free counseling and information on careers. A career professional will work with you to help you define your interests, to interpret results of any assessment you complete, to coach you on interview techniques, and to critique your résumé. It's important to schedule an appointment. By the end of your first year you should be familiar with the career center—where it is located and the counselor responsible for your academic major or interests. You might also find opportunities for internships and practicums here.

Academic Advising: More and more advisors have been trained in what is known as "developmental" advising, or helping you see beyond individual classes and working to help you plan a career search. Talking to your advisor is often the best place to start. If you have not declared a major—which is true of many first-year students, your advisor may be able to help you with that decision as well.

Faculty: On many campuses, faculty take an active role in helping students connect academic interests to careers. A faculty member can recommend specific courses in this regard. Faculty in professional curricula, such as business and other applied fields, often have direct contact with companies and serve as contacts for internships. If you have an interest in attending graduate school, faculty sponsorship is critical to admission. Developing a faculty mentor can open doors in a number of ways.

The Library: Some campuses have a separate library in the career center staffed by librarians whose job it is to help you locate career-related information resources. Of course, all campuses have a main library containing a wealth of information on careers. This is perhaps the best place to start, and the person who will be glad to help you is your reference librarian at the main desk. If you are a student on a large university campus, there will often be additional libraries that are specific to certain professional schools and colleges within the university such as business, education, law, medicine, music, engineering; these are also excellent sources of career information.

Upper-class Students: Students further along in college can help you navigate courses and find important resources. They may also have practical experience gained from internships and volunteering. Since they have tested the waters, they can alert you to potential pitfalls or apprise you of opportunities.

Student Organizations: Professional student organizations that focus on specific career interests meet regularly throughout the year. Join them now. Not only will they put you in contact with upper-class students, but their programs often include employer representatives, helpful discussions on searching for internships or jobs, and exposure to current conditions in the workplace.

ONLINE

Career Center: First go to your career center's home page and check its resources. It will have identified the best resources for students on your campus and have hot links directly to those pages.

Occupational Information Network: http:\\ online.onecenter.org. This federal government site has information on occupations, skill sets, and links to professional sites for selected occupations. This is a great place to get started thinking about your interests.

Mapping Your Future: www.mapping-your-future.org. This comprehensive site provides support for those who are just starting their career exploration.

The Riley Guide: www.rileyguide.com. This is the best site for employment resources such as interviewing, job search strategies, etc.

ACHIEVE IT! *Setting Goals for Success*

Go back to the self-assessment at the beginning of this chapter and select one to three unchecked items from the list. Use these to formulate short-term goals for yourself. Be specific about what you want to achieve and when (for example, not "become an active learner," but "find an excuse to meet with at least one of my teachers sometime next week"). Remember to choose goals that are realistic and important to you. Think about what obstacles could get in the way of achieving your goals, and make your plan. In the event you checked all items in the self-assessment, come up with one or more additional goals for this exercise.

	Goal 1	Goal 2	Goal 3
My short-term goal is . . .			
I want to achieve this goal by . . . (date)			
This goal matters because . . .			
I may encounter the following obstacles . . .			
My method for accomplishing this goal will be to . . .			

Set a Date. Put your deadline for achieving your goal(s) in your calendar. Count back ten days from your deadline and write a reminder for yourself.

Reassess. After your deadline passes, ask yourself: Did I meet this goal on time? What change has it made in my life? If I did not meet it, what am I planning to do about it?

TRY IT!   *Exercises*

The exercises at the end of each chapter will help you sharpen what we believe are the critical skills for college success: writing, critical thinking, learning in groups, planning, reflecting, and taking action. You can further explore the topic of each chapter by using your PIN to complete the exercises on the website for this text: **http://success.wadsworth.com/gardner7e/.**

WORKING TOGETHER: Work-Shadowing

Do this exercise with a partner. With your Career Center, arrange to "work-shadow" a professional in a field you think you might be interested in. Spend at least a day, preferably longer, actually observing this person. Reflect on what you observe. Did the work environment meet your expectations? Are you more or less interested in this occupation? You and your partner should then share your conclusions with the rest of the class.

EXERCISE 12.1: What Are Your Life Goals?

The following list includes some life goals that people set for themselves.[2] This list can help you begin to think about the kinds of goals you may want to set. Check the goals you would like to achieve in your life. Next, review the goals you have checked, and circle the five you want most. Finally, review your list of five goals, and rank them by priority—1 for most important, 5 for least important. Be prepared to discuss your choices in class if your instructor asks.

____ The love and admiration of friends
____ Good health
____ Lifetime financial security
____ A lovely home
____ International fame
____ Freedom within my work setting
____ A good love relationship
____ A satisfying religious faith
____ Recognition as the most attractive person in the world
____ An understanding of the meaning of life
____ Success in my profession
____ A personal contribution to the elimination of poverty and sickness
____ A chance to direct the destiny of a nation
____ Freedom to do what I want
____ A satisfying and fulfilling marriage
____ A happy family relationship
____ Complete self-confidence
____ Other:

EXERCISE 12.2: Finding Your Interests

A. Complete an interest inventory, such as the Holland Self-Directed Search, at your career center or online at www.self-directed-search.com/taketest. html (there is a fee of around $9.95 to get your results); or visit the *Princeton*

2Adapted from James D. McHolland, *Human Potential Seminar* (Evanston, IL: 1975). Used by permission of the author.

Review and take the Career Quiz (www.review.com). List your top five occupational interests based on this instrument.

B. Interview a professional in one of these fields. In the interview, find out as much as you can about the education required, skills needed to be successful, typical career opportunities, and outlook for the future. Identify five key points you learned from the interview.

EXERCISE 12.3: Using Your Career Library

Visit your campus Career Center's "career library." Many of these libraries have materials organized by Holland's model that you learned about in this chapter. This method of organization enables you to research careers that are compatible with your personality type. Talk to a career counselor about some of the jobs that interest you. Summarize in writing what you have learned.

EXERCISE 12.4: Investigating an Occupation

Using your campus Career Center, library, or the Internet, learn about a particular occupation in which you have an interest. Find out: (1) the U.S. Department of Labor projections for demand for members for this occupation; (2) the minimum entry level credentials for this occupation; (3) the salary level ranges from entry level through advanced experience levels; (4) what the work environment is like; and (5) two other important characteristics of the occupation.

EXERCISE 12.5: My Current Thinking about Career Choice

Make a list of your personal interests, preferences, characteristics, strengths, and skills. Match the list to the skills and interests demanded by successful people in a field that interests you. Note other influences that may be drawing you to that career (such as your parents' preferences). Share the notes you have prepared with a career counselor, and get some feedback on how you and your career interests mesh.

EXERCISE 12.6: Writing a Résumé and Cover Letter

A. Following the models on the website for this book, prepare two résumés, using the chronological model for one and the skills model for the other. Then, using either model, write another résumé that projects what you would like your résumé to contain five years from now.

B. Using your career center or campus library, find a professional whose career path matches your major/career interests. Write this person a cover letter to go with your résumé, and turn it in to your instructor.

WRITE ABOUT IT! My Personal Journal

This is your place to sound off, to ask your teacher to clarify part of the lesson, or to write him or her about a minor or major crisis you're experiencing. Find out if your teacher wishes you to turn in your journals. Ask if they will remain confidential. Even if the journal isn't used in your course, you can still use the format to write about and reflect on issues regarding the class, yourself, or both.

1. *What was the one major lesson you learned from reading this chapter and/or from class lecture and discussion?*

2. *What are some other important lessons about this topic?*

3. *If you believe some parts of this chapter are unimportant, spell them out here and tell why you think so. (You even might want to discuss this point with your classmates to see if they came up with a similar list.)*

4. *If anything is keeping you from performing at your peak level academically, describe what it is. Your instructor may be able to help or refer you to someone else on campus who can help.*

5. *What behaviors are you planning to change after reading this chapter? Why?*

Relationships

In this chapter YOU WILL LEARN

- How relationships are important to your success in college
- How to determine whether a serious relationship is right for you
- What kinds of relationships should be off-limits for college students
- How relationships with parents or family members change
- How to live safely on campus

What clues can you find to the relationship(s) between these two people?

Tom Carskadon of Mississippi State University contributed his valuable and considerable expertise to the writing of this chapter.

SELF-ASSESSMENT
RELATIONSHIPS

Check the items below that apply to you:

1. ____ I am seeking out friendships with other students who are different from me.

2. ____ I am aware of the pros and cons of getting serious with a romantic partner while I'm in college.

3. ____ I understand the difficulties of maintaining a long-distance relationship.

4. ____ I know why a romantic relationship with an instructor or supervisor is off-limits.

5. ____ I understand it's important to know myself before thinking about marriage.

6. ____ It's important to maintain good communication with my family members while I'm in college.

7. ____ I understand that electronic relationships can be both valuable and dangerous.

8. ____ I have established ground rules for living together with my roommate.

9. ____ I have thought seriously about whether fraternity and sorority membership is right for me.

10. ____ I know some commonsense approaches to avoiding sexual assault.

If you checked seven or fewer of the items, find someone who can help you understand why all ten items are critical. At the end of this chapter, you will be asked to set personal goals for one or more of your unchecked items. If you checked all items, you will be asked to set other goals.

What does success in college have to do with relationships? As college instructors, we have learned from our own experience and the experiences of others that the quality of the relationships students build or maintain in college can have a positive, or a negative, effect on their ability to concentrate, to feel self-confident, and to do well academically.

Relationships take many forms. If you live on campus, one of your primary relationships, for better or worse, will be with your roommate or suitemates. Another important set of relationships will be with your instructors. You may choose to get to know your instructors or to ignore them, but the quality of the interaction you have with them may affect how well you do academically.

Whether you live on or off campus, you will continue a relationship with your parents or other family members. Sometimes the assumptions and expectations that define family interactions will change, and negotiating that change is not always easy. Parents sometimes have trouble letting go of a son or daughter, and you may feel that they still want to control your life. If you are an adult with a spouse or partner, going to college will give you a new identity that may be uncomfortable or threatening to your partner. If you have children, they may not understand what's going on as your needs for study time become as important as their needs for your undivided attention.

If your friends also go to college, you will have a great deal to share and compare. But if your friends are not college students, they, too, may be threatened as you

take on a new identity. And of course, romantic relationships can support you or can create major conflict and heartbreak, depending on whether your partner shares your feelings and whether the relationship is healthy and affirming or dysfunctional.

This chapter will help you to think about all the different kinds of relationships that affect college students, including those that are established or maintained at a distance or electronically.

College Friends

One of the best things about going to college is meeting new people. In fact, scholars who study college students have found that you'll learn as much—or more—from other students whom you meet as you'll learn from professors. Although not everyone you hang out with will be a close friend, you will likely find a few relationships that are really special and may even last a lifetime. Although in the beginning it's tempting to associate with other students who dress like you dress, talk like you talk, and listen to the same music you enjoy, you will be missing out on one of the best aspects of college life if you associate only with people just like you. It's a good idea to diversity—to make friends with students who are from another state, another country, or a different racial or ethnic group.

See Exercise 13.1: Thinking about Your Friends

Getting Serious

Not only does college present an opportunity to make lots of new friends; it is also a place where romantic relationships flourish. Although some beginning college students are married or are already in long-term committed relationships, others may have their first serious romance with someone they meet on campus. If you are gay, lesbian, bisexual, or transgendered, you may find it much easier to meet romantic partners in college than you ever have before. Whatever your sexual orientation, the opportunities are like a banquet table;

some people choose to sample lots of different choices, and others settle in with just one person. Either way, you'll grow and learn a great deal about yourself and those with whom you become involved. You'll also be able to get insight regarding what it would be like to live with or marry your partner before you take that life-changing step.

You may have a relationship you feel is really special. Should you make it exclusive? Don't do so just because being with each other exclusively has become a habit. Ask yourself why you want this relationship to be exclusive. For security? To prevent jealousy? To build depth and trust? As a prelude to a permanent commitment? Before you make the decision to see only each other, make sure it is the best thing for each of you. You may find that you treat each other better and appreciate each other more when you feel free to explore other relationships.

If you are seriously thinking about marriage or long-term commitment, consider this: Studies show that the younger you are, the lower your odds of a successful marriage. Also, "trial marriage" or living together does not decrease your risk of later divorce.

TURNING POINT

Before college, my romantic partner was my priority. At that time we had more time to spend and less time apart. Now that I am in college, I place much more emphasis on other responsibilities such as school and work. It takes effort to maintain good grades and still come to terms with the fact that things have changed. There are times, for instance, when I have a break during class hours or have a day off, and I find myself giving some of that time to a school-related project and some to him. Since we have open communication, the change in shift encourages us to do the maintenance to understand and accept the situation.

Lisa H.
Bronx Community College

Above all, beware of what might be called the "fundamental marriage error": marrying before both you and your partner are certain about who you are and what you want to do in life. Many 18- to 20-year-olds change their outlook and life goals drastically as they get older. If you want to marry, the person to marry is someone you could call your best friend—the one who knows you inside and out, the one you don't have to play games with, the one who prizes your company, the one who over a period of years has come to know, love, and respect who you are and what you want to be.

See Exercise 13.2:
Looking for Love

Long-Distance Relationships

Relationships change significantly when they turn into long-distance romances. Many students arrive at college while still romantically involved with someone back home or at another school.

College is an exciting scene with many social opportunities. If you restrict yourself to a single, absent partner, you may miss out on a lot, and this often leads to cheating or resentment. Our advice for long-distance relationships: Keep seeing each other as long as you want to, but with the freedom to pursue other relationships, too.

If the best person for you turns out to be the person from whom you are separated, this will become evident, and you can reevaluate the situation in a couple of years. Meanwhile, keep your options open.

Breaking Up

In a national study of 5,000 college students conducted in 2001 by researchers at the University of California, Los Angeles, 29 percent reported they had ended a romantic relationship during their first year in college.

Breaking up is hard, but if it is time to end a relationship, do it cleanly and calmly. Don't be impulsive or angry. Explain your feelings and talk them out. If you don't get a mature reaction, take the high road; don't join someone else in the mud. If you decide to reunite after a trial separation, be sure enough time has passed for you to evaluate the situation effectively. If things fail a second time, then you really need to move on.

If your partner breaks up with you, you may find yourself sad, angry, or even depressed. Remember that you're not alone. Almost everyone has been rejected or "dumped" at some time or another. Let some time pass, be open to moral support from your friends and your family, and if necessary, pay a visit to your college counselor or a chaplain. These skilled professionals have assisted many students through similar experiences, and they can be there for you as well. Bookstores and your library will have good books on the topic of surviving a breakup. One that you might want to consider is *How to Survive the Loss of a Love* by Melba Cosgrove, Harold H. Bloomfield, and Peter McWilliams.

You may want to remain friends with your partner, especially if you have shared and invested a lot in your relationship. It will be difficult to be friends, however, until both of you have healed from the hurt and neither of you wants the old relationship back. That usually takes a year or two.

Off-Limits!

Some romantic relationships are strictly off-limits. Never become romantically involved with your teacher or someone who works over or for you. If your partner is a person who has power and influence over you, the "romance" may, in fact, be that person's need for power. Many of these relationships end in a breakup. And imagine how you would feel if your ex, who might be hurt or bitter or even want you back, still had control over your grades or your job! If you date a subordinate, when the relationship ends you may find yourself accused of sexual harassment, fired, or sued. Even dating coworkers is risky; it will be much harder to heal from a breakup if you must continue to work together.

Marriage and Parenting during College

Can marriage and parenting coexist with being a college student? The answer, of course, is yes, although linking all these identities—student, spouse, parent—will not be easy. If you are married or in a long-term relationship, with or without children, you will need to be an expert at time management. The expectations of your roles may come into conflict, and you'll need to know what comes first and when. Most college instructors will be flexible with requirements if you have genuine problems with meeting a deadline because of family obligations. But it's important that you explain your situation; don't expect your instructors to be able to guess what you need if you don't tell them. As the demands on your time increase, it is important that you and your partner share the burdens equally. You can't expect to be spoiled or pampered just because you're a student.

Occasionally, deciding to go to college can create conflict within a family. Partners and children can be threatened and intimidated if you take on a new identity and set of responsibilities. Financial pressures are likely to put an extra strain on your relationship, so both you and your partner will have to work hard at attending to each other's needs. Be sure to involve your family members in your decision to go to college; bring them to campus at every opportunity, let them read your papers and other assignments, and see if your partner can take a course too. Finally it's very important to carve out time for your partner and your family just as carefully as you schedule your work and your classes.

TURNING POINT

Since starting college I have found it difficult to balance family, school, and work. I have three children. My new saying is that there are not enough hours in the day to get everything done that needs to be done. In the beginning I was always exhausted and feeling sick. It is constantly a fight, but I cut back my work schedule and I let the chores slide. I cannot do everything by myself. I do not go out unless it is for family activities. Since I took some of the load of responsibility off my shoulders, I have felt much better and get more studying accomplished.

Tiffany E.
Lorain County Community College

See Exercise 13.3: Balancing Relationships and College

You and Your Parents

Whether you live on campus or at home, becoming a college student will change your relationship with your parents. Home will never be quite the same, and you will not be who you were before. You may find that your parents hover over you and try to make all your decisions on your behalf such as your major, where and how much you work, and what you do on weekends. In fact, some instructors and administrators have coined the term "helicopter parents" to describe these hovering behaviors. You also may find that it's really hard for you to make any decisions without talking to your parents first. While communication with your parents is important, don't let them make all your decisions. Your college or university will help you draw the line between what decisions should be yours alone, and what decisions your parents should help you make.

Many college students are living in blended families so that more than one set of parents is involved in their college experience. If your father or mother has remarried, you will have to negotiate with both family units.

So how can you have a good relationship with your parents during this period of transition? A first step in establishing a good relationship with them is to be aware of their concerns. The most common are:

- Parents fear you'll harm yourself. You may take risks that make older people shudder. You may shudder, too, when you look back on some of your stunts. Sometimes your parents have reason to worry.

- Parents think their daughter is still a young innocent. Yes, the old double standard (differing expectations for men than women, particularly regarding sex) is alive and well.

- Parents know you're older but may continue to picture you as a child. Somehow, the parental clock always lags behind reality. Maybe it's because they loved you so much as a child, they can't erase that image.

- Parents mean well. Most love their children, even if it doesn't always come out right; very few are really indifferent or abusive.

- Parents fear that you might change in some negative way and lose the values that characterize your family unit and your culture.

- Finally, parents fear that you may never come home again, and for some college students, this is exactly what happens.

Remember that parents have genuine concerns that you will understand even better when you become a parent yourself. To help your parents feel more comfortable with your life in college, try setting aside regular times to update your parents on how college and your life in general are going. Ask for and consider their advice. You don't have to take it.

Not every family is ideal. If your family is close and supportive, you are blessed. If it is even halfway normal, you will succeed. But some families are truly dysfunctional. If love, respect, enthusiasm, and encouragement are just not in the cards, look around you. Other people will give you these things, and you can create the family you need. With your emotional needs satisfied, your reactions to your real family will be much less painful.

See Exercise 13.4: Student-Parent Gripes

What should you do if the family falls apart? Divorce happens, and sometimes it happens when a son or daughter goes to college. It's hard to proceed with life as usual when the family foundation seems to be cracking under you. But remember that your parents are adults. If your father and mother decide to go their separate ways, it's not your fault, and you should not feel responsible for their happiness. Even if you're successful in determining appropriate boundaries between your life and theirs, it's hard not to worry about what's happening at home. So seek help from your campus's counseling center or from a chaplain if you find yourself in the midst of a difficult family situation.

Roommates

Adjusting to a roommate is another significant transition experience. You may make a lifetime friend or an exasperating acquaintance you wish you'd never known. A roommate doesn't have to be a best friend—just someone with whom you can share your living space comfortably. Your best friend may not make the best roommate. In fact, many students have lost friends by rooming together.

With any roommate, it's important to establish your mutual rights and responsibilities in writing. Many colleges provide contract forms that you and your roommate can use. If things go wrong later, you will have something to point to.

If you have problems, talk them out promptly. Talk directly—politely but plainly. If problems persist, or if you don't know how to talk them out, ask your residence hall counselor for help; he or she is trained to help resolve roommate conflicts.

Normally, you can tolerate (and learn from) a less than ideal situation; but if things get really bad and do not improve, insist on a change. If you are on campus, talk to your resident assistant (RA) or to a professional counselor in your campus's counseling center.

See Exercise 13.5:
Roommate Gripes

Electronic Relationships

Through electronic mail, message boards, interest groups, dating sites, and chat groups, it is possible to form relationships with people you have never met. This can be fun as well as educational. You can interact with a variety of people you might never have the opportunity to meet otherwise.

For instance, imagine having regular e-mail correspondence with the following group, as one student does, who all met online: an aspiring screenwriter in New Jersey, an undercover narcotics agent in Michigan, a professional animator in Georgia, a college teacher in Connecticut, a high school student in Arizona, a librarian in California, a strip-club bartender in Tennessee, a mother in Pennsylvania, a police officer in Australia, a flight attendant in Illinois, an entrepreneur in Louisiana, a psychologist in Colorado, a physician in training in Texas, a schoolteacher in Canada, and college students in five states and three countries.

The downside? Electronic relationships may be more transient and unpredictable than "real world" ones. People may not be what they seem. Meeting them in real life may be delightful—or disastrous. Some people assume false "electronic" identities. You could literally be corresponding with someone in prison! Be very cautious about letting strangers know your name, address, telephone number, or other personal information, and about considering face-to-face meetings.

If you find yourself spending hours every day with people on the computer, you are probably overdoing it. Don't let electronic relationships substitute for "real" ones in your life. But as a way to meet interesting people and stay in touch with those far away, electronic relationships can be uniquely valuable. By the way, your college counselors have experience helping students suffering from "computer addiction."

Finding Your Niche through On-Campus Involvement

Colleges and universities can seem huge and unfriendly places, especially if you went to a small high school or grew up in a small town. In order to feel comfortable in this new environment it is important for you to find your comfort zone or niche. It's not hard to find the place where you belong, but it will take some initiative on your part. Consider your interests, the high school activities that you enjoyed most, and choose some activities to explore. You might be interested in getting on an intramural team, in performing community service, in running for a student government office, or in getting involved in the residence hall. Or you might prefer becoming involved in a more structured campuswide club or organization.

Almost every college has numerous organizations you may join; usually you can check them out through activity fairs, printed guides, open houses, web pages, and so on. Or even better, consider attending a meeting before you make the decision to join. See what the organization is like, what the expectations of time and money are, and whether you feel comfortable with the members. And remember, new students who become involved with at least one organization are more likely to survive their first year and remain in college.

To Greek or Not to Greek?

Greek social organizations are not all alike, nor are their members. Fraternities and sororities can be a rich source of friends and support. Some students love them. But other students may find them philosophically distasteful, too demanding of time and finances, and/or too constricting. Members of Greek organizations sometimes associate exclusively with other members, and this exclusivity causes them to miss opportunities to have a more varied group of friends. Greek rush (member recruitment) on your campus may happen before you've had an opportunity to decide whether you want to go Greek or to determine which fraternity or sorority is right for you. There is nothing wrong with delaying a decision about Greek membership. In fact, we would argue that it's better to learn your way around campus and meet lots of different friends before committing to a particular organization. Fraternities and sororities are powerful social influences, so you'll definitely want to take a good look at the upper-class students in them. If what you see is what you want to be, consider joining. If not, steer clear.

If Greek life is not for you, there are many other ways to make close friends. Many campuses have residence halls or special floors for students with common interests or situations, such as first-year students; honors students; students in particular majors; students with strong ethnic or religious affiliations; students who shun tobacco, alcohol, and drugs; students interested in protecting the environment; and so on. Check these out—often they provide very satisfying experiences.

Working on Campus

One of the best ways to develop relationships with instructors and administrators on your campus is to get an on-campus job. Generally, your on-campus supervisors will be much more flexible than off-campus employers in helping you balance your study demands and your work schedule. It's possible that you won't make as much money working on campus as you would in an off-campus job, but the relationships you'll develop with influential people who really care about your success in college and who will write those all-important reference letters make the loss of a little money well worth it.

Involvement off Campus

As a first-year student, much of your time will be spent on campus, either going to class, studying, or hanging out with other students. But there are also ways that you can get involved in the surrounding community. Consider being involved in a community service project. Your college may offer service opportunities as part of first-year courses (**service learning**), or your campus's division of student affairs may have a "volunteer" or "community service" office.

While working at an off-campus job is one way to meet new people in the community, it's important that you restrict work to a reasonable number of hours per week (no more than fifteen). It's also better if your work experiences relate to your intended major, and that's more likely to happen when you work on, rather than off, campus. For instance, if you are a pre-med major, you might be able to find on-campus work in a biology or chemistry lab. That work would help you to gain knowledge and experience, and to make connections with faculty experts in these fields. Although you may feel that you have to work in order to pay your tuition or living expenses, many college students work too many hours just to support a lifestyle—to buy or maintain a brand-new car or new stereo system. It's important to maintain a reasonable balance between work and study. Don't fall into the trap of thinking, "I can do it all." Too many college students have found that "doing it all" means they don't do anything very well.

Co-op Programs

Many schools have **co-op programs** in which you spend some terms in regular classes and other terms in temporary job settings in your field. Although they usually prolong your education somewhat, these programs have many advantages. They offer an excellent preview of what work in your chosen field is actually like, thus helping you know if you have made the right choice. They give you valuable experience and contacts that help you get a job when you finish school; in fact, many firms offer successful co-op students permanent jobs when they graduate.

Alternating work and school terms may be a more agreeable schedule for you than eight or ten straight terms of classes would be, and it may help you keep your ultimate goal in mind. Co-op programs can help you pay for school, too; some co-op students, especially in technical fields, make almost as much, or even more, during their co-op terms as their professors do!

Living Safely on Campus

One of the goals of this chapter is to help you establish the kinds of relationships on campus that will give you a sense of belonging, comfort, and safety. But college is not a cocoon. Campuses are part of the real world and as such pose certain dangers and risks. It is therefore very important that you take reasonable steps to ensure your own safety and the safety of your property.

Protecting against Sexual Assault

Anyone is at risk for being raped, but the majority of victims are women. By the time they graduate, an estimated one out of four college women will be the victim of attempted rape, and one out of six will be raped. Most women will be raped by someone they know, a date or acquaintance, and most will not report the crime. Alcohol is a factor in nearly three-fourths of the incidents. Whether raped by a date or a stranger, a victim can suffer long-term traumatic effects.

Tricia Phaup of the University of South Carolina offers this advice on avoiding sexual assault:

- Know what you want and do not want sexually.
- Go to parties or social gatherings with friends, and leave with them.
- Avoid being alone with people you don't know very well.
- Trust your intuition.
- Be alert to subtle and unconscious messages you may be sending and receiving.
- Be aware of how much alcohol you drink, if any.

If you are ever tempted to force another person to have sex:

- Realize that it is never okay to force sex on someone.
- Don't assume that you know what your date wants.
- If you're getting mixed messages, ask.
- Be aware of the effects of alcohol.
- Remember that rape is morally and legally wrong.

If you have been raped, regardless of whether you choose to report the rape to the police or get a medical exam, it is very helpful to seek some type of counseling to begin working through this traumatic event.

The following people or offices may be available on or near your campus to help you deal with a sexual assault: campus sexual assault coordinator, local rape crisis center, campus police department, counseling center, student health services, women's student services office, local hospital emergency rooms, and campus chaplains.

Personal Safety

You cannot plan for every potential event that might cause injury. Each day we read about new tragedies such as airplane crashes, accidental drownings, or violent crimes. But we still fly and swim and go out at night, often finding

ourselves alone with individuals we do not know and putting ourselves at risk. Here are some commonsense ways to increase your personal safety on campus:

See Working Together: Safety Do's and Don'ts

- Find out if your campus has an escort service that provides transportation or an escort during the evening hours. Do you know the hours and days of the service and how to arrange for an escort? Use this service if you must walk alone during evening hours.

- Write down and memorize the telephone number for your campus police.

- If your campus has emergency call boxes, locate them and learn how to operate them.

- Be aware of the dark and isolated areas on campus and avoid them, especially when walking alone.

- If you're a jogger, avoid jogging alone, and wear reflective clothing for your own safety in traffic.

- If you go away overnight or for the weekend, let someone know where you will be and how to reach you in case of an emergency or in case someone becomes concerned about you.

Your behavior both on and off campus should be proactive in terms of reducing the opportunity for a crime or injury to occur. Make safety measures part of your everyday routine.

Protecting Your Property

Most campus crime involves theft. As you and other students bring more valuable items to campus, such as computers, the opportunity for theft grows. Books can be stolen and sold at bookstores, and if not properly marked, will never be recovered. Computers and other electronic items such as PDAs and iPods can be traded for cash. To reduce the chances that your property will be stolen, follow these basic rules:

- Record serial numbers of electronic equipment, and keep the numbers in a safe place.

- Mark your books on a preselected page with your name and an additional identifier such as a code other than a PIN, Social Security, or driver's license number. Remember the page where you entered the information.

- Never leave books or book bags unattended.

- Lock your room, even if you are only going out for a minute.

- Do not leave your key above the door for a friend or roommate.

- Report lost or stolen property to the proper authority, such as the campus police.

- Don't tell anyone you don't know well about your valuable possessions.

- Keep your credit or bank debit card as safe as you would your cash.

Where to Go for Help

ON CAMPUS

Counseling Center: Professional college counselors help students think and talk about their relationships and then support and advise them regarding the most appropriate courses of action. It is normal to seek such assistance. It's a rare student who doesn't have some relationship challenges in college, whether it is with roommates, friends, family, romantic partners, teachers, supervisors, and so forth. This kind of counseling is strictly confidential (unless you are a threat to the safety of yourself or others) and usually is provided at no charge, which is a great fringe benefit of being in college. But unless this is an emergency, be prepared to wait for your first appointment; these centers have very heavy caseloads due to an increase in student stressors.

Chaplains: An often underrecognized resource in terms of getting help on relationship matters is a session or more with a campus chaplain. Almost all colleges, both public and private, have religiously affiliated ministerial chaplains, who usually have specialized training in pastoral counseling. They also organize and host a number of group activities in campus religious centers that you might want to take advantage of.

Your academic advisor may be able to refer you to an appropriate chaplain or you can seek out the one who represents your faith. Most chaplains are happy to see students for counseling whether or not you attend their church, synagogue, or mosque.

Student Organizations: The variety of student groups designed to bring together students to help them with their relationships is virtually unlimited. You may find everything from Greek letter social fraternities and sororities to single parents with children to gay/lesbian/bisexual/transgendered students.

ONLINE

The University of Chicago's "Student Counseling Virtual Pamphlet Collection": http://counseling.uchicago.edu/vpc/virtulets.html. This website takes you to dozens of websites about problems in relationships. Browse among the many links to see if any information applies to you.

Healthy Romantic Relationships during College: http://www.utexas.edu/student/cmhc/booklets/romrelations/romrelations.html. The University of Texas Counseling Center offers an online brochure that explores the ups and downs of romantic relationships.

ACHIEVE IT! *Setting Goals for Success*

Go back to the self-assessment at the beginning of this chapter and select one to three unchecked items from the list. Use these to formulate short-term goals for yourself. Be specific about what you want to achieve and when. Remember to choose goals that are realistic and important to you. Think about what obstacles could get in the way of achieving your goals, and make your plan. In the event you checked all items in the self-assessment, come up with one or more additional goals for this exercise.

	Goal 1	Goal 2	Goal 3
My short-term goal is . . .			
I want to achieve this goal by . . . (date)			
This goal matters because . . .			
I may encounter the following obstacles . . .			
My method for accomplishing this goal will be to . . .			

Set a Date: Put your deadline for achieving your goal(s) in your calendar. Count back ten days from your deadline and write a reminder for yourself.

Reassess: After your deadline passes, ask yourself: Did I meet this goal on time? What change has it made in my life? If I did not meet it, what am I planning to do about it?

TRY IT!   *Exercises*

The exercises at the end of each chapter will help you sharpen what we believe are the critical skills for college success: writing, critical thinking, learning in groups, planning, reflecting, and taking action. You can further explore the topic of each chapter by using your PIN to complete the exercises on the website for this text: **http://collegesuccess.wadsworth.com/gardner7e/.**

WORKING TOGETHER: Safety Do's and Don'ts

Working in groups of four to five, create a list of "do's" and "don'ts" related to the safety of people and property on your campus. Share your group's ideas with others and create a master list. Brainstorm ways to make this list available to others on your campus and to next year's incoming class of first-year students.

EXERCISE 13.1: Thinking about Your Friends

Take inventory of the people you hang out with. Fill in the chart, using letters to identify the persons you are describing.

Friend	Things you have in common	Ways you are different	Basis for friendship	Negatives about friendship
A.				
B.				
C.				
D.				

Now review the list. If the negatives tend to outweigh the positives, what should you do about your friendship with this person? Remember that your friends have influence on you, for better or worse.

EXERCISE 13.2: Looking for Love

Read the "personal" ads in your campus or local newspaper. What questions/ issues/themes do people seem to be writing about most? What does this tell you about people's needs in relationships? Bring your paper to class and share what you learned with a small group of your classmates.

EXERCISE 13.3: Balancing Relationships and College

A. For personal writing and group discussion: If you are in a relationship, what are the greatest concerns you have about balancing your educational responsibilities with your responsibilities to your partner? What can you do to improve the situation? If the balance poses a serious problem for you, is there someone on campus from whom you can seek counseling? If you need counseling but aren't sure where to turn, ask your instructor to help you find that person.

B. If you are married and have children, write a letter to your spouse and another to your children explaining why you must often devote time to your studies instead of to them. Don't deliver the letters; read them first and keep revising them until they sound realistic and convincing. Attempt to strike a sensible balance between your commitments to family and to your future academic and professional growth. If there are other married students in your class, share letters and get reactions. Then decide whether it's prudent to actually share these thoughts with your spouse and children.

EXERCISE 13.4: Student-Parent Gripes

A. Student Gripes. In surveys, these are the most frequent student gripes about parents. Check the ones that hit closest to home for you:

___ Why are parents so overbearing and controlling, telling you everything from what to major in to whom to date?

___ Why do parents treat you like a child?

___ Why are parents so overprotective?

___ Why do parents worry so much?

___ Why do parents complain so much about money?

___ Why do parents say they want to know what's going on in your life; but when you tell them everything, they go ballistic and you never hear the end of it?

Reflect on the gripes you checked. Why do you think your parents are like that? How do your thoughts affect your relations with them?

B. Parent Gripes. Looking at things from the other side, students report the following as the most common gripes their parents have about them. Check off those that ring true for your parents:

___ Why don't you call, e-mail, and visit more?

___ Why don't you tell us more about what is going on?

___ When you are home, why do you ignore us and spend all your time with your friends?

___ Why do you spend so much time with your boyfriend (or girlfriend)?

___ Why do you need so much money?

___ Why aren't your grades better, and why don't you appreciate the importance of school?

___ Why don't you listen to us about getting into the right major and courses? You'll never get a good job if you don't.

___ What have you done to yourself? Where did you get that (haircut, piercing, tattoo, style of clothes, and so on)?

___ Why don't you listen to us and do what we tell you? You need a better attitude!

How do such statements affect you? What do you think your parents are really trying to tell you?

EXERCISE 13.5: Roommate Gripes

Residence hall authorities report that the most common areas of conflict between roommates are those listed below. Check those that are true for you:

___ One roommate needs quiet to study; the other needs music or sound.

___ One roommate is neat; the other is messy.

___ One roommate smokes; the other hates smoking.

___ One roommate brings in lots of guests; the other finds them obnoxious.

___ One roommate brings in romantic partners and wants privacy—or goes at it right in front of the other. The other is uncomfortable and feels "sexiled."

___ One roommate likes it warm; the other likes it cool.

___ One roommate considers the room a place to have fun; the other considers it a place to study.

___ One roommate likes to borrow; the other isn't comfortable lending.

___ One roommate is a morning person; the other is a night owl.

___ One roommate follows all the residence hall rules; the other breaks them.

Review this list and pick the areas where you and your roommate have conflict. Write about what you can do to improve the situation.

WRITE ABOUT IT! My Personal Journal

This is your place to sound off, to ask your teacher to clarify part of the lesson, or to write him or her about a minor or major crisis you're experiencing. Find out if your teacher wishes you to turn in your journals. Ask if they will remain confidential. Even if the journal isn't used in your course, you can still use the format to write about and reflect on issues regarding the class, yourself, or both.

1. What was the one major lesson you learned from reading this chapter and/or from class lecture and discussion?

2. What are some other important lessons about this topic?

3. If you believe some parts of this chapter are unimportant, spell them out here and tell why you think so. (You even might want to discuss this point with your classmates to see if they came up with a similar list.)

4. If anything is keeping you from performing at your peak level academically, describe what it is. Your instructor may be able to help or refer you to someone else on campus who can help.

5. What behaviors are you planning to change after reading this chapter? Why?

Diversity: Appreciating Differences among Us

In this chapter YOU WILL LEARN

- The concepts of culture, diversity, ethnicity, and multiculturalism
- The value of gaining knowledge of various ethnic and cultural groups
- The role colleges play in promoting diversity
- How to identify and cope with discrimination and prejudice on campus

What is this building? Who uses it? What clues are guiding your response?

Juan J. Flores of Folsom Lake College contributed his valuable and considerable expertise to the writing of this chapter.

SELF-ASSESSMENT:
DIVERSITY: APPRECIATING
DIFFERENCES AMONG US

Check the items below that apply to you.

1. ___ I feel capable of working or interacting with any group of people.

2. ___ I can define the terms *ethnicity*, *culture*, and *multiculturalism*.

3. ___ I identify with specific ethnic and cultural groups.

4. ___ I am open to differing worldviews and values.

5. ___ I feel uneasy when I hear and/or tell jokes aimed at "other groups."

6. ___ I have had some exposure to ethnic and/or cultural groups outside of my own.

7. ___ I make an effort to relate to people with mental, physical, or psychological disabilities.

8. ___ I have examined and understand my biases and prejudices and how they have developed.

9. ___ I actively seek out opportunities to learn about cultures and groups other than my own.

10. ___ I value the need to understand concerns that affect a variety of groups.

If you checked seven or fewer items, find someone who can help you understand why all ten items are critical. At the end of this chapter, you will be asked to set personal goals for one or more of your unchecked items. If you checked all items, you will be asked to set other goals.

At the core of the United States' value system is the belief that America is a place in which all people are welcome. This principle has created the richly diverse society in which we live today. The quilt that is America has been sewn with the fibers of many countries, and its colors shine vibrantly across the nation's landscape.

You may have heard of the "melting pot" and "salad bowl" theories: The melting pot theory promoted the blending of all cultures into one American identity, and the salad bowl theory emphasized the importance of retaining individual cultural identity while living among others. As ethnic communities began advocating for their needs in the wake of the civil rights movement, the importance of promoting cultural identity grew as did the value of celebrating diversity in American society. Today, ethnic and cultural communities have developed in every city and every state in the country, each preserving components of their heritage and providing support to their residents.

Colleges and universities serve as a microcosm of the "real world" ahead—a world that requires us all to work, live, and socialize with various ethnic and cultural groups. In few other settings do the multitudes of ethnic and cultural groups interact in such close proximity to one another as they do on a college campus. Whether you are attending a four-year university or community college, you will be exposed to new experiences and opportunities, all of which enhance learning and a deeper sense of understanding.

Through self-assessment, discovery, and open-mindedness, you can begin to understand your perspectives on diversity. This work, although difficult at times, will enhance your educational experiences, personal growth, and development. Thinking critically about your personal values and belief systems will allow you to have a greater sense of belonging, and make a positive contribution to our multi-cultural society.

The Importance of Understanding Diversity

Diversity is the variation of social and cultural identities among people existing together in a defined setting. As your journey through higher education unfolds, you will find yourself immersed in this mixture of identities. Regardless of the size of the school, going to college brings together people with differing backgrounds and experiences but with common goals and aspirations. Each person brings to campus a unique life story, upbringing, value system, view of the world, and set of judgments. You can tap these differences to enhance your experiences in the classes you will take, the organizations you will join, and the relationships you will cultivate. For many students, college is the first time they are exposed to so much diversity. Learning experiences and challenges await you both in and out of the classroom. It's a chance to learn, not only about others, but also about yourself.

Self-reflection and discovery are the keys to learning. The self-assessment activity asks some tough questions about your views of diversity, biases, and prejudices, some of which may make you a bit uncomfortable. It is safe to say that we all house some sort of bias and prejudice toward some group or value system. To say otherwise is unrealistic. Yet it is what we do with our individual beliefs that separates the average person from the racist, the bigot, and the extremist. Being open and honest in answering the self-assessment provides a foundation on which we can build. Armed with our responses, we can begin to uncover how our views came about and whether or not we want to take steps to adjust them.

TURNING POINT

Junior colleges offer a wide spectrum of diversity. Differences in cultures and beliefs become especially apparent in class debates because people's ideologies are influenced by their backgrounds. I have learned a lot more about the world around me and of the struggles that different minority groups face just by listening to my fellow students in class discussions.

Megan D.
Cabrillo College

The Sources of Our Beliefs

So just how do we acquire our **biases** and beliefs? Many of our beliefs grow out of personal experience and reinforcement. If you have had a negative

experience or endured a series of incidents involving members of a particular group, you're more likely to develop negative judgments. For example, a police officer whose involvement with a particular group has usually been negative may view all individuals of that group negatively, and this will affect his or her future interactions with them. Having repeatedly heard that "everyone" associated with a group, be it ethnic, religious, or cultural, is "that way," you may buy into that stereotype with no reason to question it. A child growing up in an environment where dislike and distrust of a group of people is openly expressed may subscribe to those very judgments without having any direct interaction with those being judged.

It may be that prior to college, you had not intermingled and coexisted with most of the groups you now see on campus. This is certainly not a shortcoming, just the background and individual experience you bring to the situation. Your community at home may not have been very diverse, although it may have *seemed* so before you got to college. Whatever your background, college gives you an opportunity to learn from a lot of different people and about their perspectives. From your roommate in the residence hall, to your lab partner in your biology class, to the members of your sociology study group, your college experience will be enriched if you allow yourself to be open to the possibility of learning from all cultural groups.

Ethnicity and Culture

Often the terms ethnicity and culture are used interchangeably, although in reality, their definitions are quite distinct. Throughout this chapter, we will use these two words together and in isolation. Before we start using the terms, it's a good idea to define them so that you're clear on what they actually mean.

Ethnicity refers to a quality assigned to a specific group of people historically connected by a common national origin or language. For example, let's look at one of the largest ethnic groups, Latinos. Latin America encompasses over thirty countries from North America to the Caribbean, all of which share the Spanish language. A notable exception is Brazil. While the national language is Portuguese, Brazilians are considered Latinos. The countries also share many traditions and beliefs, with some variations. However, we shouldn't generalize with this or any ethnic group. Not every Latino who speaks Spanish is of Mexican descent, and not every Latino speaks Spanish. Acknowledging

that differences do exist within ethnic groups is a big step in becoming ethnically aware.

Culture is defined as those aspects of a group of people that are passed on and/or learned. Traditions, food, language, clothing styles, artistic expression, and beliefs are all part of culture. With this definition in mind, we can begin to rethink the common mistake that assigns culture to only ethnic expressions. Certainly ethnic groups are also cultural groups: They share common language, foods, traditions, art, and clothing, which are passed from one generation to the next. But numerous other, nonethnic cultural groups can fit this concept of culture, too. Think of the hip-hop community. In the hip-hop world there is a common style of dress, specific terminology used in hip-hop circles, and musical and artistic expression—all of which can be learned and passed on to others.

Although we don't use the term "race" much in this chapter, it's important to discuss the idea of race as it is commonly used in everyday language. Race refers to biological characteristics shared by groups of people and includes hair texture and color, skin tone, and facial features. Making generalizations about someone's racial group affiliation is risky. For instance, can we say that an individual with black, tightly woven hair is always of African or African American descent? Certainly not, since a person of Dominican or Puerto Rican or Cuban descent can have that same black, tightly woven hair texture. Even people who share some biological features—such as similar eye shape or a dark skin—may be ethnically very distinct. For instance, people of Asian descent are not necessarily ethnically and culturally alike, since Asia is a vast region encompassing such disparate places as Mongolia, India, and Japan. Likewise, people of African descent may be from very different backgrounds; the African continent is home to fifty-three countries and hundreds of different languages, and Africans are genetically very diverse.

Making assumptions about group identity based on traits can do more harm than good. It helps to try to become more aware of the variations of ethnicity, culture, and race in our society. No one is expecting you to be an expert, now or in the future. In fact, with so much variation within groups themselves, to think you have it all figured out is fooling yourself. The best approach is to avoid making quick judgments or assigning group labels.

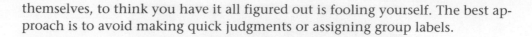

Multiculturalism in Higher Education

See Working Together:
Reflections on Identity

Acknowledging the importance of diversity to education, colleges and universities have begun to take the concepts of diversity and apply them to student learning opportunities. **Multiculturalism** is the active process of acknowledging and respecting the various social groups, cultures, religions, races, ethnicities, attitudes, and opinions within an environment. We see this in efforts by colleges to embrace an **inclusive curriculum**. Today, you can find courses with a multicultural focus in many departments of your college or university, and many have been approved to meet graduation requirements. Many colleges and universities have established specific academic departments with majors in the areas of gender studies, ethnic and cultural studies, and religious studies, to name a few.

The college setting is ideal for promoting multicultural education because it allows students and faculty of varying backgrounds to come together for the common purpose of learning and critical thinking. According to Gloria Ameny-Dixon, multicultural education in higher education can:

- Increase problem-solving skills through different perspectives applied to reaching solutions

- Increase positive relationships through achievement of common goals, respect, appreciation, and commitment to equality

- Decrease stereotyping and prejudice through contact and interaction with diverse individuals

- Promote the development of a more in-depth view of the world[1]

But colleges and universities were not always interested in the promotion of diversity and multiculturalism. As colleges and universities developed in the United States during the seventeenth and eighteenth centuries, they were geared primarily to white males. At that time, women and people of color were not given the encouragement, or even the right, to attend, although a few from both groups did find their way onto campus. Many historically black colleges developed in the southern part of the country in the 1800s. Their initial purpose was to teach freed slaves to read and write. The historically black colleges were the first opportunity most African Americans in this country had to participate in higher education. The nineteenth century gave rise to women's colleges, which were created in response to the increasing interest among women in higher education. The women's colleges developed programs of interest to their students and created services that focused on women's specific needs.

The desegregation of schools in the 1950s and the civil rights movement of the 1960s and 1970s opened the doors to colleges and universities for women and students of color. Groups that up to this time had not interacted in an academic setting began to coexist on campus. Women now outnumber men in college and university enrollment, sometimes 2 to 1, and students of color have entered higher education at increased rates as well, although the

---

[1] Gloria M. Ameny-Dixon, "Why Multicultural Education Is More Important in Higher Education Now Than Ever: A Global Perspective." McNeese State University (www.nationalforum.com).

percentage in attendance is still less than in the general population. Under-represented groups such as women and minorities had found their voices and advocated for increased educational opportunities for themselves and their communities.

College students have led the movement for a curriculum that reflects disenfranchised groups such as women, people of color, the elderly, the disabled, and gays and lesbians. By protesting, walking out of classes, and staging sit-ins at the offices of campus officials, students have demanded the hiring of more ethnic faculty, the creation of Ethnic Studies departments, and a variety of programs for academic support. These support services have increased academic access for students from ethnic and cultural groups and have helped them stay in school. They exist today in the form of multicultural centers, women's resource centers, enabling services, and numerous academic support programs. Multiculturalism in education has continued to gain momentum since it began during the civil rights movement of the 1960s. By expressing their discontent over the lack of access and representation in many of society's niches, including higher education, ethnic and cultural groups have achieved acknowledgment of their presence on campus.

We encourage you to include some courses in your schedule that have a multicultural basis. The purpose of general education is to expose you to a wide range of topics and issues, so that you can develop and express your own views. Your challenge is to step out of your comfort zone and enroll in courses that you may have not taken in the past and that sound interesting. You will gain new perspectives and may also gain an understanding of issues affecting your fellow students and community members. This awareness will serve you well in your career path; just as your college or university campus is diverse, so, too, is the workforce you will be entering in a few years. The multicultural skills you gain while in college will pay off throughout your life. Use your time in college to polish these skills and continually put them to good practice.

Diversity on Campus

See Exercise 14.1: Looking at the Curriculum

See Exercise 14.2: Diversity on Your Campus

At this point, you should be aware of the representation of numerous groups on your campus. Perhaps you have actively begun to notice the diversity around you as well as the many forms it encompasses. Be it religious affiliation, sexual orientation, gender, ethnicity, age, culture, or ability, your campus provides the opportunity to interact with and learn along with a kaleidoscope of individuals.

Student-run organizations can provide you with multiple avenues to express ideas, pursue interests, and cultivate relationships. According to our definition of culture, all student-run organizations are, in fact, culturally based and provide an outlet for the promotion and celebration of that culture. Let's take, for instance, two very different student groups, a Muslim Student Union and an Animation Club, and apply the components of culture to them. Both groups promote a belief system common among their members: The first is based on religious beliefs and the second on what constitutes animation as an art form. Both have aspects that can be taught and passed on: the teachings of the Muslim faith and the rules and techniques used in drawing. Both utilize language specific to their members. Most campus organizations bring like-minded students together and are open to those who want to become involved.

One of the best things about being on campus is the many events available to you. In order to promote learning and discovery not only inside the classroom but outside as well, colleges and universities provide programming that highlights ethnic and cultural celebrations such as Chinese New Year and Kwanzaa, topics of gender such as Taking Back the Night, and a broad range of entertainment, including concerts, art exhibits, and many others. These events expose you to new and exciting ideas and viewpoints, enhancing your education and challenging your current views.

Most college students, especially first-year students, are seeking their own niche and their own identity. Coming to college is a trying time filled with anticipation, nervousness, and optimism. Whether you are attending a school

TURNING POINT

Coming from a very homogeneous community, attending college has given me a chance to meet students from many backgrounds. It is great to share ideas with a very diverse group of people.

Kathleen B.
Lorain County Community College

close to home or farther away, living at home or on your own for the first time, the adjustment can be overwhelming. Many students have found that becoming involved in campus organizations eases the transition and helps them make connections with their fellow students.

Fraternities and Sororities

Fraternities and sororities provide a quick connection to a large number of individuals, a link to the social pipeline, camaraderie, and support. There are many fraternities and sororities to choose from, each differing in philosophy and philanthropy. Fraternities and sororities created by and for specific ethnic groups have existed for a number of years and were developed by students of color who felt the need for campus groups that allowed students to connect to their community and culture while in school. Nu Alpha Kappa Fraternity, Alpha Rho Lambda Sorority, Omega Psi Phi Fraternity, Alpha Kappa Alpha Sorority, Lamba Phi Epsilon Fraternity, and Sigma Omicron Pi Sorority are just a small list of the many ethnically based "Greek" organizations that exist across the country. Such organizations have provided many students with a means to become familiar with their campus and to gain friendships and support, while fostering and promoting their culture and ethnicity.

See Exercise 14.3: Appreciating Your Gender

Career/Major Organizations

You can explore diversity through your major and career interests as well. Organizations that focus on a specific field of study can be a great asset as you explore your interests. Interested in helping minority and majority groups interact more effectively? Consider majoring in sociology or social work. Want to learn more about human behavior? Study psychology. Join the club that is affiliated with the major you're interested in. Doing so will not only help you find out more about the major, but will also allow you make contacts in the field that can lead to career options. Many of these clubs participate in challenges and contests with similar groups from other colleges and contribute to campus activities through exhibitions and events. The Psychology Club; the Math, Engineering, and Science Association; and the Association of Student Filmmakers are examples of groups that contribute to your campus's diversity.

Political/Activist Organizations

Adding to the diversity mix on campuses are organizations pertaining to specific political affiliations and causes. Campus Republicans, Young Democrats, Amnesty International, Native Students in Social Action, and other groups provide students with a platform to express their political views and share their causes with others. Contributing to the diversity of ideas, organizations provide debating events and forums to address current issues and events.

Special-Interest Groups

Perhaps the largest subgroup of student clubs is the special-interest category, which houses everything from recreational interests to hobbies. On your campus you may find special-interest organizations like the Brazilian Jujitsu Club, the Kite Flyers' Club, the Flamenco Club, and the Video Gamer's Society. Students can cultivate an interest in bird-watching or indulge their curiosity of ballroom dance without ever leaving campus. Many of these clubs will sponsor campus events highlighting their specific interests and talents; these events provide a great way to learn about many clubs. Check out the ones you're most curious about. If a club is not available, create it yourself and contribute to the diversity on your campus! Becoming involved helps you gain valuable knowledge, expand your exposure to new ideas, make valuable contacts, and create a support network, making your time outside of class just as important as the time inside. Not all learning occurs in the classroom. The important thing is to be involved. Doing so enhances your time in college and connects you to campus.

Where to Go for Help

ON CAMPUS

The majority of colleges and university campuses have taken an active role in promoting diversity on their campuses. In the effort to ensure a welcoming and supportive environment for all students, institutions have established offices, centers, and resources with the intent of providing students with educational opportunities, academic guidance, and support networks. Look into the availability of the following resources on your campus, and visit one or more:

Office of Student Affairs
Office of Diversity
Multicultural Centers
Women's and Men's Centers
Gay, Lesbian, and Bisexual Student
   Alliances

Centers for Students with Disabilities
Academic support programs for
   under-represented groups

ONLINE

Student Now Diversity Resources: http://www.studentnow.com/collegelist/diversity.html. A list of campus diversity resources.
Diversity Web: http://www.diversityweb.org. More resources related to diversity on campus.
Tolerance.org: http://www.tolerance.org. This website, a project of the Southern Poverty Law Center, provides numerous resources about dealing with discrimination and prejudice both on and off campus.

Discrimination, Prejudice, and Insensitivity on College Campuses

College and university campuses are not immune to acts of **discrimination** and **prejudice**. The college campus is a unique setting where diverse groups of people interact and share physical as well as psychological space. Unfortunately, there are those who opt not to seek education for the common good but instead opt to respond negatively to groups that differ from their own. Acts of discrimination and prejudice have been documented on campuses across the country, much to the surprise of many in the surrounding communities. You may be shocked to hear that these acts of violence, intimidation, and stupidity occur on campuses, where the assumption is that college students are "supposed to be smarter than that."

Acts of discrimination and prejudice often arise out of hatred for other groups. Some of these acts are premeditated and occur after planning and calculation. At a Midwestern university, students arrived on campus to find racial slurs and demeaning images aimed at various ethnic groups spray-painted on the walls of the Multicultural Center. In the wake of the terrorist attack on the World Trade Center, many students of Middle Eastern descent were subjected to both violence and intimidation because of their ancestry. Reported incidents include a female student at a California university being spat upon and called a "terrorist," and hate mail being placed in the on-campus mailbox of the student-run Muslim Student Union at a private college.

While actions like these are deliberate and hateful, others occur out of lack of common sense. What may start out as an innocent joke among a few can be viewed as harmful by others. Take, for example, a party at a university on the East Coast intended to celebrate Cinco de Mayo. At a "Viva Mexico" party, the organizers asked partygoers to wear sombreros, and, upon arriving at the party, they were met with a mock-up of a border patrol station on the front lawn. In order to get into the party, students were required to crawl under or climb over a section of chain-link fencing. Student groups voiced their disapproval over this insensitivity. The organization throwing the party was subjected to campus probationary measures. At a West Coast university, an organization utilized a Greek letter, which was part of their name, to create promotional T-shirts that read, "we put the PI in Pimp." After members wore the shirts to a football game, the campus was flooded with calls from the public regarding their inappropriateness, and organization members were banned from wearing them. A Halloween party at a large university in the Midwest took a racial turn when members of a campus organization decided to dress in Ku Klux Klan outfits, while other members dressed as slaves and wore black shoe polish on their faces. The group then simulated slave hangings in front of the party. When photos of the events surfaced, the university suspended the group from campus while the community requested that the group be banned from campus indefinitely.

College and university mascots have been the subject of ongoing debates about insensitivity. Stereotypes used to identify a school and its sports teams have disturbed ethnic and cultural groups such as Native Americans for a number of years. Using mascots incorporating the bow and arrow, the tomahawk, feathers, and war paint has raised awareness about the promotion and acceptance of stereotypes associated with the "savage Indian." Some schools have responded by altering the images while retaining the mascot. Other schools have changed their mascots altogether.

Colleges and universities are working to ensure that a welcoming and inclusive campus environment awaits all students, both current and prospective. Campus resources and centers focus on providing support to and acknowledgment of the diverse student population. Campus administrations have established policies against any and all forms of discriminatory actions, racism, and insensitivity, and many campuses have adopted zero-tolerance policies in order to prohibit verbal and nonverbal harassment, intimidation, and violence. You are encouraged to find out what resources are available on your campus to protect you and other students from discriminatory and racist behavior. You may also want to find out what steps your college or university takes to promote the understanding of diversity and multiculturalism. If you've been a victim of a racist, insensitive, or discriminatory act, report it to the proper authorities.

What You Can Do to Fight Hate on Campus

Hate crimes, regardless of where they occur, should be taken very seriously. A hate crime is any prejudicial activity and can include physical assault, vandalism, and intimidation. One of the most common forms of hate crime on campus is graffiti that expresses racial, ethnic, and cultural slurs. Other incidents on campus have taken more direct and violent forms such as reported assaults on students of Middle Eastern descent following the terrorist attacks on September 11, 2001.

Whatever form these crimes take on your campus, it is important for you to assess your thoughts and feelings about their occurrence. The most important will be the answer to the following question: Will you do something or do you think it is someone else's problem? If you or a group that you belong to is the target of the hate crime, you may feel compelled to take a stand and speak out against the incident. But what if the target is not a group you associate with? Will you feel strongly enough to express your discontent with the actions taken? Or will you feel that it is "that group's problem"?

Many students, whether or not they were directly targeted in a hate crime, find strength in unity, forming action committees and making it clear that hate crimes will not be ignored or tolerated. In most cases, instead of dividing students, hate crimes bring student groups together to work toward denouncing hate. It is important not to respond to prejudice and hate crimes with violence. It is more effective to unite with fellow students, faculty, staff, campus police, and administrators to address the issue and educate the greater campus community.

How can you get involved? Work with existing campus services such as the campus police and the Multicultural Center as well as faculty and administration to plan and host educational opportunities such as training, workshops, and symposiums centered on diversity, sensitivity, and multiculturalism. Have an antidiscrimination event on campus in which campus and community leaders address the issues and provide solutions. Join prevention programs to come up with ideas to battle hate crimes on campus or in the community. Finally, look into what antidiscriminatory measures your college is employing, and decide whether they need updating or revision.

Just because you or your particular group has not been targeted in a hatecrime does not mean that you should do nothing. Challenge yourself to become involved in making your campus a safe place in which students with diverse views, lifestyles, languages, politics, religions, and interests can come

together and become educated. If nothing happens to make it known that hate crimes on campus will not be tolerated, it is anyone's guess as to who will be the next target.

A Final Look at Diversity

Diversity enriches us all. Allowing yourself to become more culturally aware and open to differing views will help you become a truly educated person. Understanding the value of working with others and the importance of open-mindedness will enhance your educational and career goals and provide gratifying experiences, both on and off campus. Making the decision to become active in your multicultural education is just that, a decision—one that will require you to be active and to sometimes step out of your comfort zones. There are many ways for you to become more culturally aware, with a variety of opportunities on your campus. Look into what cultural programming is being offered throughout the school year. From concerts to films, guest speakers to information tables, you may not have to go far to gain an insight into diversity.

Challenge yourself to learn about various groups in and around your community, at both school and home. These two settings may differ ethnically and culturally, giving you an opportunity to develop the skills needed to function in and adjust to a variety of settings. Attend events and celebrations outside of the groups with which you associate. Whether they are in the general community or on campus, this is a good way to see and hear traditions specific to the groups represented. Being exposed to new experiences through events and celebrations can be gratifying. You can also become active in your own learning by making time for travel. Seeing the world and its people can be an uplifting experience. And finally, when in doubt, ask. If done in a tactful, genuine way, the majority of people will be happy to share information about viewpoints, traditions, history, etc. It is only through allowing ourselves to grow that we really learn.

ACHIEVE IT! *Setting Goals for Success*

Go back to the self-assessment at the beginning of this chapter and select one to three unchecked items from the list. Use these to formulate short-term goals for yourself. Be specific about what you want to achieve and when (not "combat prejudice," but "make it a point to meet someone from another cultural group each week"). Remember to choose goals that are realistic and important to you. Think about what obstacles could get in the way of achieving your goals, and make your plan. In the event you checked all items in the self-assessment, come up with one or more additional goals for this exercise.

	Goal 1	Goal 2	Goal 3
My short-term goal is . . .			
I want to achieve this goal by . . . (date)			
This goal matters because . . .			
I may encounter the following obstacles . . .			
My method for accomplishing this goal will be to . . .			

Set a Date. Put your deadline for achieving your goal(s) in your calendar. Count back ten days from your deadline and write a reminder for yourself.

Reassess. After your deadline passes, ask yourself: Did I meet this goal on time? What change has it made in my life? If I did not meet it, what am I planning to do about it?

TRY IT! *Exercises*

The exercises at the end of each chapter will help you sharpen what we believe are the critical skills for college success: writing, critical thinking, learning in groups, planning, reflecting, and taking action. You can further explore the topic of each chapter by using your PIN to complete the exercises on the website for this text: **http://success.wadsworth.com/gardner7e.**

WORKING TOGETHER: Reflections on Identity

A. Reflecting on our personal identity and values is a step to increased self-awareness. Read the following questions and answer them as best you can. Remember that personal reflections are just that and there are no right or wrong answers.

- How do you identify yourself ethnically and culturally?

- How do you express yourself according to this identity?

- Are there practices or beliefs in your culture that you have difficulty subscribing to? Why?

- What aspects of your identity do you truly enjoy? In what ways are your stories similar? In what ways are they different?

B. Form work groups of four to six people. As a group, identify areas in which you all share similarities and record those on a piece of paper. Your group must all be in agreement with the items before they can be added to the list. Next, pair up with one person in your group and create a list of differences.

C. How easy or difficult was it to come up with similarities and to agree on them? To what level of depth do the group similarities go? (For example, "we all have hair" vs. "we are all religious people.") Was it easy or hard to work in pairs and identify differences? Which list was longer?

EXERCISE 14.1: Looking at the Curriculum

At this point, you may have identified some majors that interest you. Using your campus's course catalog, identify courses in those majors that focus on the topics of multiculturalism and diversity. Why do you think academic departments have included these issues in the curriculum? How would studying diversity and multiculturalism help you prepare for the field of your choice?

EXERCISE 14.2: Diversity on Your Campus

What efforts does your college or university take to ensure that students feel welcome? Enrollment statistics are typically available from the campus's Office of Institutional Research and may be accessible online. Looking at the data, which groups are represented well at your campus? Which groups are not? What efforts does the college take to increase diversity?

EXERCISE 14.3: Appreciating Your Gender

Read the following four questions pertaining to gender and create a list of answers:

- What aspects do you like about being male or female?
- What are the best things that have happened to you because you are male or female?
- What are some things that happened because you are male or female that you do not want to experience again?
- What points you would like for the opposite sex to know about males or females?

WRITE ABOUT IT! My Personal Journal

This is your place to sound off, to ask your teacher to clarify part of the lesson, or to write him or her about a minor or major crisis you're experiencing. Find out if your teacher wishes you to turn in your journals. Ask if they will remain confidential. Even if the journal isn't used in your course, you can still use the format to write about and reflect on issues regarding the class, yourself, or both.

1. What was the one major lesson you learned from reading this chapter and/or from class lecture and discussion?

2. What are some other important lessons about this topic?

3. If you believe some parts of this chapter are unimportant, spell them out here and tell why you think so. (You even might want to discuss this point with your classmates to see if they came up with a similar list.)

4. If anything is keeping you from performing at your peak level academically, describe what it is. Your instructor may be able to help or refer you to someone else on campus who can help.

5. What behaviors are you planning to change after reading this chapter? Why?

PART
5
Know Yourself!

In this chapter YOU WILL LEARN

- How to define *values*
- Distinctions between types of values
- How societal values are in conflict
- How changes in American society have forced changes in societal values
- How to put values to the test through service learning
- How the way you manage money relates to your values
- Ways to maintain financial health in college

Your reactions to the world around you help you identify your values. How does this photo make you feel?

John M. Whiteley and James B. Craig of the University of California, Irvine, and Edward Zlotkowski of Bentley College contributed their valuable and considerable expertise to the writing of this chapter.

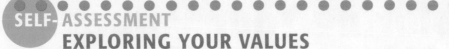

EXPLORING YOUR VALUES

Check the items below that apply to you:

1. ___ **I have thought about how my values may be challenged in college.**

2. ___ **I can cite an example of a time when my values were in conflict.**

3. ___ **I know some ways that family values have changed over the past fifty years.**

4. ___ **I know the definition of "service learning."**

5. ___ **I know why community service can be an important component of my college education.**

6. ___ **I know why "reflection" is an important component of service learning.**

7. ___ **I know my enduring values that will help me select a life partner or mate.**

8. ___ **I know whether my college or university has an honor code or rules for ethical behavior on campus.**

9. ___ **I have thought about how my values will affect the way I manage my money in college.**

10. ___ **I understand the pros and cons of credit card use.**

If you checked seven or fewer of the items, find someone who can help you understand why all ten items are critical. At the end of this chapter, you will be asked to set personal goals for one or more of your unchecked items. If you checked all items, you will be asked to set other goals.

Unlike most of the chapters in this text, this chapter deals with an abstract concept—the concept of values. If you don't already know, you'll find out why values are an integral part of who you are. We hope that by understanding how your values and the values of others may conflict with each other, you will gain a greater understanding of yourself, your friends, your family, and society at large.

The word **values** means different things to different people. For some, the word refers to specific views a person holds on controversial moral issues such as capital punishment. For others, it refers to whatever is most important to a person, such as a good job, a fancy car, or the welfare of one's family. For still others, it refers to abstractions such as truth, justice, or success.

The 2004 U.S. presidential election was said to be a referendum on "moral values," although there was no national agreement on what could be defined as "moral" or "immoral." In this chapter, we offer definitions of values, provide a framework for thinking about values, and explore ways to discover your values and apply them not only to the college experience but to life after college as well.

Defining Values

Perhaps we can best define a value as an important attitude or belief that commits us to take action, to do something. We may not necessarily act in response to others' feelings, but when we truly hold a value, we act on it.

For instance, we might watch a television program showing the devastation caused by the December 2004 tsunami in the Indian Ocean and feel sympathy or regret but take no action whatsoever. If our feelings of sympathy cause us to take action to help those who are suffering, those feelings qualify as values. Actions do not have to be overtly physical. They may involve thinking and talking continually about a problem, trying to interest others in it, reading about it, or sending letters to officials regarding it. The basic point is that when we truly hold a value, it leads us to do something.

We can also define values as beliefs that we accept by choice, with a sense of responsibility and ownership. Much of what we think is simply what others have taught us. Many things we have learned from our parents and others close to us will count as our values, but only after we fully embrace them ourselves. You must personally accept or reject something before it can become a value for you.

Finally, the idea of *affirmation*, or *prizing*, is an essential part of values. When we affirm and prize our values, we proudly declare them to be true, we readily accept the choices to which they lead, and we want others to know it. We also find ourselves ready to sacrifice for them and to establish our priorities around them. Our values govern our loyalties and commitments.

In summary, then, our values are those important attitudes or beliefs that we (1) accept by choice, (2) affirm with pride, and (3) express in action.

When Australian actor Russell Crowe was being interviewed backstage at the 2001 Oscar ceremony after having won the Best Actor award for his role in *Gladiator*, he recalled some advice he had received from his father: "You know, I'd really like you to do something at a technical college or do some kind of apprenticeship—to fall back on." Such advice from a father is not atypical. Crowe's father was reflecting the hope that his son would always have the skills to support himself and his family and would not have to worry about where the proverbial "next meal" was coming from. This valuing of security and of developing skills to help a young person fit productively into society is an example of the values that one generation, with the best of intentions and beliefs, attempts to pass on to the next. But for the next generation, these are what we call "smuggled values." As you know, Russell Crowe chose to reject his father's advice. He chose his own direction for life in terms of his own hierarchy of values, which were different from those of his father. He recalled that he told his father: "Mate, I'm really certain in my life that I'm gonna fall on my face, but it's highly unlikely that I'm ever gonna fall back." At a pinnacle of success in his career as an actor, he was expressing quite a different set of values for himself in defining his own uniqueness.

In contemporary society, many basic institutions "smuggle" or put pressure on you to choose what they believe are the "correct" values when in fact those values are often in conflict with your own. It is important for you to recognize your own values, even though they may differ from those around you.

Crowe chose to make public this brief value-laden episode from his life. But every one of us has had some version of that conversation with significant others in our lives. Pressures from family and friends to make the "right" value choices often come with the best of intentions. But within a democratic free society, a basic human right is to choose your own values. This chapter will empower you to understand more about the origins and forms of pressures on you to make particular value choices and to help you define your uniqueness.

Scholars have classified values in different ways, and it is essential to understand those different classifications. The nature of the human condition is that we are like all other people in some respects, we are like some other people in many respects, and we are like no one else in our special uniqueness. How we choose to establish values different from those of our friends, our family, our society, and its institutions is what helps us become unique.

Another Way of Looking at Values

The word *values* is used so differently in scientific and popular literature that we need to begin by explaining how we are using the concept. Values define what is deemed desirable and describe the standards someone employs to determine future directions and evaluate past actions. Authors J. P. Shaver and W. Strong state: "Values are our standards and principles for judging worth. They are the criteria by which we judge 'things' (people, objects, ideas, actions, and situations) to be good, worthwhile, desirable; or, on the other hand, bad, worthless, despicable; or, of course, somewhere in between these extremes."[1] Milton Rokeach, an important researcher whose field is the nature of values, believes that the ultimate function of human values is to provide "a set of standards to guide us in all our efforts to satisfy our needs and at the same time maintain and, insofar as possible, enhance self-esteem."[2]

Conceived in this way, values are central to determining human behavior and to influencing public and private action. Because values can be organized into hierarchies that help guide individual decisions about occupational goals and educational interests (certainly Russell Crowe and his father have different views of this), values are basic to understanding the many differences in how both people and institutions choose to act. On the institutional level, values guide decisions about where resources ought to be allocated, what policies should be formulated, and what directions institutions ought to pursue.

[1] J. P. Shaver and W. Strong, *Facing Value Decisions: Rationale-Building for Teachers* (New York: Teachers College Press, 1982), 17–34.
[2] M. Rokeach, *Understanding Human Values: Individual and Societal* (New York: The Free Press, 1979).

Types of Values

To help you with the process of analysis, there are a number of useful ways of thinking about values in practice. One approach is to distinguish among *moral values*, *aesthetic values*, and *performance values*. Another is to consider ends versus means values.

See Exercise 15.1: Evidence of Values

Moral Values

Moral values are those personal values that we generally do not attempt to force on others, but that are of immense importance to ourselves as individuals, such as, "I believe it is wrong to lie because lying shows disrespect for other people."

These moral values are used to justify our own behavior toward others (as well as to privately judge others). The college years represent a significant opportunity to focus on the choice of moral values to live by, often for the first time away from the influences of parents, siblings, and previous peer groups.

Aesthetic Values

Aesthetic values are the standards by which we judge beauty. Beauty, as used here, refers to a broad set of judgments about nature, art, music, literature, personal appearance, and so on. For example, people make different value judgments about music, about what is of value artistically, and about what types of books are worth reading. Within society, vast differences of opinion exist about the definition of proper aesthetic values and how to judge beauty—or even what beauty is.

Performance Values

There is comparatively less difference of opinion about nonmoral **performance values**, or how well a person performs to some standard, at least within most campus and other institutional cultures. The definition of performance may vary from person to person or context to context, but representative performance values are accuracy, speed, accomplishment, reward, and discipline.

These performance values can have a moral component when judgments are made about specific individuals or groups of people with similar characteristics and how they measure up to some performance standard.

Performance values influence college students through the expectations of them held by important other people in their lives. No example is closer to home for college students than the expectations of parents and teachers for a high level of academic performance. Crowe and his father, at least at the time

they had their memorable exchange, were far apart on where performance versus "security values" fit into the hierarchy of choices.

Although the Russell Crowe vignette may not be relevant to your particular relationship to your parents, instructors, or employers, it does illustrate the potential connection between performance values and the ethical standards that may be used to determine whether or not others judge your behavior to be "correct."

Means Values versus Ends Values

Values may also be classified as **means values** versus **ends values.** Ends, or *intrinsic values,* refer to ultimate goals such as a world at peace, a comfortable life, freedom, wisdom, and true friendship. Means, or *instrumental values,* are values that are used to help one attain other values such as being responsible, obedient, loving, and imaginative to ambitious, independent, and honest. When you think about your values, you should realize that they do not always separate clearly into means and ends categories. The fundamental American value of equality of opportunity, for example, is frequently offered as an intrinsic value of our society and one of the values that distinguishes the United States from totalitarian countries. But equality of opportunity can also be instrumental to the achievement of other intrinsic values, such as the enhancement of human dignity, the realization of human potential, and the liberation of the human spirit, putting it in the category of a means value.

Challenges to Personal Values in College

Most students find that college life challenges their existing personal and moral values. New students are often startled at the diversity of personal moralities found on campus. For instance, you may have been taught that it is wrong to drink alcohol, yet you find that friends whom you respect and care about see nothing wrong with drinking. At the same time, students from more liberal backgrounds may be astonished to discover themselves forming friendships with classmates whose personal values are very conservative.

When you don't approve of some aspects of a friend's way of life, do you try to change his or her behavior, pass judgment on the person, or withdraw from the relationship? Often, part of the problem is that the friend demonstrates countless good qualities and values that make the troublesome conduct seem less significant. In the process, your own values may begin to change under the influence of a new kind of relativism: "I don't choose to do that, but I'm not going to make any judgments against those who do." In cases when a friendship is affected by differing values, tolerance is generally a good goal. Tolerance for others is a central value in our society and one that often grows during college. Even so, it is easy to think of cases in which tolerance gradually becomes an indulgence of another's destructive tendencies. It is one thing to accept a friend's responsible use of alcohol at a party and quite another to fail to challenge a drunk who plans to drive you home. Sexual intimacy in an enduring relationship may be one thing; a never-ending series of one-night stands is quite another. Remember, the failure to challenge destructive conduct is no sign of friendship.

Your challenge is to balance your personal welfare, your tolerance for diversity, and your freedom of choice. It can be very enriching and rewarding to talk about values with those whose values seem to be in conflict with your own. What are the other person's true values (consciously identified, freely chosen, and actively expressed)? Do his or her current behaviors correspond to those values? Each of you can learn a great deal from talking about what you value and why. Many people flee from diversity and fail to confront conflicting value systems when, realistically speaking, the values of our society change over time and many deeply held societal values are in serious conflict. Adopting a set of values that truly make sense to you can help you move ahead with your life and enable you to consciously analyze and reflect on what is taking place in society.

Societal Values in Conflict: Value Dualisms

Societal values—values held by a society—are not necessarily consistent. And it is the nature of the human condition that individuals do not easily recognize value conflicts in themselves. Therefore, it is useful to understand that the process of choosing your values does not exist apart from the culture in which you live, and that the values in your culture and in the broader society are frequently in conflict.

See Exercise 15.2: Friends and Values

Your conflicting beliefs, or **value dualisms**, may derive from many different experiences from childhood through adolescence and into adulthood. This prolonged period of time during which you may have acquired parts of your value dualisms, coupled with the very different sources from which they derive, may help explain why such conflicts remain largely unexamined. Formal education apparently has little effect on helping you reconcile your value dualisms.

There are some common value dualisms that have existed for many years but continue to provoke different reactions. For instance, some people believe strongly that poverty should be abolished by government action while others believe that some people will always be poor because they don't work hard enough.

Apply this dualism to a contemporary problem in American society. In 2002 about 35 million U.S. citizens were living below the official poverty level, and just over 12 million of those citizens were under the age of 18. Given the immense wealth of the United States, to leave substantial percentages of its population, especially children and adolescents, to subsist in poverty is simply not a rational choice for an economically privileged civil society. Yet no one has reached a consensus on how to solve the problems of poverty and welfare, or demonstrated the political will to insist that the problems be solved.

Another values dualism relates to the importance of individual freedom versus the need for people to work together for common purposes. The value of individual freedom is essentially synonymous with the values of the United States. When seen from the perspective of people in North Korea, for example, where the rights of the state take precedence over the rights of the individual, the contrast is striking and clear. It is less clear when one examines what is happening in American society. In studies of the nation's social health, researchers have found that as of 2002, suicide among America's young people had increased 36 percent since 1970 and was triple the rate in 1950; the gap between rich and poor in America was approaching its worst point in fifty years and was the largest such gap among eighteen industrialized nations; average weekly wages, in real dollars, had declined 19 percent since 1973; the United States was leading the industrial world in youth homicide; America had more children living in poverty than any other industrial nation; 43 million Americans were without health insurance (the worst performance since records have been kept), and the number had increased by more than one-third since 1970; and violent crime remained almost double what it was in 1970, even with substantial improvements during the 1990s.

Why does the richest nation in the world have so many people who fall through the cracks? Do you think that values dualism within American society—pitting individual freedom against the common good—contributes to these statistics?

Changing Society, Changing Values

Changes in society dramatically affect both individual values and the values of society itself. Societal change was the hallmark of the twentieth century. With the information technology revolution and globalization already bringing fundamental changes to the worlds of business and education throughout the world, there is every reason to believe that change will be even more rapid in the twenty-first century.

Consider the changes in some of the fundamental institutions of American society, including family, religion, education, and the place of the United States in the global marketplace. For example, one of the major changes in American society over the past half century has been a new demographic profile due to immigration from Latin America and Asia as well as a population shift to the South and West. Another major area of change has been the extensive political realignments and major transformations in the American and world economies. Social and technological changes have reinforced each other in governing how people work, how they use their leisure time, and how they travel. Both upward and downward mobility have increased to create a larger middle class. For the first time we can remember, children may not achieve the economic level of their parents, and dual-career families have become a reality.

Moreover, local values may contrast sharply with values held at state and national levels. New ethical challenges affecting moral values are coming from such diverse sources as computer hacking, stem-cell research, white-collar crime, abortion, and the bioethical implications of cloning.

If values did not (or could not) change with the changing societal structure, we would never have progress. At the same time, it is all the more difficult to define enduring values.

The traditional family of an earlier generation does not serve as a model for society today. Many more women are working out of the home than was the case fifty years ago. As of 2004, according to the U.S. Department of Labor, 47 percent of the U.S. labor force was female. But many women still retain responsibility for the lion's share of household duties and also experience discrimination in the workplace.

If continuing changes in society are affecting values within families, what are the implications for today's college students? What do we mean by a "generation gap" between this generation of college students and the generation represented by their parents and their friends' parents? As roles of men and women within families continue to change, how does someone in college decide what enduring values will "work" for him or her? What enduring values should you seek in a "significant other"?

Service Learning and Values

At the beginning of this chapter, we noted that its focus would be on the relatively abstract concept of values. Yet one of the most effective ways to explore values is through a concept that is anything but abstract—called *service learning*.

See Exercise 15.3: Your Values and Your Family's Values

TURNING POINT

I volunteer in the community. As college students, we have gifts and energy to share, and it is energizing to get off campus and meet new people. Someday we will go back to living in the real world, so it is important not to lose touch with it.

John N.
St. Louis University

Service Learning Defined

Service learning is a teaching method that combines meaningful service to the community with curriculum-based learning.

- **Serving.** The service itself should address a *genuine community need*, as determined by existing or student-led community assessments. The service should be thoughtfully organized to solve, or make a positive contribution toward solving, a problem.

- **Linking.** In quality service learning, the service project is designed to meet not only a real community need, but also *classroom goals*. By ensuring strong linkages between the service and the learning, students are able to improve their academic skills and apply what they learn in school to the broader community and vice versa.

- **Learning.** *Reflection* is a key element of service learning. The teacher structures time and methods for students to reflect on their service experience.

In other words, service learning is both related to and yet different from two kinds of off-campus activity with which you are probably familiar: community service and internships. Like community service, service learning seeks to help others, to contribute to the common good. Indeed, students involved in service learning and in community service often work at the same community site.

But there are also important differences, such as service learning's emphasis on **reflection** (careful thought, especially the process of reconsidering previous actions, events, or decisions) and **reciprocity** (something done mutually or in return). Although a student *may* learn a lot through traditional community service, service learning does not leave such learning to chance. Instead, it surrounds the service experience with carefully designed reflection

activities to help students prepare for, process, and pull together different aspects of their experience. Because reflection and reciprocity require some kind of formal structure to make them effective, service learning often takes place in and through specially designed academic courses. Let us look at some reasons more and more students are making service learning an important part of their education.

Using Service Learning to Clarify Values

There is probably no better way for people to clarify what they really value than to put themselves in situations where their assumptions and beliefs are "tested." Suppose you've always assumed you wanted to be an accountant. You take a course with a service-learning requirement that asks you to "reconcile the books" at a local nonprofit organization. You set about introducing some method into their "madness"—and you HATE it!! Or suppose you've always believed you wanted to be a teacher, and your service-learning assignment is to teach a group of immigrant fourth-grade students how to read in English. You may find that you are able to teach these students effectively, or you may discover that you simply don't have the patience that such a job requires. In either case, you may learn that your untested beliefs about what you value in a work situation are being challenged by reality. And as a result of your experience, you've now got some important additional information with which to make your career choice.

Identifying Value Dualisms

Earlier in this chapter we discussed value dualisms, explicit—or more often implicit—conflicts between different things someone professes to believe. Service learning is one of the most powerful tools we have to bring such conflicts to consciousness. In other words, it helps an individual better understand his or her personal value system and the strength of his or her stated beliefs.

Although most students find the very experience of being on a campus a good opportunity to re-examine personal values, it's also true that most of us quickly seek out others more or less similar to us. Service learning helps to ensure that your college years really do teach you to stretch and to move outside your comfort zone.

Developing Skills

Still another set of benefits associated with service learning has to do with skills and competencies. You know you'll need to be able to think on your feet once you graduate. But how do you learn to do that in a course where the teacher frames all the problems and does most of the talking? You'd also like to improve your public speaking skills, but will in-class presentations provide you with the practice you need? And what about writing, time management, intercultural communication—not just for your classes but for the "real world"? For many students, service learning means knowing not just *about* things but *how to do* them. It juxtaposes theories and ideas with concrete personal experience, and in doing so, helps students learn how to act on their knowledge and put theory to the test. Hence, it is an especially effective way to develop critical thinking skills.

Civic Engagement

Civic engagement is participation in activities to improve your community, region, or the nation. For instance, working to register new voters is a form of civic engagement.

In February 2003, a group of Oklahoma students issued what they called a "Civic Engagement Resolution." In it they complained that ". . . higher education institutions do not provide adequate education and knowledge about our civic responsibilities. We often do not know how to address civic issues. Higher education's primary focus is to produce professionals, when instead they should be producing citizens."

Although it has become common to criticize the younger generation as politically apathetic, surveys indicate that more young people today are engaged in community service than at any time in the past. Yet they are given little guidance on how to develop their service activity into genuine civic engagement. As the Oklahoma students point out, higher education certainly is not doing its part. Service learning speaks directly to this problem. Indeed, facilitating civic engagement is one of its most important benefits.

Service learning is one of the very few teaching-learning strategies that provides an equal opportunity to succeed to all kinds of learners—not only students who learn well from books and who are perceptive listeners, but also students who learn best through active experimentation and hands-on projects. Service learning directly addresses a question often on the tip of a student's tongue: Why do I have to learn this? Because service-learning experiences let students see the utility of their knowledge even as they develop it, those experiences tend to stand out as especially meaningful—and transformative.

Practical Suggestions and Useful Resources

Whether or not you find service-learning opportunities available to you depends in part on your college or university, in part on your academic focus, and in part on you. Although the number of campuses with service-learning programs has grown tremendously over the last few years, many offer only traditional classroom learning with internships "on the side." Furthermore, faculty interest still varies greatly across areas of concentration. Many professors in the social sciences—in disciplines like sociology, psychology, and communication studies—now include in their courses at least the option of doing a service-learning project. The same is true of professors in education, the health care disciplines, and social work.

If you find willing instructors and appropriate courses, you should make sure what you are being offered is the real thing: an opportunity to *reflect* and *discuss* as well as to act, a chance to develop *citizenship* as well as professional skills. Remember the distinctions we made above, and don't confuse service learning with ordinary community service tacked on to a class or with internships that have simply been relabeled. If your school has a service-learning office, it can help you find faculty who really know how to design a valuable service-learning experience. Even if your school doesn't have such an office, you can easily do a little research on your own.

Values and You

With all of this in mind, what kinds of values do you and other college students believe should characterize a society in which you soon will play a leadership role? Does your generation of college students want to unravel some of the value dualisms discussed in this chapter? If you were to revisit some of the same issues fifty years from now, what social values would you like to see more fully actualized in practice? What dominant social values do you want to bequeath to your children? College offers a time to reflect on the purpose of learning, and on the uses to which you will put your knowledge. Values are a central element in this reflection.

College is also a time to reflect on the ethical dilemmas that confront citizens individually and as members of society. An essential goal of a college education is to cultivate a capacity for reflection about, and analysis of, issues of values in society and values in one's personal life.

College is a preparation for life as well as a career, and an opportunity for personal development, including—quite centrally—values development. It is vitally important to learn to integrate both intellectual development and personal values development.

Financial Responsibility and Values

The way you manage your financial resources in college relates to your values and those of your family. Is sound money management important to you? What about debt? When do you think it's okay to borrow money or to buy something using a credit card? These are questions that you'll grapple with, not only in college but throughout the rest of your life. Living responsibly in terms of your available resources is a wise and prudent strategy. By successfully managing your money, you'll feel better about yourself and reduce your stress, which can help you do better in classes and lead to a more successful future.

National surveys have found that most college students are worried about paying for college. But as you look at your classmates, you can assume that their financial situations are different. Some students have scholarships; other students must work to pay their tuition; still others have parents paying for their education. Many students must work to pay bills and have spending money. Some may have student loans, car payments, or credit card debt. For many students, graduating from college is a goal they can reach only with careful financial planning. It doesn't happen by chance or luck.

See Working Together: Shared Values?

Your Income and Expenses

Let's start by assessing your financial situation.

Earnings

- How much money is in your bank account?
- What is your approximate current annual income?
- What other sources of support do you have?

Debt

See Exercise 15.4: Assessing Your Financial Health

- How much money do you owe, and at what interest rate?
- How much were books and tuition this term?
- How much money have you spent on entertainment so far this month?

The Future

- When do you plan to graduate?
- How much do you think your first salary will be after college?
- How much debt will you have when you graduate?
- How long will it take you to pay off your debt?

These questions address important issues that affect your short-term and long-term financial decisions. A smart money manager would know the answer to all of these questions or have records that would reveal the answers.

Financial Aid

Financial aid to help you pay for college comes from a number of sources, including federal and state financial aid programs, institutional grants, scholarships, jobs, and private agency funds. Most of this aid is awarded to students on the basis of a demonstrated financial need and/or recognition of some identifiable talent (such as top grades for an academic scholarship).

You should become familiar with the language and terms used by financial aid professionals on your campus. Remember that although the financial aid office is there to serve you, you must become your own advocate. The following tips should help:

- File for financial aid every year. Even if you don't think you will receive aid in a certain year, you must file yearly in case you become eligible in the future.

- Meet all filing deadline dates. Financial aid is awarded from funds that are fixed. When the money has been awarded, there is usually none left for those who file late. Students who do not meet filing deadlines run a big risk of losing aid from one year to the next.

- Talk with your financial aid officer immediately if you or your family experiences a significant loss (loss of a job or death of a parent or spouse). Don't wait for the next filing period; you may be eligible for funds for the current year.

- Inquire every year about *criteria-based aid*. Many colleges and universities have grants and scholarships for students who meet specific criteria. These include grants for minority students, grants for students in specific academic majors and grants for students of single parents. Sometimes a donor will give money to the school's scholarship fund for students meeting certain other criteria, even county or state of residence. Determine if any of these fit your circumstances.

- Inquire about campus jobs throughout the year. Campus jobs become available throughout the year, not just at the beginning. If you do not have a job and want/need to work, keep asking. And remember that students who work on campus have a higher probability of graduating than students who work off campus.

- Consider asking for a reassessment. If you have reviewed your financial aid package and think that your circumstances deserve additional consideration, you can ask the financial aid office to reassess your eligibility. The office is not always required to do so, but the request may be worth your effort.

Managing Your Finances

College is a time of new experiences and new freedoms. If you're like most students, your income will be limited, but you'll suddenly have more reasons to spend. First-year students generally have some assumptions about the quality of life they want in college. That may be one reason accepting a change in lifestyle is so difficult for many of them. Even though you're almost certain to be confronted with unexpected expenses and money shortages, you can learn to handle these new responsibilities by learning how to manage your finances.

Although managing a budget may sound complicated, it doesn't have to be. To manage your budget, you need to know your spending tendencies and learn how to create a budget that keeps track of your income and expenses.

Developing a Budget

Before you can develop a budget, you will need to track and begin to understand your spending habits. In college, you'll have many expenses that recur at regular intervals, such as tuition, books, and room and board. Other expenses do not occur regularly; the costs of entertainment and clothes are difficult to track. It's easy to say at the end of the month, "I have no idea where all my money went." That's why it's important to create a system for tracking your expenses, so you can plan for major events like spring break or study abroad. And because a budget is only as good as the person who keeps it, you not only need to work hard to develop an accurate, honest budgeting method—you need to stick to it.

To help you get started, let's use two types of expenses: fixed and monthly. **Fixed expenses** are predetermined, recurring expenses, such as rent and tuition. These expenses are often large and require planning (taking money from a savings account or taking out a loan). Monthly expenses tend to be smaller and vary from month to month, such as phone charges or entertainment.

See Exercise 15.5: Creating a Monthly Budget

If you find it hard to begin making a budget, start like this: Keep track for one week of how much you spend and what you spend it on. Then take that list and place each expense into a category, such as entertainment, clothes, transportation, and so forth. Now, multiply by 4 to get your anticipated monthly expenses. This estimate will help you get started, but you will want to refine your system until it's as accurate as possible.

Now you have begun the monthly challenge of living on a budget. Remember to think ahead for things like Christmas, spring break, or plane tickets home. A good plan is a working document, that is reviewed monthly. It will probably take several months to develop a good, effective plan, but after that your budget will become part of your lifestyle. Following your budget will not only help you reduce stress but, if you stick with it, can serve you well in many ways throughout your college years.

Credit Cards and College

Beware: If you have not already been inundated with credit card offers, expect them to start rolling in. Credit card companies have increased their marketing to college students significantly over the past decade so that almost all college students have a credit card and many have multiple cards.

Credit card companies wow you with fantastic offers. Retail chain stores offer their own cards and entice potential cardholders with 10 percent or more off your next purchase. It can be difficult to make these decisions when you are just learning how to manage your money and at the same time establishing a credit history.

Using a credit card is often viewed as an effective way to establish a positive credit history. But if you don't use the card wisely, you may owe more than you can afford to pay, damage your credit history, and create credit problems that are difficult to fix. A positive credit history is an asset when applying for a loan or even a job. It is important to understand how decisions early in your credit history will affect your future. Credit cards, when used effectively, benefit the holder in many ways, but they can also be real trouble. Don't hold more credit cards than you can afford. A good rule of thumb is to not have more credit available to you than you can pay off in two months. Also, consider having only one widely accepted card, rather than several cards from a variety of retailers. Keeping your debt in one place will help you consolidate your payments and watch your spending.

Find a Way to Stay Out of Financial Trouble

Many students have problems with finances during college. It's important to be committed to resolving those problems.

Protect Your Financial Information Would you leave $50 in cash in plain sight in your residence hall room with the door wide open? Most people would not be that trusting. It is equally important that you protect your other financial resources and information as if they were cash. Credit cards and their numbers, your Social Security number, your bank statement, and your checkbook are items that can be stolen and used by other people. Keep them in a safe place out of public view. Each year, too many college students have their credit cards stolen and checks forged on their accounts. A simple way to help protect your credit card is to write the words "picture ID required" under your signature on the credit card. When a clerk checks the signature, she or he should ask for a photo ID. Another way to protect yourself is to join a credit card registry. For a small fee, this service automatically notifies all of your credit card companies when you lose a card and requests replacements. Always remember to tear up credit card receipts when you are finished with them, because receipts often contain your card number.

Be Careful When Using ATM Cards These cards come with a personal identification number (PIN) for security and protection. Keep your PIN secret. Do not use a number like your address, birth date, or phone number. People who know you may be able to guess the number. Bank studies show that about one-third of ATM frauds result because the cardholder wrote the PIN on the card or on slips of paper with the card.

Deal with Creditors Sooner Rather Than Later Do not put financial problems on the back burner. Debt will only get larger if you don't deal with it head on. As soon as you begin to experience difficulties, contact your creditors. Discuss with them why it is difficult for you to make payments. Most creditors will help you develop a more reasonable repayment plan. Don't wait until your creditors have turned your account over to a collection agency.

If you don't know what else to do, talk with someone you trust who understands your financial problems. Parents and relatives can be sources of good advice. Financial counselors also may be available to you on campus. Your financial aid office may be able to point you toward reputable people who can assist you.

Where to Go for Help

ON CAMPUS

Counselors, chaplains, academic advisors, and your own **college teachers** are all great resources for helping you sort out and think through the challenges you face in dealing with values in college—your own and those of others around you. In fact, anyone who has gotten to know you could be a person with whom you could converse on this critical topic of growth and change during college. The most important thing is to reflect on this topic and then talk about it with others. Find out if any of your teachers use **service-learning projects** as part of class.

ONLINE

Journal of College and Character: http://www. collegevalues.org/reflections.cfm. Check out this website to learn how you can contribute an essay about values to this journal pub-

lished at Florida State University, and read essays written by other college students from around the United States.

Information about Campus Honor Codes: http:// www.academicintegrity.org/ samp_honor_codes.asp. Many college and university campuses in the United States have honor codes. See this website to compare and contrast how campuses state their expectations for student moral and ethical behavior.

12 Money Management Tips for College Students: http://www.bankrate.com/brm/news/sav/ 20000814b.asp. This website offers money management tips to college students.

Top 5 Books on Student Loans and Grants, and Money Management: http://usgovinfo.about. com/cs/businessfinance/tp/collegemoney.htm. This website provides information to students and their parents about a number of valuable resources designed to help with money management and financial aid.

ACHIEVE IT!   *Setting Goals for Success*

Go back to the self-assessment at the beginning of this chapter and select one to three unchecked items from the list. Use these to formulate short-term goals for yourself. Be specific about what you want to achieve and when. Remember to choose goals that are realistic and important to you. Think about what obstacles could get in the way of achieving your goals, and make your plan. In the event you checked all items in the self-assessment, come up with one or more additional goals for this exercise.

	Goal 1	Goal 2	Goal 3
My short-term goal is . . .			
I want to achieve this goal by . . . (date)			
This goal matters because . . .			
I may encounter the following obstacles . . .			
My method for accomplishing this goal will be to . . .			

Set a Date. Put your deadline for achieving your goal(s) in your calendar. Count back ten days from your deadline and write a reminder for yourself.

Reassess. After your deadline passes, ask yourself: Did I meet this goal on time? What change has it made in my life? If I did not meet it, what am I planning to do about it?

TRY IT! *Exercises*

The exercises at the end of each chapter will help you sharpen what we believe are the critical skills for college success: writing, critical thinking, learning in groups, planning, reflecting, and taking action. You can further explore the topic of each chapter by using your PIN to complete the exercises on the website for this text: **http://success.wadsworth.com/gardner7e.**

WORKING TOGETHER: Shared Values?

List all the reasons you chose to attend college. Share your reasons in a small group. Attempt to arrive at a consensus about the five most important reasons people choose to attend college. Then rank the top five, from most important to least important.

My Group's Top 5 Reasons	Different Reasons Other Groups Listed
1.	1.
2.	2.
3.	3.
4.	4.
5.	5.

Share your final rankings with other groups in the class. How similar were the results of the groups? How different? How easy or hard was it to reach a consensus in your group? In other groups? What does this exercise tell you about the consistency of values among members of the class?

EXERCISE 15.1: Evidence of Values

One way to start discovering your values is by defining them in relation to some immediate evidence or circumstances. List ten items in your room (or apartment or house) that are important or that symbolize something important to you.

Now cross out the five items that are least important—the ones you could most easily live without. Of the remaining five, cross out two more. Rank-order the final three items from most to least important. What has this exercise told you about what you value?

EXERCISE 15.2: Friends and Values

A. Consider several friends and think about their values. Pick one who really differs from you in some important value. Write about the differences.

B. In a small group, discuss this difference in values. Explore how it's possible to be friends with someone so different.

EXERCISE 15.3: **Your Values and Your Family's Values**

The process by which we assimilate values into our own value systems involves three steps:

1. Choosing (selecting freely from alternatives after thoughtful consideration of the consequences)

2. Prizing (cherishing the value and affirming it publicly)

3. Acting (consistently displaying this value in behavior and decisions)

A. List three values your family has taught you are important. For each, document how you have completed the three-step process to make their value yours.
B. If you haven't completed the three steps, does it mean you have not chosen this value as your own? Explain your thoughts on this.

EXERCISE 15.4: **Assessing Your Financial Health**

On a separate sheet of paper, answer the questions posed on pages 305–06 as best you can. Then study your answers to get some kind of picture of your financial status. Would you say you were in excellent shape? Good shape? Fair shape? Poor shape? If you answered anything but "excellent," what steps do you think you'll need to take, and when, to improve your financial health? If your answer was "excellent," explain why you think you're in such good shape financially.

EXERCISE 15.5: **Creating a Monthly Budget**

Begin a monthly budget using the chart below. It is important to also identify fixed expenses, such as tuition and books, that you will need to save for during the year. Do this by dividing the cost of these items by 9 or 12 (depending on the number of months you will be at school).

MONTHLY BUDGET

INCOME		EXPENSES	
Sources	$	Item	$
		Clothes	
		Entertainment	
		Phone/Utilities	
		Laundry/Dry cleaning	
		Personal (toothpaste, deodorant, etc.)	
		Transportation	
		Food/Snacks	
		Other	
Total Monthly Income		**Total Monthly Expenses**	

Total Monthly Income

Total Monthly Expenses

Anticipated Difference

(+ or −)

⬤ WRITE ABOUT IT! My Personal Journal

This is your place to sound off, to ask your teacher to clarify part of the lesson, or to write him or her about a minor or major crisis you're experiencing. Find out if your teacher wishes you to turn in your journals. Ask if they will remain confidential. Even if the journal isn't used in your course, you can still use the format to write about and reflect on issues regarding the class, yourself, or both.

1. *What was the one major lesson you learned from reading this chapter and/or from class lecture and discussion?*

2. *What are some other important lessons about this topic?*

3. *If you believe some parts of this chapter are unimportant, spell them out here and tell why you think so. (You even might want to discuss this point with your classmates to see if they came up with a similar list.)*

4. *If anything is keeping you from performing at your peak level academically, describe what it is. Your instructor may be able to help or refer you to someone else on campus who can help.*

5. *What behaviors are you planning to change after reading this chapter? Why?*

Staying Healthy

Chapter 16

In this chapter YOU WILL LEARN

- The importance of managing stress
- Warning signs of depression
- Strategies for better nutrition and weight management
- The many options you have for contraception and safer sex
- The realities of alcohol use on campus
- The consequences of abusing alcohol, tobacco, and drugs

What choices have you made today to stay healthy?

Michelle Murphy Burcin of the University of South Carolina at Columbia and Providence Hospital, Columbia, SC, contributed valuable and considerable expertise to the writing of this chapter. Sara J. Corwin, JoAnn Herman, Danny Baker, Bradley H. Smith, Rick L. Gant, and Georgeann Stamper of the University of South Carolina at Columbia contributed vital material to earlier editions of this chapter.

SELF-ASSESSMENT
STAYING HEALTHY

Check the items below that apply to you or that you believe are important for college success.

1. ___ When I feel overwhelmed, I take healthy steps to deal with my stress.

2. ___ Although I am busy, taking care of myself is always a priority.

3. ___ I am conscientious about getting enough sleep, even on nights before exams.

4. ___ I exercise regularly and manage my weight to stay fit.

5. ___ I have adequate information about sex and contraception.

6. ___ I know how to avoid contracting a sexually transmitted infection.

7. ___ I don't have to drink alcohol in order to have fun.

8. ___ I have a realistic understanding of campus alcohol use and abuse.

9. ___ I don't use tobacco products, even in moderation.

10. ___ I understand the consequences of abusing legal and illegal drugs.

If you checked seven or fewer of the items, find someone who can help you understand why all ten items are critical. At the end of this chapter, you will be asked to set personal goals for one or more of your unchecked items. If you checked all items, you will be asked to set other goals.

College is a great time to explore. It's an opportunity to exercise your mind and expand your horizons. Unfortunately, for too many students it becomes an opportunity to stop exercising the body and begin expanding the waistline! Because of the newness of the college environment, you may find yourself forgetting to take care of yourself.

Most students can handle the transition to college easily using various coping mechanisms. Others drink too much or smoke too much. Some overeat or develop an eating disorder like bulimia or anorexia. Some become so stressed that their anxiety overwhelms them. Some ignore their sexual health, and then have to face a sexually transmitted infection or an unplanned pregnancy.

This chapter explores the topic of **wellness**, which is a catchall term for taking care of your mind, body, and spirit. Wellness means making healthy choices and achieving balance. Wellness includes reducing stress, keeping fit, maintaining sexual health, and taking a sensible approach to alcohol and other drugs.

Stress

When you are stressed, your body undergoes rapid physiological, behavioral, and emotional changes. Your rate of breathing may become more rapid and shallow. Your heart rate begins to speed up, and the muscles in your shoulders and forehead, the back of your neck, and perhaps across your chest begin to tighten. Your hands may become cold and/or sweaty. You may experience disturbances in your gastrointestinal system, such as a "butterfly" stomach, diarrhea, or constipation. Your mouth and lips may feel dry and hot, and you may notice that your hands and knees begin to shake or tremble. Your voice may quiver or even go up an octave.

A number of psychological changes also occur when you are under stress. You may experience changes in your ability to think, such as confusion, trouble concentrating, inability to remember things, and poor problem solving. You may experience emotions such as fear, anxiety, depression, irritability, anger, or frustration. You may have insomnia or wake up too early and not be able to go back to sleep.

Stress has many sources, but two seem to be prominent: life events and daily hassles. *Life events* are those that represent major adversity, such as the death of a parent, spouse, partner, or friend. Researchers believe that an accumulation of stress from life events, especially if many events occur over a short period of time, can cause physical and mental health problems.

The College Readjustment Rating Scale (Exercise 16.2) is a life-events scale designed especially for traditional college students. If you find that your score is 150 or higher, you have experienced a great deal of stress over the past year. You might consider what help you need or skills you must learn to be able to cope effectively.

Daily hassles are the minor irritants that we experience every day, such as losing your keys, dropping your soft drink, having three tests on the same day, quarreling with your roommate, or worrying about money.

Managing Stress

The best starting point for handling stress is to be in good shape physically and mentally. When your body and mind are healthy, it's like inoculating yourself against stress. This means you need to pay attention to diet, exercise, sleep, and mental health.

Caffeine and Stress

Your caffeine consumption can have a big impact on your stress level. In moderate amounts (50–200 milligrams per day), caffeine increases alertness and reduces feelings of fatigue, but even at this low dosage it may make you perkier during part of the day and more tired later. Consumed in larger quantities, caffeine may cause nervousness, headaches, irritability, stomach irritation, and insomnia—all symptoms of stress. Many heart patients have been told to avoid caffeine since it tends to speed up heart rates. How much caffeine do you consume? Total your caffeine intake based on these figures:

Product	Caffeine Content (mg per serving)
Coffee (5 oz. cup)	
Regular	65–115
Decaffeinated	3
Tea (6 oz. cup)	
Hot steeped	36
Iced	31
Soft Drinks (12 oz. serving)	
Red Bull	80
Jolt Cola	72
Dr Pepper	61

See Exercise 16.1: Monitoring Your Stress

See Exercise 16.2: The College Readjustment Rating Scale

(continued)

Mountain Dew	54
Coca-Cola	46
Pepsi-Cola	36
Chocolate bar	6–20 mg
Over-the-Counter Drugs	
NoDoz (2 tablets)	200
Excedrin (2 tablets)	130
Midol (2 tablets)	65

If the amount is excessive (this will vary with individuals; monitor such things as inability to sleep, high-energy mornings with tired afternoons, and so forth), think about drinking water in place of caffeine drinks, or choose the decaf version of coffee or the soft drink you like.

Exercise and Stress

Exercise is an excellent stress management technique, the best way to stay fit, and a critical part of weight loss. While any kind of recreation benefits your body and spirit, aerobic exercise is the best for stress management as well as weight management. In aerobic exercise, you work until your pulse is in a "target zone" and keep it in this zone for at least 30 minutes. You can reach your target heart rate through a variety of exercises: walking, jogging, running, swimming, biking, treadmill, or using a stair climber. What makes the exercise aerobic is the intensity of your activity. Choose activities that you enjoy so you

will look forward to your exercise time. That way, it's more likely to become a regular part of your routine.

Besides doing wonders for your body, aerobic exercise also keeps your mind healthy. When you do aerobic exercise, your body produces hormones called beta endorphins. These natural narcotics cause feelings of contentment and happiness and help manage anxiety and depression. Your mood and general sense of competence improve with regular aerobic exercise. In fact, people who undertake aerobic exercise report more energy, less stress, better sleep, weight loss, and an improved self-image.

Think about ways you can combine activities and use your time efficiently. Maybe you could leave the car at home and jog to class. Go to the gym with a friend and ask each other study questions as you work out on treadmills. Park at the far end of the lot and walk to classes or take the stairs whenever possible. Remember, exercise does not have to be a chore. Find something you enjoy doing and make it part of your daily schedule. Many campuses have recreation departments that offer activities such as intramural sports, rock climbing, aerobic classes, and much more. The most important thing about exercise is that you stay active and make it part of your day-to-day life.

Sleep and Stress

Getting adequate sleep is another way to protect you from stress. According to the National Sleep Foundation, 63 percent of American adults do not get the recommended eight hours of sleep per night. Lack of sleep can lead to anxiety, depression, and academic struggles. Researchers at Trent University in Ontario found that students who studied all week but then stayed up late on the weekends partying forgot as much as 30 percent of the material they had learned during the prior week. Try out the following suggestions to establish better sleep habits:

- If you can't sleep, get up and do something boring.
- Get your clothes and/or school materials together before you go to bed.
- Avoid long daytime naps.
- Try reading or listening to a relaxation tape before going to bed.
- Get exercise during the day.
- Sleep in the same room and bed every night.
- Set a regular schedule for going to bed and getting up.

TURNING POINT

I limit stress by not waiting until the last minute to study for an exam or assignment. I also try to have a balance of physical activities, studying, work, adequate sleep, and moderate alcohol and caffeine consumption. If I can avoid getting run down, I have a better chance of staying healthy and not missing classes.

Greg A.
De Anza College

Modifying Your Lifestyle

Modifying your lifestyle is yet another approach to stress management. You have the power to change your life so that it is less stressful. Others, such as teachers, supervisors, parents, friends, and even your children, influence you, but ultimately you control how you run your life. Lifestyle modification involves identifying the parts of your life that do not serve you well and making plans for change. For instance, if you are always late for class and get stressed about this, get up ten minutes earlier. If you get nervous before a test when you talk to a certain classmate, avoid that person before a test. Learn test-taking skills so you can manage test anxiety better.

Relaxation Techniques

See Exercise 16.3: Changing Perceptions

Relaxation techniques such as visualization and deep breathing can help you reduce stress. Learning these skills is just like learning any new skill. You need knowledge and practice. Check your course catalog, college counseling center, health clinic, student newspaper, or fitness center for classes that teach relaxation. You'll find books as well as audio tapes and CDs that guide you through relaxation techniques.

Other Ways to Relieve Stress

Here are several things you can do to improve your mental health:

- Reward yourself on a regular basis when you achieve small goals.
- Remember that there is a reason you are in a particular situation. Keep the payoff in mind.
- Laugh. A good laugh will always make you feel better.
- Get—or give—a hug.
- Pray or meditate.
- Do yoga.
- Practice a hobby.
- Purchase a pet.
- Get a massage.

See Working Together: Recommendations for Stress Management

- Say "stop!" to yourself whenever things get too intense.
- Practice deep breathing.

Depression

According to the American Psychological Association, depression is one of the most common psychiatric disorders in the United States, affecting more than 15 million adults. According to the National Institutes of Health, depression is twice as common in women as in men. Women are also more likely to seek health care for mental health issues such as depression. Depression is more than just feeling blue. It requires medical attention. If you have any of the following symptoms for more than two weeks, talk to a health care provider:

- Feelings of helplessness and hopelessness
- Feeling useless, inadequate, bad, and guilty

- Self-hatred, constant questioning of thoughts and actions
- Loss of energy and motivation
- Loss or gain in weight
- Difficulty going to sleep, or excess need for sleep
- Loss of interest in sex
- Hard time concentrating for a length of time

Suicide

College students are at especially high risk for depression as well as suicide. The CDC (Centers for Disease Control and Prevention) reports that students ages 15 to 24 are more likely than any other age group to attempt suicide. Most people who commit suicide give a warning of their intentions. The following are common signs of possible suicide:

- Recent loss and a seeming inability to let go of grief
- Change in personality—sadness, withdrawal, apathy
- Expressions of self-hatred
- Change in sleep patterns
- Change in eating habits
- A direct statement about committing suicide ("I might as well end it all.")
- A preoccupation with death

If you or someone you know threatens suicide or displays any of the above signs, please consult a mental health professional. Most campuses have counseling centers that offer one-on-one sessions as well as support groups for their students. Finally, remember there is no shame attached to high levels of stress or other anxiety-related issues. Proper counseling, medical attention, and perhaps prescription medication can help students better deal with high levels of stress.

Nutrition and Weight Management

"You are what you eat" is more than a catchphrase; it's an important reminder of the vital role diet plays in our lives. You've probably read news stories telling how more and more young people are obese than ever before in our history. The Centers for Disease Control (CDC) reports that the rates of obesity have more than doubled in the U.S. since 1990. In 1990, an estimated 11.6 percent of U.S. citizens were obese; in 2003, an estimated 24.5 percent were classified as obese. One expert, Dr. James Hill, Director of Human Nutrition at the University of Colorado, predicts that, "If obesity is left unchecked, almost all Americans will be obese by 2050." Many attribute this to the explosion of fast food restaurants, which place "flavor" and "filling" before "healthy." A Tufts University researcher found that 60 percent of college students eat too much saturated fat, which increases the risk for heart disease. Most of us do not consume sufficient amounts of fiber and whole grains either. As a result, we are more likely to have long-term health problems such as diabetes, heart disease, and cancer.

So what to do? It's not easy at first, but if you commit to a new eating regime, you will not only feel better, but you'll be healthier . . . and probably happier. Your campus may have a registered dietitian available to help you make healthy changes in your diet. Check with your student health center. Meanwhile, here are some suggestions:

- Restrict your intake of red meat, real butter, white rice, white bread, and sweets. "White foods" are made with refined flour, which has few nutrients—so you're not getting as many vitamins and minerals as you could with healthier selections. Instead, go for fish, poultry, soy products, and whole-wheat or multigrain breads. And remember that the bread that is brown in color does not equal whole wheat.

- Eat plenty of vegetables and fruits daily. These are important building blocks for a balanced diet, and they contain lots of fiber (to help fight off cancer and heart disease). Instead of fruit juices, which contain concentrated amounts of sugar, opt for the actual fruit instead. When you sit down to eat any meal (including breakfast), make sure you have at least one fruit and/or vegetable on your plate.

- Avoid fried foods—French fries, fried chicken, and so forth. Choose grilled meats instead. Avoid foods with large amounts of sugar, such as donuts.

- Keep your room stocked with healthy snacks, such as fruit, vegetables, yogurt, pretzels, and graham crackers.

- Eat a sensible amount of nuts and all the legumes (beans) you want to round out your fiber intake.

- Watch your portion size. All things need to be eaten in moderation.

- Eat breakfast! Your brain will function at a more efficient level with a power-packed meal first thing in the morning. Eating breakfast can also do wonderful things for your metabolism by jump-starting it. If you are normally not a breakfast eater, try eating just a piece of fruit or half of a bagel. You will notice a big difference in your energy level during your early morning classes. Watch out for sugar-coated cereals. Go for healthier options that are loaded with fiber. The *New York Times* reported in 2004 that many college students are eating cereal for more than just breakfast. In fact, cereal-themed restaurants are opening near some campuses. If you have cereal for lunch or dinner, remember that you need to balance the rest of your day with nutrient-packed foods.

- Always read the government-required nutrition label on all packaged foods. Check sodium content (sodium will make you retain fluids and increase your weight) and the number of fat grams. Strive for a diet with only 20 percent fat.

- Figure 16.1 shows the Healthy Eating Pyramid, designed by Walter Willett, Chairman of the Department of Nutrition at Harvard's School of Public Health. The Healthy Eating Pyramid puts exercise and weight control at the base, recommends eating whole-grain foods at most meals, and encourages eating vegetables "in abundance." This pyramid emphasizes eating lots of plant oils, like olive, canola and soy, and gives fish and poultry a higher profile than red meat, which you should consider eating sparingly.

See Exercise 16.4: Doing a Weekly Check

Obesity

People have been joking about the "freshman fifteen" forever, but it's no joke that new college students tend to gain weight during their first term. Nutrition experts at Tufts University reported that the average weight gain is 6 pounds for men and about 4.5 pounds for women during the first year of college. There are many reasons why students gain weight, some of them being increased stress, lifestyle changes, new food choices, changes in physical activity, and alcohol consumption. In addition to the nutrition tips above, other ways to avoid obesity are eating smaller meals more often, getting regular exercise, keeping a food journal (to keep track of what you are actually consuming), and being realistic about dieting.

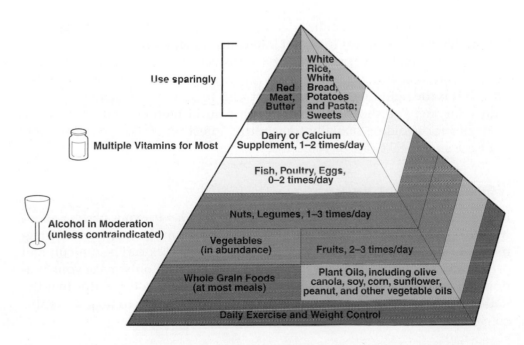

Figure 16.1
Healthy Eating Pyramid

Eating Disorders

An increasing number of college students are obsessed with their body and food intake. This obsession can lead to conditions such as anorexia, bulimia, or binge eating disorder, all of which affect women disproportionately to men. Anorexia is characterized by self-induced starvation, extreme preoccupation with food, and a body weight less than 85 percent of the healthy weight. Bulimia is characterized by cycles of bingeing (eating large amounts of food) and purging by vomiting, abusing laxatives and/or diuretics, exercising excessively, and fasting. People with a binge eating disorder do not purge the calories after the binge. Individuals with binge eating disorder tend to eat secretively and are often clinically obese.

Some of the signs and symptoms of an eating disorder are:

• Intense fear of gaining weight

• Restricting food or types of food, such as food containing any kind of fat

• Weighing less than 85 percent of expected body weight or failure to make appropriate weight gain for a period of growth

• Stopping or never getting a monthly menstrual period

• Seeing one's body as fat, even though underweight

• Overexercising

• Secrecy around food and denial of a problem with eating

If you or anyone you know is struggling with an eating disorder, please seek medical attention. Eating disorders can be life-threatening if they are not treated by a health care professional. Many colleges and universities have eating disorder case management teams to help individuals on their campus. Contact your student health center for more information, or contact the National Eating Disorder Association (www.nationaleatingdisorders.org) to find a professional in your area who specializes in eating disorder treatment.

Sexual Health

We know from numerous studies that about 75 percent of traditional-age college students have engaged in sexual intercourse at least once.

Regardless of whether you are part of this percentage, it can be helpful to explore your sexual values and to consider whether sex is right for you at this time. If it is the right time and you do not wish to become pregnant or impregnate someone, you should choose a birth control method and adopt some strategies for avoiding sexually transmitted infections (STIs). What matters most is that you take care of yourself.

Negotiating for Safer Sex

If you are sexually active, it's important that you talk with your partner about ways to protect against sexually transmitted infections and unwanted pregnancy. Communicating with your partner about safer sex can be difficult and even embarrassing initially, but this communication will only make your relationship stronger and more meaningful. The following is a list of tips that the national organization Advocates for Youth has put together to help make this conversation easier and more effective.

Sex includes communication.

- Use "I" statements when talking. For example, "I feel that abstinence is right for me at this time. Or, "I would feel more comfortable if we used a condom."

- Be assertive! Do not let fear of how your partner might react stop you from talking with him or her.

- Be a good listener. Let your partner know that you hear, understand, and care about what she or he is saying and feeling.

- Be patient with your partner, and remain firm in your decision that talking is important.

- Understand that success in talking does not mean one person getting the other person to do something. It means that you both have said what you think and feel respectfully and honestly and that you have both listened respectfully to the other.

- Avoid making assumptions. Ask open-ended questions to discuss relationship expectations, past and present sexual relationships, contraceptive use, and testing for sexually transmitted infections (STIs).

- Do not wait until you become sexually intimate to discuss safer sex with your partner. In the heat of the moment, you and your partner may be unable to talk effectively.

Sexually Transmitted Infections

The problem of STIs on college campuses has received growing attention in recent years as epidemic numbers of students have become infected. In general, STIs continue to increase faster than other illnesses on campuses today, and approximately 5 to 10 percent of visits by U.S. college students to college health services are for the diagnosis and treatment of STIs. The belief that nice young men and women don't "catch" these sorts of infections is inaccurate and potentially more dangerous than ever before. If you choose to be sexually active, particularly with more than one partner, exposure to an STI is a real possibility.

STIs are usually spread through genital contact. Sometimes, however, STIs can be transmitted through mouth-to-mouth contact. There are more than twenty known types of STIs; Table 16.1 breaks down the most common on college campuses.

As you can see from the table, many of the sexually transmitted infections have similar symptoms or no symptoms at all. Many women show no symptoms and are therefore "asymptomatic." Most health care professionals recommend that women who are sexually active be screened for all the STIs possible during their yearly pap smear. These screenings are not part of the regular annual exam and must be specifically requested.

TABLE 16.1   Sexually Transmitted Infections

SEXUALLY TRANSMITTED INFECTION	FEMALE SYMPTOMS	MALE SYMPTOMS	NUMBER OF NEW CASES ANNUALLY IN THE UNITED STATES	CURABLE OR TREATABLE
AIDS (Acquired immunodeficiency syndrome)	Symptoms appear several months to several years after contact with HIV; unexplained weight loss; white spots in mouth; yeast infections that do not go away	Symptoms appear several months to several years after contact with HIV; unexplained weight loss; white spots in mouth	40,000	Treatable
Chlamydia	Yellowish discharge; bleeding between periods; burning or pain during urination	Painful and frequent urination; watery, puslike discharge from penis	3 million	Curable
Gonorrhea	Thick yellow or gray discharge; abnormal periods or bleeding between periods; cramps or pain in lower abdomen	White, milky discharge from penis; painful, burning urination; swollen or tender testicles	800,000	Curable
Syphilis	Painless chancre; rash or white patches on skin; lymph nodes enlarge	Painless chancre; rash or white patches on skin; lymph nodes enlarge	70,000	Curable in early stages
Herpes	Burning sensation and redness at the site of infection; painful blister that will crust over, dry up, and disappear	Burning sensation and redness at the site of infection; painful blister that will crust over, dry up, and disappear	1 million	Treatable
Genital HPV (Human Papilloma Virus)	Small, bumpy warts on the sex organs and/or anus; burning or itching around sex organs	Small, bumpy warts on the sex organs and/or anus; burning or itching around sex organs	5.5 million	Treatable
Hepatitis B	Symptoms appear 1–9 months after contraction; flulike feelings that go away; tiredness; dark urine	Symptoms appear 1–9 months after contraction; flulike feelings that go away; tiredness; dark urine	120,000	Treatable
Trichomoniasis	Yellowish, unpleasant-smelling discharge accompanied by a burning sensation during urination	Watery, white drip from the penis; burning or pain during urination; need to urinate more often	5 million	Curable

Adapted from www.plannedparenthood.org and www.ashastd.org

Sources: Rebecca J. Donatelle and Larraine G. Davis, *Access To Health*, 8th ed. (San Francisco: Benjamin Cummings, 2004); Linda L. Alexander, et al., *New Dimensions in Women's Health*, 3rd ed. (Sudbury, MA: Jones and Bartlett, 2004).

Not all STIs are curable. This means that medications will help alleviate the symptoms but the virus will stay in an individual's system. Sexually transmitted infections that are left untreated can progress to pelvic inflammatory disease (PID), which is now thought to be the leading cause of infertility in women.

See Exercise 16.5: What's Your Decision?

Options for Safer Sex

There are several ways to avoid STIs and unwanted pregnancy. The most obvious is to not have sex. Even if 75 percent of college students are having sex, that still leaves 25 percent who are not. Celibacy or abstinence are options for you to consider. For some people, masturbation is a reasonable alternative to sex with a partner.

If you are sexually active, you'll be safer (in terms of STIs) if you have only one partner. Yet, you may feel that you're at a point in your life where you would prefer to have multiple relationships simultaneously. But whether you're monogamous or not, you should always protect yourself by using a condom.

In addition to being a contraceptive, the condom can help prevent the spread of STIs, including HIV. The condom's effectiveness against disease holds true for anal, vaginal, and oral intercourse. The most current research indicates that the rate of protection provided by condoms against STIs is similar to its rate of protection against pregnancy (90–99%) when used correctly and consistently for each and every act of intercourse or oral sex. Note that only latex rubber condoms and polyurethane condoms—not lambskin or other types of "natural membrane" condoms—provide this protection. The polyurethane condom is a great alternative for individuals with latex allergies. Use only a water-based lubricant (such as KY Jelly) to keep the condom from breaking.

Birth Control

Sexually active heterosexual students have to plan to prevent an unwanted pregnancy. Planning is the key. What is the best method of contraception? It is any method that you use correctly and consistently each time you have intercourse. Table 16.2 compares the major features of some of the most common methods of birth control.

Always discuss birth control with your partner so that you both feel comfortable with the option you have selected. For more information about a particular method, consult a pharmacist, your student health center, a local family planning clinic, the local health department, or your private physician. The important thing is to resolve to protect yourself and your partner each and every time you have sexual intercourse.

It is important that every college student also know about emergency contraception. What if the condom breaks or if you forget to take your birth control pill? Emergency contraception pills can reduce the risk of pregnancy if started within seventy-two hours after unprotected vaginal intercourse. According to Planned Parenthood Federation of America, if the pills are taken within seventy-two hours of unprotected intercourse they can reduce the risk of pregnancy from 75 to 89 percent. Emergency contraception does come with side effects such as nausea, vomiting, and cramping. In rare cases, serious health complications can result from emergency contraception. Be sure you ask your provider what symptoms to watch for. Most campus health centers and local health clinics are now dispensing emergency contraception to individuals in need.

TABLE 16.2   Methods of Contraception

METHOD	HOW EFFECTIVE IS THIS METHOD?	DOES IT PROTECT AGAINST HIV AND STIS?	AVERAGE COST	DO I NEED A PRESCRIPTION?
Abstinence	100%	Yes	Free	No
Cervical Cap	84%	No	$13–25	Yes
Contraceptive Injection	99%	No	$20–40 (visit to clinician); $30–75 (injection)	Yes
Diaphragm	94%	No	$13–25	Yes
Female Condom	95%	Yes	$2.50 per condom	No
Intrauterine Device (IUD)	99%	No	$175–400 (exam, insertion, and follow-up visit)	Yes
Male Condom	97%	Yes	$.50 and up	No
Norplant	99%	No	$500–750 (exam, implants, and insertion); $100–200 (removal)	Yes
NuvaRing	99%	No	$30–35 monthly	Yes
Ortho Evra (The Patch)	99%	No	$30–35 monthly	Yes
Oral Contraceptive (The Pill)	99%	No	$15–35 monthly	Yes
Spermicide	94%	No	$4–8 per kit	No
Tubal Ligation (Female Sterilization)	99%	No	$1,000–2,500	Yes
Vasectomy (Male Sterilization)	99%	No	$240–520	Yes

Adapted from www.plannedparenthood.org

Source: Rebecca J. Donatelle and Larraine G. Davis, *Access To Health*, 8th ed. (San Francisco: Benjamin Cummings, 2004).

Making Decisions about Alcohol

Even if you don't drink, you should read this information because 50 percent of college students reported helping a drunken friend, classmate, or study partner in the past year. First, remember this: A number of surveys have confirmed that your peers aren't drinking as much as you think they are, so there's no need for you to try and "catch up." Most students who try to estimate college drinking are off *by almost half*. Second, remember that, in the final analysis, it's your decision to drink or not to drink alcoholic beverages; to drink moderately or to drink heavily; to know when to stop or to be labeled as a drunk who isn't fun to be around. You should know that between 10 and 20 percent of people in the United States become addicted to alcohol at some point in their lives. Alcohol can turn people into victims even though they don't drink: people killed by drunk drivers or family members who suffer from the behavior of an alcoholic. Over the course of one year, about 20 to 30 percent of students report serious problems related to excessive alcohol use. You may have heard news reports about college students who died or were seriously or permanently injured as a result of excessive drinking. Just one occasion of heavy or high-risk drinking can lead to problems.

Drinking and Blood Alcohol Content

How alcohol affects behavior depends on the dose of alcohol, which is best measured by blood alcohol content, or BAC (see Table 16.3). Most of the pleasurable effects of alcoholic beverages are experienced at lower BAC levels, when alcohol acts as a behavioral stimulant. For most people, the stimulant level is around one drink per hour. Usually, problems begin to emerge at doses higher than .05 when alcohol acts as a sedative and begins to slow down areas of the brain. Most people who have more than four or five drinks at one occasion feel "buzzed," show signs of impairment, and are likely to be higher risks for alcohol-related problems. However, significant impairment at lower doses can occur.

How fast you drink makes a difference, too. Your body gets rid of alcohol at a rate of about one drink an hour. Drinking more than one drink an hour may cause a rise in BAC because the body is absorbing alcohol faster than it can eliminate it.

Professionals can estimate BAC from your behavior. When someone is stopped for drunk driving, police may videotape the person completing a series of tasks such as walking on a line and tipping his or her head back, or touching the nose with eyes closed. The degree of impairment shown in these tests can be presented as evidence in court.

Alcohol and Behavior

At BAC levels of .025 to .05, a drinker tends to feel animated and energized. At a BAC level of around .05, a drinker may feel rowdy or boisterous. This is where most people report feeling a buzz from alcohol. At a BAC level between .05 and .08, alcohol starts to act as a depressant. So as soon as you feel that buzz, remember that you are on the brink of losing coordination, clear thinking, and judgment!

See Exercise 16.6: Quality of Life

TABLE 16.3 Correlation of Blood Alcohol Content (BAC) with Behavior

BAC RANGE	COMMON EFFECTS ON BEHAVIOR	MAJOR DANGERS
0.00 to 0.04	Increased energy, animation	No impairment
.05 to .08	Feeling a "buzz"; slowed reflexes	4 times the risk of auto accident*
.09 to .20	Impaired walking, poor social judgment, slurred speech, nausea, fighting, vandalism, sexual aggression, blackout	25 times the risk of auto accident*; risk of indiscriminate sex
.20 to .30	Vomiting, stupor, passing out	Death from suffocation or choking on vomit
.31 to .45	Coma, shock from alcohol poisoning	Brain damage; death
.45 or higher	.45 is the fatal level for 50% of people	As the blood alcohol level rises higher than .45, death becomes more and more certain.

*Compared to a driver with a BAC of less than .01

Source: Robert Julien, *A Primer of Drug Action*, 9th ed. (New York: Worth, 2001).

Driving is measurably impaired at BAC levels *lower* than the legal limit of .08. In fact, an accurate safe level for most people may be half the legal limit (.04). As BAC levels climb past .08, you will become progressively less coordinated and less able to make good decisions. Most people become severely uncoordinated with BAC levels higher than .08 and may begin falling asleep, falling down, or slurring their speech.

Warning Signs, Saving Lives

Most people pass out or fall asleep when the BAC is above .25. Unfortunately, even after you pass out and stop drinking, your BAC can continue to rise as alcohol in your stomach is released to the intestine and absorbed into the bloodstream. Your body may try to get rid of alcohol by vomiting, but you can choke if you are unconscious, semiconscious, or severely uncoordinated.

Worse yet, at BAC levels higher than .30, most people will show signs of severe alcohol poisoning such as an inability to wake up, slowed breathing, fast but weak pulse, cool or damp skin, and pale or bluish skin. People exhibiting these symptoms need medical assistance *immediately*. If you ever find someone in such a state, remember to keep the person on his or her side with the head lower than the rest of the body. Check to see that the airway is clear, especially if the person is vomiting or if the tongue is blocking the back of the throat.

Helping an Intoxicated Friend

There are many home remedies (such as coffee, water, cold showers) for helping to sober someone up, but none have been proven to truly work. Time is the only true way because your liver can only metabolize one ounce of alcohol per hour. Harvard University has developed the following guidelines for helping an intoxicated friend:

- Never leave a drunk person alone.

- Keep her from driving, biking, or going anywhere alone.

- If he wants to lie down, turn the person on his side or stomach to prevent the inhalation of vomit.

- Don't give the person any drugs or medications to try to sober her up.

- You can't prevent the alcohol from being absorbed once it has been consumed so giving a drunk person food will only increase the risk of vomiting.

- Do not assume that a drunk is just "sleeping it off" if he cannot be awakened. This person needs urgent care.

Heavy Drinking: The Danger Zone

We know that many students have been subjected to what they may regard as exaggerated "scare tactics" by well-intentioned educators. However, there are many compelling warning indicators related to heavy drinking. Think about the following statistics and their possible application to you and your friends; the effects of heavy drinking are nothing less than a tragedy for many college students:

- 1,700 college students between the ages of 18 and 24 die each year from alcohol-related unintentional injuries, including motor vehicle crashes.

TABLE 16.4 Annual Consequences of Alcohol and Other Drug Use among All Students, All Drinkers, and Heavy Drinkers

CONSEQUENCES	PERCENT EXPERIENCING CONSEQUENCE		
	All Students	All Drinkers	Heavy Drinkers
Had a hangover	59.7	81.1	89.5
Performed poorly on a test	21.8	31.4	40.8
Trouble with police, etc.	11.7	17.4	23.7
Property damage, fire alarm	7.8	11.8	16.5
Argument or fight	29.5	42.0	52.2
Nauseated or vomited	47.1	63.9	73.5
Driven while intoxicated	32.6	47.0	57.3
Missed a class	27.9	40.9	52.9
Been criticized	27.1	37.2	45.3
Thought I had a problem	12.3	16.4	21.6
Had a memory loss	25.8	37.3	48.0
Later regretted action	35.7	49.8	60.4
Arrested for DWI, DUI	1.7	2.4	3.3
Tried, failed to stop	5.8	8.1	16.6
Been hurt, injured	12.9	18.8	25.2
Taken advantage of sexually	11.4	15.9	19.9
Took sexual advantage of someone	6.1	9.0	11.9
Tried to commit suicide	1.6	1.9	2.6
Thought about suicide	5.1	6.7	8.2

Source: Adapted with permission from C. A. Presley, P. W. Meilman, J. R. Cashin, and R. Lyeria, *Alcohol and Drugs on American College Campuses: Use, Consequences, and Perceptions of the Campus Environment,* Volume IV: 1992–94 (Carbondale: The Core Institute, Southern Illinois University).

- 599,000 students between the ages of 18 and 24 are unintentionally injured each year while under the influence of alcohol.
- More than 696,000 students between the ages of 18 and 24 are assaulted each year by another student who has been drinking.[1]

Heavy drinking, sometimes called binge drinking, is commonly defined as five or more drinks for males and four or more drinks for females on a single occasion. Presumably, for a very large person who drinks slowly over a long period of time (several hours), four or five drinks may not lead to a BAC associated with impairment. However, research suggests that in many cases the BAC of heavy drinkers exceeds the legal limit for impairment (+.08).

The academic, medical, and social consequences of heavy drinking can seriously endanger quality of life. Research based on surveys conducted by the Core Institute at Southern Illinois University (http://www.siuc.edu/~coreinst) provides substantial evidence that heavy drinkers have significantly greater risk of adverse outcomes, as shown in Table 16.4.

Among other problems, the Core data identify heavy drinking with increased risk of poor test performance, missed classes, unlawful behavior,

[1] Hingson, R., et al. "Magnitude of Alcohol-Related Mortality and Morbidity among U.S. College Students Ages 18–24: Changes from 1998–2001." *Annual Review of Public Health* 26 (2005): 259–79.

violence, memory loss, drunk driving, regretful behavior, and vandalism, compared with all drinkers and all students. At the same time, college health centers nationwide are reporting increasing occurrences of serious medical conditions—even death—resulting from excessive alcohol use:

- Alcohol poisoning causing coma and shock
- Respiratory depression, choking, and respiratory arrest
- Head trauma and brain injury
- Lacerations
- Fractures
- Unwanted or unsafe sexual activity causing STIs and pregnancies
- Bleeding intestines
- Anxiety attacks and other psychological crises
- Worsening of underlying psychiatric conditions such as depression or anxiety

If you engage in heavy drinking so long that your body can tolerate large amounts, you may become an alcoholic. According to the medical definition, someone is alcohol-dependent or alcoholic if he or she exhibits three of the following symptoms:

1. A significant tolerance for alcohol
2. Withdrawal symptoms such as "the shakes"
3. Overuse of alcohol
4. Unsuccessful attempts to control or cut down on use
5. Preoccupation with drinking or becoming anxious when you do not have a drink
6. Making new friends who drink and staying away from friends who do not drink or who do not drink to get drunk
7. Continued heavy drinking despite experiencing alcohol-related social, academic, legal, or health problems

TABLE 16.5 Comparison of Percentage of Students Reporting Alcohol-Related Problems Experienced by Light to Moderate Drinkers, Heavy Drinkers, and Frequent Heavy Drinkers

PROBLEM	LIGHT TO MODERATE DRINKERS	HEAVY DRINKERS	FREQUENT HEAVY DRINKERS
Got behind on schoolwork	9	25	48
Missed a class due to drinking	10	33	65
Argued with friends while drinking	10	24	47
Got hurt or injured	3	11	27
Damaged property	3	10	25
Got in trouble with campus police	2	5	15
Had five or more alcohol-related problems since the beginning of the school year	4	17	52

Source: Data from Henry Weschler et al., "Changes in Binge Drinking and Related Problems Among American College Students Between 1993 and 1997: Results of the Harvard School of Public Health College Alcohol Study," *Journal of American College Health* 47 (1998): 57–68.

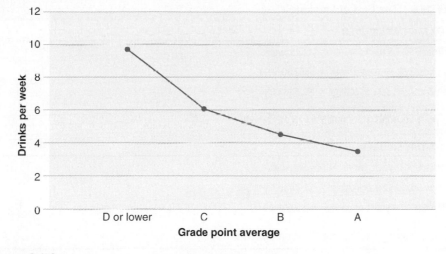

Figure 16.2
Negative Correlation between Drinks per Week and Grade Point Average

Source: Adapted with permission from C. A. Presley, P. W. Meilman, J. R. Cashin, and R. Lyeria, *Alcohol and Drugs on American College Campuses: Use, Consequences, and Perceptions of the Campus Environment,* Volume IV: 1992–94 (Carbondale: The Core Institute, Southern Illinois University).

Consequences for All

All Core Institute surveys conducted since the early 1990s have consistently shown a negative correlation between grades and the number of drinks per week—and not just for heavy drinkers. Findings, as shown in Figure 16.2, are similar for both two-year and four-year institutions.

As shown in Table 16.5, frequent heavy drinkers suffered a higher rate of problems than heavy drinkers, while heavy drinkers suffered more problems than light to moderate drinkers.

The Core Institute reports the following percentages of students who have experienced adverse effects as a result of *others'* drinking:

Study interrupted 29%

Space messed up 25%

Felt unsafe 22%

Unable to enjoy events 19%

Interfered with in other ways 32%

Tobacco—The Other Legal Drug

Tobacco use is clearly the cause of many serious medical conditions, including heart disease, cancer, and lung ailments. Over the years, tobacco has led to the deaths of hundreds of thousands of individuals. Unfortunately, cigarette smoking is on the rise among college students. The College Tobacco Prevention Resource estimates that approximately 30 percent of college students are current users, meaning they have used a tobacco product in the past thirty days. However, the greatest concern about college students and smoking is "social smoking." These are students who smoke only when hanging out with friends, drinking, or partying. The CDC reports that among 18- to 24-year-olds,

TABLE 16.6   The Cost of Smoking

1/2 PACK-A-DAY SMOKER

$3.50/pack × 3.5 packs/week = $12.25/week

$12.25/week × 52 weeks/year = $637.00/year

$637/year × 4 years of college = $2,548.00

In 25 years you will have spent $15,925 on cigarettes.

PACK-A-DAY SMOKER

$3.50/pack × 7 packs/week = $24.50/week

$24.50/week × 52 weeks/year = $1,274.00/year

$1,274/year × 4 years of college = $5,096.00

In 25 years you will have spent $31,850 on cigarettes.

28.7 percent of college students fall into the "social smoker" category.[2] Most college students feel they will be able to "give up" their social smoking habit once they graduate but, after four years of college, find that they are addicted to cigarettes. A national tobacco study reported that almost 40 percent of college students either began smoking or became regular smokers after starting college.[3]

The College Tobacco Prevention Resource reports that about 3.7 percent of college students use smokeless tobacco and that one "dip" delivers the same amount of nicotine as three to four cigarettes. Smokeless tobacco contains twenty-eight known cancer-causing substances and is associated with the same health risk as cigarette smoking. Because more women than men now smoke, the rate of cancer in women is rapidly approaching or surpassing rates in men. One explanation as to why more women smoke than men is the enormous amount of pressure on young women to stay thin. Most people would agree the health dangers of being two or three pounds heavier cannot even compare to the dangers of smoking. It has been noted that a female smoker has her first heart attack nineteen years before a nonsmoking female.

Chemicals in tobacco are highly addictive, making it hard to quit. Although young people may not worry about long-term side effects, increased numbers of respiratory infections, worsening of asthma, bad breath, stained teeth, and the huge expense should be motivations to not start smoking at all. Smoking and the use of hormonal birth control can be a deadly combination. A recent study conducted at Boston University School of Medicine showed that women who smoke and use hormonal birth control are nearly ten times more likely to have a heart attack than women who do not smoke or use one of these methods of birth control. A final reason for smokers to quit is the cost (see Table 16.6). Many institutions and local hospitals offer smoking cessation programs to help individuals addicted to nicotine to quit smoking. Contact your campus health center for more information about taking this step toward quitting.

Prescription Drug Abuse and Addiction

Researchers at the University of Michigan reported in January of 2005 that 7 percent of college students have used prescription stimulants for nonmedical purposes at some point and 4 percent have used them in the past year. Three

[2] CDC, "Prevalence of Current Cigarette Smoking among Adults and Change in Prevalence of Current and Some Day Smoking—United States, 1996–2000." *Morbidity and Mortality Weekly Report* 52:14 (April 2003): 303–07.

[3] Rigotti, N, Lee, J., and Wechsler, H. "U.S. College Students' Use of Tobacco Products: Results of a National Survey." *Journal of the American Medical Association* 284:6 (2000): 699–705.

classes of prescription drugs are the most commonly abused: opioids, central nervous system (CNS) depressants, and stimulants. Abuse of anabolic steroids is also on the rise. College students' nonmedical use of prescription pain relievers is increasing. Some individuals may engage in "doctor shopping" to get multiple prescriptions for the drugs they abuse.

Opioids include morphine, codeine, and such branded drugs as OxyContin, Darvon, Vicodin, Demerol, and Dilaudid. Opioids work by blocking the transmission of pain messages to the brain. Chronic use can result in addiction. Taking a large single dose of an opioid can cause a severe reduction in your breathing rate that can lead to death.

Taken under a doctor's care, *central nervous system (CNS) depressants* can be useful in the treatment of anxiety and sleep disorders. The flip side is that exceeding the recommended dosage can create a tolerance and the user will need larger doses to achieve the same result. If the user stops taking the drug, the brain's activity can rebound and race out of control, possibly leading to seizures and other harmful consequences.

Stimulants, such as ephedrine, Ritalin, and Dexadrine, enhance brain activity, causing an increase in alertness, attention, and energy accompanied by elevated blood pressure and increased heart rate. Legal use of stimulants to treat obesity, asthma, and other problems has dropped off as their potential for abuse and addiction has become apparent.[4] Just because a product is labeled "natural" and can be purchased over-the-counter does not mean that it is safe or worth your money. The FDA (Food and Drug Administration) does not regulate supplements like they do food or other medication, so it is very important to do thorough research and to consult your physician before starting any over-the-counter regimen.

Ritalin is prescribed for a condition called ADHD (Attention Deficit Hyperactivity Disorder) but is gaining recognition on college campuses as a "cramming drug." This prescription drug costs only about $.50 per tablet but sells on the street for as much as $15.00. College students are using Ritalin to stay awake for long periods of time to study for exams. Many students think that since it is a prescribed drug, it must be harmless. The U.S. Department of Education's Higher Education Center for Alcohol and Other Drug Abuse and Violence Prevention lists the following as possible adverse effects from abusing Ritalin: nervousness, vomiting, changes in heart rate and blood pressure, dependency, fevers, convulsions, headaches, paranoia, hallucinations, and delusions.

Another class of drugs that is of concern in the college setting is anabolic steroids. When most people think of steroids, they think about college and professional athletes. But, it is important for all college students to know and understand the dangers of these man-made substances.

According to the National Institute on Drug Abuse, steroids are taken orally or injected into the body in cycles lasting weeks or months. Steroid abuse has many major side effects, including liver tumors, cancer, jaundice, fluid retention, high blood pressure, kidney tumors, and severe acne. Most anabolic steroid users are male and therefore have gender-specific side effects including shrinking of the testicles, reduced sperm count, infertility, baldness, development of breasts, and increased risk for prostate cancer. Abusers also put themselves at risk for contracting HIV or other blood-borne viruses when using or sharing infected needles.

The abuse rate for steroids is fairly low among the general population. In 2003, the Monitoring the Future Survey found that 1.8 percent of young adults

[4] Adapted from "Prescription Drugs: Abuse and Addiction." National Institute on Drug Abuse, part of the National Institutes of Health, a division of the U.S. Department of Health and Human Services.

ages 19–28 reported using steroids at least once during their lifetimes. One-half (0.5) percent reported using steroids at least once in the past year and 0.2 percent reported using steroids in the past month.[5]

Illegal Drugs

Illegal recreational drugs, such as marijuana, cocaine, methamphetamine, Ecstasy, and heroin, are used by a much smaller number of college students and far less frequently than alcohol. Yet these drugs are significant public health issues for college students. The penalties associated with the possession or abuse of illegal drugs tend to be much more severe than those associated with underage alcohol use.

Athletic departments, potential employers, and government agencies do routine screenings for many of these illegal drugs. Future employability, athletic scholarships, and insurability may be compromised if you have a positive drug test for any of these substances. A brief summary of five of the most prevalent drugs follows.

Marijuana Marijuana has an effect on the body and its functions for between three and seven days, depending on the potency and the smoker. Like alcohol, light use will produce a pleasant high. But chronic use of marijuana can lead to a lethargic state in which users may "forget" about current responsibilities (such as going to class). Long-term use carries the same risks of lung infections and cancer that are associated with smoking tobacco.

Ecstasy MDMA, or Ecstasy, as it is known, is a synthetic—or manmade—drug. While many young people believe that MDMA is safe and offers nothing but a pleasant high for the $25 cost of a single tablet (how bad can it be if it's that cheap?), the reality is far different. Taken orally, the effects of MDMA last approximately four to six hours. Many will take a second dose when the initial dose begins to fade. Some tablets contain not only MDMA but other drugs, including amphetamine, caffeine, destromethorpin, ephedrine, and cocaine. MDMA significantly depletes serotonin—a substance in the brain that helps regulate mood, sleep, pain, emotion, and appetite, as well as other behaviors. It takes the brain time to rebuild the serotonin needed to perform important physiological and psychological functions. Of great concern is MDMA's adverse effects on the pumping efficiency of the heart. Heavy users may experience obsessive traits, anxiety, paranoia, and sleep disturbance. Another study indicates that MDMA can have long-lasting effects on memory.[6]

Heroin Numerous reports have suggested a rise in heroin use among college students. A highly addictive drug with the potential to be more damaging and fatal than other opiates, heroin is the most abused and most rapidly acting of this group. One of the most significant—and surest—effects of heroin use is addiction. The human body begins to develop tolerance to the drug on *first use*. Once this happens, the abuser must use more of the drug to achieve the same intensity. Within a short period of time, users must take the drug more and more often to alleviate the symptoms of addiction. Heroin can be injected, smoked, or snorted. Injection is the most efficient way to administer low-purity heroin. However, the availability of high-purity heroin, and the fear of infection by sharing needles has made snorting and smoking the drug more

---

[5] "2004 Monitoring the Future Survey," funded by the National Institute on Drug Abuse, National Institutes of Health, DHHS, and conducted by the University of Michigan's Institute for Social Research. For more data, go online at www.drugabuse.gov.

[6] Excerpted from "Ecstasy: What We Know and Don't Know About MDMA: A Scientific Review." National Institute on Drug Abuse, part of the National Institutes of Health (NIH), a division of the U.S. Department of Health and Human Services.

common. Some users believe that snorting or smoking heroin will not lead to addiction. They are 100 percent wrong.

Chronic users may develop collapsed veins, infection of the heart lining and valves, abscesses, and liver disease. In addition, users are at risk for pulmonary complications, including various types of pneumonia. In addition to the effects of the drug itself, users who inject heroin or share needles also put themselves at risk for contracting HIV, hepatitis B and C, and other blood-borne viruses. A heroin overdose may cause slow and shallow breathing, convulsions, coma, and possibly death.

Cocaine Cocaine or crack produces an intense experience that heightens senses. A crack high lasts only a few minutes; then the good feelings are gone. During the crash, the user may feel tired and unmotivated and find it impossible to sleep. Cocaine is highly addictive. In some instances, users have died of cardiac arrest while taking the drug.

Meth (Methamphetamine) Methamphetamine is particularly dangerous because it costs so little and is so easy to make. Much of it is being produced in makeshift labs in homes or college residences, which not only means that the quality varies from batch to batch, but that it's virtually impossible to tell what else is in the mixture.

The drug can initially produce euphoria, enhanced wakefulness, increased physical activity, and decreased appetite. Prolonged use can lead to binges, during which users take more meth every few hours for several days until they run out of the drug or become too disorganized to continue. Chronic abuse can lead to psychotic behavior, characterized by intense paranoia, visual and auditory hallucinations, and out-of-control rages that can be coupled with extremely violent behavior. Researchers have found that many former meth users experience long-term brain damage, and it is unknown whether the damage can ever be reversed.

Where to Go for Help

ON CAMPUS

Counseling Center: Professionals here will offer individual and group assistance and lots of information. Remember, their support is confidential and you will not be judged.

Health Center/Infirmary: On most campuses the professionals who staff these are especially interested in educational outreach and practicing prevention. But you should be able to receive treatment as well.

Health Education and Wellness Programs: College campuses assume and recognize that for many students, problems and challenges with alcohol, other drugs, and sexual decision making and its consequences are part of the college universe. Fellow student peer health educators who are trained and supervised by professionals can provide support. Taking part in such peer leadership is also a great way to develop and practice your own communication skills.

Campus Support Groups: Many campuses provide student support groups led by professionals for students dealing with problems related to excessive alcohol and drug use, abusive sexual relationships, and so forth.

ONLINE

Dealing with Stress: www.stress.org. Want to combat stress? Find out how at the American Institute of Stress website.

Advice from the American Dietetic Association: www.eatright.org. This website provides information on healthy eating and nutrition.

How Tobacco Affects Your Health: http://www.cancer.org. To learn more about the health effects of tobacco, visit The American Cancer Society.

The Center for Young Women's Health: http://www.youngwomenshealth.org/collegehealth10.html. This website has helpful advice on sexual health as well as other issues.

National Clearinghouse for Alcohol and Drug Information: http://www.health.org. or by calling 800-729-6686. This organization provides up-to-date information about the effects of alcohol and drug use.

DrugHelp: http://www.drughelp.org. This is a private, nonprofit referral service for drug treatment.

Methamphetamine Addiction: http://www.methamphetamineaddiction.com/methamphetamine.html. Learn more about the dangers of methamphetamine at this website.

The Centers for Disease Control and Prevention: www.cdc.gov. This website is an excellent resource for all of the topics in this chapter.

Here are some other worthy resources:

National Clearinghouse for Alcohol and Drug Information: www.health.org

National Eating Disorder Association: www.nationaleatingdisorders.org

US Government's Nutrition Information: www.nutrition.gov

Shape Up America: www.shapeup.org

National Health Information Center: www.healthfinder.org

Planned Parenthood Federation of American: www.plannedparenthood.org

US Food and Drug Administration: www.fda.gov

ACHIEVE IT! *Setting Goals for Success*

Go back to the self-assessment at the beginning of this chapter and select one to three unchecked items from the list. Use these to formulate short-term goals for yourself. Be specific about what you want to achieve and when (not "become an active learner," but "find an excuse to meet with at least one of my teachers sometime next week"). Remember to choose goals that are realistic and important to you. Think about what obstacles could get in the way of achieving your goals, and make your plan. In the event you checked all items in the self-assessment, come up with one or more additional goals for this exercise.

	Goal 1	Goal 2	Goal 3
My short-term goal is . . .			
I want to achieve this goal by . . . (date)			
This goal matters because . . .			
I may encounter the following obstacles . . .			
My method for accomplishing this goal will be to . . .			

Set a Date. Put your deadline for achieving your goal(s) in your calendar. Count back ten days from your deadline and write a reminder for yourself.

Reassess. After your deadline passes, ask yourself: Did I meet this goal on time? What change has it made in my life? If I did not meet it, what am I planning to do about it?

TRY IT! *Exercises*

The exercises at the end of each chapter will help you sharpen what we believe are the critical skills for college success: writing, critical thinking, learning in groups, planning, reflecting, and taking action. You can further explore the topic of each chapter by using your PIN to complete the exercises on the website for this text: **http://success.wadsworth.com/gardner7e**.

WORKING TOGETHER: Recommendations for Stress Management

If you could make only three recommendations to an incoming first-year college student about managing the stress of college, what would they be? Use your experience as well as what you have learned in this chapter to make your recommendations. In groups of four, compare your list with those of other students, and see if your group can agree on the three most important recommendations. Then see whether other groups in class had lists similar to yours.

EXERCISE 16.1: Monitoring Your Stress

Here's one way to learn to recognize how you feel when you are stressed. Following is a list of physical and emotional conditions that people may feel when stressed. Check the ones that best describe you. Then review those you have checked and write a paragraph describing the following: how you feel when you are under stress; how you manage the symptoms of stress; and how you attempt to deal with expected and unexpected stressors.

_____ My breathing is rapid and shallow.

_____ I feel a tightness in my chest.

_____ My pulse races.

_____ My muscles feel tense, especially around my shoulders, chest, forehead, and back of neck.

_____ My hands are cold or sweaty.

_____ I have "butterflies" in my stomach.

_____ I experience diarrhea or constipation.

_____ I have to urinate more frequently.

_____ My mouth is dry.

_____ I tremble or feel shaky.

_____ I have a quiver in my voice.

_____ Things easily confuse me.

_____ I have trouble remembering things.

_____ I have trouble solving problems.

_____ I feel irritable.

_____ I feel jittery.

_____ I have trouble concentrating.

_____ I feel overwhelmed.

_____ I am anxious about things I have to do.

_____ I feel depressed.

_____ I feel frustrated.

_____ I have insomnia.

_____ I wake up far too early and can't go back to sleep.

_____ I have noticed changes in my eating habits.

_____ I feel fatigued a good bit of the time.

EXERCISE 16.2: The College Readjustment Rating Scale

The College Readjustment Rating Scale is an adaptation of Holmes and Rahe's Life Events Scale. It has been modified for traditional-age college students and should be considered as a rough indication of stress levels and possible health consequences. In this scale, each event, such as one's first term in college, is assigned a value that represents the amount of readjustment a person has to make in life as a result of change. In some studies, people with serious illnesses have been found to have high scores on similar scales. Persons with scores of 300 and higher have a high health risk. Persons scoring between 150 and 300 points have about a 50-50 chance of serious health change within two years. Subjects scoring 150 and below have a 1 in 3 chance of a serious health change.

To determine your stress score, circle the number of points corresponding to the events you have experienced in the past six months or are likely to experience in the next six months. Then add up the circled numbers.

Event	Points
Death of spouse	100
Pregnancy for unwed female	92
Death of parent	80
Male partner in unwed pregnancy	77
Divorce	73
Death of a close family member	70
Death of a close friend	65
Divorce between parents	63
Jail term	61
Major personal injury or illness	60
Flunk out of college	58
Marriage	55
Fired from job	50
Loss of financial support for college (scholarship)	48
Failing grade in important or required course	47
Sexual difficulties	45
Serious argument with significant other	40
Academic probation	39
Change in major	37
New love interest	36
Increased workload in college	31
Outstanding personal achievement	29
First term in college	28
Serious conflict with instructor	27
Lower grades than expected	25
Change in colleges (transfer)	24
Change in social activities	22
Change in sleeping habits	21
Change in eating habits	19
Minor violation of the law (for example, traffic ticket)	15

If your score indicates potential health problems, it would be to your benefit to seriously review the stress inoculation and management techniques discussed in this chapter and select and implement some strategies to reduce your stress.[7]

EXERCISE 16.3: Changing Perceptions

Many people get overly stressed due to their negative thought patterns. The old saying, "Every negative has a positive," is very true and plays a large role in stress management. Use the following steps to help practice managing stress by changing your thoughts and perceptions.

1. Identify a stressor where perceptions can be altered.

2. Recognize the negative thoughts you are currently having in this situation.

3. Create two or three positive thoughts that you will use to deal with the stressor in the future.

4. Write down the positive thoughts and keep them with you.

5. Practice saying the positive thoughts to yourself.

6. Use the new positive thought when you encounter the stressors.

7. Practice, practice, practice. Change takes time.

EXERCISE 16.4: Doing a Weekly Check

For three days, keep a food, physical activity, and sleep journal. The goal is to write down everything you eat and/or drink during these three days as well as the amount of sleep and physical activity you get each day. The following chart may help with this exercise.

Evaluate your food journal. Did you have an even distribution among the categories? Have you met the recommendation of five fruits and/or vegetables per day? Are your grains from complex carbohydrates such as whole wheat? Did your liquids consist of high-calorie options such as soda and beer?

Review your physical activity journal at the end of the three days. Did you get thirty minutes of physical activity most days? Did you stretch after exercising? Did you work all the major muscle groups during your activity?

Analyze your sleep during the period. Did you get the recommended seven to nine hours of sleep per night? Did you follow the tips listed in this chapter regarding sleep? Did you notice a pattern between the amount of sleep you got in a given night and how well you ate? Were you as physically active on days you did not get a good night's sleep?

---

[7] Adapted with permission from T. H. Holmes and R. H. Rahe, "The Social Readjustment Scale," in Carol L. Otis and Roger Goldingay, *Campus Health Guide* (New York: CEEB, 1989).

At the end of the week, write about your experiences. Did you feel better or worse during this experiment? What will you do about your diet once this experiment is over?

	Day #1	Day #2	Day #3
Food/Drink Intake			
Breakfast			
Snack			
Lunch			
Snack			
Dinner			
Snack			
Exercise			
Type of Exercise			
How long?			
Sleep			
How many hours?			

EXERCISE 16.5: What's Your Decision?

Although you might know about the strategies to keep yourself from contracting an STI, knowledge doesn't always translate into behavior. Use the following chart to brainstorm all the reasons you can think of that people *wouldn't* practice prevention strategies of abstinence, monogamy, or condom use. Then go back over your list and consider whether each barrier would apply to you (yes, no, or maybe). In this way, you can better evaluate where you stand on the issue of safer sex and determine what areas you may need to work on to ensure that you protect yourself—always!

Barriers to Practicing Safer Sex	Does This Apply to You?

EXERCISE 16.6: Quality of Life

List five ways your or a friend's quality of life has been influenced by the drinking or substance abuse of others. In small groups, share some or all of these with others in the class. What did you find out when you compared your experiences with theirs? Did you handle the situation in a healthy manner in comparison to your group members? What would you do differently in the future?

WRITE ABOUT IT! My Personal Journal

This is your place to sound off, to ask your teacher to clarify part of the lesson, or to write him or her about a minor or major crisis you're experiencing. Find out if your teacher wishes you to turn in your journals. Ask if they will remain confidential. Even if the journal isn't used in your course, you can still use the format to write about and reflect on issues regarding the class, yourself, or both.

1. *What was the one major lesson you learned from reading this chapter and/or from class lecture and discussion?*

2. *What are some other important lessons about this topic?*

3. *If you believe some parts of this chapter are unimportant, spell them out here and tell why you think so. (You even might want to discuss this point with your classmates to see if they came up with a similar list.)*

4. *If anything is keeping you from performing at your peak level academically, describe what it is. Your instructor may be able to help or refer you to someone else on campus who can help.*

5. *What behaviors are you planning to change after reading this chapter? Why?*

Glossary

Abstract   A paragraph-length summary of the methods and major findings of an article in a scholarly journal.

Abstract conceptualization   A learner's ability to integrate observation into logically sound theories; this is one of the four stages of Kolb's Inventory of Learning Styles.

Abstract-concrete   One of two basic divisions in Kolb's Inventory of Learning Styles.

Abstractions   The bigger ideas or general principles behind a collection of facts.

Accommodators   Individuals who prefer hands-on learning. Accommodators are good at making things happen and work well with other people, although they can be pushy and impatient. This is one of the categories in Kolb's Inventory of Learning Styles.

Active experimentation   A learner's ability to make decisions, solve problems, and test what he or she has learned; this is one of the four stages of Kolb's Inventory of Learning Styles.

Active learning   Learning by doing, for example writing, speaking, creating, participating in class.

Active-reflective   One of two basic divisions in Kolb's Inventory of Learning Styles.

Aesthetic   Emphasizing beauty, art, and good taste.

Aesthetic values   The values by which we judge beauty, whether it be art, music, or appearance.

Annotate   To add critical or explanatory margin notes as you read or review a textbook.

Argument   Reason and information brought together in logical support of an idea.

Assimilators   People who like to think about abstract concepts. Assimilators enjoy courses that are highly theoretical, such as physics. This is one of the categories in Kolb's Inventory of Learning Styles.

Attention deficit disorder   A disorder characterized by difficulty organizing tasks, completing work, and following directions.

Auditory learner   A person who learns best by listening to other people talk.

Aural learner   A person who prefers to learn by hearing information. This is one of the preferences described by the VARK Learning Styles Inventory.

Autonomy   Independence. College students usually have more autonomy than they did in high school.

Behavioral interview   An interview in which the interviewer questions the candidate about past experience and how it helped the candidate learn and grow.

Bias   A negative, preconceived opinion of some person or group. The opinion may manifest itself either in attitude or in acts of discrimination.

Biorhythms   The internal biological clocks that drive our daily patterns, influencing when we are most active and alert.

Block scheduling   Scheduling courses back-to-back with no free time in between.

Brainstorming   The process of writing down everyone's ideas without comment or criticism so that the team members build on each other's ideas.

Chunking A previewing technique that involves making a list of terms from a reading assignment, dividing the list into groups of five, seven, or nine terms, and learning one group at a time.

Citation A source or author of certain material. For instance, when browsing for sources on the Internet, it is important to use only material that has citations explaining who wrote it, where it came from, and who posted it.

Civic engagement Involvement with and commitment to the community's needs and issues beyond the campus walls; becoming an involved citizen.

Civility Basic good manners, respect, and polite communication, for example in the classroom.

Co-curricular experiences Learning that occurs outside of the classroom, through on-campus clubs and groups, co-op programs, internships, or other means.

Cognitive restructuring Using positive thinking and self-talk to improve one's performance, for example on an exam.

Collaboration Working with others in the learning environment to enhance understanding for everyone.

Concrete experience Abilities that allow learners to involve themselves fully in new experiences; this is one of the four stages of Kolb's Inventory of Learning Styles.

Content skills Cognitive, intellectual, or "hard" skills, acquired as one gains mastery in an academic field. Content skills include writing proficiency, computer literacy, and foreign language skills.

Context A frame of reference that helps you refine your search for information. When conducting research, it is important to establish a context for the research, such as limiting your search to historical documents, statistics, or opinion pieces.

Convergers People who enjoy the world of ideas and theories but are able to apply them to practical situations. Convergers often major in health sciences or engineering. This is one of the categories in Kolb's Inventory of Learning Styles.

Co-op program Also called cooperative education—a program that provides an opportunity to work in academic major-related settings off campus while enrolled in college.

Cornell format A note-taking and organizing format in which one side of the page is reserved for note-taking and the other side for recall after class.

Criteria Standards for assessing potential solutions to a problem or question.

Culture Those aspects of a group of people that are passed on and/or learned.

Deep learning Understanding the why and how behind the details. Deep learning involves going beyond memorization of facts.

Developmental arithmetic disorder A learning disability characterized by difficulty recognizing numbers and symbols, memorizing mathematical facts, aligning numbers, and understanding abstract mathematical concepts.

Developmental writing disorder A learning disability that involves some or all of the areas of the brain that involve vocabulary, grammar, hand movement, and memory.

Discipline An area of academic study, such as history, mathematics, or nursing.

Discrimination Treating people differently depending on their race, ethnicity, gender, socioeconomic class, or other identifying characteristic, rather than on merit.

Divergers Individuals who are good at reflecting on situations from many viewpoints. These people are good at brainstorming and are imaginative and people-oriented, but sometimes have difficulty making decisions. This is one of the categories in Kolb's Inventory of Learning Styles.

Diversity The variation of social and cultural identities among people existing together in a defined setting.

Drop date The date by which you can drop a course without penalty, providing that you follow proper procedures.

Dyslexia A developmental reading disorder that is sometimes characterized by an inability to distinguish or separate the sounds in spoken words.

Ends values Also called *intrinsic values*, ends values refer to ultimate goals, such as getting a college degree, achieving comfortable economic status, or world peace.

Engagement Active involvement with learning and life and approaching challenges with determination.

Ethnicity A reference to a quality assigned to a specific group of people historically connected by a common national origin or language.

Examples Stories, illustrations, hypothetical events, and specific cases that provide support for the ideas in a presentation or written work.

Expressive language disorder The inability to express oneself using accurate language or sentence structure.

Extraverts Individuals who are outgoing, gregarious, and talkative, and who like to act and lead. This is one of the preferences described by the Myers-Briggs Type Indicator.

Fallacies Errors in thinking such as using false cause, attacking the arguer instead of the argument, and appealing to authority rather than relying on logic.

Faulty reasoning Illogical thinking that depends on fallacies such as false cause and hasty generalization.

Feeling types Warm, empathetic, and sympathetic individuals who value harmony above all else. This is one of the preferences described by the Myers-Briggs Type Indicator.

Field dependence/independence A concept that describes whether and to what degree learners are influenced by the surrounding environment and relationships within the classroom setting. Field independent learners tend to prefer to work autonomously. Field dependent learners tend to thrive on interpersonal interaction.

Fixed expenses Predetermined, recurring expenses, such as rent and tuition.

Freewriting Writing that is temporarily free of mechanical processes, such as punctuation, grammar, spelling, context, and so forth. Freewriting is similar to writing in a stream-of-consciousness style.

Galloping New Ignorance (GNI) The erroneous assumption that anything that exists in electronic form must be true and useful information.

Gift aid Financial aid that does not have to be repaid, such as a grant or scholarship.

Grade Point Average (GPA) The average grade of a student, calculated by dividing the grades received by the number of credits earned.

Idioms Peculiar and unique phrases that cannot be understood from the individual meanings of the words. "Pull the wool over one's eyes" is a common English language idiom.

Inclusive curriculum A curriculum that offers courses that introduce students to diverse people, worldviews, and approaches. For instance, an inclusive curriculum might include majors in the areas of gender studies, ethnic and cultural studies, and religious studies.

Information age The period of time in which we live, characterized by the central role of information in the economy, the necessity to have information retrieval and information management skills, and the explosion of available information.

Interactive learner A person who learns best by talking about and discussing information.

Introverts Quiet, sometimes shy people who prefer to reflect carefully and think through a problem before taking action. This is one of the preferences described by the Myers-Briggs Type Indicator.

Intuitive types Individuals who are excited by the meaning behind the facts and the connections between concepts. This is one of the preferences described by the Myers-Briggs Type Indicator.

Job-shadow To observe someone as he or she works, with permission.

Judging types People who strive for order and control in their environment, making plans and decisions quickly. This is one of the preferences described by the Myers-Briggs Type Indicator.

Key word A critical task word on an essay test that tells you how the question is to be answered. Examples of key words are *analyze, describe,* and *justify.*

Kinesthetic learner A person who prefers to learn through experience and practice, whether simulated or real. This term also refers to someone who learns best by doing something rather than reading about it or listening. This is one of the preferences described by the VARK Learning Styles Inventory.

Learning disabilities Disorders that affect people's ability to either interpret what they see and hear or to link information from different parts of the brain. Dyslexia is a common learning disability.

Learning styles Particular ways of learning. For example, one person's learning style may be to "split" information into small parts and another's may be to "lump" concepts together.

Liberal education Education that includes critical thinking and investigating all sides of a question or problem before reaching a conclusion.

Long-term memory Memories that you retain, divided into the categories of procedural, episodic, and semantic memory.

Mapping A previewing technique that use a wheel or branching structure to display main ideas and secondary ideas from your reading.

Means values Also called *instrumental values,* means values help one attain other values. For example, an open-admission policy is a means value that helps all students achieve the end value of an education.

Mind map A personal study device consisting of words and drawings on a single page that summarizes information about a topic.

Mnemonics Techniques to aid the memory, including acronyms, rhymes, or other bits of language that help you remember lists or phrases.

Moral values Those personal values that we generally do not attempt to force on others, but which are of immense importance to ourselves as individuals. For instance, treating others with respect is a moral value.

Multiculturalism The active process of acknowledging and respecting the various social groups, cultures, religions, races, ethnicities, attitudes, and opinions within an environment.

Multitasking Performing many tasks at once, such as eating lunch, studying, and making phone calls simultaneously.

Network To develop a chain or web of contacts and advisors who can help you achieve your academic and career goals.

Olfactory learner A person for whom smelling and tasting is an integral part of learning. For example, an olfactory learner might cook by tasting the dish and adding ingredients rather than working from a recipe.

Outsourcing The movement of jobs to individuals and companies outside of one's own. This includes hiring contractors who are not part of a company's full-time staff.

Perceiving types Individuals who are comfortable adapting to change and are prone to keeping their options open to gather more information. This is one of the preferences described by the Myers-Briggs Type Indicator.

Performance values How well a person performs to particular standards. For example, accuracy and compassion are performance values in a hospital setting.

Plagiarism A form of academic misconduct that involves presenting another's ideas, words, or opinions as one's own.

Prejudice Judging someone based on little knowledge; for example, prejudging someone based solely on his or her ethnic or racial background.

Prewriting Also called rehearsing, prewriting is preparing to write by filling your mind with information from other sources. It is generally considered the first stage of exploratory writing.

Primary sources The original research or document on a topic. For example, The Gettysburg Address is a primary source document about the Civil War.

Procrastination Putting off doing a task or assignment.

Race A term that refers to biological characteristics shared by groups of people and includes hair texture and color, skin tone, and facial features.

Read/write learning preference A preference for learning information that is displayed as words. This is one of the preferences described by the VARK Learning Styles Inventory.

Reciprocity Something done mutually or in return. For example, you might help a neighbor build a fence in reciprocity for the neighbor's helping you dig a well.

Reflection Careful thought, especially the process of reconsidering previous actions, events, or decisions; thinking about and learning from one's experience, for example with a service learning opportunity.

Reflective observation A learner's ability to reflect on his or her experience from many perspectives; this is one of the four stages of Kolb's Inventory of Learning Styles.

Returning student Students for whom several or many years have elapsed between previous and current attendance in college. Also called nontraditional students.

Self-help assistance Any type of financial aid for which you must do something in return—usually work or repayment.

Sensing types Individuals who are practical, factual, realistic, and down-to-earth. This is one of the preferences described by the Myers-Briggs Type Indicator.

Service learning Mandatory, unpaid service embedded in courses across the curriculum.

Short-term memory How many items you are able to perceive at one time. Short-term memories disappear after about 30 seconds unless they are transferred to long-term memory.

Societal values Values held by the society as a whole. For instance, a society may place a high value on universal health coverage or national security.

Sorting Part of applying information literacy to searching the Internet. Sorting is a way of sifting through available information and selecting the most relevant material.

Statistics Data used to support ideas in a speech or written work.

Stereotype An oversimplified set of assumptions about another person or group.

Subject A way of searching on the Internet that looks for information only by checking subject headings, rather than the entire document.

Supplemental Instruction (SI) Classes that provide further opportunity to discuss the information presented in lecture.

Syllabus Written class requirements or a course outline given by instructors on the first day of class to all students.

Systematic thinking Examining the outcome of abstract and creative thinking in a demanding and critical way in order to narrow down the list of possible solutions.

Tactile learner A person who learns best by using the sense of touch, for example, by typing notes after a lecture.

Testimony Quoting outside experts, paraphrasing reliable sources, and emphasizing the quality of individuals as a way to bolster an argument or support an idea.

Thinking types Logical, rational, and analytical individuals who tend to be critical and objective without involving their own or other people's feelings. This is one of the preferences described by the Myers-Briggs Type Indicator.

Transferable skills General skills that apply to or transfer to a variety of settings. Examples of transferable skills include excellent public speaking skills, using available software to maintain homepages, and providing leadership while working in a team environment.

Value dualisms Conflicting beliefs. Value dualisms often arise between what one learned as a child and what one experiences as an adult.

Values A concept that can mean any of the following: specific views a person holds on controversial moral issues; those things that are most important to a person; or abstractions such as truth, justice, or success.

Visual learner A person who learns best by reading words on a printed page or by viewing pictures, maps, charts, or videos.

Visual learning preference A preference for learning through charts, graphs, symbols, or other visual means. This is one of the preferences described by the VARK Learning Styles Inventory.

Wellness The process of taking care of one's self by making healthy choices and achieving balance in mind, body, and spirit.

Work-study award Financial aid in the form of a guaranteed job on campus.

Credits

Text Credits

Chapter 1 9: Andrew Delbanco, "Academia's Overheated Competition", The *New York Times*, March 16, 2001; 12: Bureau of the Census, 2003; 15: Adapted from *Human Potential Seminars* by James D. McHolland and Roy W. Trueblood, Evanston, IL: 1972. Used by permission of the authors.

Chapter 3 45: Herman A. Witkin, "Cognitive Style in Academic Performance and in Teacher-Student Relations" in *Individuality in Learning*, edited by Samuel Messick & Associates, San Francisco: Jossey-Bass, 1976; 45: P. Kirby, "Cognitive Style, Learning Style and Transfer Skill Acquisition" *Information Series* No. 195 (Columbus, OH: Ohio State University, National Center for Research in Vocational Education, 1979); 46: From *The Modern American College* by Chickering. Copyright © 1981 Jossey-Bass. Reprinted with permission of John Wiley & Sons, Inc.; 47: Adapted from David A. Kolb, "Learning Styles and Disciplinary Differences" in Arthur W. Chickering, *The Modern American College*, San Francisco: Jossey-Bass, 1981 (pp. 232-255); 51: Isabel Briggs Meyers, *Introduction to Type*, Sixth Edition (Palo Alto, CA: CPP, Inc., 1998); 52: From www.ldrc.ca/projects/miinventory.mitest.html; 54: © Copyright Version 5.1 (2004) held by Neil D. Fleming, Christchurch, New Zealand and Charles C. Bonwell, Green Mountain Falls, Colorado 80819 U.S.A.

Chapter 4 64-65: George Kuh. NSSE director of the National Survey of Student Engagement and Chancellor's Professor of Higher Education, Indiana University, Bloomington. From "Student Engagement: Pathways to Collegiate Success," *Viewpoint*, a publication of NSSE. Bloomington, IN: November 2004. Used by permission; 72: From a column in the *Dickens Dispatch*, the newsletter of the North Carolina Dickens Club, January 1989; 73: G. Jeffrey MacDonald. *USA Today*, May 18, 2005; 74: D. J. Levinson et al, *The Seasons of a Man's Life* (New York: Ballantine, 1978).

Chapter 5 82: Theodora J. Kalikow, "Misconceptions About the Word 'Liberal' in Liberal Arts Education," *Higher Education and National Affairs*, June 8,1998; 84: Anuradha Gokhale, "Collaborative Learning Enhances Critical Thinking," *Journal of Technology Education* 7.1 (1995); 89: A. Jerome Jewler and Bonnie Drewniany. *Creative Strategy in Advertising*, 8th ed. (Belmont, CA: Wadsworth, 2005) 89: Terrence Poltrack,

"Stalking the Big Idea," Agency, May/June 1991; 93: Excerpt on critically evaluating information on the internet from www.VirtualSalt.com. Reprinted by permission.

Chapter 8 147: Harry Lorayne. *Super Memory, Super Student: How to Raise Your Grades in 30 Days*. Little, Brown and Company, 1990; 148: W. F Brewer & J. R. Pani. "The Structure of Human Memory" in G. H. Bower's *The Psychology of Learning and Motivation: Advances in Research and Theory*, v. 17. New York: Academic Press, 1983.

Chapter 10 186: Peter Elbow, *Writing Without Teachers* (New York: Oxford University Press, 1973); 186: Robert Pirsig, *Zen and the Art of Motorcycle Maintenance* (New York: Bantam Books, 1984); 188: Donald Murray, *Learning by Teaching: Selected Articles on Writing and Teaching* (Portsmouth, NH: Boynton/Cook, 1982); 189: Niko Sylvester, *Top 10 Ways to Become a Better Writer*. http://teenwriting.about.com/od/thewritingprocess/tp/BetterWriting.htm; 189: William Zinsser, *On Writing Well* (New York: Harper Resource 25th Anniversary Edition, 2001); 191: Kaitlin Duck Sherwood, "A Beginner's Guide to Effective Email" http://www.webfoot.com/advice/email.top.html 191: Lynne Truss, *Eats, Shoots & Leaves: The Zero Tolerance Approach to Punctuation* (New York: Gotham Books, 2003).

Chapter 12 234: Adapted from John L. Holland, *Self-Directed Search Manual*, Odessa, Florida (Psychological Assessment Resources: 1985); 235: Holland's Hexagonal Model of Career Fields; 238: Used by permission of Career Passport, Michigan State University; 249: Adapted from James D. McHolland, *Human Potential Seminar* (Evanston, IL: 1975). Used by permission of the author.

Chapter 13 264: By Tricia Phaup.

Photo Credits

Chapter 1 1: © AP Photo/The Independent-Mail, Sefton Ipock; 3: © John Boykin/Photo Edit; 5: © Tom Stewart/zefa/Corbis, 7. © Gary Conner/ Index Stock Imagery; 10: © image100/Alamy; 13: © Michael Newman/PhotoEdit

Chapter 2 19: © Gary Gerovac/Masterfile; 23: © Erin Gilcrest; 34: © Bill Varie/CORBIS

Chapter 3 41: © Frances M. Roberts; 43: © Sam Pellissier/SuperStock; 46: © Bill Aron/PhotoEdit, © Chuck Savage/CORBIS; 48: © Lisa Peardon/Getty Images; 50: © Christina Micek; 51: © Alec Pytlowany/Masterfile; 53: © Bill Freeman/PhotoEdit; 58: © Reuters/CORBIS, © Mitchell Gerber/CORBIS

Chapter 4 63: © Peter Casolino/Alamy; 70: © Tom Stewart/zefa/Corbis; 72: © Horst Herget/ Masterfile; 74: © Design Pics Inc./Alamy

Chapter 5 79: © Andrew Douglas/Masterfile; 81:© David Fischer/Getty Images; 83: © Icon SMI/Corbis; 86: © Randy Faris/CORBIS; 88:© Christina Micek; 92: © ThinkStock/ SuperStock; 95: © Gary Conner/Index Open

Chapter 6 101: © Marnie Burkhart/ Masterfile; 103: © AFP/Getty Images; 106: © David Young-Wolff/Photo Edit; 110: © Horst Herget/Masterfile; 122: © Bonnie Kamin/PhotoEdit

Chapter 7 127: © Rhoda Sidney/PhotoEdit; 130: © Image Source/SuperStock; 134: © Don Smetzer/PhotoEdit; 135: © Stockbyte/SuperStock; 141: © Myrleen Ferguson Cate/PhotoEdit

Chapter 8 145: © Tony Freeman/PhotoEdit; 147: © Columbia Pictures Corporation/ZUMA/Corbis; 149: © Javier Pierini/Getty Images, © 2005 Canon U.S.A., Inc. All rights reserved.; 151: © Digital Vision/Getty Images; 152: © Sydney Shaffer/Getty Images; 155: © Jon Feingersh/CORBIS

Chapter 9 159: © Gabe Palmer/CORBIS; 163: © age fotostock/SuperStock; 164: © David Young-Wolff/PhotoEdit; 168: © Mark Richards/PhotoEdit; 169: © Big Cheese Photo/SuperStock; 175: © BananaStock/SuperStock

Chapter 10 183: © Vince Bucci/Getty Images; 185: © Christina Micek; 187: © Christina Micek; 190: © David Pollack/CORBIS; 193: © Robert Daly/Getty Images; 194: © Michael Newman/PhotoEdit; 195: © Christina Micek

Chapter 11 205: © Courtesy of the National Aeronautics and Space Administration; 207: © David Zimmerman/ Masterfile; 209: © Purestock/Alamy, © Mark Richards/PhotoEdit; 210: © Anton Vengo/SuperStock; 218:© Will & Deni McIntyre/CORBIS

Chapter 12 225: © Michael Newman/PhotoEdit; 227: © Lester Lefkowitz/CORBIS; 229: © Jon Feingersh/CORBIS; 231: © PhotoAlto/SuperStock; 233:© Bob Daemmrich/PhotoEdit; 239: © Bob Daemmrich/PhotoEdit; 240: © SW Productions/Getty Images; 245: © White Packert/ Getty Images

Chapter 13 253: © Bill Aron/PhotoEdit; 255: © Cindy Charles/PhotoEdit; 257: © Myrleen Ferguson Cate/PhotoEdit; 258: © Bonnie Kamin/PhotoEdit; 260: © age fotostock/SuperStock, © Jennifer Burrell/Masterfile; 261: © David Young Wolf/PhotoEdit; 265:© Justin Pumfrey/ Getty Images

Chapter 14 273: © Harald Sund/Getty Images; 276: © Leland Bobbé/CORBIS; 277: © Anthony Redpath/CORBIS; 279: ©Jodi Hilton/Getty Images; 282: ©Chris Nash/Getty Images; 285: © Mark Richards/PhotoEdit

Chapter 15 291: © bilderlounge/Alamy; 293: © Robert Yager/Getty Images; 295: © AFP/Getty Images; 298: © Jeff Greenberg/Photo Edit; 301: © Randy Faris/Corbis; 302: © Erik S. Lesser/Getty Images; 309: © Noel Hendrickson/Masterfile

Chapter 16 315: © Kevin Dodge/Masterfile; 318: © Stockbyte/SuperStock; 321: © Mug Shots/Corbis; 325: © Mary Kate Denny/PhotoEdit; 337: © Stephen Simpson/Getty Images

Index

Note: Figures and tables are denoted by f and t, respectively.